Learning by Doing

A Handbook for Professional Learning Communities at Work®

FOURTH EDITION

Richard DuFour
Rebecca DuFour
Robert Eaker
Thomas W. Many
Mike Mattos
Anthony Muhammad

Solution Tree | Press

a division of Solution Tree

555 North Morton Street
Bloomington, IN 47404
800.733.6786 (toll free) / 812.336.7700
FAX: 812.336.7790

email: info@SolutionTree.com
SolutionTree.com

Visit **go.SolutionTree.com/PLCbooks** to download the free reproducibles in this book.

Printed in the United States of America

Library of Congress Cataloging-in-Publication Data

Names: DuFour, Richard, 1947-2017, author. | DuFour, Rebecca Burnette, author. | Eaker, Robert E., author. | Many, Thomas W., author. | Mattos, Mike (Mike William), author. | Muhammad, Anthony, author.
Title: Learning by doing : a handbook for Professional Learning Communities at Work / Richard DuFour, Rebecca DuFour, Robert Eaker, Thomas W. Many, Mike Mattos, Anthony Muhammad.
Description: Fourth edition. | Bloomington : Solution Tree Press, [2024] | Includes bibliographical references and index.
Identifiers: LCCN 2023055996 (print) | LCCN 2023055997 (ebook) | ISBN 9781960574145 (paperback) | ISBN 9781960574152 (ebook)
Subjects: LCSH: School improvement programs—United States. | Group work in education—United States. | Team learning approach in education—United States. | Educational leadership—United States.
Classification: LCC LB2822.82 .L427 2024 (print) | LCC LB2822.82 (ebook) | DDC 371.2/070973--dc23/eng/20240125
LC record available at https://lccn.loc.gov/2023055996
LC ebook record available at https://lccn.loc.gov/2023055997

Solution Tree
Jeffrey C. Jones, CEO
Edmund M. Ackerman, President

Solution Tree Press
President and Publisher: Douglas M. Rife
Associate Publishers: Todd Brakke and Kendra Slayton
Editorial Director: Laurel Hecker
Art Director: Rian Anderson
Copy Chief: Jessi Finn
Senior Production Editor: Suzanne Kraszewski
Proofreader: Sarah Ludwig
Text and Cover Designer: Rian Anderson
Acquisitions Editors: Carol Collins and Hilary Goff
Content Development Specialist: Amy Rubenstein
Associate Editors: Sarah Ludwig and Elijah Oates
Editorial Assistant: Anne Marie Watkins

To the Solution Tree team, PLC associates, and educators across the globe who keep our parents' professional legacy alive. In addition, a heartfelt tribute to our respective children—Sam, Lee, Arlo, and Archer—who continue their grandparents' personal legacy of kindness, selflessness, and a love for learning.

—Hannah Treadway and Matt DuFour

To Douglas Rife, my professional colleague, my reading partner of many years, and, most importantly, my dear friend.

—Bob

Being a part of a project like this is gratifying. Thank you to Rick, Becky, Bob, Mike, and Anthony; it is a privilege to write with such esteemed friends and colleagues. Thank you to Douglas Rife and the rest of the Press team at Solution Tree; it is a pleasure to work with such consummate partners and professionals. And most of all, thank you to my wife, Susan, who makes it all possible with her unconditional love and support.

—Tom

To Constance Galliher—thank you for all your love and support.

—Mike

This book is dedicated to Rick and Rebecca DuFour. Thank you for giving me the gift of your minds and spirits. It is an honor to carry on your legacy. We are all better because of your positive influence on our lives. I hope that we make you proud.

—Anthony

Visit **go.SolutionTree.com/PLCbooks** to download the free reproducibles in this book.

Acknowledgments

Successful endeavors, be they writing a book or building a professional learning community (PLC), are rarely due to the actions of a single person; they require the collective efforts of many talented individuals. The fourth edition of *Learning by Doing: A Handbook for Professional Learning Communities at Work®* is truly a testament to this. We would like to thank the following people for their efforts.

The advancement of the PLC at Work process would not have been possible without the unwavering support and courageous leadership of Jeff Jones and the outstanding team at Solution Tree. Throughout the political and economic ups and downs that inevitably impact education, Jeff has remained steadfast in advancing the right work to support educators.

Every edition of *Learning by Doing*—as well as many of the most important PLC at Work resources—has been edited by Suzanne Kraszewski. It is rare to have an editor who both is exceptional at writing and has a deep understanding of the content. This book is much better because of her efforts. Douglas Rife and the publishing team at Solution Tree shepherded this book from prose to publication. Scott Brown, Renee Marshall, Alex Brownstein, and the events team have advanced this content through PLC at Work Institutes and workshops, and Shannon Ritz and the professional development team have provided on-the-ground training for schools all over the world.

We are blessed to work with a family of PLC at Work associates who continue to prove the power of the process by leading Model PLC schools and districts. Members of this team have written blogs, articles, and books that have further developed the process, many of which we reference in this edition. These colleagues also helped us update the research supporting every essential element.

And finally, we are forever grateful to our dear friends and original coauthors of this book, Richard and Rebecca DuFour. Their ideas and examples continue to inspire educators across the world, and their love and friendship live in our hearts. We hope this fourth edition honors their indelible contributions to our profession.

Table of Contents

Reproducibles are in italics.

Chapter 2

Chapter 3

Chapter 4

Chapter 5

Chapter 11

Epilogue

About the Authors

Richard DuFour, EdD, was a public school educator for thirty-four years, serving as a teacher, principal, and superintendent. During his nineteen-year tenure as a leader at Adlai E. Stevenson High School in Lincolnshire, Illinois, Stevenson was one of only three U.S. schools to win the U.S. Department of Education Blue Ribbon Award on four occasions and the first comprehensive high school to be designated a New America High School as a model of successful school reform. He received his state's highest award as both a principal and a superintendent.

A prolific author and sought-after consultant, Dr. DuFour was recognized as one of the leading authorities on helping school practitioners implement the Professional Learning Communities at Work® process in their schools and districts.

Dr. DuFour was presented the Distinguished Scholar Practitioner Award from the University of Illinois and was the 2004 recipient of the National Staff Development Council's Distinguished Service Award.

To learn more about Dr. DuFour's work, visit AllThingsPLC (https://allthingsplc.info).

Rebecca DuFour served as a teacher, school administrator, and central office coordinator. As an elementary principal, she helped her school earn state and national recognition as a Model PLC. She was coauthor of numerous books, articles, and a video series on the topic of PLCs.

Serving as a consultant for more than fifteen years, Becky brought more than thirty-five years of professional experience to her work with educators around the world who were implementing the PLC process in their own organizations.

Becky was the recipient of the Distinguished Alumni Award of Lynchburg College.

To learn more about Becky's work, visit AllThingsPLC (https://allthingsplc.info).

Robert Eaker, EdD, is professor emeritus at Middle Tennessee State University, where he also served as dean of the College of Education and as the university interim vice president and provost. Dr. Eaker is a former fellow with the National Center for Effective Schools Research and Development. He has written widely on the issues of effective teaching, effective schools, and schools and school districts functioning as professional learning communities.

Dr. Eaker is a frequent speaker at national, regional, and state meetings and regularly consults with school districts throughout North America.

To learn more about Dr. Eaker's work, visit AllThingsPLC (https://allthingsplc.info).

Thomas W. Many, EdD, works with teachers, administrators, school boards, parents, and other education stakeholders on organizational leadership, implementation and change, and PLC at Work strategies and concepts. Dr. Many's long and distinguished career includes twenty years of experience as a superintendent. He has also served as a classroom teacher, learning center director, curriculum supervisor, principal, and assistant superintendent.

When he was superintendent of Kildeer Countryside Community Consolidated School District 96 in Illinois, Dr. Many used the tenets of the PLC at Work process to ensure high levels of learning for all students. He played a key role in preparing elementary and middle-grade students to enter Adlai E. Stevenson High School, a nationally recognized PLC. Under Dr. Many's leadership, student achievement in District 96 improved every year for twelve consecutive years. More than 95 percent of all students now meet or exceed state standards. The district has been especially effective in helping students with disabilities improve their academic performance. It has become recognized as one of the premier elementary school districts in the United States.

A dedicated PLC practitioner, Dr. Many is a compelling and sought-after speaker. He has also written numerous articles and has coauthored books.

To learn more about Dr. Many's work, visit AllThingsPLC (https://allthingsplc.info) or follow @tmany96 on X, formerly known as Twitter.

Mike Mattos is an internationally recognized author, presenter, and practitioner who specializes in uniting teachers, administrators, and support staff to transform schools by implementing the response to intervention (RTI) and PLC processes. Mike co-created the RTI at Work™ model, which builds on the foundation of the PLC at Work process by using team structures and a focus on learning, collaboration, and results to successfully create systematic, multitiered systems of support that ensure high levels of learning for all students.

He is former principal of Marjorie Veeh Elementary School and Pioneer Middle School in California. At both schools, Mike helped create powerful PLCs, improving learning for all students. In 2004, Marjorie Veeh, an elementary school with a large population of historically underserved youth, won the California Distinguished School and National Title I Achieving School awards.

A National Blue Ribbon School, Pioneer is among only thirteen schools in the United States selected by the GE Foundation as a Best-Practice Partner and is one of eight schools chosen by Richard DuFour to be featured in the video series *The Power of Professional Learning Communities at Work: Bringing the Big Ideas to Life.* Based on standardized test scores, Pioneer ranks among the top 1 percent of California secondary schools and, in 2009 and 2011, was named Orange County's top middle school. For his leadership, Mike was named the Orange County Middle School Administrator of the Year by the Association of California School Administrators.

To learn more about Mike's work, visit AllThingsPLC (https://allthingsplc.info) or follow him @mikemattos65 on X, formerly known as Twitter.

Anthony Muhammad, PhD, is an author and international thought leader. He served as a practitioner for nearly twenty years as a middle school teacher, assistant principal, middle school principal, and high school principal. His tenure as a practitioner has earned him several awards as both a teacher and a principal. He also serves as an associate professor of school culture and leadership at Academica University of Applied Sciences in Amsterdam.

Dr. Muhammad is recognized as one of the field's leading experts in the areas of school culture and Professional Learning Communities at Work. The Global Gurus organization recognized him as one of the thirty most influential educational thought leaders in the world in 2021, 2022, 2023, and 2024.

Dr. Muhammad is a best-selling author. He is the author of *The Way Forward: PLC at Work and the Bright Future of Education*; *Transforming School Culture: How to Overcome Staff Division, Second Edition*; and *Overcoming the Achievement Gap Trap: Liberating Mindsets to Effect Change.* He is a coauthor of *Revisiting Professional Learning Communities at Work, Second Edition* and *Time for Change: Four Essential Skills for Transformational School and District Leaders.* He has published twenty-six articles in education journals and publications in seven countries.

To learn more about Dr. Muhammad's work, visit New Frontier 21 (www.newfrontier21.com) or follow @newfrontier21 on X, formerly known as Twitter.

To book Thomas W. Many, Mike Mattos, or Anthony Muhammad for professional development, contact pd@SolutionTree.com.

Introduction

Since the first public school in what would become the United States opened in Boston on April 23, 1635 (National Geographic Society, 2023), there has never been a shortage of initiatives aimed at improving public schools. However, with few exceptions, each has been short-lived. The Professional Learning Communities at Work® (PLC at Work) process is one exception. It has been more than twenty-five years since the 1998 publication of *Professional Learning Communities at Work: Best Practices for Enhancing Student Achievement* by Richard DuFour and Robert Eaker, and the number of schools and school districts implementing the PLC at Work process continues to show considerable growth (allthingsplc.info, 2024). Schools that have embedded PLC at Work practices can be found in every state and province in North America and increasingly throughout the world (allthingsplc.info, 2024).

What accounts for the staying power of the PLC at Work process? Why, after more than twenty-five years, does the PLC at Work process continue to grow in popularity? The primary reason is results. When embedded with fidelity and specificity, the PLC at Work process leads to improved student learning (Cottingham, Hough, & Myung, 2023; Hanson et al., 2021; Read On Arizona, 2024; Solution Tree, 2024a–j). While many factors contribute to long-term acceptance of and commitment to various improvement initiatives, by far the most powerful factor is always results. It is difficult to disagree with solid data that show increases in student learning.

In traditional schools, results are often thought of in terms of likability—whether a particular process or practice is liked by the faculty. While the PLC at Work process places a high value on administrator, faculty, and staff feelings, ultimately, the measure of results is the impact on student learning, and the PLC at Work process continues to demonstrate a positive impact on student learning in all kinds of schools of various sizes, grade levels, and socioeconomic conditions. (See "Why Should We Implement the Professional Learning Communities at Work Process?" on pages 11–12 for what the research says about the impact of the PLC at Work process.)

Contributing to the continuing popularity of PLC at Work is the reliance on collaborative teaming as the engine that drives the work. The primary structural characteristic of traditional schools is individual teachers being asked to do an increasingly difficult and complex job in isolation, by themselves. In today's schools, this is a recipe for failure and eventually contributes to low morale. The use of collaborative teaming provides teachers with an enhanced sense of hope and confidence. While an individual teacher might think, "I cannot be successful," they come to believe, "We can succeed," when working as a contributing member of a high-performing team. Teaming in a PLC at Work school gives teachers hope.

Since the primary structural characteristic of a school that functions as a PLC at Work is collaborative teaming, the vast majority of work that takes place is practitioner driven. DuFour and Eaker did not coin the term *professional learning communities*. Others had done that prior to 1998 (Hord, 1997; Little & McLaughlin, 1993). What they did do was embed processes that were both research based and, importantly, practitioner driven through action research. The result was a professional learning community "at work"—a broad framework and processes that reflect common sense. Since these processes are practitioner driven, they are doable, and most important, they have proven to be effective.

While educators in schools that have embedded the PLC at Work process value traditional research, they also place a high value on action research from practitioners within their profession. For teachers, the results of practitioner-conducted action research have a high degree of credibility. Our experience in schools has led us to believe that the fact the PLC at Work process is practitioner driven is a critical factor in its continuing success. In short, the PLC at Work process has proven sustainable because it is credible, and it is credible, in part, because it is practitioner driven.

Since the publication of the third edition of *Learning by Doing* in 2016, we, along with our colleagues and fellow practitioners, have continued to learn by doing. This fourth edition serves as an update on both our knowing and, importantly, our doing as we continue on the never-ending journey of improving student and adult learning.

What's New in This Edition

The PLC at Work process is an ongoing process in which educators work in recurring cycles of collective inquiry and action research to increase their learning and the learning of the students they serve. As authors, we continue to practice what we preach. The goal of this fourth edition is not only to update the research behind our original recommendations, but to revise and expand where we—as a profession—have learned and improved. To this end, this edition includes the following major additions.

- As a global community, we have been immeasurably impacted by the COVID-19 pandemic. Every school, educator, and student is dealing with the social, emotional, and academic repercussions of this once-in-a-century event. It would be naive at best, and downright irresponsible at worst, to not address this reality and provide context to our recommendations moving forward.
- Because the PLC at Work process is driven by job-embedded staff development for educators, we have learned much about how coaches and coaching can assist with this process. To this end, we have added to this edition a chapter on coaching in a PLC at Work. We feel blessed that original coauthor Tom Many and his colleagues Susan K. Sparks, Tesha Ferriby Thomas, and Michael J. Maffoni have been thought leaders in this area and contributed greatly to this new chapter.

- We are truly honored to add a coauthor, Anthony Muhammad, to this edition. Anthony is recognized as a "Global Guru" in the field of education (Global Gurus, 2024) and a thought leader on school culture. He has added this expertise to multiple chapters, including a significant update to the chapter on dealing with resistance.
- If our profession is going to close the learning gaps that were exacerbated by the COVID-19 pandemic, schools must provide targeted academic and behavior interventions. In this edition, we have added greater clarity on how to leverage the PLC at Work process to create a highly effective multitiered system of support (MTSS): response to intervention (RTI).
- As we reflected on the hundreds of Model PLC schools and districts around the world, and what we saw in the leadership that successfully transformed their organizations, one trait stood out as a constant: effective leaders do more than teach and support colleagues in implementing the right practices; they also continuously connect this work to our fundamental mission of helping every student succeed. Great leaders—be they teachers, support staff, or administrators—touch the hearts of those they serve. In the epilogue of this edition, we go deeper into this critical leadership trait.

These represent the major additions to this edition. But along with these are many small additions and revisions to every chapter, including many new research and resource references. We learned a lot writing this new edition—we hope you learn at least as much!

A Move From Interest to Commitment: The Issue of PLC Lite

While it is gratifying to witness the increasing popularity of the PLC at Work process, it is frustrating to observe many schools adopt the term *professional learning community* but fail to deeply embed the concepts and practices inherent in the PLC at Work process. The lack of movement from interest to a strong commitment has resulted in what is often referred to as *PLC Lite*. PLC Lite schools are, in reality, traditional schools that refer to themselves as PLCs because they adopted the popular term and made a few relatively minor changes. PLC Lite schools may enhance public relations, but they do little to improve student learning.

Becoming a high-performing PLC at Work is a journey from simply being interested to becoming deeply committed. Our colleagues Kenneth Williams and Tom Hierck (2015) offer an analogy to describe the journey from interest to commitment. To paraphrase, they observe that many educators are "flirting" with the PLC at Work process, observing the process from afar but not taking positive steps to move forward. Other educators are "dating" PLCs. They are dabbling in the work and curious about its potential, but leaving their options open so they can break up when the next hot thing comes along. Still other educators are "engaged" to the PLC at Work process. They have made a commitment to engage fully in the work and are striving to get better at it. As Williams and Hierck (2015) put it, the educators in the last category have "put a ring on it" (p. 96). Finally, we would extend the analogy to say that some educators are "married" to the PLC at Work process. This is the way of life they have chosen, and they would never return to their old ways of doing things. Their schools continue to flourish even if key leaders leave because the PLC at Work process is so deeply embedded in the school culture it has become "the way we do things around here," day in and day out.

It is time for educators to shift from an interest in the PLC at Work process to a commitment, where there are no excuses for failing to move forward. It is time to progress from flirting with PLC at Work to marrying the process. It is time to move from thinking and talking about PLCs to *doing* what PLC at Work schools and school districts actually do and continuously getting better at it—forever. The moral imperative for engaging fully in this process has never been stronger, and we do not apologize for presenting this book as what we intend it to be: a demand for action and fidelity from educators at all levels.

In this fourth edition, we recommend that readers access online reproducibles along with various tools and templates that are available at **go.SolutionTree.com/PLCbooks**. In addition, we urge readers to visit AllThingsPLC (https://allthingsplc.info) to access research, case studies, strategies, and additional tools. AllThingsPLC is also a place for educators who are on the PLC at Work journey to share ideas, issues, and materials with fellow travelers.

The Format

In this book, we continue with the format that we introduced in the second edition. Starting in chapter 2, each chapter of this handbook includes seven parts. In addition to these seven parts, we include a new eighth part in each chapter with recommended resources for digging deeper.

- Part One: The Case Study
- Part Two: Here's How
- Part Three: Here's Why
- Part Four: Assessing Your Place on the PLC Journey
- Part Five: Tips for Moving Forward
- Part Six: Questions to Guide the Work of Your Professional Learning Community
- Part Seven: Dangerous Detours and Seductive Shortcuts
- Part Eight: Digging Deeper—Recommended Resources

Part One: The Case Study

Each chapter opens with a case study describing some of the challenges that have arisen in a school or district that is attempting to implement the PLC process. The names of the schools and people described in the case studies are fictional, but the situations presented are neither fictional nor hypothetical. They represent the very real issues educators must grapple with and resolve if they are to bring the PLC process to life in their schools and districts. Readers may be tempted to skip the case studies and move quickly to solutions; we urge you to resist that temptation. A critical step in assessing alternative solutions to any problem is to come to an understanding and appreciation of the problem itself. We hope you will take the time to consider each case study carefully, reflect on the issues it presents, and generate possible strategies for addressing those issues prior to studying the rest of the chapter. Engaging in this reflective process with your colleagues will further strengthen your learning.

Part Two: Here's How

In our work with schools, we find that *how* questions come in at least two varieties. The first type represents sincere solicitations of guidance from inquirers who are willing to act, and the other typically comes in waves as a series of "Yeah, but . . ." questions. For example, after listening to an explanation of the PLC process, a teacher or administrator responds with the following.

- "Yeah, but . . . how are we supposed to find time to collaborate?"
- "Yeah, but . . . how can we give students extra time and support for learning when our schedule will not allow it?"
- "Yeah, but . . . how can this work in a school this big [or small, or poor, or urban, or rural, or suburban, or low achieving and therefore too despondent, or high achieving and therefore too complacent]?"
- "Yeah, but . . . how can we make this happen with our ineffective principal [or unsupportive central office, or adversarial teachers union]?"

These questions are less a search for ways to successfully implement the PLC process than a search for a reason to avoid implementation. As Peter Block (2003), an expert in organizational development, says, "Asking How? is a favorite defense against taking action" (p. 11). Block (2003) goes on to say, "We act like we are confused, like we don't understand. The reality is that we *do* understand—we get it, but we don't like it" (pp. 47–48). Our own work with schools has confirmed that a group that is determined not to act can always find a justification for inaction. Questions about *how* can have a positive impact only if those asking are willing to act on the answers. We challenge you, as you read this book, to begin with the attitude that you are seeking a solution for every obstacle instead of looking for an obstacle in every solution.

Therefore, the Here's How sections in this book are written for those who seek ideas, insights, and information regarding how the PLC process comes alive in the real world of schools. Part Two of each chapter describes how educators bring a particular PLC element to life in their school. It presents exemplars for schools to use as models as they work through the challenges of moving from concept to action.

We fully recognize that there is no precise recipe for school improvement (blending two parts collaboration with one part formative assessment does not work). We also understand that even the most promising strategies must be customized for the specific context of each district and each school. The most effective improvement models are those that staff have *adapted* to fit the situation in their schools and communities. In these schools and districts, "leaders use an array of strategies and tactics to accommodate the contextual realities in which they operate" (Mourshed, Chijioke, & Barber, 2010, p. 62). Therefore, the Here's How sections do not presume to present the answers to problems posed in the case studies, because the dialogue about and the struggle with those problems at the school and district levels are what result in the deepest learning and greatest commitment for teachers and administrators. Our hope is this book can serve as a tool that educators can use to initiate the dialogue and engage in the struggle.

Part Three: Here's Why

Informing others about how they can do something does not ensure they will be persuaded to do it. In fact, we are convinced that one of the most common mistakes school administrators make in the implementation of improvement initiatives is to focus exclusively on *how* while being inattentive to *why*. Leaders at all levels must be prepared to anticipate and respond to the inevitable questions and concerns that arise when educators are called on to engage in new practices. We have included Part Three in each chapter to offer useful tools—research, reasoning, and rationale—to help clarify why the initiative should be undertaken.

Throughout the book, we have provided a concise summary of research to assist in the consideration of the *why* question for a specific recommended action. Our review of research draws on, but is not limited to, the research base on education. We examine findings from studies in organizational development, change processes, leadership, effective communication, and psychology because the challenges facing contemporary leaders demand that they look outside the narrow scope of their professional field for answers. We recommend encouraging staff members to review the summaries of research and to identify any research that refutes or contradicts it. In every case, the weight of the evidence should be apparent to all who consider it.

Part Four: Assessing Your Place on the PLC Journey

In each chapter of this handbook, we'll ask you to reflect on the current conditions in your school or district and assess the alignment of those conditions with specific principles and practices of a PLC.

The assessment will present a five-point continuum.

1. **Pre-initiating stage:** The school has not yet begun to address this PLC principle or practice.
2. **Initiating stage:** The school has made an effort to address this principle or practice, but the effort has not yet begun to impact a critical mass of staff members.

3. **Implementing stage:** A critical mass of staff members are participating in implementing the principle or practice, but many approach the task with a sense of compliance rather than commitment. There is some uncertainty regarding what needs to be done and why it should be done.

4. **Developing stage:** Structures are being altered to support the changes, and resources are being devoted to moving them forward. Members are becoming more receptive to the principle, practice, or process because they have experienced some of its benefits. The focus has shifted from "Why are we doing this?" to "How can we do this more effectively?"

5. **Sustaining stage:** The principle or practice is deeply embedded in the culture of the school. It is a driving force in the daily work of staff. It is deeply internalized, and staff would resist attempts to abandon the principle or practice.

The continuum in each chapter is based on the premise that it is easier to get from point A to point B if you know where point B is and can recognize it when you get there. The sustaining stage of the continuum explains point B in vivid terms. It describes the better future your school is moving toward on its PLC journey. A journey from A to B, however, also requires some clarity regarding the starting point. The continuum is a tool to help educators assess the current position of their school or team so that they can move forward purposefully rather than fitfully.

This continuum can be administered across a district, school, or team. Many districts have converted it to an electronic format and used a simple survey tool, such as SurveyMonkey, to gather information on staff perceptions. Whatever format you use, we recommend that you begin the process by asking each individual to make anonymous, independent, and candid assessments and to offer evidence and anecdotes to support their conclusions on each characteristic presented.

Once members complete their individual assessments, the results should be compiled and shared with all participants. Staff members can then analyze the results and use them to begin a dialogue to clarify the current reality of their team, school, or district. Participants should be particularly attentive to discrepancies in responses and explore reasons for the differences. Groups tend to gloss over disagreements—one person contends the school is in the pre-initiating stage while another contends it is developing, and to avoid discussion, they merely compromise and settle for the initiating stage. Avoid that temptation. Delve into one another's thinking to see if you can clarify discrepancies and establish common ground.

Part Five: Tips for Moving Forward

Each chapter includes specific suggestions and strategies to assist with the implementation of particular PLC practices. The primary purpose of this handbook is to encourage people to act, to learn by doing. Random actions, however, do nothing to enhance the capacity of a staff to function as a PLC. The challenge facing leaders is to recognize purposeful and focused actions that contribute to the goal of improved learning for students and staff alike. Part Five offers insights regarding which actions to take and which to avoid. It identifies tactics that offer the greatest leverage for implementing PLC practices and presents research-based and practitioner-proven tips for pursuing those tactics effectively.

Part Six: Questions to Guide the Work of Your Professional Learning Community

PLC team members engage in *collective* inquiry: they learn how to learn together. But only when they focus this collective inquiry on the right questions do they develop their capacity to improve student and adult learning.

It has been said that the leader of the past knew how to tell. The leader of the future, however, will have to know how to ask. Those who lead the PLC process should not be expected to have all the answers and tell others what they must do. Leaders should instead be prepared to ask the right questions, facilitate the dialogue, and help build shared knowledge. Part Six offers some of the right questions educators should consider as they work to drive the PLC process deeper into the culture of their schools and districts.

Part Seven: Dangerous Detours and Seductive Shortcuts

The *process* of learning together is what helps educators build their capacity to create a powerful PLC. A mistake that they commonly make on the journey is to seek ways to circumvent that process. This section alerts readers to some of the most common ways educators have attempted to avoid actually doing the work of a PLC so they won't fall victim to those mistakes.

Part Eight: Digging Deeper—Recommended Resources

The PLC at Work process is a practitioner-driven movement. Since the publication of the first book on the topic in 1998 (DuFour & Eaker, 1998), hundreds of Model PLC schools and districts have continued to use collective inquiry and action research to develop better and better ways to collaboratively improve student and adult learning. This has led to numerous resources that provide additional insights, examples, and tools. At the end of each chapter, we will recommend specific resources that dig deeper into essential aspects of the chapter.

Two Companion Books

This fourth edition of *Learning by Doing* is intended to offer a comprehensive rationale for implementing the PLC process, the research that supports the various elements of the process, common mistakes people make in implementation, and specific strategies and tools for overcoming those mistakes. The key word in this description is *comprehensive*. We recognize that there may be readers who get stuck because they are looking for a quick answer to help them move forward from a specific problem.

Therefore, we have created a companion book to this edition, *Concise Answers to Frequently Asked Questions About Professional Learning Communities at Work* (Mattos, DuFour, DuFour, Eaker, & Many, 2016), to meet their needs as well. This guide on the side is arranged in a question-and-answer format by topic for easy reference. For example, if you are looking for what the research indicates is the best way to organize teams, or how a school counselor could contribute to their PLC's collaborative process, or answers to countless other specific questions, this book is the place to find what you need to know.

Additionally, our dear friend and colleague William Ferriter (2020) has written an outstanding book that is aligned with *Learning by Doing*, titled *The Big Book of Tools for Collaborative Teams in a PLC at Work*. As the title implies, this resource is full of practical, proven tools to help with the doing part of the process.

AllThingsPLC

In addition to books, Solution Tree provides a completely commerce-free digital resource—the AllThingsPLC website (https://allthingsplc.info). This free site provides detailed information on and contact information for hundreds of Model PLC at Work schools and districts across the world. Every Model PLC has effectively implemented all the essential elements of the PLC at Work process and has achieved multiple years of significant, sustained improvement in student achievement. The list of Model PLCs is searchable by level (elementary school, middle school, high school, and district), school size, demographics, and location, and these schools will gladly share what they have learned. We highly recommend utilizing this valuable resource when you want to see how the practices this book describes are being implemented in real schools.

A Journey Worth Taking

Despite the popularity of the term *professional learning community*, the *practices* of a PLC continue to represent the road less traveled in public education. Many teachers and administrators prefer the familiarity of their current path, even when it becomes apparent that it will not take them to their desired destination. We recognize it is difficult to pursue an uncharted path, particularly when it will include inevitable bumps and potholes along the way. We do not argue that the PLC journey is an easy one, but we know with certainty that it is a journey worth taking. We have seen the evidence of improved learning and heard the testimonials of teachers and principals who have been renewed by establishing common ground, a clear purpose, effective monitoring, and collaborative processes that lead to better results. These individuals describe a heightened sense of professionalism and a resurgence of energy and enthusiasm that committed people have generated while working together to accomplish what they could not do alone. As school change expert Robert Evans (1996) writes:

> Anyone who has been part of such a process, or anyone who has seen first-rate teachers engage in reflective practice together, knows its power and excitement. Opportunities to collaborate and to build knowledge can enhance job satisfaction and performance.

We do not argue that the PLC journey is an easy one, but we know with certainty that it is a journey worth taking.

> At their best, they help schools create a self-reflective, self-renewing capacity as learning organizations. (p. 232)

The following chapters will not eliminate the bumps and potholes of the PLC journey, but they will offer some guidance as to how educators can maneuver their way around and through the rough spots on the road. It has been said that a journey of a thousand miles begins with a single step. For those of you who are new to the PLC process, we urge you to take that step. And for those already on the journey, we hope the content in this new edition will assist your next steps. Let us begin together.

Why Should We Implement the Professional Learning Communities at Work® Process?

PLC at Work schools and districts are in every state and province in North America and, increasingly, throughout the world. In addition, there are more than six hundred Model PLC at Work schools and districts—those that present clear evidence of student learning after implementing PLC concepts for at least three years—in forty states in the United States, and in Canada, Australia, New Zealand, Ethiopia, Indonesia, and Singapore (AllThingsPLC.info, 2024).

The PLC at Work process can be implemented at the school, district, and state levels. There are efficacy data from every level and success stories from Model PLC schools and districts that show improved student outcomes. This document highlights just a portion of those data and stories. Visit go.SolutionTree.com/PLCbooks to find an expanded version of this reproducible and www.AllThingsPLC.info to learn more and see the evidence.

State Level

Visit www.SolutionTree.com/st-states to learn more about Solution Tree's state offices.

Arkansas

The Arkansas Division of Elementary and Secondary Education partnered with Solution Tree to launch the PLC at Work project in the 2017–2018 school year in nine schools and one district. After just two years, PLC at Work had a positive impact on achievement growth in Arkansas, particularly in mathematics. Education Northwest, a third-party research firm, measured growth on the ACT Aspire English language arts (ELA) and mathematics assessments between the year prior to implementation (2016–2017) and the end of year two (2018–2019). Education Northwest's independent evaluation validated the success of the PLC at Work process, meeting the Every Student Succeeds Act's Tier 2 evidence requirements (Hanson et al., 2021).

Since the first cohort of schools, the PLC at Work process has empowered teachers in over 300 schools and nearly 150 districts across Arkansas, with over 30 schools designated as Model PLCs at Work or Promising Practices schools. Schools have also been honored with such awards as Schools on the Move Toward Excellence, Office of Education Policy "Beating the Odds," and Reward Schools.

"The Arkansas PLC at Work model had an overall positive impact on math ACT Aspire growth, had a positive impact for specific student groups on math ACT Aspire growth, and exceeded impact on math achievement gains shown in other professional learning programs" (Hanson & Torres, 2020, p. 1). In addition, "schools have seen positive changes in student engagement," such as "increased understanding of what assessment scores indicate, increased desire to improve proficiency, improvements in . . . attendance and fewer behavior referrals, and fewer special education referrals" (Torres et al., 2020, p. 4).

California

In 2022–2023, the California Collaborative for Educational Excellence launched its Intensive Assistance Model (IAM), a three-year school-improvement project in eight schools across five districts, to build new approaches to teacher collaboration and student support. IAM's primary focus is aiding schools in implementing the PLC at Work process (Cottingham, Hough, & Myung, 2023). "This pilot has shown promise for creating schools that can quickly diagnose and collectively respond to students' needs. Five of the eight participating schools shared evidence of improved academic outcomes after the first year of implementation, along with increases in teacher satisfaction" (Cottingham et al., 2023, p. 2).

Washington

In Washington, eight schools and two districts have shown continuous improvement in student achievement, becoming Model PLCs. The Washington Association of School Administrators (WASA) and Solution Tree partnered to develop and expand the PLC at Work process across Washington schools, customizing the work by need and district size. In the 2021–2022 and 2022–2023 school years, twenty-seven districts joined the WASA PLC at Work Project—a three-year statewide project designed for district leaders to engage deeply in the PLC at Work process to address issues of equity and to support all students in learning at high levels. Recruitment is ongoing for future cohorts (Solution Tree, 2024j).

Just an investment of five days of guaranteed intervention time (twenty-five minutes per day) for students who didn't learn math content the first time is reducing the need for additional support by more than 50 percent (Solution Tree, 2024j).

District Level

During the sixth year of PLC at Work implementation at Pasadena Independent School District, 95.6 percent of preK students demonstrated emergent literacy skills in writing, and 94.4 percent demonstrated proficiency in math. From year three to year six, the percentage of students in grades 9–12 who achieved mastery in algebra rose from 75 to 90 percent. Pasadena also saw significant jumps in the percentages of students scoring a qualifying score on Advanced Placement exams in ten of fourteen subject areas (Solution Tree, 2024d).

At Southeast Polk Community School District, all elementary data points on statewide summative assessments exceeded the state average; grades 6–8 exceeded the state average in measures of ELA, math, and science; and the achievement gap in grades 7 and 8 math for students receiving free and reduced lunch narrowed by 14 percentage points (Solution Tree, 2024i).

In just three years of implementation, Lake County Schools' state ranking in graduation rate rose from fiftieth to twenty-second, with the rate increasing from 78 to 90 percent (Solution Tree, 2024h).

Tanque Verde Unified School District began their journey to implement the PLC at Work process in 2017. In their two elementary schools, the third-grade passing rates on the statewide ELA assessment jumped from 52 to 77 percent and from 60 to 75 percent between 2019 and 2022 (Read On Arizona, 2024).

School Level

Eleven Model PLC at Work schools attribute their National Blue Ribbon Schools recognition to using professional development and collaborating with Solution Tree (Solution Tree, 2024c). "There is little to no chance that a school can receive the National Blue Ribbon recognition without being focused on the three big ideas of the PLC at Work process." —Eric Twadell, superintendent, Adlai E. Stevenson High School, Illinois (Solution Tree, 2024c)

In just its second year of functioning as a PLC at Work school, Tongue River Elementary School was named a National Blue Ribbon School. Discipline referrals decreased from 256 office visits to 63 in three years. A study of a cohort of students who qualified for free and reduced lunch showed continuous improvement in English and math from third to fifth grade, 29 percent in English and 284 percent in math (Solution Tree, 2024e).

Fern Creek High School increased its test scores from the bottom 10 percent to the 76th percentile of all Kentucky schools within five years to shed its "persistently low achievement" label (Solution Tree, 2024g, p. 3).

At Greater Hartford Academy of the Arts, during the first year of PLC at Work implementation, reading scores rose from 20 to 72 percent at or above proficient, math scores rose from 42 to 68 percent at or above proficient, and writing scores rose from 56 to 80 percent at or above proficient (Solution Tree, 2024a).

With seven consecutive years of PLC at Work implementation, Esther Starkman School has outperformed the provincial averages in grade 6 ELA, math, science, and social studies—at both the acceptable standard and the standard of excellence (Solution Tree, 2024f).

After establishing itself as a PLC, Minnieville Elementary—serving a highly diverse, academically challenging, high English learner population—became the highest-performing Title I school in Prince William County and now boasts a 96 percent passing rate in both ELA and math (Solution Tree, 2024b).

CHAPTER 1

A Guide to Action for Professional Learning Communities at Work

Like the previous editions of this book, this fourth edition is grounded in the understanding that we learn best by doing. We have known this to be true for quite some time. More than 2,500 years ago, Confucius observed, "I hear and I forget. I see and I remember. I do and I understand." Most educators acknowledge that our deepest insights and understandings come from action, followed by reflection and the search for improvement. After all, most educators spent four or five years *preparing* to enter the profession—taking courses on content and pedagogy, observing students and teachers in classrooms, completing student teaching under the tutelage of a veteran teacher, and so on. Yet almost without exception, they admit that they learned more in their first semester of *teaching* than they did in the four or five years they spent preparing to enter the profession. This is not an indictment of higher education; it is merely evidence of the power of learning that is embedded in the work.

Our profession also attests to the importance and power of learning by doing in educating our students. We want students to be *actively engaged* in *hands-on, authentic exercises* that promote *experiential learning*. How odd, then, that a profession that pays such homage to learning by doing is so reluctant to apply that principle when it comes to developing its collective capacity to meet students' needs. Why do institutions created for and devoted to learning not call on the professionals within them to become more proficient in improving the effectiveness of schools by actually doing the work of school improvement? Why have we been so reluctant to learn by doing?

What Are Professional Learning Communities?

Since 1998, we have published many books and videos with the same two goals in mind: (1) to persuade educators that the most promising strategy for meeting the challenge of helping all students learn at high levels is to develop their capacity to function as a professional learning community and (2) to offer specific strategies and structures to help them transform their own schools and districts into PLCs.

It has been interesting to observe the growing popularity of the term *professional learning community*. In fact, the term has become so commonplace and has been used so ambiguously to describe virtually any loose coupling of individuals who share a common interest in education that it is in danger of losing all meaning. This lack of precision is an obstacle to implementing PLC practices because, as Mike Schmoker (2004a) observes, "clarity precedes competence" (p. 85). Thus, we begin this handbook with an attempt to clarify our meaning of the term. To those familiar with our past work, this step may seem redundant, but we are convinced that redundancy can be a powerful tool in effective communication, and we prefer redundancy to ambiguity.

We have seen many instances in which educators assume that a PLC is a program. For example, one faculty told us that each year, they implemented a new program in their school. The previous year, it had been PLC; the year prior to that, it had been Understanding by Design; and the current year, it was differentiated instruction. They had converted the names of the various programs into verbs, and the joke among the faculty was that they had been "PLCed, UBDed, and DIed."

The PLC process is not a program. It cannot be purchased, nor can it be implemented by anyone other than the staff themselves. Most importantly, it is ongoing—a continuous, never-ending process of conducting schooling that has a profound impact on the structure and culture of the school and the assumptions and practices of the professionals within it.

It is helpful to think of the school or district as the PLC and the various collaborative teams as the building blocks of the PLC.

We have seen other instances in which educators assume that a PLC is a meeting—an occasional event when they meet with colleagues to complete a task. It is not uncommon for us to hear, "My PLC meets Wednesdays from 9:00 a.m. to 10:00 a.m." This perception of a PLC is wrong on two counts. First, *the PLC is the larger organization and not the individual teams that comprise it.* While collaborative teams are essential parts of the PLC process, the sum is greater than the individual parts. Much of the work of a PLC cannot be done by a team but instead requires a schoolwide or districtwide effort. So we believe it is helpful to think of the school or district as the PLC and the various collaborative teams as the building blocks of the PLC. Second, once again, the PLC process has a pervasive and ongoing impact on the structure and culture of the school. If educators meet with peers on a regular basis only to return to business as usual, they are not functioning as a PLC. So the PLC process is much more than a meeting.

A PLC is an ongoing process in which educators work collaboratively in recurring cycles of collective inquiry and action research to achieve better results for the students they serve.

Other educators have claimed they are members of a PLC because they engage in dialogue based on common readings. The entire staff reads the same book or article, and then members meet to share their individual impressions of what they have read. But a PLC is more than a book club. Although collective study and dialogue are crucial elements of the PLC process, the process requires people to *act* on the new information.

So, what is a PLC? We argue that it is an ongoing process in which educators work collaboratively in recurring cycles of collective inquiry and action research to achieve better results for the students they serve. PLCs operate under the assumption that the key to improved learning for students is continuous job-embedded learning for educators. Transforming a traditional school into a PLC changes the very culture and structure of the school. We summarize some of these shifts in the reproducible "Cultural Shifts in a Professional Learning Community" on pages 15–17; the following section examines elements of the PLC process more closely.

Cultural Shifts in a Professional Learning Community

A Shift in Fundamental Purpose	
From a focus on teaching . . .	to a focus on learning
From emphasis on what was taught . . .	to a fixation on what students learned
From coverage of content . . .	to demonstration of proficiency
From providing individual teachers with curriculum documents such as state standards and curriculum guides . . .	to engaging collaborative teams in building shared knowledge regarding essential curriculum
A Shift in Use of Assessments	
From infrequent summative assessments . . .	to frequent common formative assessments
From assessments to determine which students failed to learn by the deadline . . .	to assessments to identify students who need additional time and support
From assessments used to reward and punish students . . .	to assessments used to inform and motivate students
From assessing many things infrequently . . .	to assessing a few things frequently
From individual teacher assessments . . .	to collaborative team-developed assessments
From each teacher determining the criteria to use in assessing student work . . .	to collaborative teams clarifying the criteria and ensuring consistency among team members when assessing student work
From an over-reliance on one kind of assessment . . .	to balanced assessments
From focusing on average scores . . .	to monitoring each student's proficiency in every essential skill
A Shift in the Response When Students Don't Learn	
From individual teachers determining the appropriate response . . .	to a systematic response that ensures support for every student
From fixed time and support for learning . . .	to time and support for learning as variables
From remediation . . .	to intervention
From invitational support outside of the school day . . .	to directed (that is, required) support occurring during the school day
From one opportunity to demonstrate learning . . .	to multiple opportunities to demonstrate learning

page 1 of 3

A Shift in the Work of Teachers	
From isolation . . .	to collaboration
From each teacher clarifying what students must learn . . .	to collaborative teams building shared knowledge and understanding about essential learning
From each teacher assigning priority to different learning standards . . .	to collaborative teams establishing the priority of respective learning standards
From each teacher determining the pacing of the curriculum . . .	to collaborative teams of teachers agreeing on common pacing
From individual teachers attempting to discover ways to improve results . . .	to collaborative teams of teachers helping each other improve
From privatization of practice . . .	to open sharing of practice
From decisions made on the basis of individual preferences . . .	to decisions made collectively by building shared knowledge of best practice
From "collaboration lite" on matters unrelated to student achievement . . .	to collaboration explicitly focused on issues and questions that most impact student achievement
From an assumption that these are "my students, those are your students" . . .	to an assumption that these are "our students"
A Shift in Focus	
From an external focus on issues outside of the school . . .	to an internal focus on steps the staff can take to improve the school
From a focus on inputs . . .	to a focus on results
From goals related to completion of projects and activities . . .	to SMART goals demanding evidence of student learning
From teachers gathering data from their individually constructed tests in order to assign grades . . .	to collaborative teams acquiring information from common assessments in order to inform their individual and collective practice and respond to students who need additional time and support
A Shift in School Culture	
From independence . . .	to interdependence
From a language of complaint . . .	to a language of commitment
From long-term strategic planning . . .	to planning for short-term wins
From infrequent generic recognition . . .	to frequent specific recognition and a culture of celebration that creates many winners

page 2 of 3

A Shift in Professional Development	
From external training (workshops and courses) . . .	to job-embedded learning
From the expectation that learning occurs infrequently (on the few days devoted to professional development) . . .	to an expectation that learning is ongoing and occurs as part of routine work practice
From presentations to entire faculties . . .	to team-based action research
From learning by listening . . .	to learning by doing
From learning individually through courses and workshops . . .	to learning collectively by working together
From assessing impact on the basis of teacher satisfaction ("Did you like it?") . . .	to assessing impact on the basis of evidence of improved student learning
From short-term exposure to multiple concepts and practices . . .	to sustained commitment to limited focused initiatives

page 3 of 3

Three Big Ideas That Drive the Work of a PLC

There are three big ideas that drive the work of the PLC process. The progress a district or school experiences on the PLC journey will largely depend on the extent to which these ideas are considered, understood, and ultimately embraced by its members.

A Focus on Learning

The first (and the biggest) of the big ideas is based on the premise that *the fundamental purpose of the school is to ensure that all students learn at high levels (grade level or higher).* This focus on and commitment to the learning of each student is the very essence of a *learning* community.

The fundamental purpose of the school is to ensure that all students learn at high levels.

When a school or district functions as a PLC, educators within the organization embrace high levels of learning for all students as both the reason the organization exists and the fundamental responsibility of those who work within it. To achieve this purpose, the members of a PLC create and are guided by a clear and compelling vision of what the organization must become in order to help all students learn. They make collective commitments, clarifying what each member will do to create such an organization, and they use results-oriented goals to mark their progress. Members work together to clarify exactly what each student must learn, monitor each student's learning on a timely basis, provide systematic interventions that ensure students receive additional time and support for learning when they struggle, and extend learning when students have already mastered the intended outcomes.

A corollary assumption is that if the organization is to become more effective in helping all students learn, the adults in the organization must also be continually learning. Therefore, structures are created to ensure staff members engage in job-embedded learning as part of their routine work practices.

There is no ambiguity or hedging regarding this commitment to learning. Whereas many schools operate as if their primary purpose is to ensure students are *taught* or are merely provided with *an opportunity* to learn, PLCs are dedicated to the idea that their organizations exist to ensure all students actually acquire the essential knowledge, skills, and dispositions of each unit, course, and grade level. Every potential organizational practice, policy, and procedure is assessed on the basis of this question: "Will this ensure higher levels of learning for our students?" All the other characteristics of a PLC flow directly from this epic shift in assumptions about the purpose of the school.

A Collaborative Culture and Collective Responsibility

The second big idea driving the PLC process is that in order to ensure all students learn at high levels, *educators must work collaboratively and take collective responsibility for the success of each student.* Working collaboratively is not optional, but instead is an expectation and requirement of employment. Consequently, the fundamental structure of a PLC is the collaborative teams of educators whose members work *interdependently* to achieve *common goals* for which members are *mutually accountable*. These common goals are directly linked to the purpose of learning for all. The team is the engine that drives the PLC effort and the primary building block of the organization.

It is difficult to overstate the importance of collaborative teams in the improvement process. It is even more important, however, to emphasize that collaboration does not lead to improved results unless people are focused on the right work. Collaboration is a means to an end, not the end itself. In many schools, staff members are willing to collaborate on a variety of topics—as long as the focus of the conversation stops at their classroom door. In a PLC, collaboration represents a systematic process in which teachers work together in order to *impact* their classroom practice in ways that will lead to better results for their students, for their team, and for their school.

In order to ensure all students learn at high levels, educators must work collaboratively and take collective responsibility for the success of each student.

Working together to build shared knowledge on the best way to achieve goals and meet the needs of those they serve is exactly what *professionals* in any field are expected to do, whether they are curing patients, winning lawsuits, or helping all students learn. Members of a *professional* learning community are expected to work and learn together.

A Results Orientation

The third big idea that drives the work of PLCs is the need for a *results orientation*. To assess their effectiveness in helping all students learn, educators in a PLC focus on results—evidence of student learning. They then use that evidence of learning to inform and improve their professional practice and respond to individual students who need intervention or extension. Members of a PLC recognize that all their efforts must ultimately be assessed on the basis of results rather than intentions. Unless their initiatives are subjected to ongoing assessment on the basis of tangible results, they represent random groping in the dark rather than purposeful improvement. As Peter Senge and colleagues (Senge, Kleiner, Roberts, Ross, & Smith, 1994) conclude, "The rationale for any strategy for building a learning organization revolves around the premise that such organizations will produce dramatically improved results" (p. 44).

Educators in a PLC focus on results—evidence of student learning.

This constant search for a better way to improve results by helping more students learn at higher levels leads to a cyclical process in which educators in a PLC:

- Gather evidence of current levels of student learning
- Develop strategies and ideas to build on strengths and address weaknesses in that learning
- Implement those strategies and ideas
- Analyze the impact of the changes to discover what was effective and what was not
- Apply new knowledge in the next cycle of continuous improvement

The intent of this cyclical process (shown in the graphic on the following page) is not simply to learn a new strategy but instead to create conditions for perpetual learning—an environment in which people view innovation and experimentation not as tasks to be

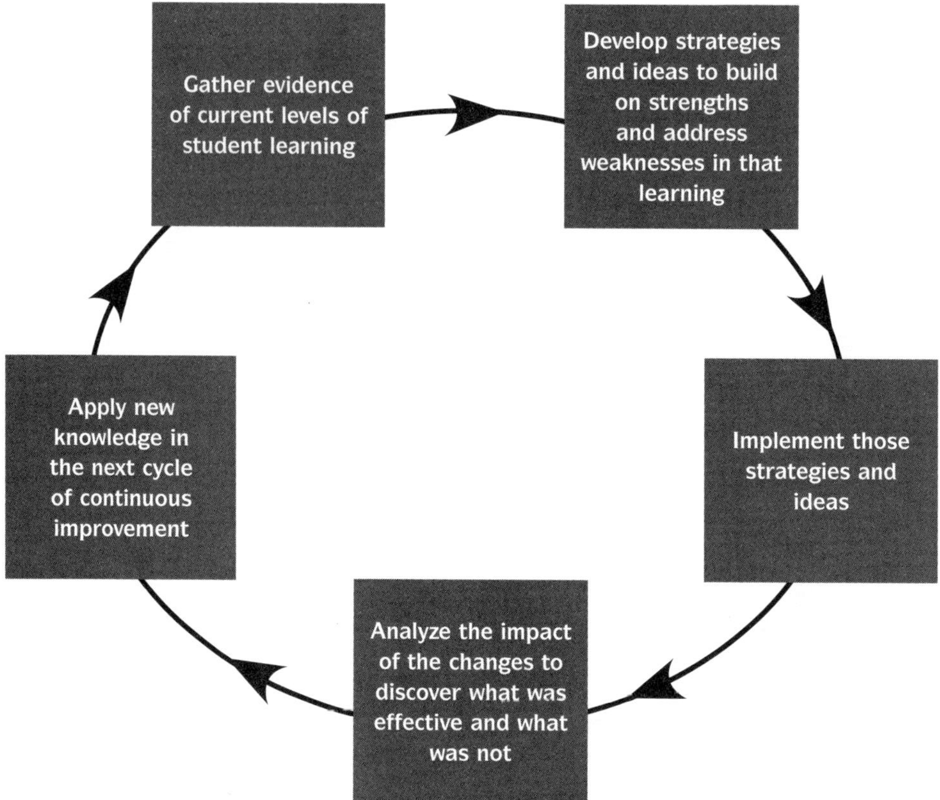

accomplished or projects to be completed but as ways of conducting day-to-day business, *forever*. Furthermore, participation in this process is not reserved for those designated as leaders; rather, it is a responsibility of every member of the organization.

This focus on results leads each team to develop and pursue measurable improvement goals for learning that align with school and district goals. It also drives teams to create a series of common formative assessments that are administered to students multiple times throughout the year to gather ongoing evidence of student learning. Team members review the results of these assessments to identify and address program concerns (areas of learning where many students are experiencing difficulty). They also examine the results to discover strengths and weaknesses in their individual teaching in order to learn from one another. Very importantly, the assessments are used to identify students who need additional time and support for learning. We will make the case that frequent common formative assessments represent one of the most powerful tools in the PLC arsenal.

A Culture That Is Simultaneously Loose and Tight

The PLC process empowers educators to make important decisions and encourages their creativity and innovation in the pursuit of improving student and adult learning. As you read through this text, you will discover that when a school functions as a PLC, teachers collectively make many of the important decisions, including the following.

- What to teach
- The sequencing and pacing of content

- The assessments used to monitor student learning
- The criteria used to assess the quality of student work
- The norms for their team
- The goals for their team

Teachers working in teams have primary responsibility for analyzing evidence of student learning and developing strategies for improvement. They each are free to use the instructional strategies that they feel will be most effective in helping students learn. Teachers have the authority to make all these important decisions because these aspects of the PLC process are said to be "loose."

At the same time, however, there are elements of the PLC process that are "tight"; that is, they are nondiscretionary and everyone in the school is required to adhere to those elements. The tight elements of the PLC process are listed in the following feature box.

Tight Elements in a PLC

1. Work in collaborative teams and take collective responsibility for student learning rather than working in isolation.
2. Implement a guaranteed and viable curriculum, unit by unit.
3. Monitor student learning through an ongoing assessment process that includes frequent, team-developed common formative assessments.
4. Use the results of common assessments to:
   - Improve individual practice
   - Build the team's capacity to achieve its goals
   - Intervene or extend on behalf of students
5. Provide systematic interventions and extensions.

The debate that has raged about whether school improvement should be top-down and driven by administrative mandates or bottom-up and left to the discretion of individuals or groups of teachers has been resolved. Neither top-down nor bottom-up works. Top-down fails to generate either the deep understanding of or the commitment to the improvement initiative that is necessary to sustain it. The laissez-faire bottom-up approach eliminates the press for change and is actually associated with a decrease in student achievement (Marzano & Waters, 2009). High-performing PLCs avoid the too-tight/too-loose trap by engaging educators in an improvement process that empowers them to make decisions at the same time that they demand adherence to core elements of the process (DuFour & Fullan, 2013). We will reference this simultaneously loose and tight culture throughout this book.

The Importance of Effective Communication

The keys to creating a PLC culture that is simultaneously loose and tight are first getting tight about the right things (as listed in the feature box) and then clearly, consistently, and unequivocally communicating what is tight. Marcus Buckingham (2005) contends that the "one thing" leaders of any organization must know to be effective is the importance of clarity. Powerful communication is simple and succinct, driven by a few key ideas, and repeated at every opportunity (Collins, 2001; Pfeffer & Sutton, 2000). Leaders must realize, however, that the most important element in communicating is congruency between their actions and their words. It is not essential that leaders be eloquent or clever, but they must demonstrate consistency between what they say and what they do (Collins & Porras, 1994; Covey, 2006; Erkens & Twadell, 2012; Fullan, 2011; Kanold, 2011; Kouzes & Posner, 1987). When leaders' actions are inconsistent with what they contend are their priorities, those actions overwhelm all other forms of communication (Kotter, 1996).

One way leaders communicate their priorities is by what they pay attention to (Kouzes & Posner, 2003; Peters & Austin, 1985). Subsequent chapters provide specific examples of leaders communicating what is valued by creating systems and structures to promote priorities, monitoring what is essential, reallocating time, asking the right questions, responding to conflict in strategic ways, and celebrating evidence of collective commitments moving their school closer to its vision.

It is important to help your staff build shared knowledge regarding your school's current status for effective communication. Addressing this critical component of a PLC helps in establishing a solid foundation. The need for clear communication is so vital to the PLC process that we present a continuum of effective communication for your consideration. "The Professional Learning Communities at Work® Continuum: Communicating Effectively" is on pages 23–24 and online at **go.SolutionTree.com/PLCbooks** as a free reproducible. Once your staff have established greater clarity regarding the current status of your communication practices, we urge you to turn your attention to the "Where Do We Go From Here?" worksheet that accompanies the continuum (on page 25 and also available for free download at **go.SolutionTree.com/PLCbooks**). It will prompt you to take the action necessary to close the knowing-doing gap.

Attention to Both Structure and Emotions

Creating and aligning the structures necessary for the implementation of the PLC at Work process is essential, but this attention to organizational structure is never enough. Ultimately, if PLCs are to be effective, leaders must focus on human emotions—how people feel—both with students and adults. Effective leaders are effective motivators, and while changing school structures might be *necessary*, those structures alone are rarely *motivators*.

The Professional Learning Communities at Work® Continuum: Communicating Effectively

DIRECTIONS: Individually, silently, and *honestly* assess the current reality of your school's implementation of each indicator listed in the left column. Consider what evidence or anecdotes support your assessment. This form may also be used to assess district or team implementation.

We understand the purpose and priorities of our school because they have been communicated consistently and effectively.

Indicator	Pre-Initiating	Initiating	Implementing	Developing	Sustaining
The school has established a clear purpose and priorities that have been effectively communicated. Systems are in place to ensure action steps aligned with the purpose and priorities are implemented and monitored.	There is no sense of purpose or priorities. People throughout the school feel swamped by what they regard as a never-ending series of fragmented, disjointed, and short-lived improvement initiatives. Changes in leadership inevitably result in changes in direction.	Key leaders may have reached agreement on general purpose and priorities, but people throughout the organization remain unclear. Furthermore, if asked to explain the priorities of the school or the strategies to achieve those priorities, leaders would have difficulty articulating specifics. Staff members would offer very different answers if pressed to explain the priorities of the school.	There is general understanding of the purpose and priorities of the school, but many staff members have not embraced them. Specific steps are being taken to advance the priorities, but some staff members are participating only grudgingly. They view the initiative as interfering with their real work.	Structures and processes have been altered to align with the purpose and priorities. Staff members are beginning to see benefits from the initiative and are seeking ways to become more effective in implementing it.	There is almost universal understanding of the purpose and priorities of the school. All policies, procedures, and structures have been purposefully aligned with the effort to fulfill the purpose and accomplish the priorities. Systems have been created to gauge progress. The systems are carefully monitored, and the resulting information is used to make adjustments designed to build the collective capacity of the group to be successful.

Indicator	Pre-Initiating	Initiating	Implementing	Developing	Sustaining
The leaders in the school communicate purpose and priorities through modeling, allocation of resources, what they celebrate, and what they are willing to confront.	There is no sense of purpose and priorities. Different people in the school seem to have different pet projects, and there is considerable in-fighting to acquire the resources to support those different projects.	Leaders can articulate the purpose and priorities of the school with a consistent voice, but their behavior is not congruent with their words. The structures, resources, and rewards of the school have not been altered to align with the professed priorities.	The school has begun to alter the structures, resources, and rewards to better align with the stated priorities. Staff members who openly oppose the initiative may be confronted, but those confronting them are likely to explain they are doing someone else's bidding. For example, a principal may say, "The central office is concerned that you are overtly resisting the process we are attempting to implement."	People throughout the school are changing their behavior to align with the priorities. They are seeking new strategies for using resources more effectively to support the initiative and are willing to reallocate time, money, materials, and people in order to move forward. Small improvements are recognized and celebrated. Leaders confront incongruent behavior.	The purpose and priorities of the school are evident by the everyday behavior of people throughout the school. Time, money, materials, people, and resources have been strategically allocated to reflect priorities. Processes are in place to recognize and celebrate commitment to the priorities. People throughout the school will confront those who disregard the priorities.

Where Do We Go From Here? Worksheet
Communicating Effectively

Indicator of a PLC at Work	What steps or activities must be initiated to create this condition in your school?	Who will be responsible for initiating or sustaining these steps or activities?	What is a realistic timeline for each step or phase of the activity?	What will you use to assess the effectiveness of your initiative?
The school has established a clear purpose and priorities that have been effectively communicated. Systems are in place to ensure action steps aligned with the purpose and priorities are implemented and monitored. The leaders in the school communicate purpose and priorities through modeling, allocation of resources, what they celebrate, and what they are willing to confront.				

Why Don't We Apply What We Know?

As we have shared our work in support of PLCs with educators from around the world, we have become accustomed to hearing the same response: "This just makes sense." It just makes sense that a school committed to helping all students learn at high levels would focus on learning rather than teaching, would have educators work collaboratively, would ensure students have access to the same curriculum, would assess each student's learning on a timely basis using consistent standards for proficiency, and would create systematic interventions and extensions that provide students with additional time and support for learning. It just makes sense that we would accomplish more working collaboratively than we do working in isolation. It just makes sense that we would assess our effectiveness in helping all students learn on the basis of results—tangible evidence that they have actually learned. It just makes sense! In fact, we have found little overt opposition to the characteristics of a PLC.

So why don't schools *do* what they already *know* makes sense? In *The Knowing-Doing Gap: How Smart Companies Turn Knowledge Into Action*, Jeffrey Pfeffer and Robert I. Sutton (2000) explore what they regard as one of the great mysteries of organizational management: the disconnect between knowledge and action. They ask, "Why does knowledge of what needs to be done so frequently fail to result in action or behavior that is consistent with that knowledge?" (Pfeffer & Sutton, 2000, p. 4).

Learning by Doing *is intended to help educators close the knowing-doing gap by transforming their schools into PLCs.*

Learning by Doing is intended to help educators close the knowing-doing gap by transforming their schools into PLCs. It reveals purposeful, realistic, actionable steps educators can take to develop their capacity to function as a PLC. It is designed to accomplish the following five objectives.

1. Help educators develop a common vocabulary and a consistent understanding of key practices in the PLC process.
2. Present a compelling argument that American educators have a moral imperative to improve their individual and collective practice.
3. Help educators assess the current reality in their own schools and districts.
4. Offer tools, templates, protocols, and sample products to help educators on their journey.
5. Eliminate excuses for inaction and convince educators that the best way to become more effective in the PLC process is to begin doing what PLCs do.

Help Educators Develop a Common Vocabulary and a Consistent Understanding of Key Practices in the PLC Process

Michael Fullan (2005) observes that "terms travel easily . . . but the meaning of the underlying concepts does not" (p. 67). Terms such as *professional learning community, collaborative teams, goals, formative assessments,* and scores of others have indeed traveled widely in educational circles. They are prevalent in the lexicon of contemporary "educationese." If pressed for a specific definition, however, many educators would be stumped. It is difficult enough to bring these concepts to life in a school or district when there *is* a shared understanding of their meaning. It is impossible when there is no common understanding and the terms mean very different things to different people within the same organization.

Developmental psychologists Robert Kegan and Lisa Laskow Lahey (2001) contend that the transformation of both individuals and organizations requires new language. They write, "The places where we work and live are, among other things, places where certain forms of speech are promoted or encouraged, and places where other ways of talking are discouraged or made impossible" (Kegan & Lahey, 2001, p. 7). As educators make the cultural shift from traditional schools and districts to PLCs, a new language emerges. Therefore, we have highlighted and defined key terms used in implementing the PLC process to assist in building shared knowledge of both critical vocabulary and the concepts underlying the terms. We have also included an online glossary at **go.SolutionTree.com/PLCbooks** that readers can freely download and distribute. We hope it will add to the precision and clarity of the emerging language that accompanies the transformation of traditional schools and districts into high-performing PLCs.

We have included an online glossary at go.SolutionTree.com/PLCbooks that readers can freely download and distribute.

Present a Compelling Argument That American Educators Have a Moral Imperative to Improve Their Individual and Collective Practice

Americans have always been critical of their public schools. But since the passage of No Child Left Behind in 2001, the media and politicians have seemed to be waging an increasingly aggressive war not just on the public school system but also on the educators within it. This legacy has continued into the second decade of the 21st century. A 2023 Gallup poll found that just 36 percent of American citizens have a favorable view of the American public school system.

We reject the notion that American schools are failing and that educators are the cause of that failure. In the first two decades of the 2000s, educators achieved some of the best results in U.S. history. Consider the following.

- Schools experienced the highest high school graduation rates in American history, and the rates improved for every subgroup of students.
- More high school students succeeded in rigorous college-level work than ever before in American history.
- Scores on the National Assessment of Educational Progress (NAEP) improved steadily since that test was first administered in the 1970s (Ravitch, 2014).
- American students scored in the top ten in the world and considerably above the international mean on Trends in International Mathematics and Science Study (TIMSS) exams (Martin, Mullis, Foy, & Stanco, 2012; Mullis, Martin, Foy, & Arora, 2012).

- From 2009, parents' satisfaction with their local schools was among the highest ever recorded in the more than four decades since *Phi Delta Kappan* and the Gallup Poll began conducting this survey (*Phi Delta Kappan*/Gallup Poll Archive, 2014).

- American students in schools with low poverty outperformed their international peers in the highest-performing countries in the world with similar poverty rates (Shyamalan, 2013).

- American students consistently gave their teachers among the highest ratings in the world on such qualities as fairness and willingness to provide them extra support (DuFour, 2015).

Contemporary American educators have accomplished more, with a more diverse student population, than any previous generation.

Contemporary American educators have accomplished more, with a more diverse student population, than any previous generation. They warrant respect rather than condemnation. We must acknowledge, however, that the COVID-19 pandemic negatively impacted much of the progress in education we have witnessed since 2000. The need to help every student succeed in school has never been greater because the consequences of failure in the K–12 system have never been more dire.

Evidence gathered in the aftermath of the COVID-19 pandemic includes devastating impacts on teacher well-being, teacher retention, new teacher preparation, student well-being, and student learning.

- The World Economic Forum found that 2.6 percent of the American workforce voluntarily left their jobs during the "Great Resignation" of 2020 and 2021, causing a national labor shortage (Ellerbeck, 2023).

- KFF (formerly known as the Kaiser Family Foundation) found that American adults reporting signs of anxiety or depression increased from 11 percent to 41.1 percent between 2019 and 2021 (Panchal, Saunders, Rudowitz, & Cox, 2023).

- A 2022 Merrimack College survey found only 12 percent of American teachers reported job satisfaction—a record low (Will, 2022).

- In the first seven months of the 2021–2022 school year, Chicago Public Schools, one of the United States' largest urban school districts, experienced an 85 percent increase in employee retirements and resignations compared to the previous school year (Koumpilova, 2022).

- The number of new teachers being prepared in traditional four-year university credentialing programs decreased nearly 30 percent from 2010 to 2020 (Goldhaber & Holden, 2020).

- In 2021–2022, 50 percent of middle school students and 56 percent of high school students reported consistent feelings of stress, anxiety, or depression (YouthTruth, 2022).

- A Harvard University study found that on average for the 2020–2021 and 2021–2022 school years, American students made about 80 percent of the academic progress they would typically make during a school year pre-pandemic (Goldhaber et al., 2022).

- The 2022 National Assessment of Educational Progress (NAEP) reported a record number of students scoring in the lowest test performance category, *below basic*, in both mathematics and reading. Collectively, this was the poorest aggregated performance on this assessment in the history of the NAEP exam (Jimenez, 2022).

Throughout most of the 20th century, a student could withdraw from high school and still have access to the middle class. In 1970, 74 percent of the middle class was composed of high school graduates and dropouts. By 2007, the middle class was composed of 31 percent high school graduates and only 8 percent dropouts (Carnevale, Smith, & Strohl, 2010).

Furthermore, many high school graduates seem unprepared for the rigors of higher education. One of America's most trusted college admissions exams, the ACT, reported that the average composite score of American high school students in 2023 reached a record low for the century at 19.5 out of a possible 36, with 43 percent of all test takers not meeting any college readiness benchmarks in mathematics, reading, writing, or science (Jones & Kallingal, 2023).

These statistics are alarming because people who are not prepared to continue learning beyond high school will be increasingly left behind in the American economy (Carnevale et al., 2010). Consider the implications for students who are unsuccessful in the K–12 system.

- As of 2019, only 44.6 percent of American high school dropouts were employed compared to 72.3 percent of college graduates (Bureau of Labor Statistics, 2019).
- In 2022, the poverty rate for high school dropouts was 25.2 percent, while bachelor's degree holders had a poverty rate of 4.3 percent (Statista, 2023).
- The Federal Reserve Bank of New York reports that a high school graduate between the ages of twenty-two and twenty-seven earns $22,000 less per year than a bachelor's degree holder in the same age group (Hardy, 2022).
- High school graduates live, on average, more than ten years longer than high school dropouts (Lee-St. John et al., 2018).
- High school dropouts are six times more likely to be incarcerated than high school graduates, and the likelihood is even higher for African American and Latino boys (Camera, 2021).
- On average, each high school dropout costs taxpayers $292,000 over their lifetime (Lynch, 2016).

PLC at Work is more important now than in any other period in American history.

So while we reject the idea that American schools are terrible and getting worse, we also acknowledge the moral imperative for improving schools so that all students are prepared for postsecondary learning. American educators must view every student as if they were their own child and provide the same education they would want for their own (DuFour, 2015). We also acknowledge the added challenges of the COVID-19 pandemic have placed educators in an unprecedented dilemma that requires unprecedented urgency. PLC at Work is more important now than in any other period in American history.

A key step in any effective improvement process is an honest assessment of the current reality—a diligent effort to determine the truth.

Help Educators Assess the Current Reality in Their Own Schools and Districts

For many educators, however, school-improvement initiatives have been plagued by uncertainty and confusion regarding both the current status of their school and what they hope it will become. As a result, efforts to reform their schools have too often been characterized by random stops and starts, rather than by purposeful progression on a path of improvement. A key step in any effective improvement process is an honest assessment of the current reality—a diligent effort to determine the truth. Educators will find it easier to move forward to where they want to go if they first agree on where they are.

Even when teachers and administrators make a good-faith effort to assess their schools, they face significant obstacles. All schools have cultures: the assumptions, beliefs, expectations, and habits that constitute the norm for a school and guide the work of the educators within it. Perhaps it is more accurate, however, to say that educators do not have *school cultures* but rather that the school cultures have *them*. Teachers and administrators are typically so immersed in their traditional ways of doing things that they find it difficult to step outside those traditions to examine conventional practices from a fresh, critical perspective. Therefore, this handbook, and particularly the continua presented throughout, is designed not only to offer specific examples of PLC practices but also to help educators frankly assess the current conditions in their schools.

Offer Tools, Templates, Protocols, and Sample Products to Help Educators on Their Journey

As we have worked in our own schools and assisted many hundreds of others, we have found that providing the right tools, templates, protocols, and sample products can help make the complex simpler and increase the self-efficacy of educators. We have attempted to gather these useful instruments in one place so that readers can access what they need at different points in the process. We hope that they are helpful, but they are not carved in stone. Feel free to adapt and modify them to make them fit your unique situations.

Eliminate Excuses for Inaction and Convince Educators That the Best Way to Become More Effective in the PLC Process Is to Begin Doing What PLCs Do

Our greatest hope in developing this handbook is that it will help educators take immediate and specific steps to close the knowing-doing gap in education by implementing the PLC process in their own schools and districts. There has never been greater consensus regarding what educators can do to improve their schools. As a profession, we know with certainty that more students learn at higher levels when:

- Their school is committed to high levels of learning for each student
- Educators have collaboratively clarified the knowledge, skills, and dispositions students are to acquire as a result of each unit, course, and grade level
- Student learning is monitored on an ongoing basis
- The school has a systematic process for providing students with extra time and support when they struggle and extended learning when they are proficient
- Educators work together to inform and improve their individual and collective practice with transparent evidence of student learning

Our greatest hope in developing this handbook is that it will help educators take immediate and specific steps to close the knowing-doing gap.

Conversely, there is simply no credible evidence that schools are more effective when educators work in isolation and the questions of what students learn, how they are assessed, and what happens when they struggle are left to the randomness of the individual teacher to whom they have been assigned.

When professionals know better, they have an obligation to do better. Our profession now clearly knows better. The weight of the evidence from research, professional organizations, high-performing districts and schools, and common sense has made it clear that schools are more effective when they operate as PLCs. It is time for educators to act on what they know. The question confronting most schools and districts is not, "What do we need to know in order to improve?" but rather, "Will we turn what we already know into action?"

Perhaps the greatest insight we have gained in our work with school districts in the United States and throughout the world is organizations that take the plunge and actually begin *doing* the work of a PLC develop their capacity to help all students learn at high levels far more effectively than schools that spend years *preparing* to become a PLC through reading or even training. Michael Fullan, who has studied school-improvement efforts from around the world, has come to a similar conclusion. He argues that educators must move quickly from conversations about mission and vision to action because "it is learning by purposeful doing that counts most" (Fullan & Quinn, 2016, p. 21).

This book is not meant to be a study guide; it is emphatically an action guide. Developing the collective capacity of educators to create high-performing PLCs demands more than book studies and workshops. It demands "the daily habit of *working together*, and you can't learn this from a workshop or course. You need to learn it by doing it and having mechanisms for getting better at it on purpose" (Fullan, 2005, p. 69). So let's examine some of the challenges of working together and consider mechanisms for getting better at it.

This book is not meant to be a study guide; it is emphatically an action guide.

CHAPTER 2

Defining a Clear and Compelling Purpose

Part One

The Case Study: Clarifying Our Purpose

Principal Cynthia Dion left the Professional Learning Community at Work Institute with the zeal and fervor of a recent convert. She was convinced that the PLC process was the best strategy for improving student achievement in her school, and she was eager to introduce the concept to her faculty at Siegfried and Roy Middle School (mascot: the Tigers).

On the opening day of school, she assembled the entire staff to share both her enthusiasm for PLCs and her plans for bringing the concept to the school. She emphasized that she was committed to transforming the school into a PLC and that the first step in the process was to develop a new mission statement that captured the new focus of the school. She presented the following draft to the staff and invited their reaction:

> It is our mission to ensure all our students acquire the knowledge and skills essential to achieving their full potential and becoming productive citizens.

The moment Principal Dion presented the statement, a teacher challenged it, arguing that any mission statement should acknowledge that the extent of student learning was dependent on students' ability and effort. Another teacher disagreed with the reference to "ensuring" all students would learn because it placed too much accountability on teachers and not enough on students. A counselor felt the proposed mission statement placed too much emphasis on academics and not enough on the emotional well-being of students. Soon it became difficult to engage the entire staff in the dialogue as pockets of conversation began to break out throughout the room. Principal Dion decided to adjourn the meeting to give staff members more time to reflect on her mission statement and promised to return to the topic at the after-school faculty meeting scheduled for the next month.

In the intervening weeks, teachers fiercely lobbied for and against different variations of the mission statement. When the staff convened for their next faculty meeting, a group of teachers proposed a compromise, a mission statement they felt would be more acceptable to the staff. It stated:

> It is our mission to give each student the opportunity to learn according to their ability and to create a school that is attentive to the emotional needs of every student.

Principal Dion expressed concern that the statement did not convey a commitment to helping all students learn; instead, it merely promised to give them the *chance* to learn. The ensuing discussion revealed significant differences of opinion, and the respective parties became more entrenched in the defense of their positions. Finally, as the time to end the meeting approached, an impatient staff member proposed a show of hands to determine support for the two different mission statements. Fifty-five percent of the staff preferred the compromise statement, 25 percent supported the mission the principal presented, and 20 percent were indifferent. Principal Dion acknowledged the decision of the majority and said the compromise statement would become the school's new mission statement.

Principal Dion remained hopeful that this mission statement would inspire new effort and commitment from the staff. As the year wore on, however, she was disappointed to see the staff return to business as usual. She became increasingly disenchanted with the PLC process. After all, she had engaged the staff in clarifying the mission of the school, just as she had been advised to do at the PLC at Work Institute. There was virtually no evidence, however, that this new mission had impacted either teacher practice or student achievement. She resolved to find another improvement model during the summer.

Reflection

Consider Principal Dion's efforts to develop a clear and compelling purpose for the school with her staff. What advice would you give Principal Dion if you were called on to mentor her as she was beginning to initiate this process with her staff?

Part Two

Here's How

Despite her good intentions and initial enthusiasm, Principal Dion struggled with two significant factors that adversely impacted her efforts.

1. The process she utilized in attempting to build consensus
2. Her failure to shift the dialogue beyond the philosophical debate about the school's mission to the specific actions needed to move forward

How would leaders of a high-performing PLC work to build consensus, and what steps would they take to move from dialogue to action?

Create a Guiding Coalition

Those who hope to lead the PLC process must begin by acknowledging that no one person will have the energy, expertise, and influence to lead a complex change process until it becomes anchored in the organization's culture and gains the support of key staff members. Robert J. Marzano, Timothy Waters, and Brian McNulty (2005) refer to this group as the "leadership team." John Kotter (2012) describes them as the "guiding coalition," and Jim Collins (2001) simply reminds leaders that they must first "get the right people on the bus." Although the terminology may vary, according to the Wallace Foundation (2013):

> A broad and longstanding consensus in leadership theory holds that leaders in all walks of life and all kinds of organizations, public and private, need to depend on others to accomplish the group's purpose and need to encourage the development of leadership across the organization. (p. 9)

Principal Dion made a mistake in thinking she was personally responsible for selling the faculty on her version of a new mission statement. If a mission is to be truly shared, it must be co-created, not sold, and co-creation requires a process that fully engages others. Before bringing the issue to the full faculty, Principal Dion should have first developed a small cadre of staff members to serve as her guiding coalition. She should have selected members on the basis of their influence with their peers. Kerry Patterson, Joseph Grenny, David Maxfield, Ron McMillan, and Al Switzler (2008) have found that, in most organizations, who supports an idea is typically more important than the quality of the idea itself. Roughly 15 percent of the members of an organization are the "opinion leaders"—people who are so knowledgeable, respected, and trustworthy that their position has a major influence on the rest of the group (Patterson et al., 2008). If Principal Dion had organized this guiding coalition, worked through the issues with its members, built consensus among them that the school's mission must commit to ensuring learning for all, and secured them as allies of and champions for the new mission, the likelihood of winning the faculty's support would have been much greater. The bottom line for principals is this: if you can't persuade a small group of people of the merits of an idea and enlist their help, there is little chance you will persuade the larger group.

If a mission is to be truly shared, it must be co-created, not sold, and co-creation requires a process that fully engages others.

Choose the Right Forum

In presenting the proposal to the entire staff at one time, Principal Dion used a forum—a large group—that was ill suited to the dialogue that facilitates consensus. Most people will have questions when significant change is proposed, and they will want those questions answered before they are willing to give their consent for moving forward. The large-group forum she used in the case study allowed those skeptical of the proposal to dominate the discussion before the idea had been fully considered. A more intimate venue with a small number of staff would have been more effective.

Principal Dion might have asked teachers to meet in small groups with her or representatives of the guiding coalition during a preparation period so they could engage in this dialogue, particularly if she was willing to cancel an after-school faculty meeting to compensate teachers for their lost time. She might have hired enough substitute teachers to free small groups of teachers to meet with her during the school day. Her effort to build support for her idea through a presentation was unlikely to succeed. Building consensus requires conversations, not presentations; dialogue, not monologue.

Build Shared Knowledge

The biggest process mistake Principal Dion made was her failure to build shared knowledge among the staff. Although she had apparently learned of concepts and strategies at the PLC at Work Institute that convinced her of the benefits of a PLC, she did nothing to share that learning with her colleagues in the school. A cardinal rule of decision making in a professional *learning* community is that prior to making a decision, people must first build shared knowledge; that is, they must *learn together*. When all staff members have access to the same information, it increases the likelihood that they will arrive at similar conclusions. Conversely, if uninformed people are asked to make decisions, they will make uninformed decisions. Without access to pertinent information, they resort to debating opinions or retreating to a muddied middle ground.

A cardinal rule of decision making in a professional **learning** *community is that prior to making a decision, people must first build shared knowledge; that is, they must* **learn together.**

Working with her guiding coalition, Principal Dion might have presented information to help the staff assess the current reality of the school. For example, she could have presented data to help paint a picture of the school's current reality. The data picture worksheet ("A Data Picture of Our School," pages 37–39) assists in the gathering and presentation of information to clarify the existing conditions of the school. Anecdotes and stories about students who were not being successful could also have helped establish what the school experience was like for some students.

In addition, the coalition could have presented staff with a synthesis of research on characteristics of high-performing schools such as PLCs (clear academic goals for every student, ongoing monitoring of student learning, systematic interventions, and high expectations for student achievement) to support the premise that schools are most effective when staff members define their purpose as helping students learn rather than ensuring they are taught. The staff might have heard testimonials from other schools that had adopted PLC practices or conducted site visits to see a PLC in action. Principal Dion and the guiding coalition could have framed all this information around a moral imperative by providing a picture of what happens when students fail in the K–12 system, and by challenging the staff to consider if these outcomes would be acceptable for the students in both their personal and professional lives. Time spent up front building shared knowledge results in faster, more effective, and most importantly, more committed action later in the improvement process (Grenny, Patterson, McMillan, Switzler, & Gregory, 2022; Patterson, Grenny, McMillan, & Switzler, 2002).

Arrive at Consensus on Consensus

Principal Dion hoped to build consensus on a new mission statement. In our work with schools, however, we have found that most schools do not have consensus on

A Data Picture of Our School

School Name:

Indicator	**Year 20__-20__**	**Year 20__-20__**	**Year 20__-20__**	**Facts About Our Data**
Student Achievement Results				
Based on Our School Assessment Data				
Based on Our District Assessment Data				
Based on Our State or Provincial Assessment Data				
Based on Our National Assessment Data				
Student Engagement Data				
Average Daily Attendance				
Percentage of Students in Extracurricular Activities				
Percentage of Students Using School's Tutoring Services				
Percentage of Students Enrolled in Most Rigorous Courses Offered				
Percentage of Students Graduating Without Retention				
Percentage of Students Who Drop Out of School				

page 1 of 3

A Data Picture of Our School

Student Engagement Data (continued)				
Indicator	**Year 20__-20__**	**Year 20__-20__**	**Year 20__-20__**	**Facts About Our Data**
Other Areas in Which We Hope to Engage Students, Such as Community Service				
Discipline				
Number of Referrals / Top Three Reasons for Referrals				
Number of Parent Conferences Regarding Discipline				
Number of In-School Suspensions				
Number of Detentions / Saturday School				
Number of Out-of-School Suspensions				
Number of Expulsions				
Other				
Survey Data				
Student Satisfaction or Perception Assessment				
Alumni Satisfaction or Perception Assessment				

page 2 of 3

A Data Picture of Our School

Survey Data (continued)				
Indicator	**Year 20__-20__**	**Year 20__-20__**	**Year 20__-20__**	**Facts About Our Data**
Parent Satisfaction or Perception Assessment				
Teacher Satisfaction or Perception Assessment				
Administration Satisfaction or Perception Assessment				
Community Satisfaction or Perception Assessment				
Demographic Data				
Percent Free and Reduced Lunch				
Percent Mobility				
Percent Special Education				
Percent English as a Second Language				
Percent White (Not of Hispanic Origin)				
Percent Black				
Percent Hispanic				
Percent Asian				
Percent Native American				

when they have consensus. We ask a straightforward question: "How do you define *consensus* when your staff consider a proposal?" The responses we hear vary greatly within the same school. We have established a continuum of consensus based on the typical responses. Consider the following continuum and select the point at which you feel you have reached agreement on a proposal in your own school.

We have arrived at consensus in our school when:

1. All of us can embrace the proposal
2. All of us can endorse the proposal
3. All of us can live with the proposal
4. All of us can agree not to sabotage the proposal
5. We have a majority—at least 51 percent—in support of the proposal

The most common outcome of this survey is a staff distributed all along the continuum because members do not have consensus on the definition of consensus. Disagreements and allegations are inevitable when a faculty does not understand the standard that must be met in order to make a collective decision.

We advise staffs to reject all points on the five-point continuum we just presented. In our view, it is difficult to maintain that you have the group's consent to move forward with a simple majority—a standard that can disregard the perspective of 49 percent of the group. On the other hand, every other point on the continuum goes beyond consensus when it calls for "all of us" to reach a level of agreement. While it is wonderful to strive for unanimity, there is a difference between unanimity and consensus. In the real world of schools, if all of us must agree before we can act, if any staff member can veto taking action, we will be subjected to constant inaction, a state of perpetual status quo.

A group has arrived at consensus when it meets two criteria.

The definition of *consensus* that we prefer establishes two simple standards that must be met in order to move forward when a decision is made. A group has arrived at consensus when it meets two criteria.

1. All points of view have not merely been heard but been actively solicited.
2. The will of the group is evident *even to those who most oppose it.*

This definition can, and typically does, result in moving forward with a proposal despite the fact that some members of the organization are against it. However, as Patrick Lencioni (2005) writes, "Waiting for everyone on a team to agree intellectually on a decision is a good recipe for mediocrity, delay, and frustration" (p. 51). An insistence on unanimity conflicts with the action orientation of a PLC.

If the standards for consensus we recommend had been applied in the case study, Principal Dion and the guiding coalition could have engaged in small-group dialogues to address concerns. At some point, however, they would have also presented a specific proposal such as this:

> It is our mission to ensure all our students acquire the knowledge and skills essential to achieving their full potential and becoming productive citizens.

Each small group is then *randomly* divided into two groups. The first is asked to work together to create a comprehensive list of all the reasons the faculty should oppose the proposal. The second group is called on to create a comprehensive list of all the reasons the staff should support the proposal. At this point, personal feelings about the proposal do not come into play. Each staff member is to engage in an intellectual exercise to list all the possible pros and cons regarding the specific idea under consideration.

In the next step of the process, the first group presents all the reasons members listed to oppose the suggestion. Members of the second group are asked to listen attentively until the opposed group has completed its list, and then they are invited to add to that list with other objections that might not have been identified. The process is then repeated with the proponent group announcing its comprehensive list in support of the decision, and the group responsible for listing objections is invited to add to it. Throughout this listing of the pros and cons, staff should not question or debate individual points; staff members should list points without comment. If this is done correctly, no one will know where any staff member personally stands on the issue, but all points of view will now have been heard.

The next step is to determine the will of the group. A quick and simple way to do so is to use the *fist to five* strategy. Once everyone is clear on the proposal, and all pros and cons have been offered, each person is asked to indicate a level of support, as shown in the feature box.

A quick and simple way to determine the will of the group is to use the* fist to five *strategy.

Fist to Five Strategy

- **Five fingers:** I love this proposal. I will champion it.
- **Four fingers:** I strongly agree with the proposal.
- **Three fingers:** The proposal is OK with me. I am willing to go along with it.
- **Two fingers:** I have reservations and am not yet ready to support this proposal.
- **One finger:** I am opposed to this proposal.
- **Fist:** If I had the authority, I would veto this proposal, regardless of the will of the group.

The facilitator for the process ensures that everyone understands the issue under consideration and how to express themselves through fist to five. Then the facilitator asks all members of the small group to simultaneously express their position by raising their hand with the number of fingers best expressing their level of support. Each participant is then able to ascertain the support for the proposal by looking around the room. If participants do not support the proposal, or the vote is too close to determine the will of the group at a glance, the proposal does not go forward. Pilot projects may be run, more time may be taken to build shared knowledge, and in time, the proposal may be presented again; however, if support is not readily apparent, the standard of consensus has not been met.

If, however, it is evident that it is the will of the group to move forward (hands with three, four, and five fingers clearly outnumber fists and hands with one and two fingers), consensus has been reached, and all staff members will be expected to honor the decision.

There are certainly variations on this format. For example, if the technology is available, staff could vote anonymously and have the tally reported instantly. If there are concerns about intimidation, an anonymous paper vote may be appropriate, as long as the process for counting the votes is accepted as fair by all concerned. It may be prudent to have the teachers' association appoint a representative to attend all the meetings in case concerns emerge about the accuracy of the reporting. But while the format may vary, one thing does not: decision making is easier, more effective, and less likely to end in disputes about process when a staff has a clear, operational definition of consensus.

Live Your Mission

The biggest mistake Principal Dion and her staff made was confusing *writing* a mission statement with *living* a mission. No school has ever improved simply because the staff wrote a mission statement. In fact, we have found no correlation between the presence of a written mission statement, or even the wording of a mission statement, and a school's effectiveness as a PLC. The words of a mission statement are not worth the paper they are written on unless people begin to *do* differently.

The words of a mission statement are not worth the paper they are written on unless people begin to do differently.

What could Principal Dion and the guiding coalition have done to bring the mission to life in their school? First, after engaging staff in building shared knowledge on the specific practices and characteristics of schools where all students learn at high levels, she might have asked them to describe in vivid detail the school they hoped to create. Once the staff could describe that school, the principal and her guiding coalition could have then led the staff in a discussion of the specific commitments each member would need to honor in order to become the school they had envisioned. Principal Dion might have modeled a willingness to make commitments by identifying the specific things she was prepared to do to support the effort to transform the school. She could have shared her commitments with the staff and asked for their reactions, revisions, and additions. Members of the guiding coalition could have then led the staff in a process to clarify their collective commitments.

Principal Dion might also have asked the faculty to identify the indicators that should be monitored to assess their progress in creating their agreed-on school. They could have established benchmarks for what they hoped to achieve in the first six months, the first year, and the first three years. Each teacher team could have been asked to establish specific team goals that, if accomplished, would contribute to achieving schoolwide goals and to moving the school toward the ideal the staff had described.

Of course, all this dialogue would impact the school only if purposeful steps were taken to demonstrate that creating the school of their hopes, honoring their commitments, and achieving their goals were the collective responsibilities of every staff member. How is that message best communicated? The most powerful communication is a function of not what is written or said, but rather, once again, what is *done*. As James A. Autry (2001), author of *The Servant Leader*, writes:

> Those around you in the workplace—colleagues and employees—can determine who you are only by observing what you do. . . . The only way you can manifest your character, your personhood, and your spirit in the workplace is through your behavior. (p. 1)

Or, to paraphrase Ralph Waldo Emerson, what you do stands over you all the while and thunders so loudly that we cannot hear what you say.

Consider seven specific actions the principal and staff might have taken to convey their commitment to improving their school.

1. **Initiating structures and systems to foster qualities and characteristics consistent with a learning-centered school:** When something is truly a priority in an organization, people do not hope it happens; they develop and implement systematic plans to ensure that it happens. For example, if the leadership team was committed to creating a collaborative culture, it could take steps to organize teachers into teams, build time for collaboration into the contractual workday, develop protocols and parameters to guide the work of teams, and so on. True priorities are not left to chance but are carefully and systematically addressed.

2. **Creating processes to monitor critical conditions and important goals:** In most organizations, what gets monitored gets done. A critical step in moving an organization from rhetoric to reality is to establish the indicators of progress to be monitored, the process and timeline for monitoring them, and the means of sharing results with and getting input from people throughout the organization. For example, if the staff agreed student learning was the priority in their school, creating procedures to monitor each student's learning on a timely and systematic basis would be imperative.

3. **Reallocating resources to support the proclaimed priorities:** Marshall McLuhan (1994) observed, "Money talks because money is a metaphor" (p. 136). The actual legal tender may have little intrinsic value, but how it is expended, particularly in times of scarcity, reveals a great deal about what is valued. Money, however, is not the only significant resource in an organization, and in contemporary public education, time is even scarcer than money. Giving teachers time to collaborate and providing students who are struggling with additional time and support for learning are prerequisite conditions for a PLC (Battelle for Kids, 2013; Farbman, Goldberg, & Miller, 2014; Fulton & Britton, 2011; National Governors Association Center for Best Practices [NGA], Council of Chief State School Officers [CCSSO], & Achieve, 2008; Robinson, 2010; Tucker, 2014). Decisions about the spending of precious resources are some of the most unequivocal ways organizations communicate what is important. Had Principal Dion and the guiding

coalition created a schedule that provided teachers with time to collaborate and students with time for additional support for learning when they experienced difficulty, they would have sent the message that teacher collaboration and student learning were priorities in the school.

The questions an organization poses—and the effort and energy spent in the pursuit of answers—not only communicate priorities but also turn members in a particular direction.

4. **Posing the right questions:** The questions an organization poses—and the effort and energy spent in the pursuit of answers—not only communicate priorities but also turn members in a particular direction. In too many schools, the prevalent question is, "What is wrong with these students?"—a question that typically has little impact on improving student achievement. Principal Dion and her staff could have conveyed their commitment to student learning by devoting time to the pursuit of the four critical questions of the PLC process.
    a. What knowledge, skills, and dispositions should every student acquire as a result of this unit, this course, or this grade level?
    b. How will we know when each student has acquired the essential knowledge and skills?
    c. How will we respond when some students do not learn?
    d. How will we extend the learning for students who are already proficient?
5. **Modeling what is valued:** Example is still the most powerful teacher. If Principal Dion hopes the staff will make a commitment to high levels of learning for all students, she must demonstrate her own commitment by focusing on learning with laser-like intensity and constantly keeping the issue before the faculty. If she hopes to build a culture in which teachers collaborate, she must engage the staff in collaborative decision making and provide the time and support essential for effective collaboration. As one study concluded, "The single most powerful mechanism for creating a learning environment is that the leadership of the organization be willing to model the approach to learning that they want others to embrace" (Thompson, 1995, p. 96).
6. **Celebrating progress:** When an organization makes a concerted effort to call attention to and celebrate progress toward its goals, commitments members demonstrate in day-to-day work, and evidence of improved results, people within the organization are continually reminded of the priorities and what it takes to achieve them. Furthermore, these celebrations provide real-life models by which people can assess their own efforts and commitment. If Principal Dion used every opportunity to publicly celebrate positive, forward-moving steps on the journey of school improvement, the faculty would soon learn what was noted, appreciated, and valued in their school.
7. **Confronting violations of commitments:** If Principal Dion hopes to convey what is important and valued, she must be prepared to confront

those who act in ways that are contrary to the priorities of the school and the commitments of the staff. Leaders who are unwilling to promote and defend improvement initiatives put those initiatives at risk. A leader of the PLC process cannot verbally commit to a school mission of learning for all but then allow individuals within the organization to act in ways that are counterproductive to this commitment. Not only will allowing these actions negatively impact student learning, but staff members who supported the new school mission will become skeptical because the school leadership is hedging on its commitment. We will address both celebration and confrontation more fully in chapter 10 (page 249).

A leader of the PLC process cannot verbally commit to a school mission of learning for all but then allow individuals within the organization to act in ways that are counter-productive to this commitment.

Part Three

Here's Why

Engaging members of an organization in reflective dialogue about the fundamental purpose of the organization, as Principal Dion attempted to do, can be a powerful strategy for improvement. In fact, the first question any organization must consider if it hopes to improve results is the question of purpose (Drucker, 1992). Why does our organization exist? What are we here to do together? What exactly do we hope to accomplish? What is the business of our business (American Society for Quality, n.d.; Champy, 1995; Senge et al., 1994)?

Research on effective organizations, effective leadership, and effective schools supports the idea that a shared sense of purpose is key to high performance. (See "Why Should We Clarify Our Mission?" on page 46 for what the research says about shared purpose.)

To close that gap, educators must move beyond writing mission statements to clarifying the vision, values (that is, collective commitments), and goals that drive the daily workings of the school and aligning all their practices accordingly.

The Foundation of a PLC

Imagine that the foundation of a PLC rests on the four pillars of mission, vision, values, and goals (see the graphic on page 47). Each of these pillars asks a different question of the educators within the school. When teachers and administrators have worked together to consider those questions and reach consensus regarding their collective positions on each question, they have built a solid foundation for a PLC. Much work remains to be done, for these are just a few of the thousands of steps that must be taken in the never-ending process of continuous improvement. But addressing these questions increases the likelihood that all subsequent work will have the benefit of firm underpinnings. If staff members have not considered the questions, have done so only superficially, or are unable to establish common ground regarding their positions on the questions, any and all future efforts to improve the school will stand on shaky ground.

Why Should We Clarify Our Mission?

"There is no point in thinking about changes in structure until the school achieves reasonable consensus about its intellectual mission for children" (Newmann & Wehlage, 1996, p. 295).

"Members of great organizations think they are 'on a mission from God. [They] always believe that they are doing something vital, even holy . . . something worthy of their best selves. Their clear collective purpose makes everything they do seem meaningful and valuable'" (Bennis & Biederman, 1997, p. 204).

"In the effective school, there is a clearly articulated mission of the school through which the staff shares an understanding of and a commitment to the school's goals, priorities, assessment procedures, and accountability. . . . The issue of mission is one that must receive substantial discussion" (Lezotte, 2002, pp. 4–5).

"Contrary to popular wisdom, the proper first response to a changing world is NOT to ask, 'How should we change,' but rather, 'What do we stand for and why do we exist?' This should never change. And then feel free to change everything else. Put another way, visionary companies distinguish between their core values and enduring purpose (which should never change) from their operating practices and business strategies (which should be changing constantly in response to an ever-changing world)" (Collins & Porras, 1994, p. xiv).

The Wallace Foundation study of effective district leadership found that district offices that had a positive influence on schools and student achievement established a clear purpose that was widely shared (Leithwood et al., 2009).

"The most deeply motivated people—not to mention those that are most productive and satisfied—hitch their desires to a cause larger than themselves. . . . Nothing bonds a team like a shared mission. The more that people share a common cause . . . the more your group will do deeply satisfying and outstanding work" (Pink, 2011, pp. 131, 174).

Research examining successful schools reveals that they share the characteristics of modern high-performance workplaces that foster cultures built on teamwork and shared mission (Anrig, 2013).

A "persuasive and valuable" mission statement "gives people a context" for their actions and empowers them "to support one another's efforts" and fully engage their talents and imagination (Halvorson, 2014, p. 38).

"Leaders need the ability to develop a shared moral purpose and meaning as well as a pathway for attaining that purpose. . . . Great leaders connect others to the reasons they became educators—their moral purpose" (Fullan & Quinn, 2016, p. 17).

Educators who believe that merely clarifying or reaffirming their mission will somehow improve results are certain to be disappointed. In fact, in many schools, developing a mission statement has served as a substitute, rather than a catalyst, for meaningful action. Merely drafting a new mission statement does not automatically change how people act, and therefore, writing a mission statement does nothing to close the knowing-doing gap (Pfeffer & Sutton, 2000).

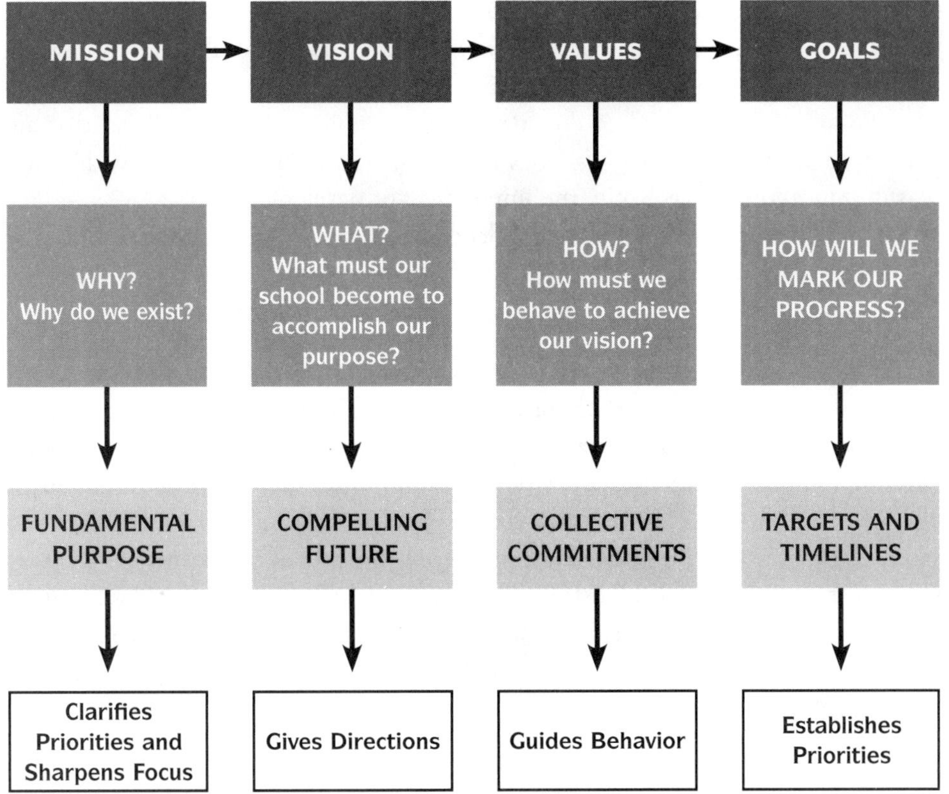

Mission

"Why do we exist?"

As we have stressed, the mission pillar asks the question, "Why?" More specifically, it asks, "Why do we exist?" The intent of this question is to help reach agreement regarding the fundamental purpose of the school. This clarity of purpose can help establish priorities and becomes an important factor in guiding decisions. In a learning-centered school, ensuring that all students learn must be at the heart of its mission. However, leaders of high-performing PLCs must go beyond ensuring that learning is at the heart of their school or district.

While proclaiming that learning is the primary reason the school exists is crucial, declaring a learning mission alone is inadequate. It provides direction and can be the centerpiece for decision making, but by itself, it is not particularly motivational. The question of why must push members of a PLC to examine why they are so adamant about ensuring student learning. Is it because of the pressure to raise test scores? Is it because it is good for public relations? The answer to such questions must center on the affective side of schooling, and this almost always means understanding and communicating that we as a school care for every student and every adult—a lot—and because we care so much, members of PLCs go to extraordinary lengths to ensure every single student knows we want them to learn.

Vision

The vision pillar asks, "What?"—that is, "What must we become in order to accomplish our fundamental purpose?" In pursuing this question, a staff attempts to create a compelling, attractive, realistic future that describes what they hope their school will

"What must we become in order to accomplish our fundamental purpose?"

become. Vision provides a sense of direction and a basis for assessing both the current reality of the school and potential strategies, programs, and procedures to improve on that reality. Equally important, a clear vision statement can lead to the creation of a "stop-doing list," comprised of the current school policies and procedures that are misaligned with ensuring higher levels of student learning. Researchers within and outside education routinely cite the importance of developing a shared vision. (See page 49, "Why Should We Describe the School or District We Are Trying to Create?") Burt Nanus's (1992) conclusion is typical: "There is no more powerful engine driving an organization toward excellence and long-range success than an attractive, worthwhile and achievable vision of the future, widely shared" (p. 3).

The very first standard for school administrators drafted by the National Policy Board for Educational Administration (2015) calls on education leaders to collaboratively develop a shared mission and vision and to promote the success of every student by facilitating the development, articulation, implementation, and stewardship of a vision of learning that is shared and supported by the school community. A comprehensive review of research found that "setting direction" through the identification and articulation of a shared vision accounted for the largest proportion of a principal's impact on student achievement (Leithwood, Louis, Anderson, & Wahlstrom, 2004).

Collective Commitments (Values)

In their study of high-performing organizations, Jim Collins and Jerry Porras (1994) found that although creating a vision can be a helpful step in the improvement process, it is never sufficient. Teachers and administrators must also tackle the collective commitments they will make and honor in order to achieve the shared vision for their school or district. The third pillar of the foundation, the values pillar, clarifies these collective commitments. It does not ask, "Why do we exist?" or "What do we hope to become?" Rather, it asks, "How must we behave to create the school that will achieve our purpose?" In answering this question, educators shift from offering philosophical musings on mission or their shared hopes for the school of the future to making commitments to act in certain ways—starting today. Clarity on this topic guides the individual and collaborative work of each staff member and outlines how each person can contribute to the improvement initiative. When members of an organization understand the purpose of their organization, know where it is headed, and then pledge to act in certain ways to move it in the right direction, they don't need prescriptive rules and regulations to guide their daily work. Policy manuals and directives are replaced by commitments and covenants. As a result, members of the organization enjoy greater autonomy and creativity than their more rigidly supervised counterparts.

"How must we behave to create the school that will achieve our purpose?"

Leaders benefit from clearly defined commitments as well. When leaders in traditional hierarchical structures address an employee's inappropriate behavior and demand change, their rationale tends to be "because the rules say we have to do it," or "because I am the boss, and I said so." If, however, the members of the organization have specified collective commitments, leaders operate with the full weight of the moral authority of the group behind them. Inappropriate behavior is presented to the offender as a violation of collective commitments, and the leader moves from the role of "boss" to the promoter and protector of what members have declared as important or sacred. Furthermore, the leader is not alone in insisting that collective commitments be honored. A values-driven

Why Should We Describe the School or District We Are Trying to Create?

"At both school and district levels, administrative tasks essential to teachers' learning and learning communities include building a shared vision and common language about practice" (McLaughlin & Talbert, 2006, p. 80).

"The very best leaders understand that their key task is inspiring a shared vision, not selling their own idiosyncratic view of the world" (Kouzes & Posner, 2006, p. 108).

"A vision builds trust, collaboration, interdependence, motivation, and mutual responsibility for success. Vision helps people make smart choices, because their decisions are made with the end result in mind. . . . Vision allows us to act from a proactive stance, moving toward what we want. . . . Vision empowers and excites us to reach for what we truly desire" (Blanchard, 2007, p. 22).

In order for a school to move forward, its faculty need to develop an understood and agreed-on purpose and sense of direction. "If you don't have a common, agreed-on destination, then everyone is left to [their] own devices to imagine one—a scenario that results in unharnessed and unfocused efforts" (Gabriel & Farmer, 2009, p. 46).

A key responsibility of an educational leader is "developing and delivering a compelling picture of the school's future that produces energy, passion, and action in yourself and others. [A vision is] one of your most potent leadership tools for the development of coherent and sustainable actions" (Kanold, 2011, pp. 6–7).

In identifying five key functions of principals, the Wallace Foundation (2013) listed shaping a vision of academic success as the first of those functions. It concludes, "Effective principals are responsible for establishing a schoolwide vision of commitment to high standards and the success of all students" (Wallace Foundation, 2013, p. 7).

"Shared vision emerges from a collaboratively defined understanding of what constitutes worthwhile student learning, with all members of the PLC working together on problems around that common vision" (Fulton & Britton, 2011, p. 14).

A powerful vision results in inspiration, aspiration, and perspiration. It inspires people to rally around a greater purpose. It challenges educators to articulate the school they aspire to create. It leads to action, beginning with building shared knowledge of what it will take to reduce the gap between the current reality of their school and the school described in the vision (Williams & Hierck, 2015).

"The better people can envision where they are going, the more they can focus on specific initiatives that will make that vision a reality" (Kotter International, 2015, p. 17).

Shared vision emerges when there is clarity of purpose and "continuous collaborative conversations that build shared language, knowledge, and expectations" (Fullan & Quinn, 2016, p. 29).

culture generates internal accountability by which people throughout the organization create a positive peer pressure to act in accordance with public commitments.

Finally, achieving agreement about what we are prepared to start *doing*, and then *implementing* that agreement, is, by definition, the key step in closing the knowing-doing gap. We believe that clarifying collective commitments is one of the most important and, regrettably, least utilized strategies in building the foundation of a PLC. There is, once again, considerable evidence in organizational and educational research to support that belief. (See page 51, "Why Should We Articulate Collective Commitments?")

Goals

"How will we know if all of this is making a difference?"

The final pillar of the foundation asks members to clarify the specific goals they hope to achieve as a result of their improvement initiative. The goals pillar identifies the targets and timelines that enable a staff to answer the question, "How will we know if all of this is making a difference?"

Goals provide staff members with a sense of their short-term priorities and the steps to achieve the benchmarks. Effective goals foster both the results orientation of a PLC and individual and collective accountability for achieving the results. They help close the gap between the current reality and where the staff hope to take the school (the shared vision).

Furthermore, goals are absolutely essential to the collaborative team process. We define a team as a group of people working *interdependently* to achieve a *common goal* for which members are *mutually accountable*. In the absence of a common goal, there can be no true team. Effective goals generate joint effort and help collaborative teams clarify how their work can contribute to schoolwide or districtwide improvement initiatives.

When schools create short-term goals and routinely celebrate as those goals are achieved, they foster a sense of confidence and self-efficacy among the staff. Confidence is merely "the expectation of success" (Kanter, 2005, p. 22), and when people expect to be successful, they are more likely to put forth the effort to ensure it. Thus, goals play a key role in motivating people to honor their commitments so the school moves closer to fulfilling its fundamental purpose of learning for all students. We will have more to say about goals in chapter 5 (page 119), but, once again, educational researchers and organizational theorists consider measurable goals a key element in improvement.

The key to effective leadership and a healthy organization is clarity regarding the purpose of the organization, the future it is creating, the specific actions members can take immediately to make progress on short-term goals and achieve the long-term purpose, and the indicators of progress the organization will track (Buckingham, 2005). When educators have addressed each of the four pillars we have referenced in this chapter and arrived at a shared understanding of and commitment to each pillar, they have the benefit of a solid foundation for all the future efforts in building their PLC.

The final document articulating the shared mission, vision, collective commitments, and goals need not be lengthy. Brevity and specificity are preferred over verbosity. We provide you with two examples of very serviceable foundation statements. (See pages 52–53, which feature "The Foundation of Anywhere High School" and the statements for Boones Mill Elementary School in Franklin County, Virginia, from when Becky was principal.)

Why Should We Articulate Collective Commitments?

With the democratization of organizations, especially schools, the leadership function becomes one of creating a "community of shared values" (Lezotte, 1991, p. 3).

"Values describe how we intend to operate, on a day-to-day basis, as we pursue our vision. . . . Values are best expressed in terms of behavior: If we act as we should, what would an observer see us doing? . . . When values are made a central part of the organization's shared vision effort, and put out in full view, they become like a figurehead on a ship: a guiding symbol of the behavior that will help people move toward the vision" (Senge et al., 1994, p. 302).

Both profit and nonprofit organizations should be grounded in "a timeless set of core values and an enduring purpose" (Collins & Porras, 1994, p. xxiv).

"The language of complaint essentially tells us, and others, what it is we can't stand. The language of commitment tells us (and possibly others) what it is we stand for" (Kegan & Lahey, 2001, p. 32).

High-performing districts "tended to rely more on a common culture of values to shape collective action than on bureaucratic rules and controls. The shared values typically focused on improvement of student learning as the central goal" (Elmore, 2000, p. 26).

"Values provide guidelines on how you should proceed as you pursue your purpose and picture of the future. They answer the question . . . 'How?' They need to be clearly described so that you know exactly what behaviors demonstrate that the value is being lived" (Blanchard, 2007, p. 30).

Values must be driven into the policy, the decision making, and ultimately the culture of the organization; otherwise, value statements are just words. When values become part of an employee's DNA, they not only guide day-to-day work but also empower employees to act in unique situations (Berry & Seltman, 2008, 2017).

"Values represent the commitments to action necessary to ensure the vision is realized. . . . In the best PLC cultures, vision and values ultimately become the driving force behind the decision-making process that takes place every day" (Kanold, 2011, p. 13).

To bring a mission statement to life, "educators must be willing to transparently communicate their commitment to students as it relates to their stated mission and challenge one another to live up to that commitment" (Muhammad & Hollie, 2012, p. 28).

The key to values' impacting the organization in a positive way is that people have to "live by them, reinforce them every day, and not tolerate behavior that is at odds with them" (Bryant, 2014).

The Foundation of Anywhere High School

Our Mission: To help *all* of our students achieve the high levels of learning required for success in college or post-secondary training

Our Vision: The policies, programs, and practices of Anywhere High School reflect its commitment to helping all students learn at high levels.

As a Result of That Commitment:

- The staff constantly seeks out the most promising practices that support student learning.
- The school is characterized by a collaborative culture in which educators take collective responsibility for helping all students learn at high levels.
- The collaborative team is the fundamental structure of the school.
- Students are provided a guaranteed and viable curriculum, unit by unit.
- The learning of each student is monitored on an ongoing basis through daily formative assessment in the classroom and team-developed common formative assessment for each unit.
- The school has systems in place to ensure that evidence of student learning is used to—
    - Provide timely, diagnostic, and directive support for students who are struggling
    - Enrich and extend learning for students who demonstrate they are highly proficient
    - Inform individual educators regarding their strengths and weaknesses in helping students to learn at high levels
    - Alert a collaborative team to areas of concern in student learning that warrant the attention of the entire team
- The school supports educators' continuous learning and ongoing professional development.
- The school has a strong partnership with parents and provides parents with the information they need to monitor and support the learning of their children.

Our Collective Commitments: In order to fulfill our fundamental purpose and become the school we describe in our vision statement, each member of the staff commits to the following—

- I will be a positive, contributing member of my collaborative team.
- I will teach the essential learnings of our agreed-upon curriculum, unit by unit.
- I will monitor each student's learning on an ongoing basis through classroom and team-developed formative assessments.
- I will use evidence of student learning to inform and improve my practice and to better meet the needs of individual students.
- I will work with my colleagues to achieve our SMART goals.
- I will seek out the most promising practices to support student learning.
- I will keep parents informed of the progress of their children.

Our Schoolwide Goals: We will monitor the following indicators to mark our progress—

- Reduce the failure rate.
- Increase the percentage of students pursuing and being successful in the most rigorous curriculum in each program.
- Increase student achievement on local, state, and national high-stakes assessments.
- Increase the percentage of our graduates who experience success in postsecondary learning.

Boones Mill Elementary School: Hand in Hand We All Learn

Mission

It is the mission of Boones Mill Elementary School to ensure high levels of learning for each student. Through mutual respect within the total school community, our children will grow and learn in a positive atmosphere where faculty, staff, students, and parents together are enthusiastic about the teaching and learning process.

Vision

We believe that the most promising strategy for achieving the mission of our school is to develop our capacity to function as a professional learning community. We envision a school in which staff:

- Unite to achieve a common purpose and SMART goals
- Work together—interdependently—in collaborative teams
- Seek and implement promising strategies for improving student learning on a continuous basis
- Monitor each student's progress on a frequent basis
- Demonstrate a personal commitment to the academic success and general well-being of each student

Collective Commitments

In order to achieve the shared vision of our school, Boones Mill staff have made the following collective commitments.

1. Study, clarify, align, and pace state resource guides, assessment blueprints, and district curriculum guides.
2. Develop and implement local common formative assessments to monitor each student's learning.
3. Develop, implement, and evaluate team professional enhancement plans aligned to our SMART goals to target specific instructional areas in need of improvement.
4. Engage in meaningful, job-embedded staff development to enhance our professional skills.
5. Utilize a variety of instructional strategies to promote success for all students.
6. Initiate individual and small-group instructional programs to provide additional learning time for all students.
7. Provide parents with resources, strategies, and information to help students succeed.

Schoolwide Goals

1. To improve student achievement in language arts in each grade level as measured by performance on local, district, state, and national assessments
2. To improve student achievement in math in each grade level as measured by performance on local, district, state, and national assessments

Part Four

Assessing Your Place on the PLC Journey

It is important to help your staff build shared knowledge regarding your school's current status in addressing the critical step on the PLC journey of establishing a solid foundation. We have created a tool to assist you in that effort. "The Professional Learning Communities at Work® Continuum: Laying the Foundation" is available on pages 55–57 and at **go.SolutionTree.com/PLCbooks** as a free reproducible. Once your staff have established greater clarity regarding the current status of your PLC foundation, we urge you to turn your attention to the "Where Do We Go From Here?" worksheet that accompanies the continuum (on page 58 and also available for free download at **go.SolutionTree.com/PLCbooks**). It will prompt you to take the action necessary to close the knowing-doing gap.

Part Five

Tips for Moving Forward: Building the Foundation of a PLC

1. **Move quickly to action:** Remember that you will not progress on the PLC continuum or close the knowing-doing gap until people in the school or district begin to "do" differently. We have seen educators devote years to studying, debating, rewording, and revising different elements of the foundation, thereby giving the illusion of meaningful action. In most instances, a staff should be able to consider and resolve all the questions of the foundation in a matter of weeks. They may need to return to the foundation in the future to make changes as the vision becomes clearer, the need for additional commitments arises, or new goals emerge. Perfection is not the objective; action is. Once again, the school or district that actually does the work of a PLC will develop its capacity to help all students learn far more effectively than the school or district that spends years preparing to be a PLC.

2. **Build shared knowledge when asking people to make a decision:** Asking uninformed people to make decisions is bound to result in uninformed decisions. Members of a PLC resolve issues and answer important questions by asking, "What information do we need to examine together to make a good decision?" and then building shared knowledge regarding that information. In a profession, decisions should be guided by research-based best practices that will best serve the clients' needs—in this case, our students. Learning together is, by definition, the very essence of a *learning* community. Furthermore, giving people access to the same

The Professional Learning Communities at Work® Continuum: Laying the Foundation

DIRECTIONS: Individually, silently, and *honestly* assess the current reality of your school's implementation of each indicator listed in the left column. Consider what evidence or anecdotes support your assessment. This form may also be used to assess district or team implementation.

We have a clear sense of our collective purpose, the school we are attempting to create to achieve that purpose, the commitments we must make and honor to become that school, and the specific goals that will help monitor our progress.

Indicator	Pre-Initiating	Initiating	Implementing	Developing	Sustaining
Shared Mission It is evident that learning for all is our core purpose.	The purpose of the school has not been articulated. Most staff members view the mission of the school as teaching. They operate from the assumption that although all students should have the opportunity to learn, responsibility for learning belongs to the individual student and will be determined by his or her ability and effort.	An attempt has been made to clarify the purpose of the school through the development of a formal mission statement. Few people were involved in its creation. It does little to impact professional practice or the assumptions behind those practices.	A process has been initiated to provide greater focus and clarity regarding the mission of learning for all. Steps are being taken to clarify what, specifically, students are to learn and to monitor their learning. Some teachers are concerned that these efforts will deprive them of academic freedom.	Teachers are beginning to see evidence of the benefits of clearly established expectations for student learning and systematic processes to monitor student learning. They are becoming more analytical in assessing the evidence of student learning and are looking for ways to become more effective in assessing student learning and providing instruction to enhance student learning.	Staff members are committed to helping all students learn. They demonstrate that commitment by working collaboratively to clarify what students are to learn in each unit, creating frequent common formative assessments to monitor each student's learning on an ongoing basis, and implementing a systematic plan of intervention when students experience difficulty. They are willing to examine all practices and procedures in light of their impact on learning.

Indicator	Pre-Initiating	Initiating	Implementing	Developing	Sustaining
Shared Vision We have a shared understanding of and commitment to the school we are attempting to create.	No effort has been made to engage staff in describing the preferred conditions for the school.	A formal vision statement has been created for the school, but most staff members are unaware of it.	Staff members have participated in a process to clarify the school they are trying to create, and leadership calls attention to the resulting vision statement on a regular basis. Many staff members question the relevance of the vision statement, and their behavior is generally unaffected by it.	Staff members have worked together to describe the school they are trying to create. They have endorsed this general description and use it to guide their school improvement efforts and their professional development.	Staff members can and do routinely articulate the major principles of the school's shared vision and use those principles to guide their day-to-day efforts and decisions. They honestly assess the current reality in their school and continually seek more effective strategies for reducing the discrepancy between that reality and the school they are working to create.
Collective Commitments (Shared Values) We have made commitments to each other regarding how we must behave in order to achieve our shared vision.	Staff members have not yet articulated the attitudes, behaviors, or commitments they are prepared to demonstrate in order to advance the mission of learning for all and the vision of what the school might become.	Administrators or a committee of teachers have created statements of beliefs regarding the school's purpose and its direction. Staff members have reviewed and reacted to those statements. Initial drafts have been amended based on staff feedback. There is no attempt to translate the beliefs into the specific commitments or behaviors that staff will model.	A statement has been developed that articulates the specific commitments staff have been asked to embrace to help the school fulfill its purpose and move closer to its vision. The commitments are stated as behaviors rather than beliefs. Many staff object to specifying these commitments and prefer to focus on what other groups must do to improve the school.	Staff members have been engaged in the process to articulate the collective commitments that will advance the school toward its vision. They endorse the commitments and seek ways to bring them to life in the school.	The collective commitments are embraced by staff, embedded in the school's culture, and evident to observers of the school. They help define the school and what it stands for. Examples of the commitments are shared in stories and celebrations, and people are challenged when they behave in ways that are inconsistent with the collective commitments.

Indicator	Pre-Initiating	Initiating	Implementing	Developing	Sustaining
Common School Goals We have articulated our long-term priorities, short-term targets, and timelines for achieving those targets.	No effort has been made to engage the staff in establishing school improvement goals related to student learning.	Goals for the school have been established by the administration or school improvement team as part of the formal district process for school improvement. Most staff would be unable to articulate a goal that has been established for their school.	Staff members have been made aware of the long-term and short-term goals for the school. Tools and strategies have been developed and implemented to monitor the school's progress toward its goals. Little has been done to translate the school goal into meaningful targets for either collaborative teams or individual teachers.	The school goal has been translated into specific goals that directly impact student achievement for each collaborative team. If teams are successful in achieving their goals, the school will achieve its goal as well. Teams are exploring different strategies for achieving their goals.	All staff members pursue measurable goals that are directly linked to the school's goals as part of their routine responsibilities. Teams work interdependently to achieve common goals for which members are mutually accountable. The celebration of the achievement of goals is part of the school culture and an important element in sustaining the PLC process.

Where Do We Go From Here? Worksheet
Laying the Foundation

Indicator of a PLC at Work	What steps or activities must be initiated to create this condition in your school?	Who will be responsible for initiating or sustaining these steps or activities?	What is a realistic timeline for each step or phase of the activity?	What will you use to assess the effectiveness of your initiative?
Shared Mission It is evident that learning for all is our core purpose. **Shared Vision** We have a shared understanding of and commitment to the school we are attempting to create. **Collective Commitments (Shared Values)** We have made commitments to each other regarding how we must behave in order to achieve our shared vision. **Common School Goals** We have articulated our long-term priorities, short-term targets, and timelines for achieving those targets.				

information increases the likelihood that they will arrive at the same conclusions. All staff should have direct access to user-friendly information on the current reality in their school or district as well as access to summaries of the best practices and best thinking regarding the issue under consideration. School and district leaders must take responsibility for gathering and disseminating this information, but all staff should be invited to present any information for distribution that they feel is relevant.

3 **Use the foundation to assist in day-to-day decisions:** Addressing the foundation of a PLC will impact the school only if it becomes a tool for making decisions. Posting a mission statement in the building or inserting a vision statement or goals into a strategic plan does nothing to improve a school. When proposals are considered, the first questions that the group should ask are—

- Is this consistent with our purpose?
- Will it help us become the school we envision?
- Are we prepared to commit to do this?
- Will it enable us to achieve our goals?

An honest assessment of these questions can help shorten debate and lead the group to the right conclusion.

4 **Use the foundation to identify existing practices that should be eliminated:** Once your foundation has been established, use it to identify and eliminate any practices that are inconsistent with its principles. As Jim Collins (2001) writes—

> Most of us . . . have ever-expanding "to do" lists, trying to build momentum by doing, doing, doing—and doing more. And it rarely works. Those who build the good-to-great companies, however, made as much use of "stop doing" lists as "to do" lists. They displayed a remarkable amount of discipline to unplug all sorts of the extraneous junk. (p. 139)

5 **Translate the vision of your school into a teachable point of view:** Effective leaders create a "teachable point of view"—a succinct explanation of the organization's purpose and direction that can be illustrated through stories that engage others emotionally and intellectually (Tichy, 1997). They have a knack for making the complex simple in ways that give direction to those in the organization (Collins, 2001). They use simple language, simple concepts, and the power of common sense (Pfeffer & Sutton, 2000). Develop a brief teachable point of view that captures the vision of your school in a message that is simple, direct, and jargon-free. Practice presenting the vision until articulating it becomes second nature.

6 **Write value statements as behaviors rather than beliefs:** "We believe in the potential and worth of each of our students" is a morally impeccable statement; however, it offers little insight into what a

staff is prepared to do to help each student realize that potential. Another difficulty with belief statements is their failure to assign specific, personal responsibility. A staff may agree with the statement, "We believe in a safe and orderly environment," but feel it is the job of the administration to create such an environment. Simple, direct statements of what we commit to do are preferable to the most eloquent statements of our beliefs. For example, "We will monitor each student's learning on a timely basis and provide additional time and support for learning until the student becomes proficient" helps clarify expectations far more effectively than assertions about the potential of every student.

7 **Focus on yourself rather than others:** In our work with schools, we have found that educators rarely have difficulty articulating steps that could be taken to improve their schools, but they call on others to take them. Parents need to be more supportive, students need to be more responsible, the district needs to reduce class size, the state or province needs to provide more funding, and so on. This external focus on what others must do fails to improve the situation and fosters a culture of dependency and resignation (Sparks, 2007). Furthermore, we cannot make commitments on behalf of others; we can only make them for ourselves. Members of a PLC have an internal focus that acknowledges there is much within their sphere of influence that they could do to improve their school. They create a culture of self-efficacy and optimism by concentrating on what is within their collective power to do.

8 **Recognize that the process is nonlinear:** Although we present the four pillars sequentially, the process of clarifying purpose, vision, collective commitments, and goals is nonlinear, nonhierarchical, and nonsequential. Working on the foundation is cyclical and interactive. Writing purpose and vision statements can help shape commitments and goals, but it is not until those commitments are honored and goals are achieved that the purpose and vision become more real, clearer, and more focused.

9 **Remember it is what you do that matters, not what you call it:** Henry Mintzberg (1994) advises, "Never adopt a technique by its usual name . . . call it something different so that you have to think it through for yourself and work it out on your own terms" (p. 27). When concepts take on a label, they accumulate baggage. People get the impression that a proposal represents the latest fad, or they settle for a superficial understanding rather than really engaging in an assessment of the underlying ideas. There are schools and districts throughout North America that call themselves professional learning communities yet demonstrate none of the characteristics of a PLC. There are schools that could serve as Model PLCs yet are unfamiliar with the term. We are not advocating that faculties be asked to vote to become a PLC or take a PLC pledge. In fact, it may be more helpful to never use the *PLC* term. What is important is that we first engage staff members in building shared knowledge of certain key assumptions and critical practices and then call on them to act in accordance with that knowledge.

Part Six

Questions to Guide the Work of Your Professional Learning Community

To assess your effectiveness in building a solid foundation for a PLC, ask:

1. Have we created a guiding coalition to help implement and sustain our PLC?

2. Have we established an understood and accepted working definition of when we have reached consensus?

3. Did we build shared knowledge throughout the organization before asking people to make a decision?

4. Did we engage in dialogue rather than monologue—conversations rather than presentations—to provide people throughout the organization with ample opportunity to ask their questions and raise their concerns?

5. Have we created a process to allow dissenting points of view to be heard in a nonacrimonious way?

6. Have the staff embraced the premise that the purpose of their school is to ensure high levels of learning for all students?

7. Have the staff established the conditions they must create in the school to help all students learn at high levels?

8. Have the staff translated their aspirations for the school and their desire to help all students learn at high levels into collective commitments about how each individual can contribute to the school's vision and mission?

9. Have the staff established the school's short-term and long-term goals to serve as benchmarks of progress on their PLC journey?

10. Has the discussion to clarify the mission, vision, values (collective commitments), and goals led to specific actions designed to move the school closer to its vision?

11. Has the school initiated structural changes and reallocated resources to support the new vision?

12. Has the school created a process for monitoring progress toward the vision?

13. Are the four critical questions of a PLC driving the work of people throughout the school?

14. Do we celebrate our progress, model our commitments, and confront violations of the commitments?

page 2 of 2

Part Seven

Dangerous Detours and Seductive Shortcuts

Beware of mission statements that hedge on the collective commitment to promote high levels of learning for all students. References to "providing students with an opportunity to learn" or "helping each student learn according to the best of their ability" are subtle ways of distancing a school from a focus on the achievement of each student. Educators must do more than give students the chance to learn; they must align their practices to promote learning. They must reject the fixed mindset that attributes accomplishments to innate abilities or dispositions that cannot be enhanced. They must instead embrace the *growth* mindset—the belief that students can cultivate their abilities and talents through their own additional effort and the support of their educators (Dweck, 2006, 2016).

Educators must do more than give students the chance to learn; they must align their practices to promote learning.

Do not equate writing a mission statement with establishing a shared purpose for your school. Your shared purpose is ultimately revealed by what you do. The completion of a mission statement indicates not that your work is over, but rather that it has just begun. The tenets of a mission statement must be translated into specific, actionable steps that bring the mission to life. Remember the advice of Jim Collins (1996), who writes:

> [Leaders] spend too much time drafting, wordsmithing, and redrafting vision statements, mission statements, values statements, purpose statements, aspiration statements, and so on. They spend nowhere near enough time trying to align their organizations with the values and visions already in place. . . . When you have superb alignment, a visitor could drop into your organization from another planet and infer the vision without having to read it on paper. (p. 19)

Part Eight

Digging Deeper—Recommended Resources

The following resources delve deeper into the topic of defining a clear and compelling purpose.

- *Revisiting Professional Learning Communities at Work: Proven Insights for Sustained, Substantive School Improvement, Second Edition* by Richard DuFour, Rebecca DuFour, Robert Eaker, Mike Mattos, and Anthony Muhammad (2021)
- *In Praise of American Educators: And How They Can Become Even Better* by Richard DuFour (2015)

- *Powerful Guiding Coalitions: How to Build and Sustain the Leadership Team in Your PLC at Work* by Bill Hall (2022)
- *Creating and Protecting the Shared Foundation of a Professional Learning Community at Work* (video workshop) by Richard DuFour, Rebecca DuFour, Tim Brown, and Mike Mattos (2016)

Final Thoughts

The consideration of the questions of purpose, vision, commitments, and goals can help a staff lay the foundation for a professional learning community, but important work remains to be done. The fundamental structure and the engine that drives the PLC process is not the individual educator but a collaborative team. In the next chapter, we examine how to create genuine collaborative *teams* rather than congenial groups.

CHAPTER 3
Building a Collaborative Culture

Part One

The Case Study: Are We Engaged in Collaboration or "Coblaboration"?

Principal Joe McDonald was puzzled. He knew that building a collaborative culture was the key to improving student achievement. He could cite any number of research studies to support his position. He had worked tirelessly to promote collaboration and had taken a number of steps to support teachers working together. He organized each grade level in Nemo Middle School (nickname: the Fish) into an interdisciplinary team composed of individual mathematics, science, social studies, and language arts teachers. He created a schedule that gave teams time to meet together each day. He trained staff in collaborative skills, consensus building, and conflict resolution. He emphasized the importance of collaboration at almost every faculty meeting. He felt he had done all the right things, and for three years, he had waited patiently to reap the reward of higher levels of student learning. But to his dismay and bewilderment, every academic indicator of student achievement that the school monitored had remained essentially the same.

Principal McDonald decided to survey the faculty to see if he could discover why all the collaboration had yielded no gains in student achievement. The satisfaction survey he developed revealed that, with very few exceptions, teachers felt their collaborative time had strengthened the bonds between teachers. Specialist teachers—those in art, music, physical education, technical education, and special education—were less enthusiastic and expressed some resentment about being lumped together in one collaborative team. In general, however, teachers seemed to enjoy working together.

Principal McDonald then decided to make a concerted effort to personally observe the workings of the teams. At the first meeting he attended, a seventh-grade team focused on the behavior of a student who had become increasingly disruptive. The team agreed to schedule a parent conference so it could present its concerns to the parent as a group. An eighth-grade team brainstormed strategies for achieving the team goal of reducing disciplinary referrals for tardiness to class. At a meeting of a second seventh-grade team, he observed a lively debate about whether members should accept late work from students, and if so, how many points they should deduct for each day the work was late. The fourth team he observed assigned roles and responsibilities to each member to ensure all the tasks associated with an upcoming field trip were addressed.

By the end of the fourth meeting, Principal McDonald had a revelation: there had been no gains in student achievement because the collaborative teams addressed topics that were only remotely related to student learning! Armed with this insight, he convened a meeting of the faculty and shared his conclusion that teams needed to shift the focus of their dialogues to curriculum, assessment, and instruction.

His proposal met with less than wild enthusiasm. Teachers pointed out that each interdisciplinary team member taught different content. How could a seventh-grade science teacher engage in meaningful work on curriculum, assessment, and instruction with a seventh-grade social studies teacher? The team of specialist teachers was even more emphatic that it was impossible for them to have meaningful conversations on those topics because of the different courses they taught. Teachers argued that since they did not share content with the colleagues on their team, it made sense that they would use their team time to focus on the one thing they did have in common: their students.

Other teachers accused Principal McDonald of abandoning the middle school concept and its commitment to the whole child. One highly emotional teacher charged Principal McDonald with selling out—disregarding the emotional well-being of the student in the pursuit of higher test scores.

The staff's reaction genuinely stunned Principal McDonald. He had always believed they enjoyed working together in their teams, and he assumed that merely shifting the focus of their collaboration would be a relatively simple matter. It now appeared, however, that although the staff were happy to collaborate regarding some aspects of the school's program, they were either disinterested in or adamantly opposed to addressing others. Dispirited, he retreated to his office to ponder next steps.

Reflection

Why did Principal McDonald's efforts to build a collaborative culture in his school go awry? What steps might he take to improve the situation?

Part Two

Here's How

The situation in this school reflects one of the most pervasive problems in building PLCs. Many educators have gradually, sometimes grudgingly, come to acknowledge that collaborating with one's colleagues is preferable to working in isolation. Slowly, structures have been put in place to support collaboration. Staff members are increasingly assigned to teams, given time for collaboration during their contractual day, and provided with training to assist them as they begin the challenge of working together. Administrators and teachers alike take pride that the goal has been accomplished: professionals in the building are collaborating with each other on a regular basis. The anticipated gains in student achievement, however, often fail to materialize.

We cannot stress this next point too emphatically: the fact that teachers collaborate will do nothing to improve a school. The pertinent question is not, "Are they collaborating?" but rather, "What are they collaborating about?" Collaboration is not a virtue in itself, and building a collaborative culture is simply a means to an end, not the end itself. The purpose of collaboration—to help more students achieve at higher levels—can only be accomplished if the professionals engaged in collaboration are focused on the *right work.*

The purpose of collaboration—to help more students achieve at higher levels—can only be accomplished if the professionals engaged in collaboration are focused on the right work.

What is the right work that would focus the collaborative efforts of a team committed to higher levels of learning for all students? Once again, we return to the four questions that drive the work of a PLC.

1. **What is it we want our students to know and be able to do?** Have we identified the essential knowledge, skills, and dispositions each student is to acquire as a result of each unit of instruction?
2. **How will we know if each student has learned it?** Are we using formative assessment in our classrooms on an ongoing basis? Are we gathering evidence of student learning through one or more team-developed common formative assessments for each unit of instruction?
3. **How will we respond when some students do not learn it?** Can we identify students who need additional time and support by the student, by the standard, and for every unit of instruction? Do we use evidence of student learning from common formative assessments to analyze and improve our individual and collective instructional practice?
4. **How will we extend the learning for students who have demonstrated proficiency?** Can we identify students who have reached identified learning targets to extend their learning?

Principal McDonald must first form an alliance with key staff members to build a deeper understanding of the real purpose of their collaboration and then create supports and parameters to guide staff dialogue to the right topics. He must do more than assign people to teams and hope for the best. If Principal McDonald is to build the capacity of the staff to function as members of high-performing teams, he must demonstrate reciprocal accountability by providing those teams with the focus, support, and resources to be successful.

Clarifying Key Terms

Educators who are asked to work in collaborative teams will continue to struggle unless they come to a shared understanding of key terms. Principal McDonald must clarify that in asking educators to work in teams, he is asking them to work interdependently to achieve a common goal for which members are mutually accountable. Furthermore, since a school's mission is to ensure high levels of learning, the team's goals must be explicitly and directly tied to that purpose. A collection of teachers does not truly become a team until members must rely on one another to accomplish a goal that none could achieve individually. We will have more to say about the importance of goals in chapter 5 (page 119).

A collection of teachers does not truly become a team until members must rely on one another to accomplish a goal that none could achieve individually.

In asking teachers to collaborate, Principal McDonald is asking them to engage in a systematic process in which they work together, interdependently, to analyze and impact their professional practice in order to improve individual and collective results. A systematic process is a combination of related parts, organized into a whole in a methodical, deliberate, and orderly way, toward a particular aim. It is not intended to be invitational or indiscriminate. Those who develop systematic practices do not hope things happen a certain way; they create specific structures to ensure certain steps are taken.

A deeper understanding of the meaning and purpose of teams and collaboration could help the educators in this school recognize that they have not been focusing on the right work in the right way.

Creating Meaningful Teams

One way Principal McDonald can support teachers in the effort to create high-performing collaborative teams is to ensure that each staff member is assigned to a meaningful team. Principals must recognize that the task of building a collaborative culture requires more than bringing random adults together in the hope they will discover a topic of conversation. The fundamental question in organizing teams is, "Do team members have a shared responsibility for responding to the four critical questions in ways that enhance students' learning?"

Much work will remain in terms of helping teams develop their capacity to improve student learning, but that outcome is far more difficult to achieve without organizing teams appropriately.

Examining Possible Team Structures

Let's examine some possible team structures that support meaningful collaboration.

Same Course or Grade Level

The best team structure for improving student achievement is simple: a team of teachers who teach the same course or grade level. These teachers have a natural common interest in exploring the critical questions of learning. Furthermore, considerable research indicates that this structure is best suited for the ongoing professional learning that leads to improved student achievement (Gallimore, Ermeling, Saunders, & Goldenberg, 2009; Little, 2006; Robinson, 2010; Saphier, King, & D'Auria, 2006; Stigler & Hiebert, 2009; Wei, Darling-Hammond, Andree, Richardson, & Orphanos, 2009). In some instances, however, a single person may be the only teacher of a grade level or content area (such as in very small schools or courses outside the core curriculum). How does the only first-grade teacher or the only art teacher in a school become a member of a meaningful collaborative team?

The best team structure for improving student achievement is simple: a team of teachers who teach the same course or grade level.

Vertical Teams

Vertical teams link teachers with those who teach content above and below that of their students. For example, the sole first-grade teacher could join the kindergarten and second-grade teachers to create the school's primary team. The team members would work together to:

- Clarify the essential outcomes for students in kindergarten, first grade, and second grade
- Develop assessments for the students in each grade level
- Analyze the results of each assessment
- Offer suggestions for improving results
- Take collective responsibility for each other's students during a common block of time designated for intervention and enrichment

In this structure, each teacher has the benefit of two *critical friends* who can offer suggestions for improvement as the team examines indicators of student achievement. Furthermore, when teachers examine evidence indicating students are having difficulty with a particular skill in the grade level beyond the one they are teaching, they can adjust their own instruction, pacing, and curriculum to better prepare students for that content.

Vertical teams can also cut across schools. A middle school band director, for example, could join the high school band director to create a vertical team responsible for creating a strong band program. An elementary school art teacher could work with the middle school art teacher to clarify the prerequisite skills students should acquire before they enter the middle school art program. The K–12 vertical team format can be a powerful tool for strengthening the program of an entire district.

Virtual Teams

Proximity is not a prerequisite for an effective collaborative team. Teachers can use technology to create powerful partnerships with colleagues across the district, state,

Proximity is not a prerequisite for an effective collaborative team.

province, or world. As Ken Blanchard (2007) concludes in his study of effective organizations, "There is no reason that time and distance should keep people from interacting as a team. With proper management and the help of technology, virtual teams can be every bit as productive and rewarding as face-to-face teams" (p. 173). Any teacher with access to a computer can create a virtual team of colleagues who teach the same course or grade level by using virtual collaboration tools—such as Zoom or Google Chat—to engage in real-time dialogue with teammates. Using technology, the team members can clarify what students should learn, develop common pacing guides, create common assessments, and share information regarding the learning of their students. Principals in the same district can facilitate the process by coordinating with their colleagues to provide a common planning period for singleton teachers in different schools. For example, all the elementary physical education teachers in the district can become a team to answer the critical questions of learning related to their content area of expertise.

Furthermore, most professional organizations will assist teachers in finding colleagues to form a collaborative team. For example, the College Board has created electronic discussion groups for each area of the Advanced Placement (AP) program along with sample syllabi, course descriptions, free-response questions, and tips for teaching the AP content. The ubiquity of and easy access to technology mean every teacher is able to engage in powerful collaboration even without the benefit of having a colleague in the building who teaches the same content.

Interdisciplinary Teams

The interdisciplinary team model used in the case-study school can be an effective structure for collaboration, but only if certain steps are taken to change the nature of the conversation. If teachers share no common content or objectives, they will inevitably turn their attention to the one thing they do have in common: their students. A seventh-grade team's discussions regarding Johnny's behavior and Mary's attitude can be appropriate and beneficial, but at some point, the team must clarify the knowledge, skills, and dispositions Johnny and Mary are to acquire as a result of their seventh-grade experience.

In an interdisciplinary structure, each team in the school should be asked to create an overarching curricular goal that members will interdependently work to achieve.

Therefore, in an interdisciplinary structure, each team in the school should be asked to create an overarching curricular goal that members will interdependently work to achieve. For example, Principal McDonald could make staff aware of the power of nonfiction writing to improve student achievement in mathematics, science, social studies, and reading (Reeves, 2006, 2020). He could then ask each grade-level team to develop a goal to increase student achievement by becoming more effective in the instruction of nonfiction writing. As members of the seventh-grade team worked together to achieve this goal, they would confront a series of questions, such as the following.

- How can we integrate nonfiction writing into each of our different subject areas?
- What criteria will we use to assess the quality of student writing?
- How will we know if we are applying the criteria consistently?

- What are the most effective ways to teach nonfiction writing?
- Is there a team member with expertise in this area who can help the rest of us become more effective?
- How will we know if our students are becoming better writers?
- How will we know if the focus on writing is impacting achievement in our respective courses?
- What strategies will we put in place for students who struggle with nonfiction writing?
- How can we enrich the learning experience for students who are already capable writers?
- Are there elements of the seventh-grade curriculum we can eliminate or curtail to provide the necessary time for greater emphasis on nonfiction writing?

Principal McDonald could also foster a greater focus on learning if he created a schedule that allowed teachers to meet in content-area teams as well as in grade-level teams. Once again, research finds the grade-level or course structure to be the most conducive to meaningful dialogue and the continuing professional learning of a team. Middle schools make a mistake when they put all their eggs in the interdisciplinary basket. A seventh-grade mathematics teacher can certainly benefit from conversations with colleagues who teach language arts, social studies, or science, but just as certainly, that mathematics teacher can also benefit from conversations with other mathematics teachers. The best middle schools utilize both team structures to focus on and improve the academic achievement of their students.

Logical Links

Specialist teachers can become members of grade-level or course-specific teams that are pursuing outcomes linked to their areas of expertise. A physical education teacher could join a sixth-grade team in an effort to help students learn percentages. Each day, the teacher could help students learn to calculate their free throw percentage in basketball or their batting average in baseball. A music teacher we know joined the fourth-grade team and wrote a musical based on key historical figures students were required to learn that year. A special education teacher joined a biology team because of the difficulties her students were experiencing in that course. She disaggregated the scores of students with special needs on each test, and she became a consultant to the team on supplementary materials, instructional strategies, and alternative assessments to help special education students achieve the course's intended outcomes. She then worked as a member of the special education team to help her colleagues recognize the specific biology skills and concepts that were causing difficulty for students in special education. She provided colleagues with resources and ideas for supporting students in those areas during their resource period with their special education teacher.

Specialist teachers can become members of grade-level or course-specific teams that are pursuing outcomes linked to their areas of expertise.

Site Intervention Teams

A site intervention team leads the school's focused efforts concerning the specific students in need of intensive reinforcements (Buffum et al., in press). These students often have needs in multiple areas, including:

- Foundational reading and writing
- Number sense
- Speaking English (or the primary language of the school community)
- Academic and social behaviors
- Health and home

Creating an intervention team comprised of staff members who have expertise in these areas will provide the school the best chance to diagnose, target, prioritize, and monitor the intervention needs of students. Potential team members include administrators, special education staff, counselors, psychologists, speech-language pathologists, and subject specialists.

Like any other team, a site intervention team uses the four critical questions of the PLC at Work process to focus on the individual needs of struggling students. Equally important, the team can use evidence of individual student learning to identify more effective teaching practices, which will help each team member improve their practices. (See chapter 8, page 197, for a detailed examination of intervention in a PLC at Work.)

Team Structures

- **Same-course or grade-level teams** are those in which, for example, all the geometry teachers or all the second-grade teachers in a school form a collaborative team.
- **Vertical teams** link teachers with those who teach content above or below that of their students.
- **Virtual teams** use technology to create powerful partnerships with colleagues across the district, state, province, or world.
- **Interdisciplinary teams** found in middle schools and small high schools can be an effective structure if members work interdependently to achieve an overarching curricular goal that will result in higher levels of student learning.
- **Logical links** put teachers together in teams that are pursuing outcomes linked to their areas of expertise.
- **Site intervention teams** are comprised of educators with diverse expertise who work collaboratively to focus on the individual needs of the school's students who are most at risk.

In short, teachers should be organized into structures that allow them to engage in meaningful collaboration that is beneficial to them and their students. Once again, the fundamental question in organizing teams is this: "Do team members have a shared responsibility for responding to the four critical questions in ways that enhance students' learning?" The effectiveness of any particular team structure will depend on the extent to which it supports teacher dialogue and action aligned with those four questions.

Teachers should be organized into structures that allow them to engage in meaningful collaboration that is beneficial to them and their students.

Making Time for Collaboration

Reciprocal accountability demands that leaders who ask educators to work in collaborative teams provide those educators with time to meet during their contractual day. We believe it is insincere for any district or school leader to stress the importance of collaboration and then fail to provide time for it. One of the ways in which organizations demonstrate their priorities is through the allocation of resources, and in schools, one of the most precious resources is time. Thus, school and district leaders must provide teachers with time to do the things they are being asked to do.

School and district leaders must provide teachers with time to do the things they are being asked to do.

We also recognize that many districts face real-world constraints in providing time for collaboration. Releasing students from school so that teachers can collaborate may create childcare hardships for some families. In fact, we have seen several instances where community pressure has put an end to collaborative time for teachers. In almost every instance, what sparked the opposition was not the fact that teachers were collaborating, but that the strategy for providing collaborative time created problems for families. Other districts have paid teachers to extend their school day in order to provide time for collaboration, but often that time is lost when money gets tight. Furthermore, this strategy conveys the message that collaboration is an add-on to the teacher workday rather than an integral part of teaching. Hiring substitute teachers to give teacher teams time to work together is a possible strategy but may be cost prohibitive in some districts—and it gives teachers the added burden of creating plans for the substitutes. Furthermore, teachers and administrators alike are often reluctant to lose precious instructional time so that teachers can meet in teams. Nonetheless, we have worked with school districts throughout North America that have been able to create regularly scheduled weekly time for collaboration within real-world parameters: they bring teachers together during their contractual day while students are on campus, in ways that do not cost money and that result in little to no loss of instructional time.

The issue of finding time for collaboration has been addressed effectively—and often—in the professional literature, which is readily available for those who are sincerely interested in exploring alternatives. Learning Forward alone has addressed the issue hundreds of times in its publications, and AllThingsPLC (https://allthingsplc.info) lists hundreds of schools that have created time for teachers to collaborate in ways that don't cost money, result in significant loss of instructional time, or require the school to be shut down. The following strategies do not form a comprehensive list; rather, they illustrate some of the steps schools and districts have taken to create the prerequisite time for collaboration.

Common Preparation

Build the master schedule to provide daily common preparation periods for teachers of the same course or department. Each team should then designate one day each week to engage in collaborative, rather than individual, planning.

Parallel Scheduling

Schedule common preparation time by assigning the specialists (physical education teachers, librarians, music teachers, art teachers, instructional technologists, guidance counselors, foreign language teachers, and so on) to provide lessons to students across an entire grade level at the same time each day. The team should designate one day each week for collaborative planning. Some schools build back-to-back specials classes into the master schedule on each team's designated collaborative day, thus creating an extended block of time for the team to meet. Specials teachers must also be given time to collaborate.

Adjusted Start and End Times

Gain collaborative time by starting the workday early or extending the workday one day each week. In exchange for adding time to one end of the workday, teachers get the time back on the other end of that day. For example, on Tuesdays, all staff at Adlai E. Stevenson High School in Lincolnshire, Illinois, begin their workday at 7:30 a.m. rather than the normal 7:45 a.m. start time. From 7:30 to 8:30 a.m., the entire faculty engages in collaborative team meetings. Classes, which usually begin at 8:05 a.m., are delayed until 8:30 a.m. on Tuesdays. Students who can arrange for their own transportation arrive to school then. Buses run their regular routes so that no parent is inconvenienced, and students are delivered to the school at 7:40 a.m. Administrative and noninstructional staff supervise students upon their arrival in a variety of optional activities (such as breakfast, library and computer research, open gym, study halls, and tutorials) until classes begin. To make up for the twenty-five minutes of lost instructional time, five minutes is trimmed from five of the eight fifty-minute class periods. The school day ends at the usual time (3:25 p.m.), and again, buses run on their regular schedules. Because they began work fifteen minutes early (7:30 rather than 7:45 a.m.), Stevenson teachers are free to leave fifteen minutes earlier than the normal conclusion of their workday (3:30 rather than 3:45 p.m.). By making these minor adjustments to the schedule one day each week, the entire faculty is guaranteed an hour of collaborative planning without extending their workday or workweek by a single minute.

Shared Classes

Combine students across two different grade levels or courses into one class for instruction. While one teacher or team instructs the students, the other team engages in collaborative work. The teams alternate instructing and collaborating to provide equity in learning time for students and teams. Some schools coordinate shared classes so older students adopt younger students and serve as mathematics and literacy buddies, tutors, and mentors during shared classes.

Group Activities, Events, and Testing

Teacher teams coordinate activities that require student supervision rather than instructional expertise, such as watching an instructional video, conducting resource lessons, reading aloud, attending assemblies, or testing. Nonteaching staff members supervise students while teachers engage in team collaboration.

Banked Time

Over a designated period of days, extend the instructional minutes beyond the required school day. After you have banked the desired number of minutes, end the instructional day early to allow for faculty collaboration and student enrichment. For example, in a middle school, the traditional instructional day ends at 3:00 p.m., students board buses at 3:20 p.m., and the teachers' contractual day ends at 3:30 p.m. The faculty may decide to extend the instructional day until 3:10 p.m. By teaching an extra ten minutes for nine days in a row, they bank ninety minutes. On the tenth day, instruction stops at 1:30 p.m., and the entire faculty has collaborative team time for two hours. The students remain on campus and are engaged in clubs, enrichment activities, assemblies, and so on that a variety of parent and community partners sponsor and that the school's nonteaching staff co-supervise.

In-Service and Faculty Meeting Time

Schedule extended time for teams to work together on staff development days and during faculty meeting time. Rather than requiring staff to attend a traditional whole-staff in-service session or sit in a faculty meeting while directives and calendar items are read aloud, shift the focus and use of these days and meetings so team members have extended time to learn with and from each other.

Making Time for Collaboration

- Provide common preparation time.
- Use parallel scheduling.
- Adjust start and end times.
- Share classes.
- Schedule group activities, events, and testing.
- Bank time.
- Use in-service and faculty meeting time wisely.

Clarifying the Right Work

A very important way in which Principal McDonald could support his teams and increase the likelihood of their success would be to ensure they are clear on the nature of the work to be done. It is not difficult to assign teachers to meaningful teams and provide them with time to collaborate. But educators arrive at a fork in the road in the PLC process when they determine how they will use that collaborative time.

Once again, merely assigning teachers to groups will not improve a school, and much of what passes for collaboration among educators is more aptly described as coblaboration, a term David Perkins (2003) coined. Ineffective or unproductive team meetings create cynicism and sour teachers' attitudes toward teaming while simultaneously reinforcing the norms of isolation so prevalent in our schools (Boston Consulting Group, 2014). Those who hope to improve student achievement by developing the capacity of staff to function as a PLC must create and foster the conditions that move educators from mere work groups to high-performing collaborative teams.

Those who hope to improve student achievement by developing the capacity of staff to function as a PLC must create and foster the conditions that move educators from mere work groups to high-performing collaborative teams.

In a PLC, the process of collaboration is specifically designed to impact educator practice in ways that lead to better results. Over and over again, we have seen schools in which staff members are willing to collaborate about any number of things—dress codes, tardy policies, the appropriateness of Halloween parties—provided they can return to their classrooms and continue to do what they have always done. Yet in a PLC, the reason teachers are organized into teams, provided with time to work together, and asked to focus on certain topics and complete specific tasks is so that when they return to their classrooms, they will possess and utilize an expanded repertoire of skills, strategies, materials, assessments, and ideas to impact student achievement in a more positive way.

One of the most important elements of reciprocal accountability that district and school leaders must address is establishing clear parameters and priorities that guide teamwork toward the goal of improved student learning.

Therefore, one of the most important elements of reciprocal accountability that district and school leaders must address is establishing clear parameters and priorities that guide teamwork toward the goal of improved student learning. The "Critical Issues for Team Consideration" worksheet (pages 77–78) is a useful tool toward that end. First, it directs the team's attention to issues that impact practice and, thus, student achievement. Second, it calls on the team to generate products that flow directly from the dialogue and decisions regarding those issues. Those products, in turn, are crucial to helping Principal McDonald monitor the progress of teams. Even if teams are doing the right work, they may not be doing the work well. Principal McDonald must put a process in place to monitor each team's work—the *products* of their work (the quality of what they produce), their *processes* (how they do their work), and most important, the *results* of their work (the effects of their work on student learning). Without a process for monitoring teams, the principal will not know when a team is struggling and will be unable to fulfill their responsibility of helping each team succeed in what members are being called on to do (Eaker & Sells, 2016).

Creating the position of team leader is another way Principal McDonald could support teams' work. Team leaders serve as the liaisons between the principal and the faculty. McDonald should regularly meet with these leaders; practice, clarify, and rehearse how leaders can lead the teams through each of the eighteen critical issues for team consideration (pages 77–78); and share problems, concerns, and successes (Eaker & Sells, 2016).

Principal McDonald might have avoided some of the initial confusion regarding how teams were expected to use their time had he presented them with the "Critical Issues for Team Consideration" worksheet and then worked with the team leaders to help them establish a timeline for the completion of team products. Imagine if the principal and staff had created the following timeline to guide the dialogue of teams.

Critical Issues for Team Consideration

Team Name:

Team Members:

Use the following rating scale to indicate the extent to which each statement is true of your team.

1	2	3	4	5	6	7	8	9	10

Not True of Our Team **Our Team Is Addressing This** **True of Our Team**

1. ______ We have identified team norms and protocols to guide us in working together.
2. ______ We have analyzed student achievement data and established SMART goals to improve on this level of achievement we are working interdependently to attain. (SMART goals are specific and strategic, measurable, attainable, results oriented, and time bound. SMART goals are discussed at length on page 121.)
3. ______ Each team member is clear on the knowledge, skills, and dispositions (that is, the essential learning) that students will acquire as a result of our course or grade level and each unit within the course or grade level.
4. ______ We have aligned the essential learning with state and district standards and the high-stakes assessments required of our students.
5. ______ We have identified course content and topics we can eliminate to devote more time to the essential curriculum.
6. ______ We have agreed on how to best sequence the content of the course and have established pacing guides to help students achieve the intended essential learning.
7. ______ We have identified the prerequisite knowledge and skills students need in order to master the essential learning of each unit of instruction.
8. ______ We have identified strategies and created instruments to assess whether students have the prerequisite knowledge and skills.
9. ______ We have developed strategies and systems to assist students in acquiring prerequisite knowledge and skills when they are lacking in those areas.
10. ______ We have developed frequent common formative assessments that help us determine each student's mastery of essential learning.
11. ______ We have established the proficiency standard we want each student to achieve on each skill and concept examined with our common assessments.

page 1 of 2

12. ______ We use the results of our common assessments to assist each other in building on strengths and addressing weaknesses as part of an ongoing process of continuous improvement designed to help students achieve at higher levels.

13. ______ We use the results of our common assessments to identify students who need additional time and support to master essential learning, and we work within the systems and processes of the school to ensure they receive that support.

14. ______ We have agreed on the criteria we will use in judging the quality of student work related to the essential learning of our course, and we continually practice applying those criteria to ensure we are consistent.

15. ______ We have taught students the criteria we will use in judging the quality of their work and provided them with examples.

16. ______ We have developed or utilized common summative assessments that help us assess the strengths and weaknesses of our program.

17. ______ We have established the proficiency standard we want each student to achieve on each skill and concept examined with our summative assessments.

18. ______ We formally evaluate our adherence to team norms and the effectiveness of our team at least twice each year.

By the end of . . .

- The second week of school, we will present our team norms
- The fourth week of school, we will present our team SMART goal
- The sixth week of school, we will present our list of the essential knowledge, skills, and dispositions our students will acquire during this semester
- The eighth week of school, we will present our first common assessment
- The tenth week of school, we will present our analysis of the results from the common assessment, including areas of strength and strategies for addressing areas of concern

Clearly established expectations and timelines are of tremendous benefit to teams. Members lose no time debating, "Why are we here?" or focusing on the trivial because they have been guided toward conversations specific to teaching and learning. Furthermore, by gathering and reviewing team products with team leaders on a regular basis, Principal McDonald could monitor the teams' progress without micromanaging them. We highly recommend that principals and team leaders use the "Critical Issues for Team Consideration" worksheet or a similar tool to help clarify exactly what collaborative teams are expected to do by when and to monitor the progress the teams are making.

Establishing Collective Commitments to Enhance the Effectiveness of Teams

A reluctance to change their traditional classroom practices is not the only reason educators tend to drift away from substantive conversations about teaching and learning if parameters are not in place to guide their work. Conversations about the trivial are safer. If teachers are to work collaboratively to clarify the essential learning for their courses and grade levels, write common assessments, and jointly analyze the results, they must overcome the fear that they may be exposed to their colleagues and principals as ineffective. After all, you were hired for your professional expertise, but what if the results from a common assessment demonstrate that while your colleagues' students are successful, your students are not? We have seen evidence that some teachers would prefer not to know their strengths and weaknesses in relation to their colleagues' because it is not worth the risk of being exposed and vulnerable.

If teachers are to work collaboratively to clarify the essential learning for their courses and grade levels, write common assessments, and jointly analyze the results, they must overcome the fear that they may be exposed to their colleagues and principals as ineffective.

In his review of the dysfunctions of a team, Patrick Lencioni (2003) contends that the first and most important step in building a cohesive and high-performing team is the establishment of vulnerability-based trust. Individuals on effective teams learn to acknowledge mistakes, weaknesses, failures, and the need for help. They also learn to recognize and value the strengths of other team members and are willing to learn from one another.

The fear of vulnerability leads to the second team dysfunction: avoidance of productive conflict. Dysfunctional teams prefer artificial harmony to insightful inquiry and advocacy. As a result, they avoid topics that require them to work interdependently. Even decisions that would appear to require joint effort fail to generate genuine commitment from individuals on the team. Members settle for the appearance of agreement rather than pushing each other to pledge to honor the agreement through their actions. The avoidance of conflict and lack of commitment lead to yet another dysfunction of a team: avoidance of accountability. Team members are unwilling to confront peers who fail to work toward team goals or to honor team decisions. Finally, since members are unwilling to commit to purpose, priorities, and decisions, and are unwilling to hold each other accountable, they inevitably are inattentive to results. When groups demonstrate the five dysfunctions of a team—the inabilities to (1) establish trust, (2) engage in honest dialogue regarding disagreements, (3) make commitments to one another, (4) hold each other accountable, and (5) focus on results—the team process begins to unravel (Lencioni, 2003).

Leaders can help teams avoid these dysfunctions in several ways. First, and very importantly, they can model vulnerability, enthusiasm for meaningful exploration of disagreements, articulation of public commitments, a willingness to confront those who fail to honor decisions, and an unrelenting focus on and accountability for results. For example, Principal McDonald could acknowledge that he made a mistake in his initial approach to creating high-performing teams and admit that he needs the help of the faculty in altering the team process so that it benefits students. He could invite open dialogue about specific proposals to refocus teams on matters impacting learning and help build shared knowledge regarding the advantages and disadvantages of each proposal. He could make commitments to the staff regarding what he is prepared to do to support their efforts and address their concerns. He could demonstrate his commitment to the decisions they reach by confronting those who violate them. Finally, he could clarify the indicators they would monitor as a school to maintain their focus on results.

Furthermore, Principal McDonald could help staff members engage in professional dialogue designed to address the dangers of a dysfunctional team. Teams benefit from clarity regarding not only the purpose of their collaboration but also how they will work together and what is expected of each member. Once again, simply putting people in groups does not ensure a productive, positive experience for participants. Most educators can remember a time when they worked in a group that was painfully inefficient and excruciatingly ineffective. But teams increase their likelihood of performing at high levels when they clarify their expectations of one another regarding procedures, responsibilities, and relationships.

Teams increase their likelihood of performing at high levels when they clarify their expectations of one another regarding procedures, responsibilities, and relationships.

All groups establish norms—ground rules or habits that govern the group—whether or not they take the time to reflect on and articulate the norms they prefer for their team. But when individuals work through a process to create explicitly stated norms, and then commit to honor those norms, they increase the likelihood they will begin to function as a collaborative team rather than as a loose collection of people working together.

Team norms are intended to serve not as rules but rather as collective commitments—public agreements shared among the members (Kegan & Lahey, 2001). Effective teams do not settle for "sorta" agreements; they identify the very specific commitments members have made to each other.

Here again, learning community members will begin the challenging task of articulating collective commitments for each team by building shared knowledge of best practices and strategies for implementing those practices. For example, one study of high-performing teams (Druskat & Wolff, 2001) found that members consistently demonstrate high emotional intelligence in the following characteristics.

- **Perspective taking:** Members are willing to consider matters from the other person's point of view.
- **Interpersonal understanding:** Members demonstrate accurate understanding of other group members' spoken and unspoken feelings, interests, and concerns.
- **A willingness to confront:** Members speak up when an individual violates commitments, but they confront the person in a caring way aimed at building consensus and shared interpretations of commitments.
- **A caring orientation:** Members communicate positive regard, appreciation, and respect. A close personal relationship is not a prerequisite of an effective team, but mutual respect and validation are critical.
- **Team self-evaluation:** The team is willing and able to evaluate its effectiveness.
- **Feedback solicitation:** The team solicits feedback and searches for evidence of its effectiveness from external sources as part of a process of continuous improvement.
- **A positive environment:** The team focuses on staying positive—a positive affect, positive behavior, and the pursuit of positive outcomes. Members cultivate positive images of the group's past, present, and future.
- **Proactive problem solving:** Members actively take the initiative to resolve issues that stand in the way of accomplishing team goals.
- **Organizational awareness:** Members understand their connection to and contribution to the larger organization.
- **The building of external relationships:** The team establishes relationships with others who can support their efforts to achieve their goals.

We also recommend that team members have an honest and open dialogue about the expectations they bring to the process by asking each other to reflect on and discuss their past experience with groups. Ask each participant to describe a time when they were a member of a group, committee, or task force that proved to be a negative experience. Then ask each participant to explain the specific behaviors or conditions that made it so negative. Next, invite each participant to describe a personal experience in which they felt the power and synergy of an effective team. Record the answers, and turn the group's attention to identifying commitments that would prevent the negative and promote the positive aspects of team membership if all participants pledged to honor those norms.

We offer the following six tips for creating norms.

1. **Each team should create its own norms:** Asking a committee to create norms all teams should honor is ineffective. Norms are collective commitments that members make to each other, and committees cannot make commitments for us. Furthermore, norms should reflect the experiences, hopes, and expectations of a specific team's members.

2. **Norms should be stated as commitments to act or behave in certain ways rather than as beliefs:** The statement, "We will arrive to meetings on time and stay fully engaged throughout the meetings," is more powerful than, "We believe in punctuality."

3. **Norms should be reviewed at the beginning and end of each meeting for at least six months:** Norms impact the work of a team only if they are put into practice over and over again until they become internalized. Teams should not confuse writing norms with living norms.

4. **Teams should formally evaluate the effectiveness of their norms at least twice a year:** This assessment should include exploration of the following questions.

    - Are we adhering to our norms?
    - Do we need to establish a new norm to address a problem occurring on our team?
    - Are all members of the team contributing to its work?
    - Are we working interdependently to achieve our team goal?

5. **Teams should focus on a few essential norms rather than creating an extensive laundry list:** Less is more when it comes to norms. People do not need a lot of rules to remember, just a few commitments to honor.

6. **One of the team norms should clarify how the team will respond if one or more members are not observing the norms:** Violations of team norms must be addressed. Failure to confront clear violations of the commitments members have made to each other will undermine the entire team process. We will address the issue of how to confront violations in chapter 10 (page 249).

When done well, norms can help establish the trust, openness, commitment, and accountability that move teams from the trivial to the substantive. No team should work without the benefit of these clearly defined collective commitments. Neglecting to establish norms that clarify expectations is a major reason teams fail (Blanchard, 2007, 2019).

Leaders can and should take each of the purposeful steps presented in this chapter.

1. Creating teams on the basis of a common responsibility for pursuing the critical questions of learning
2. Providing them with time to collaborate
3. Guiding them to the most powerful questions that impact learning
4. Asking teams to create specific products that should flow naturally from the dialogue of a team focused on the right work
5. Helping them create collective commitments that facilitate the trust, openness, and clarity of expectations essential to effective teams

When done well, norms can help establish the trust, openness, commitment, and accountability that move teams from the trivial to the substantive.

Those steps can help create the structure for meaningful team dialogue; however, two more critical steps must be taken to help turn the focus of the team to improved student learning.

6. Encouraging collaborative teams to develop and pursue SMART goals
7. Ensuring individual teachers and teams have access to relevant and timely information

These steps will be addressed in subsequent chapters.

Monitoring the Work of Teams

A question that leaders in PLCs frequently ask is, "How do we monitor the work of teams?" Monitoring the work of teams, both individually and collectively, is done in much the same way student work is monitored. That is, monitoring should be *frequent* and *timely*, and be both *formative* and *summative*. The focus of monitoring should primarily be on student learning results (student by student and skill by skill), products that teams produce, and each team's SMART goals.

Effectively monitoring the work of teams requires a clear understanding of what the particular work in which each team is engaged should look like when successfully completed. This understanding enables the use of high-quality examples of the work that the teams will engage in, and allows monitoring activities to be conducted against predetermined standards.

Like students, teams will learn at different rates and in different ways. And like students, some teams will need additional support, while others will need to extend their learning and effectiveness. Additionally, leaders should frequently recognize and celebrate the work of teams in meaningful ways. Like individuals, teams want to be recognized and appreciated for doing complex and difficult work well.

Part Three

Here's Why

The very reason any organization is established is to bring people together in an organized way to achieve a collective purpose that cannot be accomplished by working alone.

Why is it so important to organize a staff into collaborative teams in which people work interdependently to achieve common goals rather than continuing the long-standing tradition of teacher isolation? The very reason any organization is established is to bring people together in an organized way to achieve a collective purpose that cannot be accomplished by working alone. As Jeffrey Pfeffer and Robert Sutton (2000) write, "Interdependence is what organizations are all about. Productivity, performance, and innovation result from *joint* action, not just individual efforts and behavior" (p. 197). The degree to which people are working together in a coordinated, focused effort is a major determinant of the effectiveness of any organization, and the inability to work interdependently has been described as the "biggest opponent" and the "mortal enemy" of those who confront complex tasks in their daily work (Patterson et al., 2008, p. 192). Certainly, there are few tasks more complex than accomplishing something that has never been done—helping all students learn at high levels.

Furthermore, the collaborative team has repeatedly been cited in organizational literature as the most powerful structure for promoting the essential interdependence of an effective enterprise. Experts on effective teams offer very consistent advice regarding the benefits of teams (see page 86, "Why Should We Use Teams as Our Basic Structure?").

As we mentioned earlier in this chapter, simply organizing people into teams does not improve a school. Steps must be taken to ensure that those team members engage in collaboration on the issues that most impact student learning. Education research repeatedly links collaborative cultures with school improvement. In fact, the case for teachers working together collaboratively is so compelling that we are unaware of any credible research explicitly opposed to the concept (see page 87, "Why Should We Collaborate?").

We have, however, heard individuals oppose providing educators with time to collaborate. They typically frame their objection by arguing the time a teacher spends collaborating with colleagues is time they could have spent teaching students and, thus, represents unproductive time. Once again, research from both organizational development and education refutes that position. Effective organizations and effective schools build time for reflection and dialogue into every process. The goal is not merely to do more of what we have always done (regardless of its effectiveness) but to create a culture of continuous improvement and to discover ways to become better at achieving our purpose, forever (Black, Harrison, Lee, Marshall, & Wiliam, 2004; Champy, 1995; Collins & Porras, 1994; Darling-Hammond, 1996; Dolan, 1994; Goldsmith, 1996; Kouzes & Posner, 1987; Schein, 1996).

Common sense advises, however, that collaborative time can be squandered if educators do not use that time to focus on issues most directly related to teaching and learning. Michael Fullan's (2001) caution should be self-evident: "Collaborative cultures, which by definition have close relationships, are indeed powerful, but unless they are focusing on the right things they may end up being powerfully wrong" (p. 67).

Effective leaders will direct the work of teams to the critical questions because those are the conversations that have the biggest impact on student achievement. Clarifying what students must learn, monitoring each student's learning, responding to students who need additional time and support for learning, and challenging students who have already mastered the intended outcomes are the most critical tasks in a school. It is therefore imperative that educators interdependently work to become more skillful in these critical areas and that these questions become the priority within and among collaborative teams.

School and district leaders should also be prepared to provide the research rationale regarding why collaborative teams should establish the norms or collective commitments to clarify their expectations of one another and guide their collective efforts (see page 88, "Why Should We Create Norms?").

Part Four

Assessing Your Place on the PLC Journey

It is important to help your staff build shared knowledge regarding your school's current status in addressing the critical step on the PLC journey of building a collaborative culture. We have created a tool to assist you in that effort. "The Professional Learning Communities at Work® Continuum: Building a Collaborative Culture Through High-Performing Teams" is on pages 89–90 and online at **go.SolutionTree.com/PLCbooks** as a free reproducible. Once your staff have established greater clarity regarding the current status of your collaborative teams, we urge you to turn your attention to the "Where Do We Go From Here?" worksheet that accompanies the continuum (on page 91 and also available for free download at **go.SolutionTree.com/PLCbooks**). It will prompt you to take the action necessary to close the knowing-doing gap.

Why Should We Use Teams as Our Basic Structure?

"Empowered teams are such a powerful force of integration and productivity that they form the basic building block of any intelligent organization" (Pinchot & Pinchot, 1993, p. 66).

"Teams are recognized as a critical component of every enterprise—the predominant unit for decision making and getting things done. . . . Working in teams is the norm in a learning organization" (Senge et al., 1994, pp. 354–355).

Teams "bring together complementary skills and experience that . . . exceed those of any individual on the team." Teams are more effective in problem solving, "provide a unique social dimension that enhances . . . work," motivate, and foster peer pressure and internal accountability (Katzenbach & Smith, 1993, p. 18).

"In the most innovative [organizations], teaming *is* the culture. . . . Today's leaders must therefore build a culture where teaming is expected and begins to feel natural." (Edmondson, 2013).

"The ability to develop and support high-functioning teams schoolwide is essential to ensuring improved and inspired learning for all learners—adults or children" (D'Auria, 2015, p. 54).

"A team can make better decisions, solve more complex problems, and do more to enhance creativity and build skills than individuals working alone. . . . They have become the vehicle for moving organizations into the future. . . . Teams are not just nice to have. They are hard-core units of the production" (Blanchard, 2007, p. 17).

"Educators work alone more than any other professionals in modern America. Most professions have come to recognize the value of teamwork as a better way to understand and solve 'problems of practice.' . . . Fortunately, there appears to be new interest in forms of collaboration among educators. . . . 'Professional learning communities' are increasingly popular" (Wagner, 2007).

"Influencers increase the capacity of others by asking them to work in teams with interdependent relationships. . . . We increase capacity when we work together rather than in isolation" (Patterson et al., 2008, p. 183).

"We now have compelling evidence that when teachers team up with their colleagues they are able to create a culture of success in schools, leading to teaching improvements and student learning gains. The clear policy and practice implication is that teaching is a team sport" (Fulton & Britton, 2011, p. 4).

Why Should We Collaborate?

"The single most important factor for successful school restructuring and the first order of business for those interested in increasing the capacity of their schools is building a collaborative internal environment" (Eastwood & Louis, 1992, p. 215).

"When groups, rather than individuals, are seen as the main units for implementing curriculum, instruction, and assessment, they facilitate development of shared purpose for student learning and collective responsibility to achieve it" (Newmann & Wehlage, 1995, p. 38).

"[High-achieving schools] build a highly collaborative school environment where working together to solve problems and to learn from each other become cultural norms" (WestEd, 2000, p. 12).

"The key to ensuring that every child has a quality teacher is finding a way for school systems to organize the work of qualified teachers so they can collaborate with their colleagues in developing strong learning communities that will sustain them as they become more accomplished teachers" (National Commission on Teaching and America's Future, 2003, p. 7).

"Collaboration and the ability to engage in collaborative action are becoming increasingly important to the survival of public schools. Indeed, without the ability to collaborate with others, the prospect of truly repositioning schools . . . is not likely" (Schlechty, 2009, p. 237).

"It is time to end the practice of solo teaching in isolated classrooms" (Fulton, Yoon, & Lee, 2005, p. 4).

Teacher collaboration in strong professional learning communities improves the quality and equity of student learning, promotes discussions that are grounded in evidence and analysis rather than opinion, and fosters collective responsibility for student success (McLaughlin & Talbert, 2006).

"Quality teaching is not an individual accomplishment, it is the result of a collaborative culture that empowers teachers to team up to improve student learning beyond what any one of them can achieve alone" (Carroll, 2009, p. 13).

High-performing, high-poverty schools build deep teacher collaboration that focuses on student learning into the culture of the school. Structures and systems are set up to ensure teachers work together rather than in isolation, and "the point of their collaboration is to improve instruction and ensure all students learn" (Chenoweth, 2009, p. 17).

Teachers should be provided with more time for collaboration and embedded professional development during the school day and year. Expanding time for collaboration during the school day "facilitates the development of effective professional learning communities among teachers" (Farbman et al., 2014, p. 25).

"When teachers work together on collaborative teams, they improve their practice in two important ways. First, they sharpen their pedagogy by sharing specific instructional strategies for teaching more effectively. Second, they deepen their content knowledge by identifying the specific standards students must master. In other words, when teachers work together they become better teachers" (Many & Sparks-Many, 2015, p. 83).

"We must stop allowing teachers to work alone, behind closed doors and in isolation in the staffrooms and instead shift to a professional ethic that emphasizes collaboration. We need communities within and across schools that work collaboratively to diagnose what teachers need to do, plan programs and teaching interventions and evaluate the success of the interventions" (Hattie, 2015b, p. 23).

Why Should We Create Norms?

Teams improve their ability to grapple with the critical questions when they clarify the norms that will guide their work. These collective commitments represent the "promises we make to ourselves and others, promises that underpin two critical aspects of teams—commitment and trust" (Katzenbach & Smith, 1993, p. 60).

Explicit team norms help to increase the emotional intelligence of the group by cultivating trust, a sense of group identity, and belief in group efficacy (Druskat & Wolff, 2001).

"When self-management norms are explicit and practiced over time, team effectiveness improves dramatically, as does the experience of team members themselves. Being on the team becomes rewarding in itself—and those positive emotions provide energy and motivation for accomplishing the team's goals" (Goleman, Boyatzis, & McKee, 2004, p. 182).

Norms can help clarify expectations, promote open dialogue, and serve as a powerful tool for holding members accountable (Lencioni, 2005).

Referring back to the norms can help "the members of a group to 're-member,' to once again take out membership in what the group values and stands for; to 'remember,' to bring the group back into one cooperating whole" (Kegan & Lahey, 2001, p. 194).

Inattention to establishing specific team norms is one of the major reasons teams fail (Blanchard, 2007).

After looking at over a hundred teams for more than a year, researchers concluded that understanding and influencing group norms were the keys to improving teams. Researchers noted two norms that all good teams generally shared. First, members spoke in roughly the same proportion. Second, the good teams were skilled at intuiting how others felt based on their tone of voice, expressions, and other nonverbal cues (Duhigg, 2016).

The Professional Learning Communities at Work® Continuum: Building a Collaborative Culture Through High-Performing Teams

DIRECTIONS: Individually, silently, and *honestly* assess the current reality of your school's implementation of each indicator listed in the left column. Consider what evidence or anecdotes support your assessment. This form may also be used to assess district or team implementation.

We are committed to working together to achieve our collective purpose of learning for all students. We cultivate a collaborative culture through the development of high-performing teams.

Indicator	Pre-Initiating	Initiating	Implementing	Developing	Sustaining
We are organized into collaborative teams in which members work interdependently to achieve common goals that directly impact student achievement. Structures have been put in place to ensure: 1. Collaboration is embedded in our routine work practice. 2. We are provided with time to collaborate. 3. We are clear on the critical questions that should drive our collaboration. 4. Our collaborative work is monitored and supported.	Teachers work in isolation with little awareness of the strategies, methods, or materials that colleagues use in teaching the same course or grade level. There is no plan in place to assign staff members into teams or to provide them with time to collaborate.	Teachers are encouraged but not required to work together collaboratively. Some staff may elect to work with colleagues on topics of mutual interest. Staff members are congenial but are not co-laboring in an effort to improve student achievement.	Teachers have been assigned to collaborative teams and have been provided time for collaboration during the regular contractual day. Teams may be unclear regarding how they should use the collaborative time. Topics often focus on matters unrelated to teaching and learning. Some teachers believe the team meeting is not a productive use of their time.	Teachers have been assigned to collaborative teams and have been provided time for collaboration on a weekly basis during the regular contractual day. Guidelines, protocols, and processes have been established in an effort to help teams use collaborative time to focus on topics that will have a positive impact on student achievement. Team leaders are helping lead the collaborative process, and the work of teams is monitored closely so assistance can be provided when a team struggles. Teams are working interdependently to achieve goals specifically related to higher levels of student achievement and are focusing their efforts on discovering better ways to achieve those goals.	The collaborative team process is deeply engrained in the school culture. Staff members view it as the engine that drives school improvement. Teams are self-directed and very skillful in advocacy and inquiry. They consistently focus on issues that are most significant in improving student achievement and set specific, measurable goals to monitor improvement. The collaborative team process serves as a powerful form of job-embedded professional development because members are willing and eager to learn from one another, identify common problems, engage in action research, make evidence of student learning transparent among members of the team, and make judgments about the effectiveness of different practices on the basis of that evidence. The team process directly impacts teacher practice in the classroom, helping each teacher clarify what to teach, how to assess, and how to improve instruction.

Indicator	Pre-Initiating	Initiating	Implementing	Developing	Sustaining
We have identified and honor the commitments we have made to the members of our collaborative teams in order to enhance the effectiveness of our team. These articulated collective commitments or norms have clarified expectations of how our team will operate, and we use them to address problems that may occur on the team.	No attention has been paid to establishing clearly articulated commitments that clarify the expectations of how the team will function and how each member will contribute to its success. Norms do emerge from each group based on the habits that come to characterize the group, but they are neither explicit nor the result of a thoughtful process. Several of the norms have an adverse effect on the effectiveness of the team.	Teams have been encouraged by school or district leadership to create norms that clarify expectations and commitments. Recommended norms for teams may have been created and distributed. Norms are often stated as beliefs rather than commitments to act in certain ways.	Each team has been required to develop written norms that clarify expectations and commitments. Many teams have viewed this as a task to be accomplished. They have written the norms and submitted them, but do not use them as part of the collaborative team process.	Teams have established the collective commitments that will guide their work, and members have agreed to honor the commitments. The commitments are stated in terms of specific behaviors that members will demonstrate. The team begins and ends each meeting with a review of the commitments to remind each other of the agreements they have made about how they will work together. They assess the effectiveness of the commitments periodically and make revisions when they feel that will help the team become more effective.	Team members honor the collective commitments they have made to one another regarding how the team will operate and the responsibility of each member to the team. The commitments have been instrumental in creating an atmosphere of trust and mutual respect. They have helped members work interdependently to achieve common goals because members believe they can rely upon one another. The commitments facilitate the team's collective inquiry and help people explore their assumptions and practices. Members recognize that their collective commitments have not only helped the team become more effective, but also made the collaborative experience more personally rewarding. Violations of the commitments are addressed. Members use them as the basis for crucial conversations and honest dialogue when there is concern that one or more members are not fulfilling commitments.

Where Do We Go From Here? Worksheet
Building a Collaborative Culture Through High-Performing Teams

Indicator of a PLC at Work	What steps or activities must be initiated to create this condition in your school?	Who will be responsible for initiating or sustaining these steps or activities?	What is a realistic timeline for each step or phase of the activity?	What will you use to assess the effectiveness of your initiative?
We are organized into collaborative teams in which members work interdependently to achieve common goals that directly impact student achievement. Structures have been put in place to ensure: 1. Collaboration is embedded in our routine work practice. 2. We are provided with time to collaborate. 3. We are clear on the critical questions that should drive our collaboration. 4. Our collaborative work is monitored and supported. We have identified and honor the commitments we have made to the members of our collaborative teams in order to enhance the effectiveness of our team. These articulated collective commitments or norms have clarified expectations of how our team will operate, and we use them to address problems that may occur on the team.				

Part Five

Tips for Moving Forward: Building a Collaborative Culture Through High-Performing Teams

1. **Create meaningful teams:** Ensure that teams are created on the basis of shared responsibility for pursuing the critical questions of teaching and learning with a particular group of students—for example, by course or by grade level.

2. **Make time for collaboration:** Work with staff to find creative ways to provide more time for team collaboration, including ways of using existing time more effectively.

3. **Develop widespread leadership:** Disperse leadership more widely by identifying team leaders for any teams with more than three people. Meet with team leaders on a regular basis to identify problematic areas of the process, and develop strategies for resolving those problems.

4. **Make decisions on the basis of evidence:** Ask teams to build shared knowledge—to learn together—as they approach each new task in the collaborative process.

5. **Build the capacity of teams to succeed in the PLC process by providing them with essential tools:** Make supporting research, templates, protocols, exemplars, worksheets, and timelines available to teams to assist them in each step of the process.

6. **Continually assess the progress of teams:** Monitor the work of each team through ongoing assessment of their products, regular meetings with team leaders, and formal self-evaluations. Respond immediately to a team that is having difficulty.

7. **Lead by example:** Building-level leadership teams should model everything being asked of the collaborative teams, including meeting on a regular basis, staying focused on issues with the greatest impact on student achievement, establishing and honoring collective commitments, and working toward SMART goals.

8. **Coach collaborative teams:** Provide collaborative teams with coaching focused on improving their ability to collaborate and implement the essential elements of the PLC process with fidelity.

9. **Expand the knowledge base available to teams:** Look for ways to link teams with relevant resources inside and outside your building.

10. **Celebrate teams:** Make teams the focus of recognition and celebration (see chapter 10, page 249). Take every opportunity to acknowledge the efforts and accomplishments of teams.

Part Six

Questions to Guide the Work of Your Professional Learning Community

To promote a collaborative culture in your school or district, ask:

1. Have we organized our staff into collaborative teams?

2. Have teams been organized on the basis of common courses and common grade levels whenever possible?

3. If we have used the interdisciplinary team structure, have team members identified specific and overarching student achievement goals, and do they use those goals to guide their work?

4. Have specialist teachers and singleton teachers found meaningful collaborative teams?

5. Have we avoided assigning people to teams whose disparate assignments make it difficult, if not impossible, to focus on the critical questions of learning?

6. Have we provided time for teachers to meet in their collaborative teams on a regular basis?

7. Do teams focus on the critical questions of learning identified on the "Critical Issues for Team Consideration" (page 77) worksheet?

8. Are teams asked to submit specific products according to a designated timeline? Do these products reflect their focus on the critical questions?

9. What systems are in place to monitor the teams' work and effectiveness on a timely basis?

10. Has every team developed explicit norms that clarify the commitments members have made to one another regarding how they will work together as a team?

11. Do team members honor the norms they have established? Have they established a process for responding when a member fails to honor the norms?

12. Have we given teams the knowledge base, time, and support essential for their effectiveness?

13. Have we provided teachers with opportunities for job-embedded coaching of collaborative teams within the context of their regular and routine responsibilities?

Part Seven

Dangerous Detours and Seductive Shortcuts

Many schools and districts organize educators into what are simply groups rather than teams. Unless educators are working interdependently to achieve a common goal for which members are mutually accountable, they are not a team.

Unless educators are working interdependently to achieve a common goal for which members are mutually accountable, they are not a team.

Beware of artificial teams. We have seen schools create the "leftover team" that combines unrelated singleton teachers on the pretext that they will function as a collaborative team. The likelihood that this disparate group will actually function as a collaborative team is extremely remote. Work with singletons to make them members of meaningful teams, even if the teams are vertical or electronic and include members outside the building.

Most importantly, remember that a collaborative team will have no impact on student achievement unless its members are co-laboring on the right work. Systems must be in place to clarify what teams are to accomplish, monitor their progress, and provide assistance when they struggle.

Part Eight

Digging Deeper—Recommended Resources

The following resources delve deeper into the topic of forming collaborative teams, especially for small schools and singleton staff members.

- *How to Develop PLCs for Singletons and Small Schools* by Aaron Hansen (2015)
- *Singletons in a PLC at Work: Navigating On-Ramps to Meaningful Collaboration* by Brig Leane and Jon Yost (2022)
- *PLC at Work and Your Small School: Building, Deepening, and Sustaining a Culture of Collaboration for Singletons* by Breez Longwell Daniels (2020)
- *Yes We Can! General and Special Educators Collaborating in a Professional Learning Community* by Heather Friziellie, Julie A. Schmidt, and Jeanne Spiller (2016)
- *Collaboration for Career and Technical Education: Teamwork Beyond the Core Content Areas in a PLC at Work* by Wendy Custable and Paul C. Farmer (2020)

- *Virtual PLCs at Work: A Guide to Effectively Implementing Online and Hybrid Teaching and Learning* by Paul C. Farmer and Dennis King (2022)
- *Professional Learning Communities at Work and Virtual Collaboration: On the Tipping Point of Transformation* by Richard DuFour and Casey Reason (2016)
- *A New Way: Introducing Higher Education to Professional Learning Communities at Work* by Robert Eaker and Debra Sells (2016)

Final Thoughts

A collaborative culture does not simply emerge in a school or district; leaders *cultivate* collaborative cultures when they develop the capacity of their staff to work as members of high-performing teams. People throughout the organization, however, must always remember that collaboration is a means to an end—to higher levels of learning—rather than the end itself. The end in a PLC is higher levels of learning for all students.

The next chapter explores opportunities for developing high-performing collaborative teams through coaching. The argument for embracing the practice of coaching teams is simple: if collaborative teams are the foundation, the basic building block, and the engine that drives PLCs, then creating highly effective collaborative teams by coaching them on improving their PLC practice becomes a high priority for school leaders.

CHAPTER 4

Coaching Collaborative Teams

Part One

The Case Study: When Workshops Are Not Enough

Lee Lambert had been principal of Glacier Mountain Middle School (nicknamed the Yetis) for six years. He loved his job, but he often thought to himself, "The name of our school is so fitting. Things move so slowly around here." Lately, however, he was feeling like the school was finally making progress. It was slow, with small steps forward, but things were finally starting to happen with the school's PLC at Work initiative.

The faculty at Glacier Mountain had previously embraced the PLC process as the school's overarching improvement strategy. Lambert and a team of teacher leaders had designed a comprehensive plan to promote the PLC process, the faculty had expressed support for the idea, and the district office had approved a significant increase in funding for professional development. The good news was that little real resistance had emerged thus far.

A delegation of faculty members attended a two-day conference devoted to developing high-quality PLCs. Principal Lambert provided additional support by devoting all the school's allocated professional development days to a series of in-depth, whole-faculty training sessions with an outside consultant. The district also endorsed the use of release time, and individual teams started meeting during the first semester. The faculty's initial feedback had been positive, but after an early surge of enthusiasm, progress slowed, and there were signs the initiative was beginning to get bogged down. Still, Principal Lambert was looking forward to the guiding coalition's scheduled meeting to discuss how the PLC at Work initiative was going.

As Principal Lambert called the meeting to order, he asked the guiding coalition to talk about the initiative's progress and to identify what could be done to further support it. He asked the assistant principal to capture the group's input, suggestions, and observations on chart paper.

The team leader of the mathematics department began by suggesting, "We should revisit the evaluation results from the last training session to look for insights." He wondered, "Maybe we haven't provided teachers with enough background knowledge to understand the core competencies." The school's counselor and newest member of the guiding coalition asked if everyone was really on board with "this whole PLC thing" and suggested a survey of the faculty's feelings about the idea might be beneficial.

A long-tenured member of the social studies team, who had a reputation of being curmudgeonly, mumbled something under his breath; Principal Lambert asked him to speak up. He said, "All of this is a waste of time. I have more important things to do than sit in meetings." He continued, "Instead of norms and four questions, let's talk about the amount of texting our students do! I mean, there must be some orthopedic surgeon out there predicting dire consequences—carpal tunnel syndrome is nothing compared to the problems future generations will have with their opposable thumbs." The science team leader agreed, adding, "Kids pay more attention to dance videos on their cell phones than the lessons I teach." The room became silent.

After a moment, a teacher raised her hand and said, "Honestly, I'm not sure I know what a good PLC looks like. How do I know if I'm even *PLCing* the right way?" Another teacher chimed in: "I agree. We need more training. We need to learn more before we can ever think about being successful." A third team member suggested teachers had spent enough time attending workshops and argued, "If they *really* want us to do all of this, we need more release time."

Decorum in the room unraveled as everyone began speaking at the same time. Principal Lambert refocused the meeting by reviewing what the assistant principal had captured on chart paper. He said, "We agree we've learned a lot and the initial training sessions during the conference and customized workshops have been beneficial. All that learning has sparked some interest, created common language, and promoted a shared understanding of why the PLC process is important." Principal Lambert continued, "We also agree that the initiative is losing momentum and we're not seeing consistent or lasting changes. We've done all the workshops and conferences, but it's not transferring from theory into practice. What are we missing?"

Reflection

What would you say if you were a member of the Glacier Mountain guiding coalition? Why do you think all the training wasn't resulting in more changes in the faculty's professional practice? What next steps would you recommend Principal Lambert consider?

Part Two

Here's How

School leaders take a risk when they assume that all teachers understand the PLC process (many don't) or that all teachers are comfortable working in PLCs (many aren't). For some teachers, the PLC process is exciting; for others, it feels irrelevant, contrived, and downright challenging—especially in schools where teacher isolation has become ingrained in the culture. Developing an effective PLC requires the acquisition of knowledge and skills coupled with ongoing job-embedded support over an extended period of time.

It's a mistake to assume that attending a couple of workshops will ensure teachers are willing and able to be productive members of a PLC. Bruce Joyce and Beverly Showers (2002) have found that teachers incorporate only 5 percent of what they learn from traditional workshops into their professional practice. However, when traditional professional development opportunities are combined with coaching, the transfer rate of new knowledge and skills increases to 95 percent.

One study of teachers in California found that when coaching was added to traditional forms of professional development (workshops and conferences), the percentage of teachers who implemented new skills rose from 10 percent to 95 percent (Cornett & Knight, 2009). After reviewing thirteen scientific studies, Bryan Goodwin and Meagan Taylor (2019) reported similar results: "Basically, without coaching, teachers brought little of what they learned in workshops back into classrooms." These studies demonstrate that teachers are unlikely to develop new ways of working together by simply attending a workshop, a conference, or some other traditional form of professional development. They need more; they need coaching.

Teachers are unlikely to develop new ways of working together by simply attending a workshop, a conference, or some other traditional form of professional development. They need more; they need coaching.

Using Coaching Cycles

The most common way to organize the coaching of collaborative teams is through coaching cycles. Coaching cycles have been around a long time; Joellen Killion and colleagues (2020) cite examples of their use from the 1970s. As Andrew Miller (2019) points out, "Coaching cycles are still tried-and-true ways to support professional learning." The coaching cycle "provides a clear roadmap for growth and improvement, along with ongoing support and feedback to help teachers achieve their goals and improve their practice over time" (International Coaching Federation, 2023).

A simple definition of a *coaching cycle* is a structured process whereby a coach and a teacher team work together to improve the team's professional practice. The literature is filled with different frameworks, formats, and models for coaching, and most contain the same basic components; all coaching cycles guide a team through a circular and recursive process designed to improve their practice.

All coaching cycles guide a team through a circular and recursive process designed to improve their practice.

Coaching cycles differ from traditional coaching approaches. The International Coaching Federation (2023) suggests, "Traditional coaching typically involves a coach offering feedback and advice to a coachee based on their expertise and experience."

These coaching approaches tend to "rely heavily on the teachers' and coaches' perceptions as the measure of effectiveness" (Many, Maffoni, Sparks, & Thomas, 2018, p. 17).

According to the International Coaching Federation (2023), a key difference between coaching cycles and traditional coaching is that "the coaching cycle is focused on specific goals and outcomes to enhance student learning"—in this case, a team's PLC practices. In contrast to a traditional coaching approach, coaching cycles are grounded in an agreed-on standard of PLC best practice and a detailed analysis of the team's professional practice. The International Coaching Federation (2023) continues:

> In a coaching cycle, the coachee [team] works with the instructional coach to identify clear, measurable goals, and then the coach helps the coachee [team] to develop a plan to achieve those goals. The plan is then implemented, and progress is monitored and evaluated throughout the cycle.

Researchers and practitioners alike have found that coaching cycles increase the likelihood of success. Diane Sweeney (2021) believes that organizing coaching in cycles creates the kind of structure necessary for successful collaboration. Kenny McKee (2022) cites studies (Shidler, 2009; Sweeney, 2018) that support his belief that teachers who receive coaching through coaching cycles achieve better results than teachers who participate in the traditional coaching approach. Donna Spangler (2023) suggests that combining coaching cycles with PLC implementation "leverages the strengths of both approaches, resulting in a dynamic and holistic strategy for improving teaching practices and student outcomes."

Tools for Coaching

Strategy implementation guides (SIGs) and pathways tools are extremely valuable for use in coaching cycles (Many et al., 2018). The *SIG* is an agreed-on standard of PLC best practice that helps leaders and teams identify and monitor team progress toward their goal. A *pathways tool* guides teams through a series of probing questions related to the PLC process and serves as an invaluable tool when teams conduct a gap analysis. Visit **go.SolutionTree.com/PLCbooks** to see sample SIGs and pathways tools. For more information on how teams and schools can create their own SIGs and pathways, see chapters 3 and 5 of the book *Amplify Your Impact: Coaching Collaborative Teams in PLCs at Work* (Many et al., 2018).

These team coaching cycles include five steps (Many, Maffoni, Sparks, & Thomas, 2022).

1. **Gather data and evidence regarding the team's PLC practice:** In this step, the coach observes a team meeting, paying particular attention to the essential elements of the PLC process. The coach collects artifacts or products developed by the team during their team meetings and provides nonjudgmental feedback about the level of the team's PLC practice for their consideration.

2. **Develop an evidence-based assessment of the team's current reality:** Using a SIG (or a similar document that represents an agreed-on standard of PLC best practice), the coach and team reach consensus on the team's level of performance for each element of the PLC process, choose an area of the PLC process the team wants to improve, and set an improvement goal.

3. **Reach consensus on an improvement goal or best next steps:** Referring to the pathways tool (or a similar tool that describes different steps to take in each element of the PLC process), the coach and team conduct a gap analysis and identify the precise characteristic or specific next step or steps the team needs to address to accomplish the improvement goal identified in the previous step.

4. **Provide feedback and facilitate professional development:** The coach works with the team to provide feedback and facilitate SIG- and pathway-grounded professional development regarding any new learning or experiences the team might require to make progress toward the goal of improved practice. Consider using a plan-do-study-act (PDSA) cycle to support this step.

5. **Apply the new learning to improve the team's PLC practice:** The coach and team reflect on lessons learned during the coaching cycle, celebrate any progress the team has made toward accomplishing the goal, and decide whether the goal has been accomplished or more work is needed. If continued work is needed, the coaching cycle is repeated.

For a more detailed exploration of team coaching cycles, see *Energize Your Teams: Powerful Tools for Coaching Collaborative Teams in PLCs at Work*, pages 33–38 (Many et al., 2022).

The team coaching cycle (Many et al., 2022) provides opportunities for all three actions that Sweeney (2013) believes are required in an effective coaching cycle: (1) it promotes in-depth work with teacher teams over an extended time, (2) it is grounded in data or some agreed-on standard of best practice, and (3) it provides regular opportunities for feedback and planning. After participating in a coaching cycle, a team should be able to affirmatively answer a few questions.

- Did the team learn something new or become more proficient at some existing aspect of the PLC process? The team should be able to identify or describe a change in the team's PLC practice.
- Has the team reached consensus on what each team member needs to do to continue improving their PLC practice? The team should be able to articulate what is the best next step or steps.
- Did the team identify what plans or procedures are in place to ensure their lessons learned (changes in practice) become habits of their professional practice?

Coaching the PLC Process With Fidelity

The coaching cycle provides a framework for coaching collaborative teams. Strategy implementation guides and pathways—both tools that are embedded in the coaching cycle—have proven to be extremely valuable when coaching teams (Many et al., 2018). The SIG (used in step 2 of the coaching cycle) represents an agreed-on standard of PLC best practice that helps teams highlight their relative strengths and vulnerabilities before setting an improvement goal. The pathways (used in step 3 of the coaching cycle) guide teams through a series of probing questions related to the PLC process, helping them identify, describe, and monitor progress toward their improvement goal.

The most common SIG consists of a simple matrix of five rows and three columns. The five rows, which feature anchor statements, reflect the five prerequisites of a PLC: (1) collaborative teams, (2) a guaranteed and viable curriculum, (3) common assessments, (4) the use of data to improve teaching and learning, and (5) more time and support to ensure all students learn (DuFour, 2015; Many et al., 2018). The three columns, which feature indicators, define three levels of proficiency (beyond proficient, proficient, and below proficient). Using the SIG to identify their strengths and vulnerabilities, teams set specific improvement goals and monitor progress as they move through the coaching cycle. The simple act of creating a SIG is an excellent way to build shared knowledge while simultaneously creating common language about important elements of the PLC process.

The pathways align with the SIG and provide teams with a series of cascading questions describing the tasks associated with the prerequisites of a PLC. Once teams decide which of the prerequisites they want to work on, they choose the corresponding pathway. Coaches then use the pathways to guide the teams through a process of reflecting on their practice until the team members identify a question they can't answer or a task they don't know how to accomplish. That single question or task becomes the focus of the coaching cycle.

Using the SIG and pathways promotes a higher level of fidelity to the important elements of the PLC process. These tools ensure the coaching cycle stays focused, remains on target toward the goal, and reinforces the standard of PLC best practice teams aspire to.

Coaching From an Asset Perspective

Coaching cycles, specifically those supported with a SIG and pathways, promote coaching from an asset perspective, which means providing observational, growth-oriented feedback reflective of the team's strengths. In a 2019 *Harvard Business Review* article titled "The Feedback Fallacy," Marcus Buckingham and Ashley Goodall report that the brain reacts to judgmental feedback based on individual (or team) weaknesses by shutting down. The same research shows the brain responds positively to observational feedback based on individual (or team) strengths. What is clear is that if the goal of coaching collaborative teams is improving teaching and learning, it is incumbent on principals, coaches, and teacher leaders to place a higher priority on strength- or asset-based feedback, which is at the very heart of an effective coaching cycle.

While remaining focused on sharing observational and growth-oriented feedback, coaches can and should differentiate their feedback during the coaching cycle based on the needs of the team at that time. The feedback might need to be more direct when a team is beginning to learn new skills or concepts. For example, a coach might say, "The first part of the strategy went pretty well; let's try using the next part and keep track of what happens." As the team continues to develop, the coach's feedback might shift to a collaborative approach. In this situation, a coach might say, "We all agree that we're making progress. Here are a couple of ideas we can consider for the next unit." Finally, as the team matures, engaging in more reflective feedback might be most appropriate. The coach's feedback might begin with a question like, "You're all feeling good about the results you got on the last assessment. What still needs to be done to accomplish the goal you set at the start of this coaching cycle?"

An effective coaching cycle, focused on the team's strengths and assets, results in a positive and growth-oriented experience that builds the teacher team's capacity to readily engage in collective inquiry and continuous improvement. Done well, coaching cycles shift the conversation from fixating on *what's wrong* to focusing on *what's next* in a collective and continuous effort to improve the team's professional practice.

At some point, however, leaders will inevitably hear, "This all sounds great, but who will be doing all this coaching?" which is another way of asking, "Who can coach?" Should coaching be delegated to those with the formal title of coach? Can principals coach? What about other administrators, department chairs, or lead teachers—can they be effective coaches? Is it OK for teachers to coach other teachers? The answer to the question of who can and who should coach has become a persistent myth associated with the practice of coaching collaborative teams; a lot of misinformation, misinterpretation, and misunderstanding surrounds this issue. Fortunately, plenty of research-based evidence and practitioner-driven experience is available to help answer the question of who can coach.

The literature has long supported the fact that people other than those formally designated as coaches can engage in the coaching process (Dennison, 2021; Knight, van Nieuwerburgh, Campbell, & Thomas, 2019; Psencik, 2011; Showers & Joyce, 1996). A meta-analysis of sixty studies (Kraft, Blazar, & Hogan, 2018) concludes, "The role of coach may be performed by a range of personnel, including administrators, master teachers, curriculum designers, external experts, and classroom teachers" (p. 9). Practitioners Tesha F. Thomas and Jennifer Parker (in press) remind educators that "one does not need the title of 'coach' to take on a coaching role"; they observe that "principals, teacher leaders, and members of a guiding coalition are all examples of positions that regularly include coaching responsibilities, despite the absence of the word 'coach' in the title." To ensure sufficient resources (personnel) are available to support widespread access to coaching, school leaders recruit a variety of people to fill coaching roles, including administrators, principals, department chairs, grade-level leads, and the teachers themselves.

Part Three

Here's Why

The reason to coach someone, whether it be in music, sports, or any other worthwhile endeavor, is to maximize an *individual's* potential to succeed. It's no different in schools; we coach teachers in order to maximize their impact on student achievement. The reason to collaborate, regardless of the setting, is to maximize a *team's* potential to perform at high levels. In schools, collaboration blends the talents of teachers on a team in order to improve their professional practice and, ultimately, to improve student achievement. The answer to "Why coach collaborative teams?" touches on both coaching and collaboration; if we acknowledge that coaching and collaboration are compatible, even complementary constructs, it follows that if coaching individual teachers is good, then coaching collaborative teams is better! We provide you with a small sample of the research showing the importance of coaching collaborative teams on page 105, "Why Should We Coach Collaborative Teams?"

The phrase most often used to describe the idea that working together is better than working alone has been attributed to Aristotle: "The whole is greater than the sum of its parts." You may have also heard, "The smartest person in the room is the room," and "None of us is as smart as all of us." These popular idioms reflect what research shows: working together is better than working alone. Robert Marzano and colleagues (2016) speak directly to the importance of collaboration by stating unequivocally, "Working together produces better results than working alone" (p. 8). They (2016) go on to advocate for the greater use of collaborative structures, arguing that "distributed knowledge, collective capacity, and shared responsibility [qualities found on highly effective collaborative teams] are much more powerful than the abilities of even the best teacher working in isolation" (p. 10).

On highly effective collaborative teams, each individual member benefits from the talent and expertise of the other members to the point where the entire team is more effective, more productive, and more impactful than any individual teacher could ever hope to be by themselves. As an example of how this works, imagine during a team meeting, one teacher's suggestion triggers another teacher's experience, which triggers another teacher's insights, and so on until the team produces a collective solution that is better than any single teacher could have created on their own. We've learned that the best thinking almost always comes from the collective wisdom of the group.

For years, we have argued that collaborative teams are the foundation, the fundamental building block, and the engine that drives the PLC process (Eaker & Dillard, 2017). It can be said that team meetings are ground zero for the PLC process; they are where the work gets done.

Why Should We Coach Collaborative Teams?

"Coaching models that rely solely on one-on-one interactions between the coach and the teacher do not show as much promise as those that incorporate small-group [team] learning" (Neufeld & Roper, 2003, p. 20).

"We have great success when coaches work with individuals, but we can go further faster when we work with teams" (Delehant, 2007).

Leaders should work to "create a culture where coaching occurs formally and informally, between people at all levels, within and across functions and departments" (Evans, 2011, p. 36).

"If teachers are the most significant factor in student success, and principals are second, then coaches are third. All three, working in coordinated teams, will be required to bring about deep change. The work of coaches is crucial because they change the culture of the school as it relates to instructional [and professional] practice" (Fullan & Knight, 2011, p. 4).

"[Teachers] build the capacity to support one another over time when the coach is not available, and so long-term change becomes more sustainable" (Killion, Harrison, Bryan, & Clifton, 2012, p. 160).

"We believe that coaching and collaboration form the link that connects great leadership, great teaching, and great learning" (Johnson, Leibowitz, & Perret, 2017, p. 11).

"Coaching is considered a key lever for improving teachers' classroom instruction and for translating knowledge into new classroom practices" (Kraft et al., 2018, p. 8).

"Coaching creates conditions of excellence by increasing collaboration, individualizing support and improving teacher effectiveness faster than traditional professional development techniques" (Lupoli, 2018).

"There is a growing body of evidence showing that coaching teachers is an effective form of professional development" (Thomas, 2019, p. 33).

"Coaching is about intentionally and strategically building skill. It is not about leaving notes and hoping" (Sonbert, 2020, p. 41).

"To coach your team, focus on interpersonal skills and interactions instead of on individual development (as you tend to do with individually-focused coaching). The way people act with their teammates, and the way they communicate with one another—these are important drivers of effective team performance" (MindTools, n.d.).

"The approach [coaching teams] creates an environment of agency and accountability, with a healthy balance between challenges and support" (Siang & Canning, 2023).

"By working with a coach, team members can learn how to better understand and appreciate each other's strengths, and how to use those strengths to support the team as a whole" (Blackbyrn, 2024).

In team meetings, teachers make meaning of their practice, build a common language, discuss how to implement new strategies, and assess what effect instruction has had on learning. In fact, teachers are "most likely to gather [their] knowledge about teaching from fellow teachers" (Basileo, 2016, p. 3). Carrie R. Leana (2011) has found that teachers are "almost twice as likely to turn to their peers as to the experts designated by the school district [content or curriculum coordinators], and four times more likely to seek advice from one another than from their principal" (p. 33). If, as the literature suggests, a teacher's primary source of ideas to improve their instructional practice is other teachers, then the value of a highly effective collaborative team takes on even greater importance. Lindsey Devers Basileo (2016) observes that "a high-functioning PLC focused on the right work will act, in essence, as a kind of knowledge-generation system for teachers, where the effect of professional development is accelerated and refined through collective focus on learning within the team" (p. 3). These findings make a persuasive case for *why* leaders should embrace the coaching of collaborative teams.

Besides the fact that highly effective collaborative teams can have a greater impact on student learning than individual teachers, and they are an important source of information for teachers looking to improve their professional practice, there is a growing body of evidence that shows various aspects of coaching and collaboration positively impact collaborative cultures and the development of PLCs. Coaching collaborative teams promotes the following.

- **Development of a collaborative culture:** Coaching teams allows teachers to learn in collaboration with their colleagues and coaches (Neufeld & Roper, 2003). It helps shift school cultures to be more collaborative, supportive, and transparent (Killion, Bryan, & Clifton, 2020; Killion et al., 2012).
- **Deeper understanding of the essential elements of the PLC process:** Coaching teams supports the PLC process by promoting a commitment to building shared knowledge, collective inquiry, and continuous improvement (Killion et al., 2012). Coaching has also been linked to creating common language, shared knowledge, and adherence to team norms (Joyce & Showers, 2002).
- **An asset orientation:** Coaching teams leverages a team's strengths and successes (assets) rather than fixing a teacher's weaknesses and failures (deficits; Sweeney, 2013).
- **Greater access to resources and expertise:** Coaching teams encourages team members to learn from and with a coach (and each other) while sharing their own insights and experiences, thereby multiplying the impact of the coach's knowledge and expertise (Annenberg Institute for School Reform, 2004; Killion et al., 2012, 2020).
- **Increased synergy between and among teachers:** Coaching teams builds teachers' capacity to support each other. In the event that problems arise

when the coach is unavailable, teachers can turn to their colleagues for help (Basileo, 2016; Killion et al., 2012, 2020; Leana, 2011).

- **More cost-effective use of resources:** Coaching teams is efficient; rather than improving professional practice one teacher at a time using a one-on-one format, it improves teacher effectiveness several teachers at a time using a one-on-many format (Killion et al., 2012, 2020; Knight, 2012).
- **Deeper understanding of instructional strategies and approaches:** Coaching promotes the development of instructionally focused cultures (Neufeld & Roper, 2003) and improves teachers' classroom instruction (Kraft et al., 2018). It also promotes deeper understanding of the purpose of a new strategy or approach, more skillful use of the new strategy or approach, and successful implementation of the new strategy or approach (Joyce & Showers, 2002).

Coaching has the potential to transform teaching and learning in positive ways, but only if leaders are wise about how to maximize that potential. Joellen Killion and colleagues (2012) explain, "Team coaching intends to move information into practice, just as one-on-one coaching does. Working one-on-one is a less efficient way, however, to make a substantive difference for teachers and students" (p. 159). Michael Fullan and Jim Knight (2011) posit that "school improvement will fail if the work of coaches remains at the one-to-one level" (p. 4). They describe coaches as system leaders and argue for expanding the impact of coaches, suggesting, "It's time to recast their role as integral to whole-system reform" (Fullan & Knight, 2011, p. 4).

Coaching has the potential to transform teaching and learning in positive ways, but only if leaders are wise about how to maximize that potential.

Coaching teams offers a solution to access and capacity problems that can limit impact with individual coaching. As Tom Many, Michael J. Maffoni, Susan K. Sparks, and Tesha Ferriby Thomas (2020) write:

> It is unlikely that schools will ever have enough coaches to support *all* the needs of *all* the teachers *all* the time; the impact of a school's coaching efforts, however, can be doubled, tripled, even quadrupled if the focus of a school's coaching efforts shifts from [coaching] individual teachers to collaborative teams. (p. 35)

Coaching collaborative teams—moving from one-on-one delivery to one-on-many settings—certainly provides coaches with opportunities for greater impact.

DuFour and Marzano (2011) suggest the time has come to shift from "helping individuals become more effective in their isolated classrooms, to creating a new collaborative culture based on interdependence, shared responsibility, and mutual accountability" (p. 67). Such a shift necessitates the recalibration of traditional thinking about coaching. It requires schools to move from their reliance on models that primarily coach individual teachers toward improving their instructional practice, and to adopt models that coach collaborative teams toward improving the efficacy of their collaboration. The good news is that this shift has already started, as a growing number of schools are incorporating the coaching of collaborative teams into their professional development plans (Galey, 2016; Steeg, 2016; Steiner & Kowal, 2007).

Part Four

Assessing Your Place on the PLC Journey

It is important to help your staff build shared knowledge regarding your school's current status in addressing the critical step on the PLC journey of coaching collaborative teams. We have created a tool to assist you in that effort. "The Professional Learning Communities at Work® Continuum: Coaching Collaborative Teams" on pages 109–110 is also available at **go.SolutionTree.com/PLCbooks** as a free reproducible. Once your staff have established greater clarity regarding the current status of your collaborative teams, we urge you to turn your attention to the "Where Do We Go From Here?" worksheet that accompanies the continuum (on page 111 and also available for free download at **go.SolutionTree.com/PLCbooks**). It will prompt you to take the action necessary to close the knowing-doing gap.

Part Five

Tips for Moving Forward: Coaching Collaborative Teams

1. **Coach to leverage the power of collaboration:** Traditional coaching models seek to improve teacher effectiveness one teacher at a time. Team coaching seeks to improve several teachers simultaneously and capitalizes on the synergy of the group to promote higher levels of learning. Teachers' preferred source of ideas to improve their practice is other teachers. Leaders can leverage those relationships by promoting the kinds of team meetings where teachers share, develop, and exchange ideas, resources, and strategies.

2. **Coaching cycles are effective:** Use coaching cycles to organize team coaching. Research shows that the use of coaching cycles increases the likelihood of success and is more effective than traditional coaching approaches.

3. **Coach against an agreed-on standard of PLC best practice:** The goal is to help teams deepen their PLC practice. To do this, provide teams and coaches with some kind of rubric or continuum—such as a SIG and pathways. These tools serve as a guide or agreed-on standard of PLC best practice and create a frame of reference for feedback.

The Professional Learning Communities at Work® Continuum: Coaching Collaborative Teams

DIRECTIONS: Individually, silently, and *honestly* assess the current reality of your school's implementation of each indicator listed in the left column. Consider what evidence or anecdotes support your assessment. This form may also be used to assess district or team implementation.

Collaborative teams engage in coaching focused on improving their professional practice.

Indicator	Pre-Initiating	Initiating	Implementing	Developing	Sustaining
To capitalize on the tremendous potential of the PLC process, leaders promote and support the development of highly effective collaborative teams. Collaborative teams receive coaching on improving their professional practice associated with the PLC process.	A collaborative culture exists in name only, and team meetings are held but seen as a compulsory obligation thrust upon teachers by their principal. Coaching is not available, nor is it considered a viable option for individuals or teams of teachers who wish to improve their professional practice.	The basic structures of a PLC are in place, and a collaborative culture is growing. Team time is built into the day, and teams meet to talk about students. Initial efforts to identify essential standards, develop common assessments, and interventions are underway. Access to any coaching is voluntary and delivered using an individualized format. Teachers have expressed a willingness to talk with a coach about providing more direct support for the PLC process.	A collaborative culture has been established, the structures of a PLC are in place, and teachers are meeting in teams. Coaching based on the coach's expertise and experience is available, but it is individualized, episodic, and dependent on who asks for help. Most instructional coaches are serving as de facto team leaders. To provide more support for the PLC process, a few teams agreed to be part of a pilot project using coaching cycles	Collaboration is embedded in the school's culture. Most teams accept coaching, but participation is voluntary. Teams set common data-based goals, which they pursue interdependently, and use quarterly cycles to organize the coaching that is designed to improve their PLC practices. There is confusion around who can coach and the different roles administrators can play in coaching teams. A committee of the faculty has drafted an agreed-on standard of PLC	All teams embrace coaching, not because they need to improve but because they want to improve. Coaching is viewed as the primary vehicle for the delivery of professional development. Many administrators now incorporate coaching behaviors into their supervisory responsibilities and actively participate in coaching. Teams can articulate the benefits of coaching and have examined their core beliefs about continuous improvement, collective inquiry, and an action orientation with a focus on results.

Indicator	Pre-Initiating	Initiating	Implementing	Developing	Sustaining
			to coach teams. A committee of the faculty has begun drafting an agreed-on standard of PLC best practice (SIG) and is working on a progression of skills (pathway) for each of the essential elements of a PLC.	best practice (SIG) and a progression of skills (pathway) that breaks down the essential elements of a PLC. Coaches combine feedback from the consulting and collaborative stances to help teams and are expected to provide professional development on the PLC process.	Teams are regularly engaged in coaching to improve their PLC practices using multistep and recursive coaching cycles. Each team shares and collectively pursues a common data-based goal related to the improvement of some aspect of the PLC process. The faculty has published and is using an agreed-on standard of PLC best practice (SIG) and a progression of skills (pathway) for each essential element of the PLC process. Coaches provide teams with feedback from the consulting, collaborative, and reflective stances.

Where Do We Go From Here? Worksheet Coaching Collaborative Teams

Indicator of a PLC at Work	What steps or activities must be initiated to create this condition in your school?	Who will be responsible for initiating or sustaining these steps or activities?	What is a realistic timeline for each step or phase of the activity?	What will you use to assess the effectiveness of your initiative?
To capitalize on the tremendous potential of the PLC process, leaders promote and support the development of highly effective collaborative teams. Collaborative teams receive coaching on improving their professional practice associated with the PLC process.				

4 **Shift more resources to coaching collaborative teams:** The answer is not coaching individual teachers *or* collaborative teams; it's coaching individual teachers *and* collaborative teams. However, leaders should shift more of their coaching resources to the coaching of collaborative teams.

5 **Coach the PLC process with fidelity:** Coach teams toward the goal of improving their ability to collaborate with each other and implement the essential elements of the PLC process with fidelity. Coaching individuals on improving their instructional methods and their use of curricular materials is helpful, but both can and do change over time. The ability to function as a high-performing PLC builds capacity that positively impacts teaching and learning in any setting, now and in the future.

6 **Coach from an asset perspective:** Coaching is different from evaluating. Rather than offering judgmental feedback focused on identifying deficiencies the team should fix, provide descriptive feedback focused on building the team's strengths. Articulate what the team did well, highlight what they learned, and encourage the team to consider what they might do next to promote higher levels of student learning. The mantra, "It's not what's wrong, it's what's next," should guide the interactions.

7 **Coaching teams is a process, not an event:** To paraphrase a wise comment Bob Eaker once shared, leaders should remember that the PLC process is complex but not complicated; it is simple but not simplistic. Becoming a highly effective PLC requires a concerted effort over time to coach teams on a few fundamental elements. When collaborative teams function at high levels, they are more effective and efficient, and student learning is impacted in positive ways.

Part Six

Questions to Guide the Work of Your Professional Learning Community

To ensure collaborative teams receive coaching designed to improve their PLC practice, ask:

1. What evidence was used to determine the appropriateness of, readiness for, and rationale behind coaching collaborative teams to improve their PLC practice?

2. What opportunities have the faculty and staff had to explore their beliefs about continuous improvement and collective inquiry? Have we created a culture where every teacher believes they can coach and be coached in the interest of improving their practice?

3. How confident are we that the faculty and staff have heard and understood the rationale for why coaching collaborative teams to improve their PLC practice will result in higher levels of learning?

4. What evidence can we cite that indicates the faculty and staff have reached consensus on the benefits of coaching collaborative teams? Have teachers received adequate opportunities to ask questions, provide input, and express concerns?

5. Have we reached consensus on an agreed-on standard of PLC best practice? Has that information been documented and shared with the faculty and staff in the form of a SIG or some other rubric or continuum?

6. How will we know what support teams need? Have we created pathways or a similar document that provides teams with a detailed breakdown of the PLC process? Do we have a system in place that allows—even encourages—teams to ask for help with specific aspects of the PLC process?

7. Do we have the tools in place to support the use of coaching cycles as the primary way for organizing and delivering coaching support? Can teams conduct a gap analysis to assist with identifying an improvement goal that includes a plan and clear direction regarding best next steps?

8. Have we given teams the knowledge base, time, and support essential for their effectiveness? Have we provided teachers with opportunities for job-embedded coaching of collaborative teams within the context of their regular and routine responsibilities?

9. How will we monitor the progress of this initiative? What is our vision of success, and how will we measure and evaluate the success of the team coaching program?

Part Seven

Dangerous Detours and Seductive Shortcuts

When coaching collaborative teams, the most dangerous detour is also one of the most seductive shortcuts. Those coaching teams must resist the temptation to become the de facto team leaders. In turn, leaders must remind the faculty and staff that the appropriate role of those coaching teams is to help, support, guide, assist, and facilitate the development of the team; it is not to *lead* the team. When coaches fill the role of team leader, they risk creating a form of learned helplessness, diminishing the team's potential to develop ownership and efficacy, and removing any opportunity for team members to grow into leadership roles.

It is also tempting for leaders to take matters into their own hands and become overly prescriptive. For example, in a well-intended effort to save time and create greater clarity, coaches might publish expectations for collaborative team meetings. Unfortunately, instead of being considered a starting place or a set of initial recommendations, the expectations become rigid rules that limit the effectiveness of the team's collaborative efforts.

Leaders should also not be lured into the trap of setting arbitrary minimums and maximums regarding things like the duration of and the number of steps in a coaching cycle or the number of coaching relationships any one person can manage. There is no consensus on exactly what an effective team coaching cycle should look like, and this lack of agreement generates lots of practical questions.

For example, a common question is, "How long is a coaching cycle?" The literature is full of recommendations but little agreement on how long a coaching cycle should last. Some experts suggest cycles of four to six weeks, others recommend longer cycles lasting six to eight weeks, and still others argue short two- to three-week cycles are most effective. In fact, they are all correct! Shorter cycles are appropriate for single topics or units, while longer cycles are appropriate for implementation of new curricula, processes, or methods. The truth is that the length of a coaching cycle depends on many factors, including topic complexity, team needs, and school traditions. Perhaps Michael Cary Sonbert (2020) provides the best advice, saying coaching cycles should be "short enough to feel urgent and long enough to allow change to happen" (p. 102).

Some schools might be stuck on how many steps are in a coaching cycle. Almost all cycles are based on a BDA (before, during, and after) framework, but just as the length of a coaching cycle can vary, so, too, can the number of steps or stages in a coaching cycle. Some models advocate three or four steps, others (such as the cycle included in this chapter) suggest five steps, and still others identify six or more steps or stages. The number of steps or stages is not what really matters; what matters is that the implemented coaching cycle guides the team through a recursive and reflective process for improving their practice.

Some schools get stuck on determining how many teams a single coach can manage at once. Seeking an arbitrary number is a waste of time. Having too many coaching relationships can be overwhelming, and having too few can be an ineffective use of resources. The maximum number of teams or teachers a coach can simultaneously work with depends on team needs, teacher experience, cultural complexities, and what other resources might be available. There may be times when the coach needs to schedule multiple visits with a team or an individual member of the team; whatever the number of teams or teachers a coach works with, it must allow the coach to meaningfully interact with the team at least once a week. What is more important than the *number* of coaching relationships is the *effectiveness* of those relationships. As Linda Shidler (2009) says, it is "the type and quality of interaction" in the coaching relationships that matters most (p. 459).

Part Eight

Digging Deeper—Recommended Resources

The following resources delve deeper into the topic of coaching collaborative teams.

- *Amplify Your Impact: Coaching Collaborative Teams in PLCs at Work* by Thomas W. Many, Michael J. Maffoni, Susan K. Sparks, and Tesha Ferriby Thomas (2018)
- *How Schools Thrive: Building a Coaching Culture for Collaborative Teams in PLCs at Work* by Thomas W. Many, Michael J. Maffoni, Susan K. Sparks, and Tesha Ferriby Thomas (2020)
- *Energize Your Teams: Powerful Tools for Coaching Collaborative Teams in PLCs at Work* by Thomas W. Many, Michael J. Maffoni, Susan K. Sparks, and Tesha Ferriby Thomas (2022)
- *Make It Happen: Coaching With the Four Critical Questions of PLCs at Work* by Kim Bailey and Chris Jakicic (2019)
- *Mathematics Coaching and Collaboration in a PLC at Work* by Timothy D. Kanold, Mona Toncheff, Matthew R. Larson, Bill Barnes, Jessica Kanold-McIntyre, and Sarah Schuhl (2018)

Final Thoughts

What is often missing from the launch of coaching initiatives is a heavy dose of common sense. Coaching collaborative teams is a promising practice that holds great potential, but at this time, the practice is in its early stages of development, and there are few absolutes. Certainly, leaders should start with some structure; for example, begin with a five-step coaching cycle that lasts four weeks. Once the coaching cycle is complete, gather some feedback about the experience, and if there is evidence of a better way, leaders should be willing to explore it. Such collaboration is an example of the very essence of the PLC process—teams of teachers engaging in collective inquiry and continuous improvement combined with an action orientation to produce the desired results.

Whatever decisions are made about coaching collaborative teams should be intentional and learning centered. For example, if a coaching cycle is too short or too long to make an impact, adjust it. There is nothing magical about the number of steps in a coaching cycle; it is based on what actions will help the team learn and grow. Once those are decided, the number of steps becomes self-evident. Still, if after a few cycles, the team feels the number of steps in a cycle is overwhelming or inadequate, change it. Regardless of the specifics, coaching should be frequent, focused, and effective enough to positively impact the team's professional practice.

The next chapter addresses the challenge of focusing on prerequisite requirements essential to effective teams—working interdependently on a common SMART goal for which members are mutually accountable.

CHAPTER 5
Creating a Results Orientation

Part One

The Case Study: Creating a Results Orientation at the School, Team, and Teacher Levels

When Aretha Ross was hired as superintendent of Supreme School District, the board of education made it clear that its strategic plan for school improvement was the pride of the district. Every five years, the board engaged the community and staff in a comprehensive planning process intended to provide a sense of direction for the district and all its schools and programs. A committee of key stakeholders oversaw the creation of the plan during a six-month development process. Each member was responsible for periodically reporting back to the group they represented to ensure accurate representation and ongoing communication. The committee held a series of community focus groups to solicit feedback from hundreds of parents, analyzed quantitative data, and generated qualitative data through a series of surveys to the community, staff, and parents. The district mission statement provided the foundation of the document:

> It is the mission of our schools to provide a rigorous academic curriculum in a safe, caring, and enjoyable learning environment that enables each and every child to realize their potential and become a responsible and productive citizen and lifelong learner fully equipped to meet the challenges of the 21st century.

The plan provided the vision for the district and its schools, as well as core beliefs, strategic goals, key objectives, operational principles, and performance outcomes. With its adoption by the board of education, it became the blueprint for school improvement in the district. Each school was then called on to create an extensive annual school-improvement plan (SIP) aligned with the district's strategic plan.

Superintendent Ross was impressed by the effort that went into the strategic planning process, and by the heft of the resulting document, but she was curious to see how it was implemented in the schools. In late October, she scheduled a meeting with Harry Lee Lewis, principal of Elvis Presley Elementary School (nickname: the Kings), to discuss the improvement process of that school.

Principal Lewis explained that the SIP the staff adopted the previous month was linked to the district goal of "preparing students to succeed as members of a global community and global economy." The Presley School Improvement Committee had analyzed the results from the previous state assessment of third and fifth graders and concluded that word analysis was an area of weakness for students. The committee reasoned that students would not be prepared to succeed as members of a global community if they were not proficient in such an important skill. So the committee recommended that the staff adopt a school-improvement goal of "improving student achievement in word analysis as indicated on the state assessment." The faculty had agreed to this with little debate. Principal Lewis assured Superintendent Ross that this process was the standard procedure in all the district's schools.

The explanation of this improvement process troubled Superintendent Ross somewhat. She realized the state assessment wasn't administered to students until third grade, and she questioned how much impact the school's goal was having on the primary grade levels. Furthermore, she questioned whether the SIP process described to her fostered the commitment to continuous improvement she hoped to see in every school.

Superintendent Ross decided to do some informal investigating by visiting the third-grade team at Presley as its members met in their weekly meeting. She asked if they felt teachers in other grade levels were helping address the language arts goal established by Presley's School Improvement Committee. After some awkward silence, the team members admitted they did not remember the goal and asked if she could remind them of it.

Superintendent Ross did not want to generalize based on one school, so she made arrangements to visit four other schools that week. In each, she discovered a similar situation. She was convinced that despite the board's affection for the strategic plan, it was neither impacting practice in the classroom nor contributing to a culture of continuous improvement. She knew there was little reason to believe students would achieve at higher levels until principals and teachers became much more interested in and responsible for improved results. What she did not know was what steps the district might take to foster a results orientation.

Reflection

How does a school or district create a results orientation among administrators and teachers—the very people who are called on to improve results?

Part Two

Here's How

As we have repeatedly listed, a results orientation is one of the big ideas of a professional learning community. However, organizations do not focus on results; the people within them do—or they do not. There is little evidence to suggest that centralized, formal strategic planning creates such an orientation. In fact, one comprehensive study of strategic planning over a thirty-year period chronicled its failure to impact results (Mintzberg, 1994).

If formal, district-led strategic planning processes do not create a results orientation, would handing the improvement process over to schools be a more effective alternative? The Consortium on Productivity in the Schools (1995) answers that question with a resounding "no," and concludes:

> Site-based management cannot overcome failures in other parts of the educational system. . . . Site based management does not substitute for the lack of stable, limited, and well-defined goals for the school. . . . [Otherwise] the agendas of [site-based school improvement] tend to drift into non-academic and administrative matters. (p. 47)

The challenge for Superintendent Ross and for any leader who hopes to improve student achievement by creating a results orientation is to engage all members of the organization in establishing goals that, if achieved, will result in higher levels of student learning. We have found that the best way to help people throughout a school district truly focus on results is to insist that every collaborative team establish SMART goals that align with school and district goals.

We have found that the best way to help people throughout a school district truly focus on results is to insist that every collaborative team establish SMART goals that align with school and district goals.

Creating Clarity About SMART Goals

Once again, we begin with what should now be a familiar refrain: "Clarity precedes competence."

Before teams can create SMART goals, members must be in agreement about the meaning of the term. It is another of those terms that can mean many different things to different people within an organization. While district and school goals tend to be broad goal statements, the *SMART goal* acronym (Conzemius & O'Neill, 2014) provides much-needed clarity for the kinds of goals teams pursue. Goals are SMART when they are:

- Strategic (aligned with the organization's goals) and specific
- Measurable
- Attainable

- Results oriented
- Time bound (specifying when the goal will be achieved)

Superintendent Ross could help her staff gain confidence in their ability to develop SMART goals if she had the leadership teams both at the central office and in each building demonstrate reciprocal accountability by providing each collaborative team with:

- The rationale as to why SMART goals are so important in the PLC process
- Tools and templates for establishing SMART goals
- Examples and nonexamples of SMART goals
- Criteria for assessing the quality of the SMART goals they develop
- Tips for developing good SMART goals

Leadership teams at both levels would also need to develop plans for monitoring each collaborative team's SMART goals and providing assistance whenever a team struggles to complete the task.

SMART Goals Are

Strategic and specific
Measurable
Attainable
Results oriented
Time bound

Aligning Team SMART Goals to School and District Goals

A district that has stipulated its fundamental mission is to help all students learn at high levels could adopt such ongoing goals as these.

- We will help all students successfully complete every course and every grade level and demonstrate proficiency on local, state, and national assessments.
- We will eliminate the gaps in student achievement that are connected to race, socioeconomic status, and gender.

Those broad, overarching district goals could then be translated into school goals such as the following.

- We will reduce the failure rate in each grade level (or course) in our school.

- We will increase the percentage of students meeting or exceeding proficiency on district and state assessments in each course or grade level in our school.
- We will increase the number of students who have access to and succeed in the most rigorous curriculum we offer.

The critical step in this process is to then ensure that each collaborative team translates one or more of the school goals into a SMART goal that drives the work of the team. As we discussed earlier, the definition of a team is a group of people working interdependently *to achieve a common goal* for which members are held mutually accountable. Thus, by definition, team members must be working toward a shared goal, and since the mission of the district and school is to improve student learning, that goal should focus specifically and directly on evidence of student learning.

Team SMART goals aligned to the school goals should stipulate both the past level of performance and the improvement goal for the indicator being monitored. Consider these examples.

- **Our reality:** Last year, 76 percent of the first-grade students scored at the proficient or advanced levels in mathematics, as measured by our district's end-of-year mathematics assessment.

  Our SMART goal: By the end of this school year, at least 81 percent of the first-grade students will score at the proficient or advanced levels in mathematics, as measured by our district's end-of-year mathematics assessment.

- **Our reality:** Last year, 68 percent of the freshman English students earned a final grade of C or better.

  Our SMART goal: By the end of this school year, at least 75 percent of the freshman English students will earn a final grade of C or better.

- **Our reality:** Last year, 89 percent of the eighth-grade science students scored at the proficient or advanced levels in science, as measured by our state's eighth-grade science assessment.

  Our SMART goal: By the end of this school year, at least 93 percent of the eighth-grade science students will score at the proficient or advanced levels in science, as measured by our state's eighth-grade science assessment.

- **Our reality:** Last year, 35 percent of the students in our school enrolled in at least one AP course. Seventy-three percent of those students scored 3, 4, or 5 (passing scores) on the end-of-course national AP exams.

  Our SMART goal: This year, 48 percent of the students in our school will enroll in at least one AP course. At least 75 percent of those students will score 3, 4, or 5 (passing scores) on the end-of-course national AP exams.

Balancing Attainable Goals With Stretch Goals

When building a results-oriented culture, leaders must find a balance between the attainable goals teams feel they can achieve in the short term and stretch goals—goals so ambitious they could not possibly be achieved unless practices within the organization change significantly (Tichy, 1997). Stretch goals have also been referred to as *BHAGs*: *Big Hairy Audacious Goals* (Collins & Porras, 1994). Attainable goals are intended to document incremental progress and build momentum and self-efficacy through short-term wins. Stretch goals are intended to inspire, to capture the imagination of people within the organization, to stimulate creativity and innovation, and to serve as a unifying focal point of effort.

Stretch goals are effective only if they stimulate action—if people begin to behave in new ways. Pronouncements without action are hopes, not goals. Furthermore, stretch goals must be goals, not mission statements. They must set specific targets rather than offer vague expressions or beliefs. A perfect example of a stretch goal is President Kennedy's assertion in 1961 that the United States would land a man on the moon before the end of the decade. Notice he did not say, "We need to do something to strengthen the space program," or "We believe in the potential of space." He established a BHAG that included a specific target.

"We believe in high levels of learning for all students" is not a stretch goal. "We will ensure all students demonstrate proficiency on the state assessment," "We will eliminate achievement gaps based on socioeconomic status," and "We will ensure the academic success of every student in every grade level" are examples of stretch goals because they are stated as targets.

If schools and districts limit themselves to the pursuit of attainable goals, they run the risk of never moving outside their comfort zones. . . . On the other hand, if the only goals educators pursue are stretch goals, teachers and principals are prone to give up in hopelessness.

If schools and districts limit themselves to the pursuit of attainable goals, they run the risk of never moving outside their comfort zones. Organizations are unlikely to experience dramatic improvement if they are content with creeping incrementalism—slowly inching forward over time. If the only goals educators pursue are easily attainable, the focus shifts to how good we have to be rather than how good we can be.

On the other hand, if the only goals educators pursue are stretch goals, teachers and principals are prone to give up in hopelessness. If educators perceive goals as unrealistic to the point of being unattainable, and there are no successes to celebrate, they will be discouraged from taking action to achieve those goals.

We have found that in the early stages of building a PLC, celebrating small wins is key to sustaining the effort, and attainable goals are an essential element of results-oriented small wins. Therefore, we strongly recommend that goals established by collaborative teams be attainable and include short-term goals that serve as benchmarks of progress. Teams should feel reasonably confident they have the capacity to achieve their goals. They should be able to say, "We have reason to believe that if we seek and implement best practices, we will achieve our team goal."

Furthermore, frequent feedback and intermittent reinforcement are two factors that help sustain the effort essential to achieving goals. A team that establishes a goal of improving student performance on a state test receives neither feedback nor reinforcement for almost a year unless it establishes some short-term goals. For example, consider the team that analyzes the results from the common formative assessment its members administered in the first unit of the previous school year. Its members determine that 64 percent of students were able to meet the established standard for writing proficiency by the end of October. That team sets a goal that at least 75 percent of students will meet that standard by the same date this year. In this instance, a short-term goal can inform the team of progress and create a basis for celebration prior to the end of the school year.

District goals, however, should be clearly linked to the purpose of learning for all students, should establish challenging targets, and should require innovation and long-term commitment if they are to be achieved. District goals should be so bold that they require the development of new capacities. A few district goals, such as those listed in this chapter, are long-term stretch goals representing a life's work rather than a short-term project. Therefore, the district leadership should commit to these goals year after year until they are achieved. New hot topics will be touted on the professional development circuit, political leaders will come and go, and special interest groups will demand schools pay more attention to their causes. Rather than reacting to each shift in the wind by placing more initiatives on their schools, the central office staff must help buffer the schools from the constant turbulence so educators can stay the course.

Focusing on Results, Not Activities

Once again, a school that defines its purpose as "high levels of learning for all students" will insist that teams include the language of learning in their goals. This is contrary to the traditional approach of writing goals that focus on evidence of what teachers will do rather than on evidence of what students will learn. Statements such as, "We will integrate technology into our course," "We will align our curriculum with the newly adopted textbook," "We will increase the use of cooperative learning activities," and "We will solicit more parent involvement," may describe worthwhile initiatives, but they do not represent goals. If the purpose of these initiatives is to increase student learning, that purpose should be explicitly stated in a goal. Effective team goals will help answer the question, "How will we know if our strategies are resulting in gains in student learning?" The goals will focus on the intended outcome rather than on the strategies to achieve the outcome.

The "SMART Goal Worksheet" reproducibles (pages 126–132) provide examples of how different district and school goals might be translated into SMART goals for collaborative teams. A blank "SMART Goal Worksheet" appears on page 133. Note that when this process is in place, a team that accomplishes its SMART goal contributes to the ongoing improvement of its school and its district.

SMART Goal Worksheet: Third-Grade Team

School: George Washington Elementary **Team Name:** Third Grade **Team Leader:** Theresa Smith

Team Members: Ken Thomas, Joe Ramirez, Cathy Armstrong, Amy Wu

District Goals:

- We will increase student achievement and close the achievement gap in all areas using a variety of indicators to document improved learning on the part of our students.

School Goals:

- We will improve student achievement in language arts as measured by local, district, state, and national indicators.

Team SMART Goal	Strategies and Action Steps	Who Is Responsible	Target Date or Timeline	Evidence of Effectiveness
Our Current Reality: Last year, 85 percent of our students met or exceeded the target score of 3 on our state's writing prompt in May. **Our SMART Goal:** This year, at least 90 percent of our students will meet or exceed the target score of 3 on our state's writing prompt in May.	**Curriculum** 1. Clarify and pace essential student learning outcomes in writing using standards documents, curriculum guides, assessment blueprints and data, and the wish list of skills from the fourth-grade team.	All members of our team	October 15	Lists of essential student learning outcomes and pacing guide Increased results for all students on team, district, state, and national indicators

Team SMART Goal	Strategies and Action Steps	Who Is Responsible	Target Date or Timeline	Evidence of Effectiveness
	Assessments 2. Develop, implement, and collaboratively score grade-level formative writing prompts to: a) Frequently monitor each student's learning of essential writing outcomes b) Provide students with multiple opportunities to demonstrate progress in meeting and exceeding learning targets in writing c) Learn with and from each other better ways to help students become proficient writers	All members of our team	October–May Checkpoints at midpoint of each grading period District benchmark assessments at end of each semester	Common writing prompts Common writing rubric Increased results for all students on team, district, state, and national indicators
	3. Provide students with writing assignments in all subject areas, and utilize a variety of instructional strategies to help students learn all essential writing skills.	All members of our team Principal Resource staff Volunteers	Daily, September–May	Intervention/enrichment schedule Student learning results
	4. Initiate individual and small-group sessions to provide additional intervention and enrichment focused on writing.	All members of our team	Daily, September–May	Intervention/enrichment schedule Student learning results

Team SMART Goal	Strategies and Action Steps	Who Is Responsible	Target Date or Timeline	Evidence of Effectiveness
	5. Provide parents with resources and strategies to help their children succeed as writers.	All members of our team	First semester workshop: 10/20 Second semester workshop: 1/19 Newsletters End-of-grading-period conferences	Number of parents in attendance Study guides and newsletters
	Staff Development 6. Develop, implement, and evaluate our team action research project in writing to improve our individual and collective ability to help our students learn to write at high levels. Use information from our common formative assessments to identify staff development needs and engage in ongoing, job-embedded staff development in the area of writing.	All members of our team	Weekly collaborative team meetings Staff development days Faculty meeting sessions Additional professional learning time by request	Common assessments Quarterly reviews Midyear progress reports End-of-year team evaluations Increased results for all students on team, district, state, and national indicators

page 3 of 3

SMART Goal Worksheet: Eighth-Grade Mathematics

School: Thomas Jefferson Middle School **Team Name:** Eighth-Grade Mathematics **Team Leader:** Chris Rauch

Team Members: Chris Carter, Dolores Layco, Mary Fischer

District Goals:

- We will increase student achievement and close the achievement gap in all areas using a variety of indicators to document improved learning on the part of our students.

School Goals: We will—

1. Reduce the failure rate in our school.
2. Increase the percentage of students scoring at or above the established proficiency standard on the state assessment in all areas.

Team SMART Goal	Strategies and Action Steps	Who Is Responsible	Target Date or Timeline	Evidence of Effectiveness
Our Current Reality: Last year, 24 percent of our students failed one or more semesters of mathematics, and 31 percent of our students were unable to meet the state proficiency standard in mathematics. **Our SMART Goal:** This year, we will reduce the percentage of failing grades to 10 percent or less and the percentage of students unable to meet state standards to no more than 15 percent.	We will align each unit of our mathematics program with state standards, study the results of the last state assessment, identify problem areas, and develop specific strategies to address those areas in our course.	Entire team	We will complete the analysis on the teacher workday prior to the start of the year. We will review our findings prior to the start of each new unit.	Written analysis of state assessment and strategies to address weaknesses
	We will develop common formative assessments and administer them every three weeks. These assessments will provide repeated opportunities for students to become familiar with the format used on the state assessment.	Entire team	Formative assessments will be created prior to the start of each unit of instruction throughout the year. They will be administered on a day designated by the team.	Student performance on team-endorsed common assessments

Team SMART Goal	Strategies and Action Steps	Who Is Responsible	Target Date or Timeline	Evidence of Effectiveness
	After each common assessment, we will identify any student who does not meet the established proficiency standard and will work with the counselor to have those students reassigned from study hall to the mathematics tutoring center.	Members of entire team will request tutoring as their supervisory responsibility; team leader will work with the counselor after each assessment.	Assessments will be administered every three weeks. Students will be assigned to the tutoring center within one week of assessment.	Daily list of students receiving tutoring in mathematics
	We will replace failing grades from our common assessments with the higher grade earned by students who are able to demonstrate proficiency in key skills on subsequent forms of the assessment after completing tutoring.	Entire team will create multiple forms of each assessment. Tutors will administer the assessment after a student has completed the required tutoring.	Multiple forms of an assessment will be created prior to the start of each unit of instruction. Tutors will administer the second assessment within two weeks of a student's assignment to the tutoring center.	Compilation of results from subsequent assessments
	We will examine the results of each common assessment to determine which member of the team is getting the best results on each skill, and then share ideas, methods, and materials for teaching those skills more effectively.	Each member of the team	Ongoing throughout the year each time a common assessment is administered	Analysis of findings after each common assessment is administered Decrease in the failure rate Increase in percentage of students proficient on state assessment

SMART Goal Worksheet: American Government

School: John Adams High School **Team Name:** American Government **Team Leader:** Tom Botimer

Team Members: Dan Hahn, Andy Bradford, Nick Larsen, Helen Harvey

District Goals:

1. We will increase student achievement and close the achievement gap in all areas using a variety of indicators to document improved learning on the part of our students.
2. We will provide more students with access to our most rigorous curriculum in each subject area and grade level.

School Goals: We will increase by at least 10 percent the number of students earning credit in—

1. Advanced Placement courses
2. Capstone courses in a departmental sequence

Team SMART Goal	Strategies and Action Steps	Who Is Responsible	Target Date or Timeline	Evidence of Effectiveness
Our Current Reality: All students must complete a semester of American Government as a graduation requirement. Last year, only 10 percent of the graduating class fulfilled that requirement by enrolling in AP American Government.	We will make a presentation in each section of United States History, encouraging students to enroll in AP American Government and listing the advantages for doing so.	Team leader will coordinate the schedule for these presentations with the team leader for United States History. Each member of the team will assist in making these presentations and will distribute a written list of advantages created by the team.	Complete presentations by the end of January prior to students registering for their courses for next year	The presentation has been made in every United States History class.

Team SMART Goal	Strategies and Action Steps	Who Is Responsible	Target Date or Timeline	Evidence of Effectiveness
Our SMART Goal: At least 20 percent of the current junior class will enroll in and earn a score of 3, 4, or 5 on the AP American Government exam by the end of next school year.	We will coordinate with the guidance department to ensure that when counselors register students for classes, they encourage any student who receives an A at the end of the first semester of United States History to enroll in AP American Government.	Team leader will attend the counselors' team meeting to enlist their support, explain advantages of the AP program, and share the team's strategies for supporting students in AP American Government.	End of first semester	Minutes of meeting
	We will advise parents of the benefits of AP American Government.	The team will draft a letter to parents of students who earn an A in United States History at the end of the semester. The letter will list the advantages of completing this course while in high school for any student planning on attending college. It will also include the team's strategy to provide students with additional support. The team will also create a flyer on the benefits of the AP program to be distributed during parent open house.	The flyer will be created for distribution at the open house in early October. The letter will be sent at the end of the first semester.	Completed documents
	We will create study groups to review material prior to the comprehensive assessments we administer every six weeks.	The team will create the common comprehensive assessments. Each member will be responsible for conducting one study group to help students review for these tests. Study groups will be held on three evenings in the week prior to the test.	Ongoing throughout the semester	Completion of common assessments and student performance on common assessments The number of students earning honor grades on the AP exam in American Government will double over last year's total.

SMART Goal Worksheet

School: **Team Name:** **Team Leader:**

Team Members:

District Goals:

School Goals:

Team SMART Goal	Strategies and Action Steps	Who Is Responsible	Target Date or Timeline	Evidence of Effectiveness

Part Three

Here's Why

There is no evidence that formal strategic planning leads to improved results.

Why should educators abandon traditional strategic planning and focus instead on ensuring that each collaborative team in every school is working toward SMART goals that are specifically linked to a few school and district goals? Most simply, because there is no evidence that formal strategic planning leads to improved results. In his study of "great" organizations, Jim Collins (2001) was unable to discover any link between formal planning and organizational effectiveness. Jeffrey Pfeffer and Robert Sutton (2000) were even more emphatic in their conclusion: "Existing research on the effectiveness of formal planning efforts is clear: Planning is essentially unrelated to organizational performance" (p. 42). In his study of strategic planning in education, Douglas Reeves (2009) actually found a negative correlation between formal, district-led strategic planning and improved student achievement.

Whereas effective leaders are skillful in making the complex simple, strategic planning almost inevitably makes the simple complex. The one thing most strategic plans for school districts have in common is their girth. Voluminous tomes place far too many initiatives on schools and obscure rather than clarify priorities. The ambiguity and interchangeable use of terms add to the confusion. How many people can assert with confidence that they can specify the differences between a strategic goal, a key objective, and a performance outcome? Furthermore, strategic plans often serve as barriers to the relentless action orientation of effective organizations (Pfeffer & Sutton, 2000). Far too many school districts confuse developing or possessing a plan with taking meaningful action to ensure that something actually happens. Michael Fullan (2010) offers succinct advice to those hoping to improve their schools and districts: "Beware of fat plans" (p. 24).

The biggest factor in the ineffectiveness of formal strategic planning rests on its faulty underlying assumption: some people in organizations (the leaders) are responsible for thinking and planning, while others (the workers) are responsible for carrying out those plans. This separation of thought and action is the antithesis of a learning community, which requires widely dispersed leadership and strategic thinkers throughout the organization (Fullan, 2005). Asking employees to follow a five-year strategic plan chartered by others does little to generate a focus on or commitment to improved results. Engaging those employees in a process of continuous improvement where they establish their own short-term goals, develop their own plans to achieve them, act on those plans, and make frequent adjustments based on their analysis of evidence is much more likely to instill a results orientation throughout the organization.

Not only do collaborative teams represent the optimum setting for the pursuit of meaningful SMART goals, but SMART goals also represent an essential tool in developing powerful collaborative teams. Teams benefit when they have a few key goals that clarify the results they seek and how each member can contribute to achieving those results (Lencioni, 2005; Schaffer & Thomson, 1992). They are more effective when they see how their goals and their efforts are linked to the larger organization (Druskat & Wolff, 2001). They are strengthened by the accomplishment and celebration of short-term wins (Collins, 2001; Katzenbach & Smith, 1993; Kotter & Cohen, 2002; Kouzes & Posner, 1987). They are more committed, empowered, and motivated when they set their own targets and create their own plans to achieve them (Amabile & Kramer, 2011; Axelrod, 2002; Pink, 2011).

In short, there is *nothing* more important in determining the effectiveness of a team than each member's understanding of and commitment to the achievement of results-oriented goals for which the group hold one another mutually accountable. Helping a team translate a long-term purpose into specific, measurable, short-term goals (SMART goals), and then helping members develop the skills to achieve those goals, is one of the most important steps leaders can take in building a group's capacity to function as a high-performing collaborative team (Katzenbach & Smith, 1993). Furthermore, as teams achieve their short-term goals, it creates the opportunity to celebrate progress and builds commitment to the PLC process. We provide you with a small sample of the research showing the importance of team-developed goals (see page 136, "Why Do We Need SMART Goals?").

In short, there is* nothing *more important in determining the effectiveness of a team than each member's understanding of and commitment to the achievement of results-oriented goals for which the group hold one another mutually accountable.

Part Four

Assessing Your Place on the PLC Journey

It is important to help your staff build shared knowledge regarding your school's current status in addressing the critical step on the PLC journey of creating a results orientation. We have created a tool to assist you in that effort. "The Professional Learning Communities at Work® Continuum: Using School Improvement Goals to Drive Team Goals" is on page 137 and available at **go.SolutionTree.com/PLCbooks** as a free reproducible. Once your staff have established greater clarity regarding the current status of your collaborative teams, we urge you to turn your attention to the "Where Do We Go From Here?" worksheet that accompanies the continuum (on page 138 and also available for free download at **go.SolutionTree.com/PLCbooks**). It will prompt you to take the action necessary to close the knowing-doing gap.

Why Do We Need SMART Goals?

"According to research, goal setting is the single most powerful motivational tool in a leader's toolkit. Why? Because goal setting operates in ways that provide purpose, challenge, and meaning. Goals are the guideposts along the road that make a compelling vision come alive. Goals energize people. Specific, clear, challenging goals lead to greater effort and achievement than easy or vague goals do" (Blanchard, 2007, p. 150).

"Goal setting is one of the simplest and most effective organizational interventions that can be used to increase employee performance" (O'Hora & Maglieri, 2006, p. 132).

"[Schools with teachers who learn and students who achieve] use clear, agreed-upon student achievement goals to focus and shape teacher learning" (WestEd, 2000, p. 12).

"Collegial support and professional development in schools are unlikely to have any effect on improvement of practice and performance if they are not connected to a coherent set of goals that give direction and meaning to learning and collegiality" (Elmore, 2003, p. 60).

California elementary schools that outperformed schools with similar student populations assigned a high priority to student achievement, set measurable goals for improved student achievement, and had a well-defined plan to improve achievement (Williams et al., 2005).

"[Consistently higher performing high schools] set explicit academic goals that are aligned with and often exceed state standards" (Dolejs, 2006, p. 1).

"Our investigations suggest it is critical to define and publish a protocol that articulates specific inquiry functions: jointly and recursively identifying appropriate and worthwhile goals for student learning; finding or developing appropriate means to assess student progress toward those goals; bringing to the table the expertise of colleagues and others who can assist in accomplishing these goals; planning, preparing, and delivering lessons; using evidence from the classroom to evaluate instruction; and, finally, reflecting on the process to determine next steps" (Gallimore et al., 2009, pp. 548–549).

"One of the greatest challenges to team success is the inattention to results. . . . But there is no getting around the fact that the only measure of a great team—or a great organization—is whether it accomplishes what it sets out to accomplish. . . . When it comes to how a cohesive team measures its performance, one criterion sets it apart from noncohesive ones: its goals are shared across the entire team" (Lencioni, 2012, pp. 65–66).

Schools that have the greatest impact on student learning establish clear and measurable goals focused on improving overall student achievement at the school level. "Data are analyzed, interpreted, and used to regularly monitor progress toward school achievement goals" (Marzano, Warrick, & Simms, 2014, p. 57).

"The problem is not the absence of goals in districts and schools today but the presence of too many that are ad hoc, unconnected, and ever-changing. . . . [They are too often fragmented and so] people see them as discrete demands with little or no connection to . . . their daily work. . . . The solution lies in developing limited goals, persisting, and avoiding distractors. . . . These leaders . . . [use goals] to establish continuous focused direction" (Fullan & Quinn, 2016, pp. 20–21).

The Professional Learning Communities at Work® Continuum: Using School Improvement Goals to Drive Team Goals

DIRECTIONS: Individually, silently, and *honestly* assess the current reality of your school's implementation of each indicator listed in the left column. Consider what evidence or anecdotes support your assessment. This form may also be used to assess district or team implementation.

We assess our effectiveness on the basis of results rather than intentions.

Indicator	Pre-Initiating	Initiating	Implementing	Developing	Sustaining
The members of each of our collaborative teams are working interdependently to achieve one or more SMART goals that align with our school goals. Each team has identified specific action steps members will take to achieve the goal and a process for monitoring progress toward the goal. The identification and pursuit of SMART goals by each collaborative team are critical elements of the school's continuous improvement process.	Goals have not been established at the district or school level. Teams are not expected to establish goals.	Teams establish goals that focus on adult activities and projects rather than student learning.	Teams have been asked to create SMART goals, but many teachers are wary of establishing goals based on improved student learning. Some attempt to articulate very narrow goals that can be accomplished despite students learning less. Others present goals that are impossible to monitor. Still others continue to offer goals based on teacher projects. There is still confusion regarding the nature of and reasons for SMART goals.	All teams have established annual SMART goals as an essential element of their collaborative team process. Teams have established processes to monitor their progress, and members work together in an effort to identify strategies for becoming more effective at achieving the team's SMART goal.	Each collaborative team of teachers has established both an annual SMART goal and a series of short-term goals to monitor their progress. They create specific action plans to achieve the goals, clarify the evidence that they will gather to assess their progress, and work together interdependently to achieve the goal. This focus on tangible evidence of results guides the work of teams and is critical to the continuous improvement process of the school. The recognition and celebration of efforts to achieve goals help sustain the improvement process.

Where Do We Go From Here? Worksheet Using School Improvement Goals to Drive Team Goals

Indicator of a PLC at Work	What steps or activities must be initiated to create this condition in your school?	Who will be responsible for initiating or sustaining these steps or activities?	What is a realistic timeline for each step or phase of the activity?	What will you use to assess the effectiveness of your initiative?
The members of each of our collaborative teams are working interdependently to achieve one or more SMART goals that align with our school goals. Each team has identified specific action steps members will take to achieve the goal and a process for monitoring progress toward the goal. The identification and pursuit of SMART goals by each collaborative team are critical elements of the school's continuous improvement process.				

Part Five

Tips for Moving Forward: Using Goals to Focus on Results

1. **Remember less is more:** Limit the number of district and school initiatives, and make certain the initiatives reflect the priority of high levels of learning for all students.

2. **Tie all goals to district goals:** Assuming the district has created learning-focused goals, require each school to pursue a few schoolwide goals and each collaborative team within the school to establish a limited number of SMART goals (two or three) that specifically align with the school and district goals.

3. **Provide goal-setting templates for every team:** The templates should reinforce the premise that the team must (a) focus on improving results rather than implementing activities and (b) clarify how goal achievement will be attained, monitored, and measured.

4. **Make certain that goals are team goals rather than individual goals:** Remember that an effective goal will require team members to work interdependently in order to achieve it. Members should be able to clarify both individual and collective responsibilities.

5. **Ensure team goals are established by teams rather than for teams:** Teams should be expected to create and write goals that align with school and district goals, that represent continuous improvement, and that are consistent with specified parameters. However, each team should enjoy considerable autonomy in articulating its goals.

6. **Monitor work toward a goal by requiring teams to create specific products that are directly related to achieving the goal:** Typical products include collective commitments or norms, aligned curriculum, common assessments, collective analysis of results, improvement plans, and so on.

7. **Celebrate progress:** Plan for, seek out, and celebrate small wins.

8 **Consider affective goals as well as academic goals:** The high levels of learning a school or team seeks for its students need not be limited to academic areas. Affective areas aligned to essential social and academic behaviors (responsibility, empathy, self-efficacy, independence, and so on) are perfectly legitimate areas for establishing goals. Because these behaviors should be demonstrated schoolwide, these goals should usually be written by and include the entire faculty. However, there is a tendency when establishing such goals to be content with the implementation of new programs or the nobleness of the cause. Neither the completion of projects nor the unassailability of good intentions should substitute for results-oriented goals. Teams must discipline themselves to address the question, "How will we know our students are achieving this goal?" for every goal they establish.

9 **Include stretch goals in direct goals:** These goals will be so challenging that people throughout the organization will be called on to build new capacities in order to achieve them.

10 **Be wary of the complacency that can set in once a stretch goal has been achieved:** An organization can easily drift into "we have arrived" mode when it has succeeded in the pursuit of a challenging goal (Collins & Porras, 1994). Combat that tendency and promote continuous improvement by celebrating the accomplishment and then creating a new stretch goal.

Part Six

Questions to Guide the Work of Your Professional Learning Community

To promote the commitment to a results orientation in your school or district, ask:

1. What evidence do we have that district goals are directly impacting the work of schools and collaborative teams within the school?

2. Does every collaborative team have a goal that aligns with district and school goals?

3. Are team goals SMART: strategic and specific, measurable, attainable, results oriented, and time bound?

4. Is there a plan in place to monitor each team's progress? Does the plan include monitoring the team's products as it works toward its goals?

5. Are teams provided with relevant and timely feedback regarding their progress? Remember that goals are effective motivators, but only if teams receive feedback.

6. Is a plan in place to identify, acknowledge, and celebrate small wins as teams make progress toward their goals?

7. Do district goals include stretch goals?

Part Seven

Dangerous Detours and Seductive Shortcuts

Beware of goals that are so narrow they can be accomplished even if students learn less. For example, a team that establishes a SMART goal of improving student performance in the skill of capitalization could achieve that goal even if their students' reading comprehension or writing proficiency actually declines. Be certain to establish goals that focus on the knowledge and skills that are most essential in the given content or grade level.

If a goal can be accomplished without students learning at higher levels (for example, "Our team will create four new common assessments"), it is not a SMART goal.

Beware of morally impeccable goals that are impossible to monitor. A team that announces its goal is to help its students become lifelong learners has certainly established a noble goal, but unless it can identify the specific indicators it will monitor to assess students' progress as lifelong learners, it has not yet established a SMART goal.

Finally, beware of goals that do not require students to learn at higher levels. Once again, educators are accustomed to focusing on what they will do rather than the knowledge and skills that students will demonstrate. If a goal can be accomplished without students learning at higher levels (for example, "Our team will create four new common assessments"), it is not a SMART goal.

Part Eight

Digging Deeper—Recommended Resources

The following resource delves deeper into the topic of creating a results orientation.

- *The Handbook for SMART School Teams: Revitalizing Best Practices for Collaboration, Second Edition* by Anne E. Conzemius and Jan O'Neill (2014)

Final Thoughts

The way in which a school or district structures its planning and goal-setting process can help or hinder the adoption of the PLC process. When a school has organized its faculty into meaningful teams, provided them with time to collaborate, helped each team clarify its commitments to its members, and established SMART goals that require them to work interdependently and demonstrate mutual accountability, the teams are well positioned to begin their collective inquiry into the critical questions that will drive their work. We turn our attention to the first of those questions—What do we want our students to learn?—in the next chapter.

CHAPTER 6

Establishing a Focus on Learning

Part One

The Case Study: What Do We Want Our Students to Learn?

Principal Dan Matthews had successfully worked with a task force of committed teachers to build support for the professional learning community process among the staff of Genghis Khan High School (nickname: the Fighting Horde). The task force drafted and the staff approved a new vision statement, endorsed their collective commitments, and established school-improvement goals. The vision statement called for a school in which teachers would deliver a "guaranteed and viable curriculum" in each course that provided all students with access to the same knowledge, concepts, and skills regardless of the teacher to whom they were assigned. Principal Matthews and the task force hoped to use the vision statement as a catalyst for action. He asked department chairs to help teachers work together in their collaborative teams to clarify the most essential learning for students by asking, "What knowledge, skills, and dispositions should each student acquire as a result of this course and each unit of instruction within this course?"

After a few weeks, the department chairs proposed modifications to Principal Matthews's request. The mathematics chair reported that teachers felt the state standards already clarified what students were to learn, and they saw no point in addressing a question that had already been answered. The English chair informed Principal Matthews that several teachers from her department had been members of the committee that wrote the district's language arts curriculum, and they felt their work was being dismissed as irrelevant or ineffective. The head of the social studies department complained that the teachers in her department were unable to agree on the most essential learning for students because so many were personally invested in particular units they refused to abandon. After considerable discussion, the principal accepted the following three recommendations of the department chairs.

1. Every teacher would be provided with a copy of the state standards and the district curriculum guide for their curricular area.
2. Teachers would be asked to adhere to the state and district guidelines.
3. Teacher teams would no longer be required to clarify the essential learning of their courses.

Reflection

Consider the efforts of Principal Matthews and the task force to engage teachers in clarifying the essential outcomes of their courses. If you were called on to consult with the school, what advice would you offer?

Part Two

Here's How

The principal and task force in this case study confronted a common dilemma: there were certain important tasks in which they hoped to engage the staff in order to further their agreed-on commitment to learning for all students; however, they wanted the staff to be part of the process and to feel empowered as the school moved forward.

- Should they insist that the faculty develop common outcomes for their courses, or should they abandon a process vital to a PLC because of the objections raised by the staff?
- Is the school better served by a culture of control that demands adherence to certain practices or a culture of freedom that encourages individual or departmental autonomy?

In their study of high-performing organizations, Collins and Porras (1994) discovered ineffective organizations succumb to the "Tyranny of Or"—"the rational view that cannot easily accept paradox, that cannot live with two seemingly contradictory forces at the same time. We must be A or B, but not both" (p. 44). High-performing organizations, however, reject this false dichotomy and embrace the "Genius of And" by demonstrating the ability to honor both extremes at the same time. Collins and Porras (1994) clarified that the Genius of And "is not just a question of 'balance' because balance implies going to the midpoint—fifty-fifty. A visionary company does not seek the gray of balance, but seeks to be distinctly both 'A' and 'B' at the same time" (p. 45).

If Principal Matthews and his task force were to apply these findings to their situation, they would create a school culture that was simultaneously loose and tight, as we described in chapter 1 (page 13). Schools and districts need not choose between demanding adherence to certain core principles and practices and empowering the staff. Certain critical issues must be addressed, and certain important tasks must be accomplished in a PLC. The school or district is tight in those areas, demanding faithfulness to specific principles and practices.

At the same time, however, individuals and teams can benefit from considerable autonomy in terms of how things get done on a day-to-day basis because the school or district is loose about much of the implementation. Members of the school have the benefit of clear parameters that provide direction and coherence to the improvement process; however, they are also given the freedom and tools to make their own contribution to that process. This autonomy allows the school community to benefit from the insights and expertise of those who are called on to do the actual work.

The question, "Learn what?" is one of the most significant questions the members of a PLC will consider. In fact, the entire PLC process is predicated on all educators having a deep understanding of what each student must know and be able to do as a result of every unit of instruction. Therefore, a "tight" expectation the school must establish is that every teacher will be called on to collaborate with colleagues to clarify the first critical question, "What is it we want our students to learn?"

The question, "Learn what?" is one of the most significant questions the members of a PLC will consider.

By the same token, if Principal Matthews intends to hold collaborative teams accountable for establishing a guaranteed and viable curriculum, he has a responsibility to provide them with the clarity, parameters, resources, support, and rationale to help them succeed in what they are being asked to accomplish. Let's consider how Principal Matthews might work with team leaders to address those questions.

If teams are going to create a guaranteed and viable curriculum, members must be clear on what the term represents. Members of the collaborative teams should understand that a "guaranteed and viable curriculum" (1) gives students access to the same essential learning outcomes regardless of who is teaching the class and (2) can be taught in the time allotted (Marzano, 2003). It does not mean that teachers must adhere to lockstep pacing, by which members teach from the same page on the same day. It does not mean that all teachers must use the same instructional strategies or same materials. It does mean that during a unit presented within a specific team-established window of time (for example, three weeks), each team member will work to ensure every student acquires the knowledge and skills the team has agreed are most essential for that unit.

In many schools and districts, educators settle for creating the illusion of a guaranteed curriculum by providing all teachers with a copy of state or district standards; they pretend that the mere distribution of the same curriculum document ensures a guaranteed curriculum. In a PLC, the first step educators take when making decisions is to *learn together*. As we argue in *Concise Answers to Frequently Asked Questions About Professional Learning Communities at Work*:

***In a PLC, the first step educators take when making decisions is to* learn together.**

> Merely providing teachers with a copy of the state standards for their grade level does not ensure all students will have access to a guaranteed curriculum that can be taught in the amount of time

> available for teaching. Teachers may ignore the standards, assign different priorities to the standards, vary dramatically in how much time they devote to the standards, [have] huge discrepancies in what the standard looks like in terms of student work, and possess significant differences in their ability to teach the standards. (Mattos et al., 2016, p. 77)

There are no shortcuts; establishing a guaranteed and viable curriculum requires that teachers engage in a process of collective inquiry.

There are no shortcuts; establishing a guaranteed and viable curriculum requires that teachers engage in a process of collective inquiry. Principal Matthews and the faculty should embrace a process that includes the following six steps.

1. Collectively study the standards using a variety of internal and external resources.
2. Reach consensus on the highest-priority standards by differentiating standards that are "nice to know" from those that all students "must know."
3. Clarify how the highest-priority standards (or essential learnings) are translated into the specific knowledge, skills, and dispositions that all students must demonstrate.
4. Establish what proficiency for each standard or essential learning looks like.
5. Establish common pacing guides and agreed-on assessment schedules.
6. Commit to one another that they will actually teach that agreed-on curriculum.

In order to support the task of creating a guaranteed and viable curriculum, Principal Matthews should provide all staff members with the pertinent resources to help them address the question of "Learn what?" Some of the resources Principal Matthews should provide to assist teacher teams in creating a guaranteed and viable curriculum include the following.

- Copies of current state (or provincial) standards
- Recommended standards from professional organizations (for example, from the National Council of Teachers of Mathematics)
- District curriculum guides
- A list of prerequisite skills that colleagues in the next course or grade level have established as essential for success at that level
- Assessment frameworks (how students will be assessed on district, state [or provincial], and national assessments)
- Data on student performance on past assessments
- Examples of student work and of specific criteria that could be used in judging the quality of student work
- Recommendations and standards for workplace skills

- Recommendations on standards and curriculum design from authors such as Douglas Reeves, Heidi Hayes Jacobs, Robert J. Marzano, Grant Wiggins, and Jay McTighe

When developing a guaranteed and viable curriculum, teachers continually refine and clarify their understanding of what all students should know and be able to do as they move from prioritizing and unwrapping standards to identifying specific learning targets, to creating *I can* statements for students.

When developing a guaranteed and viable curriculum, teachers continually refine and clarify their understanding of what all students should know and be able to do.

Prioritizing the Standards

Standards refer to the general knowledge, skills, and dispositions that students are expected to acquire as a result of the teaching and learning process. Typically developed by content specialists external to the school, standards are often complex and densely worded statements that describe global outcomes for each content area.

Developing a guaranteed and viable curriculum requires prioritization of these standards and recognition of the fact that while all standards are important, some standards are more important than others. As Sharon V. Kramer (2015) writes:

> Although they are more targeted, the Common Core standards and other new or revised state standards are far too many to learn in a school year. Teams must collaborate to determine which of the standards are essential from those that are nice to know or peripheral. Essential standards do not represent all that teachers teach. They represent the minimum a student must learn to reach high levels of learning. They serve to establish the focus for assessing student learning and implementing interventions when students do not learn. Teachers are not creating a list but building shared knowledge of what the most important skills, concepts, and understandings are that will result in higher levels of achievement. This is about focus, focus, focus. (p. 21)

For schools, the question is not whether teachers should prioritize the standards. For years, individual teachers have made decisions about what they will teach and what they will skip. The question confronting schools is, Will teachers engage in a rational, focused, and collaborative process designed to identify the most essential standards (the ones that all students must learn), or will the critical task of prioritizing the standards be relegated to an informal process based on the personal preferences of individual educators?

Larry Ainsworth (2015a) offers a helpful process to guide educators in establishing the priority standards. He recommends that teachers working in grade-level or course-specific teams apply a four-part test to each of the standards proposed by their state, province, or district.

1. **Does the standard have endurance?** Are students expected to retain the knowledge and skill beyond the unit and the course?

2. **Does the standard have leverage?** Will the students be able to apply the standard in more than one subject area?

3. **Does the standard prepare students for success at the next level?** Has this standard been identified as an essential prerequisite skill in the next course or grade level?

4. **Will the standard prepare students for success on high-stakes external exams?** Is this a concept or skill that students are most likely to encounter on state or provincial exams, college entrance exams, or occupational competency exams?

Collaborative team members must go beyond the mere study of the standards for their course or grade level.

It should be evident that in order to answer these questions, collaborative team members must go beyond the mere study of the standards for their course or grade level. They must also engage in vertical articulation with their colleagues above and below their course or grade level to clarify prerequisite skills. They must also become students of the high-stakes external exams to become familiar with the content and format of those exams. High-stakes examinations can have a profound impact on both a student's advancement in school and their access to educational and occupational opportunities. Therefore, teams should engage in collective study of the content, format, and rigor of these exams to help increase their students' likelihood of success.

As collaborative teams consider each standard, Ainsworth (2015b) recommends that they underline the teachable concepts (important nouns and noun phrases) and capitalize the skills (verbs) students are to demonstrate. He offers the following examples (NGA & CCSSO, 2010a, 2010b):

> RI.6.6: DETERMINE an author's point of view or purpose in a text and EXPLAIN how it is conveyed in the text.
>
> 2.NBT.9: EXPLAIN WHY addition and subtraction strategies work, USING place value and the properties of operations.

We recommend that teams consider a fifth question during their review of standards.

5. **What content do we currently teach that we can eliminate from the curriculum because it is not essential?**

Principal Matthews could help foster a new mindset in the school if he asked each team to identify content it was removing from the curriculum each time the team planned a unit of instruction.

Creating a Process for Identifying Nonessential Curriculum

When Tom Many works with schools, he uses a simple process called *Keep, Drop, Create* to engage teachers in dialogue regarding a guaranteed and viable curriculum.

At least once each quarter, teachers devote a grade-level or departmental meeting to analysis of the intended curriculum versus the implemented curriculum. Each team member brings their lesson plan books and a copy of the essential curriculum. Three pieces of butcher paper are posted on the wall of the meeting room and labeled with one of the three categories: (1) Keep, (2) Drop, or (3) Create. Each team member is then given sticky notes in three colors—yellow for Keep, pink for Drop, and green for Create—and is asked to reflect honestly on their teaching.

Teams begin their analysis using their lesson plans (either digital or hard copies) to consider what was actually taught (the implemented curriculum) and copies of state, provincial, or district curriculum guides to review the intended curriculum. Topics identified in the essential curriculum documents and included in each teacher's lesson plans are recorded on the Keep page. Topics identified as essential but not addressed in a teacher's lesson plans (either because the topics have not yet been taught or because they have been omitted) are listed on the Create page. Finally, topics included in a teacher's lesson plans but not reflected in the essential curriculum documents are put on the Drop page.

This process assists teams not only in discovering curriculum gaps and topics that must be addressed in upcoming units, but also in creating a stop-doing list of topics that are nonessential. As teachers engage in this activity over time, they become clearer, more consistent, and more confident in their response to the question, "What must our students know and be able to do as a result of this unit we are about to teach?"

Visit the website of Kildeer Countryside Community Consolidated School District 96 (www.kcsd96.org/curriculum/curriculum-frameworks) to review the guaranteed and viable curriculum of a district that has used this approach.

The process of prioritizing the standards has significant benefits. It creates greater clarity about what teachers will teach, which in turn promotes more efficient planning and sharing of resources. Perhaps the greatest benefit of prioritizing the standards is that it encourages teachers to embrace more in-depth instruction by reducing the pressure to simply cover the material.

The process of prioritizing the standards has significant benefits.

Identifying the Learning Targets

Once teams have established the essential standards, they should create learning targets to clarify the desired outcome of an individual lesson or series of lessons. As our colleague Nicole Dimich (2015) points out, "Learning goals [targets] tightly align to the standards, representing the learning students need to reflect the essence of the standards" (p. 27).

It is through the simple yet powerful process of unwrapping standards that teams come to understand what each standard requires that teachers should teach and students should learn. A single standard typically includes multiple learning targets. Thus, it is virtually impossible for teams to determine if a curriculum is viable—if it can be taught in the amount of time that is available to teach—unless teachers first develop a deep, rich understanding of how many learning targets each standard contains. The goal of unwrapping the standards is not to create another list of ministandards (teachers have enough lists!); it is to get at what Dimich (2015) refers to as the "essence" of each standard.

It is through the simple yet powerful process of unwrapping standards that teams come to understand what each standard requires that teachers should teach and students should learn.

Creating *I Can* Statements

Rick Stiggins (2004) encourages teachers to translate learning targets into student-friendly statements called *I can* statements, which help students understand their progress toward mastery of the standard. Developing *I can* statements serves a number of important purposes. These statements clarify for students what they are learning—what they should know and be able to do—in language students can understand. They enable students to monitor and assume major responsibility for their own learning, a practice associated with a 32 percentile point gain in student achievement (Marzano, 2010).

Developing *I can* statements also helps teachers sharpen both their own understanding of what students are expected to do in order to demonstrate their learning, and the level of rigor necessary to demonstrate proficiency. These statements help teams develop appropriate formats for formative and summative assessments and enhance specificity regarding the kind of support that will benefit students who are experiencing difficulty.

I can statements can also be a valuable resource for parents, providing them with a clear explanation of what their child is expected to know and be able to do. These statements can assist parents in their support of their own child's learning. Tracy Nelson formerly from White River School District in Buckley, Washington, provides examples of team-developed *I can* statements based on power standards from the following Common Core State Standards for grade 3 (NGA & CCSSO, 2010a). Not only does White River use *I can* statements as a tool to keep parents informed about their child's learning, but students in White River use the statements to monitor and improve their own learning (such as in the chart on page 151). Students keep *I can* statements as part of their portfolio, and after formative assessments, students fill out forms, such as the example chart, to track the skills they have mastered as well as those requiring additional work.

Standards for Grade 3

RI.3.2: Determine the main idea of a text; recount the key details and explain how they support the main idea.

W.3.2: Write informative/explanatory texts to examine a topic and convey ideas and information clearly.

SL.3.2: Determine the main ideas and supporting details of a text read aloud or information presented in diverse media and formats, including visually, quantitatively, and orally.

Target	Not Yet (1)	Starting To (2)	Yes! (3)
I can identify the main topic of the text.			
I can identify main ideas about a topic.			
I can identify details that support main ideas.			
I can determine which details are important (key) and which are less important.			
I can explain why details I identified are key details that support the main idea.			
I can listen to text to determine topic, main ideas, and details.			
I can read about a topic of interest and organize my thinking using topic, main ideas, and details.			
I can organize and clearly communicate my thinking about a topic orally.			
I can plan my informational writing using a topic, main ideas, and details.			
I can organize and clearly communicate my thinking about a topic in writing.			

Clarifying What Proficient Student Work Will Look Like

Once a team has agreed that a particular standard is essential, its members must also clarify what represents proficient student work. White River School District engages teachers in a process to clarify essential standards by asking them to address the question, "What would this standard, if mastered, *look like* in terms of student work?" This strategy of clarifying standards through the lens of student work leads teams through a natural progression of questions.

Once a team has agreed that a particular standard is essential, its members must also clarify what represents proficient student work.

- What is it we want our students to learn?
- What is the evidence we expect students to generate in order to demonstrate proficiency?
- What will proficient student work look like?
- What will our assessments look like in order to gather the appropriate evidence?

A very important lesson team members must learn in working together is that it is impossible to establish a guaranteed and viable curriculum unless and until they have agreed on what constitutes proficient work. As John Hattie (2012) concludes in his book *Visible Learning for Teachers: Maximizing Impact on Learning*, a synthesis of the research on factors that impact student learning:

> One of the major messages from *Visible Learning* is the power of teachers learning from and talking to each other about planning—learning intentions, success criteria, what is valuable learning, progression, what it means to be "good at" a subject. . . . Only by having some common understanding of what it means to be "good at" something can the resulting debates about forms of evidence, quality of teaching, and student outcomes make sense. . . . Sharing a common understanding of progression is the most critical success factor in any school; without it, individualism, personal opinions, and "anything goes" dominate. (p. 60)

Determining what successful student work should look like enables teams to do a number of important things during the instructional process. First, they can provide students with *high-quality examples*, thus allowing students to see what their work should look like. The use of high-quality examples also speeds up the learning process and improves the quality of the initial work that students produce.

Second, clarifying what student work looks like is a valuable tool when teams develop common formative assessments. Because teams know exactly what they are assessing and what it should look like, they are able to develop formative assessments that directly align with the essential expectations for student learning. The same holds true for teams developing summative assessments. Importantly, knowing what student work should look like allows for more precise additional time, support, and extension of learning since teams can more easily assess student work in relation to the quality of work that they expect.

Last, agreement on what student work should look like improves the use of common scoring and allows for more accurate grading of student work.

Determining Proficiency and Beyond

Collaborative teacher teams must avoid the trap of thinking that "proficiency" is the ultimate expectation all students should reach.

Collaborative teacher teams must avoid the trap of thinking that "proficiency" is the ultimate expectation all students should reach. It is incumbent on teacher teams to determine what "beyond proficiency" looks like. Marzano Resources offers proficiency scales tied to critical concepts to assist teams with this challenge. Visit the Marzano Resources website (www.marzanoresources.com/educational-services/critical-concepts) to learn the process for identifying and articulating critical concepts in English language arts, mathematics, and science.

Pacing the Guaranteed and Viable Curriculum

After teams have prioritized and unwrapped the standards, translated learning targets into *I can* statements, and reached consensus on what proficiency looks like, they turn their attention to pacing. Grant Wiggins (2012) observes that the pacing of curriculum (1) is a dynamic, not static process that (2) should concern itself first and foremost with the pace of the learner, not the teacher. His observations align perfectly with our belief that the fundamental purpose of school is learning, not teaching.

The pacing of a guaranteed and viable curriculum concentrates on designing an instructional sequence for the highest-priority standards as identified earlier in the process. It also requires that teams focus on teaching, as opposed to simply covering, the curriculum.

Pacing is another topic for the crucial conversations teams must engage in; it simply cannot be delegated to external consultants, textbook publishers, or even district-level administrators. Many districts publish district-level pacing guides that serve as good starting places for team discussions, but pacing guides that mandate strict adherence to rigid schedules and timelines promote covering the curriculum as opposed to teaching the curriculum.

We believe teams must have the autonomy to adjust pacing based on students' needs. According to Jane L. David (2008), "The best pacing guides emphasize curricular guidance instead of prescriptive pacing" (p. 88). She continues, "Constructive pacing guides assume differences in teachers, students, and school contexts. They adjust expectations through frequent revisions based on *input from teachers*" (David, 2008, p. 88, emphasis added).

Teams must have the autonomy to adjust pacing based on students' needs.

The best way for teachers to have input in their curriculum's pacing is by using the results of their common formative assessments. Once a team has established an assessment schedule for the unit, they may decide that proficiency is demonstrated when 80 percent of the students achieve 80 percent mastery on a common assessment. If only 55 percent of the students demonstrate 80 percent mastery, the team should consider slowing down and exploring new ways to teach the skills.

Committing to Each Other and the Curriculum

The "Learn what?" question is simply too vital to the PLC process to be left to either individual teachers or those outside the school. Constant collective inquiry into this question is a professional responsibility of every faculty member in a PLC. Thus, the challenge of developing and implementing a guaranteed and viable curriculum is a *both* top-down *and* bottom-up process (Eaker & Keating, 2012).

On the one hand, district- and school-level leaders must provide guidelines, resources, training, examples, and feedback to assist teachers in sharpening their understanding of what is essential for their students to be able to do and know (from the top down). On the other hand, the actual development and implementation of a guaranteed and viable curriculum must be grounded in the work of collaborative teacher teams that bring their collective expertise to the task (from the bottom up).

Opportunity to learn is a powerful factor in student learning. This concept rests on the logical proposition that students are most likely to learn what they are taught and will have a difficult time learning things that they are not taught (Marzano et al., 2014). Leaving the "Learn what?" question to individual teachers deprives students of an equal opportunity to learn and results in an inequitable educational lottery in which the knowledge and skills a student acquires depend on the teacher to whom that student has been assigned. As our colleague Tim Brown asserts in his work at PLC at Work Institutes, a guaranteed and viable curriculum represents more than a list of intended outcomes (Brown & Ferriter, 2021). It is the promises we as educators make to our students about what we will ensure that they learn.

Developing and implementing a guaranteed and viable curriculum is the essential cornerstone for making the cultural shift from a focus on teaching content to a focus on the deep, rich, rigorous learning of each student.

In summary, developing and implementing a guaranteed and viable curriculum is the essential cornerstone for making the cultural shift from a focus on teaching content to a focus on the deep, rich, rigorous learning of each student. Implementing a guaranteed and viable curriculum is a process, not an event. Effective teams realize that the actual implementation of a guaranteed and viable curriculum is an ongoing process of examining and sharpening the focus on what students should know and what the learning should look like in student work.

Identifying, Teaching, Assessing, and Supporting Essential Behaviors

As we have stressed throughout this book, the fundamental purpose of a PLC is to ensure every student learns at high levels. To achieve this goal, students will undoubtedly need to master the essential behaviors required for success in school and beyond. The foundation of a highly effective school is a safe, orderly, and collaborative culture (Lezotte & Snyder, 2011; Marzano et al., 2014); as student misbehavior decreases, teacher efficacy and student engagement increase (Collie, Shapka, & Perry, 2012). This requires a school staff to answer PLC critical question one through the lens of behavior: "What are the essential behaviors, dispositions, and mindsets all students must master for their success?" Essential behaviors that students must acquire might include those described in the chart on page 155 (Hannigan, Hannigan, Mattos, & Buffum, 2021).

Acedemic Behaviors	
Skill	**Requirement**
Metacognition	Having knowledge of and beliefs about one's thinking
Self-concept	Believing in one's abilities
Self-monitoring	Planning, preparing for, and continuing learning
Motivation	Initiating and maintaining interests in tasks
Strategy	Organizing and memorizing knowledge
Volition	Staying motivated and engaged in learning (Many educators refer to this as demonstrating *grit*.)
Social Behaviors	
Skill	**Requirement**
Responsible verbal and physical interactions with peers and adults	Social responsibility, honesty, compassion, respect, self-regulation, and self-control
Appropriate language	Self-awareness, communication, civility, and character
Respect for property and materials	Skills that demonstrate empathy and respect
Independently staying on a required task	Skills that demonstrate on-task behavior and self-monitoring
Regular attendance	Skills that demonstrate punctuality, time management, and accountability

Source: Hannigan et al., 2021, p. 18.

The six previously described steps related to essential academic standards (page 146) are equally applicable to essential behaviors, with one significant difference: the entire staff should be involved in the process of identifying, teaching, assessing, and supporting students in mastering essential behaviors. This is because essential behaviors are outcomes that schools want students to demonstrate across the campus—in the classroom, on the playground, during transitions, on the bus, in the cafeteria, and so on. This is best achieved when students experience consistency of expectations from every adult in the school.

Part Three

Here's Why

Reciprocal accountability requires leaders not only to help educators understand how to address a task, but also to make the case for why the task is essential.

Reciprocal accountability requires leaders not only to help educators understand how to address a task, but also to make the case for why the task is essential. Schools are most effective when the people throughout the organization are clear regarding their fundamental purpose. Educators can play a role in the success of their organizations when they know how to perform their specific tasks and they understand why they do them—how their work contributes to a larger purpose (DuFour & Fullan, 2013). This clarity of purpose directs their day-to-day actions and decisions. As Jim Collins (2001) notes, "Great organizations simplify a complex world into a single organizing idea, a basic principle or concept that unifies and guides everything" (p. 91).

In chapter 2 (page 33), we argued that the fundamental purpose—the single organizing idea—that unifies and guides the work of a PLC is ensuring high levels of learning for all students. No school or district can accomplish that purpose unless it can answer the question, "Exactly what is each student expected to learn?" School districts are most effective when these questions are addressed in a systematic way by the professionals most responsible for ensuring learning: classroom teachers.

The premise that every teacher needs to know what they must teach and what students must learn is found in virtually every credible school-improvement model (see page 157, "Why Should We Ensure Students Have Access to a Guaranteed and Viable Curriculum?"). It only makes sense that teachers are most effective in helping all students learn when they are clear regarding exactly what their students must know and be able to do as a result of the course, the grade level, and each unit of instruction.

This finding presents schools and districts with an important question: "What is the best way to ensure each teacher knows what students must learn?" One approach is to provide each teacher with a copy of the standards that have been established for their subject area or grade level as well as a district curriculum guide for addressing those standards. The assumption behind this practice is that if the right documents are distributed to individual teachers, each will teach the same curriculum as their colleagues. This assumption lingers despite decades of evidence that it is erroneous. Almost every veteran educator would agree with the research that there is a huge discrepancy between the intended curriculum and the implemented curriculum (Marzano, 2003). The former specifies what teachers are called on to teach; the latter reflects what is actually taught. The idea that all students within the same school have access to the same curriculum has been described as a "gravely misleading myth" (Hirsch, 1996, p. 26), and district curriculum guides have been characterized as "well intended, but fundamentally fictional accounts" of what students are actually learning (Jacobs, 2001, p. 20).

Why Should We Ensure Students Have Access to a Guaranteed and Viable Curriculum?

To improve student achievement, educators must determine the *power standards*—learning standards that are most essential because they possess the qualities of endurance, leverage, and readiness for success at the next level; "the first and most important practical implication of power standards is that leaders must make time for teachers to collaborate within and among grade levels to identify the power standards" (Reeves, 2002, p. 54).

"The staff in the effective school accepts responsibility for the students' learning of the *essential curricular goals*" (Lezotte, 2002, p. 4, emphasis added).

Professional learning communities are characterized by an academic focus that begins with a set of practices that bring clarity, coherence, and precision to every teacher's classroom work. Teachers work collaboratively to provide a rigorous curriculum that is crystal clear and includes a compact list of learning expectations for each grade or course and tangible exemplars of student proficiency for each learning expectation (Saphier, 2005).

The first step in curriculum development is to "identify desired results. What should students know, understand, and be able to do? What content is worthy of understanding? What 'enduring' understandings are desired? What essential questions will be explored? [This step] calls for clarity about priorities" (Tomlinson & McTighe, 2006, pp. 27–28).

One of the keys to improving schools is to ensure teachers "know the learning intentions and success criteria of their lessons, know how well they are attaining these criteria for all students, and know where to go next in light of the gap between students' current knowledge and understanding and the success criteria"; this can be maximized in a safe and collaborative environment where teachers talk to each other about teaching (Hattie, 2009, p. 239).

"Implementing a strategy of common, rigorous standards with differentiated resources and instruction can create excellence and equity for all students" (Childress, Doyle, & Thomas, 2009, p. 133).

A high-reliability school provides students with a guaranteed and viable curriculum focused on enhancing student learning. The curriculum is focused enough that it can be adequately addressed in the time available to teachers. All students have the opportunity to learn the critical content of the curriculum. Individual teachers do not have the option to disregard or replace content that has been designated as essential (Marzano et al., 2014).

"The only way the curriculum in a school can truly be guaranteed is if the teachers themselves, those who are called upon to deliver the curriculum, have worked collaboratively to do the following:

- Study the intended curriculum.
- Agree on priorities within the curriculum.
- Clarify how the curriculum translates into student knowledge and skills.
- Establish general pacing guidelines for delivering the curriculum.
- Commit to one another that they will, in fact, teach the agreed-upon curriculum" (DuFour & Marzano, 2011, p. 91).

"If we want to mobilize concerted action and a deep shift in practice then governments, districts, and schools need to develop clarity of outcomes and build shared understanding of these by educators, students, and parents" (Fullan & Quinn, 2016, p. 83).

To ensure all students have an opportunity to master the same essential learning, school and district leaders . . . must engage every teacher in a collaborative process to study, to clarify, and most importantly, to commit to teaching the curriculum.

To ensure all students have an opportunity to master the same essential learning, school and district leaders must do more than deliver curriculum documents to teachers. They must engage every teacher in a collaborative process to study, to clarify, and most importantly, to commit to teaching the curriculum. All teachers should be expected to clarify essential learning with their colleagues—even in states or provinces with delineated standards and in districts with highly developed curriculum guides. They should do so because of the following five reasons.

1. **Collaborative study of essential learning promotes clarity:** Even if individual teachers take the time to review state (or provincial) and district curriculum standards, it is unlikely they will interpret those standards consistently. Dialogue clarifying what standards mean and what they look like in the classroom helps promote a more consistent curriculum.
2. **Collaborative study of essential learning promotes consistent priorities:** Just because teachers consistently interpret a learning standard does not guarantee they will assign the same priority to the standard. One teacher may conclude a particular standard is very significant and devote weeks to teaching it, while another teacher may choose to spend only a day on the same standard.
3. **Collaborative study of essential learning is crucial to the common pacing required for common formative assessments:** If teachers have not agreed on the meaning and significance of what they are being asked to teach, they will not be able to establish common pacing in their courses and grade levels. Common pacing is a prerequisite for common formative assessments, which, as we will demonstrate in the next chapter, are among the most powerful tools for improvement available to a school.
4. **Collaborative study of essential learning can help establish a curriculum that is viable:** A significant barrier to clarity regarding essential learning for students is curriculum overload (Consortium on Productivity in the Schools, 1995; Reeves, 2004). One analysis has concluded it would take up to twenty-three years to adequately cover all the standards that have been established at the state and national levels (Marzano, 2003). As a result, individual teachers are constantly making decisions regarding what content to omit in their classrooms, making it difficult for subsequent teachers to know what has been taught and what has not (Stevenson & Stigler, 1992). If teachers work together to make these decisions, they can establish a curriculum that they can teach in the allotted time, and they can clarify the scope and sequence of the curriculum with colleagues who teach the preceding and subsequent courses or grade levels.
5. **Collaborative study of essential learning creates ownership of the curriculum among those who are called on to teach it:** Attempts to create a guaranteed curriculum for every student throughout a state, province, or district often produce a uniform intended curriculum but do little to address the *implemented* curriculum. Teachers throughout North America often feel neither ownership of nor accountability for the content they are being asked to teach. They were not meaningfully involved in the

> process of creating that content, and they often critique the decisions of those who were: state or provincial departments of education, district committees, central office curriculum coordinators, and so on. Others do not debate the merits of the curriculum; they simply ignore it. A guaranteed curriculum exists in theory but not in fact.

Certainly, teachers' ownership of and commitment to the curriculum their students are expected to master play an important role in the quality of student learning. Successful implementation of any course of study requires people who care about intended outcomes and have a determination to achieve them. Teachers need to be convinced of the value of the skills they are teaching. As the Organisation for Economic Co-operation and Development (OECD, 2009) advises, "Involving teachers themselves and drawing on their expertise . . . is a first step towards ensuring their commitment to [the skills they are teaching] as well as being essential for tapping into their knowledge and experience" (pp. 16–17).

Successful implementation of any course of study requires people who care about intended outcomes and have a determination to achieve them.

Collaborative Study of Essential Learning . . .

- Promotes clarity
- Promotes consistent priorities
- Is crucial to the common pacing required for formative assessments
- Can help establish a curriculum that is viable
- Creates ownership of the curriculum among those who are asked to teach it

Ownership and commitment are directly linked to the extent to which people are engaged in the decision-making process (Axelrod, 2002). Stephen R. Covey (1989) was emphatic on this point, writing, "Without involvement there is no commitment. Mark it down, asterisk it, circle it, underline it. *No involvement, no commitment*" (p. 143). As a result, there is a direct correlation between participation and improved results (Wheatley, 1999). Attempting to bring about significant school change without first engaging in meaningful dialogue with those who will be called on to do the work creates a context for failure.

So what is the best way to engage staff in an improvement process? The greatest ownership and strongest level of commitment flow to the smallest part of the organization to which each member belongs because that is where people's engagement levels are highest. Teachers are de facto members of their state or provincial systems of education, but they feel greater allegiance to their local district than they do to the state or province. Most teachers, however, feel greater loyalty to their individual school than to their district. Teachers are likely to feel even greater allegiance to their department than to their school. If their department has been organized into teams, they probably feel greater loyalty to their teammates than to the department as a whole. It is at the team level that teachers have the greatest opportunity for engagement, dialogue, and decision making.

When teachers have collaboratively studied the question, "What must our students learn?" when they have created common formative assessments as a team to monitor student learning on a timely basis, and when they have promised each other to teach essential content and prepare students for the assessments, they have exponentially increased the likelihood that the agreed-on curriculum will actually be taught.

We are not advocating that a teacher team should be free to disregard state, provincial, or district guidelines and pursue its own interests. We are instead contending that a powerful way to bring the guidelines to life is to create processes to ensure every teacher becomes a true student of them.

When school leaders establish clear expectations and parameters like those we listed earlier in this chapter, they create a process that promotes consistency and engages teachers in ways that encourage ownership and commitment. Those guidelines also demand accountability because a team must be able to demonstrate that its decisions have led to more students achieving at higher levels as measured by multiple indicators. Furthermore, the team format itself promotes accountability. Teachers recognize that failure to address agreed-on content will adversely impact their students when they take common assessments and will prevent the team from achieving its goals. Few teachers will be cavalier about letting down their students and their teammates, particularly when evidence of their failure to honor commitments is readily available with each common assessment.

For too long, administrators have settled for the illusion of uniformity across the entire district.

For too long, administrators have settled for the illusion of uniformity across the entire district: they dictated curriculum to schools while teachers provided students in the same course or grade level with vastly different experiences. Effective leaders will view engagement with the question, "What do we want our students to know and be able to do?" as a professional obligation incumbent on every teacher, and they will create the processes and parameters to promote far greater consistency in the implemented curriculum.

Part Four

Assessing Your Place on the PLC Journey

It is important to help your staff build shared knowledge regarding your school's current status in addressing the critical step on the PLC journey of creating a focus on learning. We have created a tool to assist you in that effort. "The Professional Learning Communities at Work® Continuum: Clarifying What Students Must Learn" is on page 161 and available at **go.SolutionTree.com/PLCbooks** as a free reproducible. Once your staff have established greater clarity regarding the current status of your collaborative teams, we urge you to turn your attention to the "Where Do We Go From Here?" worksheet that accompanies the continuum (on page 162 and also available for free download at **go.SolutionTree.com/PLCbooks**). It will prompt you to take the action necessary to close the knowing-doing gap.

The Professional Learning Communities at Work® Continuum: Clarifying What Students Must Learn

DIRECTIONS: Individually, silently, and *honestly* assess the current reality of your school's implementation of each indicator listed in the left column. Consider what evidence or anecdotes support your assessment. This form may also be used to assess district or team implementation.

We acknowledge that the fundamental purpose of our school is to help all students achieve high levels of learning, and therefore, we work collaboratively to clarify what students must learn.

Indicator	Pre-Initiating	Initiating	Implementing	Developing	Sustaining
We work with colleagues on our team to build shared knowledge regarding state, provincial, or national standards; district curriculum guides; trends in student achievement; and expectations for the next course or grade level. This collective inquiry has enabled each member of our team to clarify what all students must know and be able to do as a result of every unit of instruction.	Teachers have been provided with a copy of state, provincial, or national standards and a district curriculum guide. There is no process for them to discuss curriculum with colleagues and no expectation they will do so.	Teacher representatives have helped to create a district curriculum guide. Those involved in the development feel it is a useful resource for teachers. Those not involved in the development may or may not use the guide.	Teachers are working in collaborative teams to clarify the essential learning for each unit and to establish a common pacing guide. Some staff members question the benefit of the work. They argue that developing curriculum is the responsibility of the central office or textbook publishers rather than teachers. Some are reluctant to give up favorite units that seem to have no bearing on essential standards.	Teachers have clarified the essential learning for each unit by building shared knowledge regarding state, provincial, or national standards; by studying high-stakes assessments; and by seeking input regarding the prerequisites for success as students enter the next grade level. They are beginning to adjust curriculum, pacing, and instruction based on evidence of student learning.	Teachers on every collaborative team are confident they have established a guaranteed and viable curriculum for their students. Their clarity regarding the knowledge and skills students must acquire as a result of each unit of instruction, and their commitment to providing students with the instruction and support to achieve the intended outcomes, give every student access to essential learning.

Where Do We Go From Here? Worksheet
Clarifying What Students Must Learn

Indicator of a PLC at Work	What steps or activities must be initiated to create this condition in your school?	Who will be responsible for initiating or sustaining these steps or activities?	What is a realistic timeline for each step or phase of the activity?	What will you use to assess the effectiveness of your initiative?
We work with colleagues on our team to build shared knowledge regarding state, provincial, or national standards; district curriculum guides; trends in student achievement; and expectations for the next course or grade level. This collective inquiry has enabled each member of our team to clarify what all students must know and be able to do as a result of every unit of instruction.				

Part Five

Tips for Moving Forward: Clarifying and Monitoring Essential Learning

1 **Remember less is more:** Remember that the main problem with curricula in North America is not that the curricula do not do enough, but rather that the curricula attempt to do too much. As Douglas Reeves (2005) writes, "While academic standards vary widely in their specificity and clarity, they almost all have one thing in common: there are too many of them" (p. 48). We recommend that teams start by identifying the eight to ten most essential standards they will expect students to achieve in their course or subject area for that semester. There is nothing sacred about that total; it is merely meant to serve as a guideline for team dialogue.

2 **Focus on proficiency in key skills—not coverage:** Teachers throughout North America are confronted with a multitude of standards, and they fear that any one of them may be addressed on state or provincial tests. Therefore, they focus on covering the content rather than ensuring students become proficient in the most essential skills. But not all standards are of equal importance. Some are vital to a student's success, and others are simply nice to know. By focusing on essential skills, teachers prepare students for 80 to 90 percent of the content that will be addressed on state or provincial tests and provide students with the reading, writing, and reasoning skills to address any question that could appear (Reeves, 2002).

Part Six

Questions to Guide the Work of Your Professional Learning Community

To clarify essential learning, ask:

1. What is it we want all students to know and be able to do as a result of this course, grade level, or unit of instruction?

2. How can we be sure each student has access to the same knowledge and skills regardless of who is teaching the course?

3. What knowledge and which skills in our curriculum pass the four-part test: (a) endurance, (b) leverage, (c) necessity for success at the next level, and (d) likelihood to be assessed on high-stakes external tests?

4. What material can we eliminate from our curriculum?

5. How should we pace the curriculum to ensure that all students have the opportunity to master the essential learning?

6. Have we agreed on what proficient student work looks like? Can we consistently apply our agreed-on criteria for student work to ensure students receive reliable feedback?

Part Seven

Dangerous Detours and Seductive Shortcuts

It is the process of team members collaboratively building shared knowledge and collectively making decisions about curriculum and assessment that results in adult learning and improved professional practice. Beware of any action that removes teachers from the process or minimizes their role, because in every instance, the impact of the process will be diminished. Examples of shortcuts that are frequently used to circumvent this critical collaborative team dialogue include the following.

- Distributing state or provincial and district guidelines to individual teachers as a substitute for team dialogue
- Assigning a committee of teachers to establish the curriculum and present it to their colleagues
- Purchasing the curriculum
- Allowing the textbook to determine the curriculum

It is the process of team members collaboratively building shared knowledge and collectively making decisions about curriculum and assessment that results in adult learning and improved professional practice.

Teachers and administrators both may argue that teachers are too busy to clarify curriculum or create assessments. They may assert that having someone else do the work provides teachers with an important service. Some may argue that teachers lack the knowledge and skills to do the work well. It is certainly true that school leaders will need to provide collaborative teams of teachers with time, resources, and training to assist them in this important work. Once again, however, the critical question, "What must our students learn?" must be systematically addressed by the professionals most responsible for ensuring learning—classroom teachers. It is by engaging in the process that teachers learn, so do not remove them from the process.

Part Eight

Digging Deeper—Recommended Resources

The following resources delve deeper into the topic of establishing a focus on learning.

- *Kid by Kid, Skill by Skill: Teaching in a Professional Learning Community at Work* by Robert Eaker and Janel Keating (2015)
- *Simplifying the Journey: Six Steps to Schoolwide Collaboration, Consistency, and Clarity in a PLC at Work* by Bob Sonju, Maren Powers, and Sheline Miller (2024)

- *You Can Learn! Building Student Ownership, Motivation, and Efficacy With the PLC at Work Process* by Tim Brown and William M. Ferriter (2021)
- *What About Us? The PLC at Work Process for Grades PreK–2 Teams* by Diane Kerr, Tracey A. Hulen, Jacqueline Heller, and Brian K. Butler (2021)
- *Literacy in a PLC at Work: Guiding Teams to Get Going and Get Better in Grades K–6 Reading* by Paula Maeker and Jacqueline Heller (2023)
- *Behavior Solutions: Teaching Academic and Social Skills Through RTI at Work* by John Hannigan, Jessica Djabrayan Hannigan, Mike Mattos, and Austin Buffum (2021)

Final Thoughts

When teachers work together to establish clarity regarding the knowledge, skills, and dispositions all students are to acquire as a result of each course, grade level, and unit of instruction, schools take a significant step forward on their PLC journey. When those same teachers establish frequent common formative assessments that provide timely feedback on each student's proficiency, their schools advance even further, because these assessments help identify students who are experiencing difficulty in their learning. We turn our attention to common formative assessments in the next chapter.

CHAPTER 7

Creating Team-Developed Common Formative Assessments

Part One

The Case Study: How Do We Know If They Have Learned It?

Principal Anne Burnette and the leadership team of Boone's Farm Elementary (nickname: the Moonshiners) were frustrated that their two-year effort to implement the professional learning community process in their K–5 school had no impact on student achievement. They had the sense that their school was stuck, but they were uncertain as to how to improve the situation. So Principal Burnette and her team went to a PLC at Work Institute looking for ideas. They learned that team-developed common formative assessments served two important purposes. The first was to better meet individual students' needs through timely and targeted intervention or extension. The second was to help teachers improve their individual and collective teaching practice. They came away from the institute with a clear message: team-developed common formative assessments are the linchpin of the PLC process and, when used properly, the key to improving both student and adult learning.

The institute energized Principal Burnette and her team. They acknowledged that their grade-level teams were not using team-developed common formative assessments, and they were convinced that addressing this oversight in their process would finally lead to improved student achievement. They met with the faculty to present the rationale for common formative assessments, provided examples of how teams could use the results to intervene for students and analyze their instructional practices, and shared websites where teams could access assessment items for each subject of their grade level. Teachers were receptive, and each grade-level team agreed that members would administer a common formative assessment for a unit in reading within the next month.

At the end of a month, Principal Burnette met with each team to review its use of common assessments and to see if members required any additional support. She was surprised to discover that the kindergarten, first-grade, and second-grade teams had all decided to use the Dynamic Indicators of Basic Early Literacy Skills (DIBELS) as their common assessment rather than create one of their own. The third-grade team had created a common assessment for their students; however, they continued to group students during the daily intervention and enrichment block based on their scores on the SRA Reading Laboratory program the school had purchased, rather than on evidence of learning from the common assessment. The fourth- and fifth-grade teams had each developed common assessments for their grade level, and every teacher used the results of those assessments to assign students to the appropriate placement during their daily intervention and enrichment block. There was no evidence, however, that any of the grade levels were using transparent results from assessments to analyze and impact their instructional practice. It was evident to Principal Burnette that the assessment process was not yet leading to the desired outcomes in her school.

Reflection

The staff of Boone's Farm Elementary had not objected to the idea of common formative assessments, and each grade level had taken some initial steps to use common assessments. Principal Burnette was convinced, however, that the school was not yet properly using this assessment process. How should she respond?

Part Two

Here's How

Because clarity precedes competence, the staff of Boone's Farm Elementary will struggle in their attempt to develop and implement a common formative assessment process until they establish a shared understanding of what that process entails. Using a common assessment means students who are in the same curriculum and are expected to acquire the same knowledge, skills, and dispositions will be assessed using the same instrument or process at the same time, or within a very narrow window of time. If the assessment is a pencil-and-paper test, it will be the same pencil-and-paper test. If the assessment is performance based, the assessment will focus on the same performance, and teachers will use the same criteria in judging the quality of student work.

In the PLC process, the team develops one or more common assessments for each unit of instruction.

State assessments, district benchmark assessments, Advanced Placement exams, and universal screening instruments are examples of common assessments. But these tests rarely perfectly align to the essential standards that a teacher team has identified for a specific unit of study. Therefore, in the PLC process, the team develops one or more common assessments for each unit of instruction.

The proposal to use common assessments often leads to the question, "But what about students who have been identified as having special needs?" The answer to this question is found in the student's individualized education plan (IEP). If that plan indicates the student's condition is *so profound* that the student is not expected to achieve the intended outcomes of the grade level or course, but instead is pursuing entirely different goals or learning outcomes, there will be no need to administer the common assessment to this student. Their assessment will be based on the learning outcomes established in the IEP. Considering that less than 1 percent of students in the United States are classified in special education as "profoundly disabled," denying a student access to grade-level common assessments should be a rare occurrence at most schools. Typically, a student with special needs should be expected to acquire the same knowledge and skills as the other students in the class but will need additional support services in order to do so. In that case, the student will take the common assessment, but, once again, the IEP will specify accommodations or modifications that should be applied. If, for example, a student's IEP stipulates the student should have extended time to take the test or the test should be read to the student, those accommodations will apply.

Formative Assessments

The use of the formative assessment process is typically contrasted with the use of summative assessments. Rick Stiggins (2005) distinguishes between the two by saying that a summative assessment is an assessment *of* learning while a formative assessment is an assessment *for* learning. As he explains, educators utilize the formative assessment process when they use assessment to help students understand the following three items.

1. The achievement target they are aspiring to
2. Where they are now in relation to that expectation
3. How to close the gap between the two

The OECD (as cited in Looney, 2005) defines formative assessment as "frequent, interactive assessments of students' progress and understanding to identify learning needs and adjust teaching appropriately" (p. 21). Dylan Wiliam (2018) advises that an assessment is formative:

> to the extent that evidence about student achievement is elicited, interpreted, and used by teachers, learners, or their peers to make decisions about the next steps in instruction that are likely to be better, or better founded, than the decisions they would have made in the absence of that evidence. (p. 48)

A summative assessment gives the student the opportunity to prove what they have learned. . . . A formative assessment gives the student the opportunity to improve their learning.

We think the following helps clarify the difference between summative and formative assessments: A summative assessment gives the student the opportunity to *prove* what they have learned by a certain deadline, and it results in a dichotomy—pass or fail, proficient or not proficient. A formative assessment gives the student the opportunity to *improve* their learning because it informs both the teacher and the student as to appropriate next steps in the learning process.

There are several misunderstandings about formative assessment. Often, educators think of formative assessment as an event or a test rather than an ongoing process. Effective teachers use formative assessment almost minute by minute during instruction to check for student understanding so they know where to go next with instruction. Formative assessments that give both the teacher and students insights as to what should come next in the teaching and learning process occur when teachers:

- Randomly direct purposeful questions to students and have others in the class respond to the answers
- Ask students to write their answers in their notes as the teachers circulate around the room to determine student responses
- Have students use clickers, whiteboards, and exit slips to gain insight into student thinking
- Create signals for students to indicate their level of understanding

In high-performing PLCs, the assessment process must also include team-developed common formative assessments as team members attempt to answer the second critical question of PLCs: "How do we know our students are learning?" The team members then use the evidence of student learning from their common formative assessments to inform their individual and collective practice in four ways.

The team members use the evidence of student learning from their common formative assessments to inform their individual and collective practice in four ways.

1. To inform each teacher of individual students who need intervention because they are struggling to learn or who need enrichment because they are already proficient
2. To inform students of the next steps they must take in their learning
3. To inform each team member of their individual strengths and weaknesses in teaching particular skills so each of them can provide help or solicit help from colleagues on the team
4. To inform the team of areas where many students are struggling so that the team can develop and implement better strategies for teaching those areas (DuFour & DuFour, 2012)

Another misunderstanding about common formative assessments is that the content of an assessment or when an assessment takes place determines whether the assessment is formative. A short quiz that is given to students early in a unit can be summative if it is used only to assign a grade. A comprehensive exam at the end of a unit can be formative if it is used to identify students who are struggling to demonstrate proficiency in a particular skill or concept, if those students are required to keep working on the skill or concept through the school's systematic intervention plan until they become proficient, and if those students are given another opportunity to demonstrate that they have learned. In this scenario, a student who fails an assessment after three weeks of instruction but is able to demonstrate proficiency in the fourth week after engaging in systematic interventions is assigned a grade that reflects proficiency. In this situation, the end-of-unit assessment is part of the formative process. Thus, how the results are used, or what happens *after* the assessment, is what determines whether the assessment is part of a formative process.

Finally, in too many schools, team-developed common formative assessments are viewed as tools for determining which students need interventions but not as powerful tools for informing and improving teacher practice. All the steps in the PLC process are intended to provide a teacher team with transparent evidence of student learning so team members can determine which instructional strategies are working and which are not. This collective analysis of the evidence enables team members to make informed adjustments to their teaching. So we want to stress that unless collaborative teams are using evidence of student learning to inform and improve their individual and collective professional practice, their school is not fully engaged in the PLC process.

All the steps in the PLC process are intended to provide a teacher team with transparent evidence of student learning so team members can determine which instructional strategies are working and which are not.

Protocols and Tools to Guide the Work of Collaborative Teams

By providing teachers with protocols to guide their work, Principal Burnette can help make analyzing evidence of student learning for the improvement of student and adult learning part of the school's organizational routine. Protocols ensure all voices are heard on the critical issue at hand, and they help members look closely at evidence of student learning, examine success as well as failure, and become skillful in facilitating dialogue on the right work (McDonald, Mohr, Dichter, & McDonald, 2007). Put more simply, "a protocol creates the structure that makes it safe for teachers to ask challenging questions of each other" (Quate, n.d.).

Most protocols consist of a structured format that includes a tentative time frame and specific guidelines for communication among team members. All protocols do two things: "they provide a structure for conversation—a series of steps that a group follows in a fixed order—and specify the roles different people in the group will play" (Larner, 2007, p. 104).

An example of a protocol adapted from the Collaborative Assessment Conference comes from Harvard University's Project Zero (cited in McDonald et al., 2007) and includes the following six steps.

1. Team members examine evidence of student learning or examples of student work in silence and take notes on their observations.
2. The team leader asks, "What did you see?" Members are asked to make factual, nonevaluative statements.
3. The team leader asks, "What questions does this evidence of student learning raise for you?" Members speculate about students' thought processes and gaps in their understanding.
4. Members discuss implications for their teaching.
5. Members establish action plans to act on their learning.
6. Members share their reactions to and assessment of the meeting.

Teams can also use protocols to create a safe environment for an individual teacher to pose a problem and seek the help of their colleagues. For example, teams at Adlai

E. Stevenson High School use a six-step tuning protocol called Descriptive Review as a way to support one another (Blythe, Allen, & Powell, 2015).

1. **Introduction:** A team member presents the results of an assessment or examples of student work to teammates (five minutes).

2. **Teacher presentation:** Team members review the presented work as the presenting member explains their concerns or questions. No interruptions or questions are allowed during this presentation (ten minutes).

3. **Clarifying questions:** Participants may ask clarifying questions, but again, no discussion is allowed at this point (five minutes).

4. **Feedback:** The team members discuss the work together, giving three kinds of feedback each in separate intervals. The presenting teacher listens and takes notes while their colleagues talk (ten minutes).

   The feedback must directly relate to the assessment or examples of student work at hand. The three kinds of feedback include the following.

   a. *Warm feedback*—Positive points associated with the work

   b. *Cool feedback*—Questions, doubts, or possible gaps in the work

   c. *Hard feedback*—Challenges related to the work

5. **Reflection:** The presenting teacher responds to team members' feedback, highlighting new insights, seeking clarifications, and identifying changes to be made (ten minutes).

6. **Debrief:** The team leader solicits feedback regarding the team's perceptions of the process (five minutes).

There are also excellent tools to help teams focus on the right work that are less formulaic than protocols.

Teams should also return to the results of their analysis when they prepare to teach the same unit in the next school year. They should examine where students experienced difficulty on the assessment, their theories as to why students struggled, and the corrective actions they took to improve their ability to teach that skill or concept. They would then set a short-term SMART goal for the unit to improve on the student achievement levels from the previous year (an example of that tool is the "SMART Goal Worksheet" on page 133). This ongoing effort to use evidence of past students' learning to get better results in the present is the essence of the continuous improvement process that drives the work of collaborative teams in a PLC. The most helpful resource we have seen for protocols and tools to guide the work of collaborative teams is *Common Formative Assessment: A Toolkit for Professional Learning Communities at Work, Second Edition* by Kim Bailey and Chris Jakicic (2023). We highly recommend it.

Deeper Learning

Although initially almost all U.S. states endorsed the Common Core State Standards and the complementary assessments created by the Partnership for Assessment of Readiness for College and Careers (PARCC) and the Smarter Balanced Assessment Consortium (SBAC; now known as Smarter Balanced), these standards and assessments have largely become disfavored. There is general consensus among policymakers and educators alike that assessments of student learning must focus less on recall of information, become more rigorous, and call on students to demonstrate deeper learning.

The National Research Council's Committee on Defining Deeper Learning and 21st Century Skills stipulates that *deeper learning* is "the process through which an individual becomes capable of taking what was learned in one situation and applying it to new situations (i.e., transfer) . . . by developing cognitive, interpersonal, and intrapersonal competencies" (as cited in Pellegrino & Hilton, 2012, p. 5). The Hewlett Foundation defines deeper learning as preparing students to "master core academic content, think critically, solve complex problems, work collaboratively, communicate effectively, direct their own learning, and develop an academic mindset" (as cited in Vander Ark & Schneider, 2014, p. 37).

Norman Webb has classified Depth of Knowledge (DOK) criteria into the following four levels, with levels 3 and 4 representing deeper learning (Francis, 2022). The levels are as follows.

- **DOK 1:** Recall of a fact, term, concept, or procedure—basic comprehension
- **DOK 2:** Application of concepts or procedures involving some mental processing
- **DOK 3:** Applications requiring abstract thinking, reasoning, or more complex inferences
- **DOK 4:** Extended analysis or investigation that requires synthesis and analysis across multiple contexts and nonroutine applications

If educators are to help students acquire deeper knowledge and skills, they must create assessments that provide timely information on each student's proficiency in these key areas of learning. The first step in the process of creating these assessments is the first step in every aspect of the PLC process—educators must *learn together*. They must engage in collective inquiry regarding how to monitor deeper learning for their students. They must become students of assessments that are intended to provide insights into a student's ability to apply their knowledge and skills.

If educators are to help students acquire deeper knowledge and skills, they must create assessments that provide timely information on each student's proficiency.

Principal Burnette can help the teams in this collective inquiry by providing them with clear parameters and guidelines for creating assessments that will call on students to demonstrate deeper learning. Such guidelines might call on teams to:

- Create a specific minimum number of common assessments to use in their course or grade level during the semester to ensure student learning is monitored on a timely basis

- Include multiple levels of knowledge questions on each assessment
- Demonstrate how each item on the assessment is aligned to an essential outcome of the course or grade level
- Specify the proficiency standard for each skill or concept so that teachers and students alike are able to identify, with precision, where the student needs help
- Clarify the conditions for administering the test consistently
- Ensure that demonstration of proficiency on the team assessment will be highly correlated with success on high-stakes testing at the district, state, provincial, or national level
- Assess a few key concepts frequently rather than many concepts infrequently

Once again, when Principal Burnette calls on teachers to create new common formative assessments, reciprocal accountability demands she must support their efforts by providing them with time to address the task and resources to help them build quality assessments. Such resources might include:

- State or provincial assessment frameworks to make sure staff are familiar with the format and rigor of the state or provincial tests
- Student performance data on past indicators of achievement
- Examples of rubrics for performance-based assessments
- Recommendations from assessment experts such as Rick Stiggins, W. James Popham, Dylan Wiliam, and Larry Ainsworth
- Tests that individual team members developed

Team members should work together to become students of more rigorous assessments to learn about both their format and their content.

A powerful tool Principal Burnette can provide to teams is ready access to websites that support educators in developing more rigorous assessments. Team members should work together to become students of more rigorous assessments to learn about both their format and their content. The following are examples of such websites.

- National Center for Research on Evaluation, Standards, and Student Testing (CRESST; https://cresst.org/areas-of-work/#Evaluation)
- New Meridian (https://resources.newmeridiancorp.org)
- Smarter Balanced (https://smarterbalanced.org)
- National Center for Education Statistics (NCES; https://nces.ed.gov/nationsreportcard)
- OECD's Programme for International Student Assessment (PISA; www.oecd.org/pisa)

Assessment experts agree that the best way for educators to build their capacity to create quality assessments is to address the challenge as collaborative team members rather than as individuals. The collaborative team structure is described as essential in any effort to build the assessment literacy of educators (Stiggins, 1999), the best way to support teachers in learning how to use powerful classroom assessments (Wiliam, 2007), and "the best way to accomplish a schoolwide implementation of formative assessment" (Popham, 2008, p. 119). Teams should have the autonomy to develop the kind of assessments they believe will result in valid and authentic measures of their students' learning. They should have autonomy in designating the proficiency targets for each skill; however, they should also be called on to demonstrate that student success on their assessments is strongly correlated with success on other indicators of achievement the school is monitoring.

Assessment experts agree that the best way for educators to build their capacity to create quality assessments is to address the challenge as collaborative team members rather than as individuals.

Common Mistakes

Principal Burnette must resist any effort to exempt teachers from working together to create the frequent common formative assessments that enable a team to verify the proficiency of each student in each essential skill. Frequent monitoring of each student's learning is a critical element of effective teaching, and no teacher should be absolved from that task or allowed to assign responsibility for it to state test makers, central office coordinators, or textbook publishers.

Finally, it is critical that Principal Burnette and the administrative team commit to the staff that they will not use the common assessment data to formally or informally evaluate teacher performance in a punitive way. When teachers compare results on a common assessment, invariably one teacher is going to have the lowest scores. This delineation should be interpreted as meaning that the instructional practices used did not best meet students' learning needs, not that the teaching was inferior. If teachers fear that common assessment data will be used to negatively evaluate or publicly humiliate them, then they have every right to resist engaging in the process.

Assessment of Essential Behaviors

If a school is committed to ensuring every student masters the behaviors needed for future success, then it must have a timely and systematic process to assess each student's progress on the behaviors the school has identified as essential. Like assessing essential academic standards, assessing essential behaviors includes the following.

- **Common assessments:** "Being respectful" is a commonly identified essential behavior. Respectfulness cannot be measured with a multiple-choice test—it is an outcome that must be observed. Yet different staff members often show significant variance in what they think respectful student behavior looks like. If a school is going to commonly assess behavior, staff must first agree on what respectful behavior looks like in different situations—in the classroom, on the playground, and during a school assembly, for example—to create a respect rubric that staff members can use to teach and assess this essential behavior.

- **Formative assessments:** Like the results of academic assessments, assessments of students' behaviors must be used in a formative way. Students will undoubtedly make behavior mistakes. Remember that these mistakes are opportunities; they represent a way for educators to identify students who need extra time and support to master essential behaviors—not just a way to refer misbehaving students for punitive disciplinary consequences.

Finally, remember that a professional learning community regularly gathers evidence of student learning to assess the actions of the adults. Which practices, policies, and procedures are increasing student achievement, and which ones are not? This results orientation is not different for essential behaviors. The school leadership team should frequently review schoolwide behavior information—such as attendance data and discipline referrals—to identify areas of need.

Part Three

Here's Why

The creation of frequent, high-quality common formative assessments by teachers who are collaborating to help a group of students acquire agreed-on knowledge and skills is one of the most powerful, high-leverage strategies for improving student learning available to schools. Such assessments serve a distinctly different purpose than the state and provincial tests that have become the norm in North America. State and provincial tests typically serve as summative assessments: attempts to determine whether students have met intended standards by a specified deadline. They are assessments of learning, typically measuring many things infrequently. They can provide helpful information regarding the strengths and weaknesses of curricula and programs in a district, school, or department, and they often serve as a means of promoting institutional accountability. The infrequency of these end-of-process measurements, however, limits their effectiveness in providing the timely feedback that guides teacher practice and student learning (Stiggins & DuFour, 2009).

Formative assessments are part of an ongoing process to monitor each student's learning on a continuous basis. Formative assessments typically measure a few things frequently and are intended to inform teachers of the effectiveness of their practice and to inform students of their next steps in the scaffolding of learning. When done well, formative assessment advances and motivates, rather than merely reports on, student learning. The clearly defined goals and descriptive feedback provide students with specific insights regarding how to improve, and the growth that students experience helps build their confidence as learners (Stiggins & DuFour, 2009).

The case for formative assessment is compelling (see page 177, "Why Should We Use Formative Assessments?"). The case for team-developed common formative assessments as a powerful tool for school improvement is also compelling (see page 178, "Why Should We Use Common Assessments?").

Why Should We Use Formative Assessments?

"There is strong and rigorous evidence that improving formative assessment can raise standards of pupils' performance. There have been few initiatives in education with such a strong body of evidence to support a claim to raise standards" (Black & Wiliam, 2004, p. 20).

"Studies have demonstrated assessment *for* learning rivals one-on-one tutoring in its effectiveness and that the use of assessment particularly benefits low-achieving students" (Stiggins, 2004, p. 27).

"Assessment for learning . . . when done well, this is one of the most powerful, high-leverage strategies for improving student learning that we know of. Educators collectively at the district and school levels become more skilled and focused at assessing, disaggregating, and using student achievement as a tool for ongoing improvement" (Fullan, 2005, p. 71).

"[Formative assessments are] 'one of the most powerful weapons in a teacher's arsenal.' An effective standards-based, formative assessment program can help to dramatically enhance student achievement throughout the K–12 system" (Marzano, 2006, back cover).

Effective use of formative assessment, developed through teacher learning communities, promises not only the largest potential gains in student achievement but also a process for affordable teacher professional development (Wiliam & Thompson, 2008).

"Deeper learning is enhanced when formative assessment is used to: (1) make learning goals clear to students; (2) continuously monitor, provide feedback, and respond to students' learning progress; and (3) involve students in self- and peer assessment" (Pellegrino & Hilton, 2012, p. 166).

"Formative assessment works. That's right: Ample research evidence is now at hand to indicate emphatically that when the formative-assessment process is used, students learn better—lots better. It's really not surprising that formative assessment works so well. What is surprising is how few U.S. teachers use the process" (Popham, 2013, p. 29).

"Teachers are reluctant to persist in implementing new practices in the absence of evidence that what they're doing makes a positive difference. Therefore, it's important to build some mechanism into the implementation process to show teachers that these new practices are working. . . . Because teachers have the most confidence in evidence they gather themselves, results from classroom formative assessments provide an ideal feedback source" (Guskey, 2014).

The major purpose of assessment in schools should be to provide interpretative information to teachers and school leaders about their impact on students, so that these educators have the best information possible about what steps to take with instruction and how they need to change and adapt. Using assessments as feedback for teachers is powerful. And this power is truly maximized when the assessments are timely, informative, and related to what teachers are actually teaching (Hattie, 2015c).

Why Should We Use Common Assessments?

Reviews of accountability data from hundreds of schools reveal the schools with the greatest gains in achievement consistently employ common assessments, nonfiction writing, and collaborative scoring by faculty (Reeves, 2004).

Powerful, proven structures for improved results are at hand. "It starts when a group of teachers meets regularly as a team to identify essential and valued student learning, develop common formative assessments, analyze current levels of achievement, set achievement goals, and then share and create lessons and strategies to improve upon those levels" (Schmoker, 2004a, p. 48).

The schools and districts that doubled student achievement added another layer of testing—common formative or benchmark assessments. These assessments were designed to provide detailed and concrete information on what students know and do not know with respect to specific learning targets (Odden & Archibald, 2009).

The key to improved student achievement was moving beyond an individual teacher looking at his or her classroom data. Instead, it took getting same-grade teacher teams to meet, analyze the results of each interim assessment to understand what concepts in the curriculum were posing difficulty for students, share ideas, figure out the best interventions, and actually follow up in their classrooms (Christman et al., 2009).

In schools that help students burdened by poverty achieve remarkable success, teachers work in collaborative teams to build common formative assessments and use the data to identify which students need help and which need greater challenges. But they also use data to inform teachers' practice, to discuss why one teacher is having success in teaching a concept and others are not, and what the more successful teacher can teach his or her colleagues (Chenoweth, 2009).

"High-growth schools and districts use frequent, common short-cycle assessments—at least every three to six weeks. Teachers create formative assessments before developing their lessons for a unit and clarify success criteria. The importance of focusing the attention of teachers on formative assessment practices and developing and using short-cycle common assessments was one of the most consistent findings of the study" (Battelle for Kids, 2013).

One of the most effective ways educators can use formative assessments is by collaboratively creating common formative assessments with grade-level or course-level colleagues to assess student understanding of the particular learning intentions and success criteria currently in focus within a curricular unit of study. Common formative assessments afford teacher teams a clear lens through which to see their instructional impact on student learning (Ainsworth, 2014).

We argue that the benefits of using team-developed common assessments for formative purposes are so powerful that no teacher team should be allowed to opt out of creating them. We are not suggesting that these assessments take the place of the ongoing checks for understanding that should occur in individual teachers' classrooms each day. Furthermore, schools should certainly use a variety of assessments: tests that individual teachers develop, district tests, state or provincial tests, national tests, tests that accompany textbooks, and so on. But school leaders should never let the presence of these other assessments excuse teams from making common formative assessments for the following seven reasons.

We argue that the benefits of using team-developed common assessments for formative purposes are so powerful that no teacher team should be allowed to opt out of creating them.

1. **Common assessments promote efficiency for teachers:** If all students are expected to demonstrate the same knowledge and skills regardless of the teacher to whom they are assigned, it only makes sense that teachers would work together to assess student learning. For example, suppose four third-grade teachers will assess their students on four reading skills during a unit. Having each teacher develop activities or questions for one skill and present them for team review, feedback, and, ultimately, agreement about their inclusion on the common assessment would be more efficient than having each teacher work separately to create items on all four skills, thereby duplicating their colleagues' efforts. It is ineffective and inefficient for teachers to operate as independent subcontractors who are stationed in proximity to others yet work in isolation. Those who are called on to complete the same task benefit by pooling their efforts.

2. **Common assessments promote equity for students:** When schools utilize common assessments, they are more likely to—

    - Ensure that students have access to the same essential curriculum
    - Use common pacing
    - Assess the quality of student work according to the same criteria

    It is ironic that schools and districts often pride themselves on fairly and consistently applying rules and policies while, at the same time, they ignore tremendous inequities in both the learning opportunities students are given and the criteria by which students' learning is assessed. Schools will continue to have difficulty helping all students achieve high standards if the teachers within them do not develop the capacity to define a standard with specificity and assess it with consistency.

3. **Common assessments represent a powerful strategy for determining whether the guaranteed curriculum is being taught and, more importantly, learned:** Douglas Reeves (2004) refers to teacher-made common formative assessments as the "best practice in assessment" (p. 71) and the "gold standard in educational accountability" (p. 114) because they promote consistency in expectations and provide timely, accurate, and specific feedback to both students and teachers. Furthermore, as teachers work together to study the elements of effective assessment and critique one another's ideas for assessment, they improve their assessment literacy. Perhaps most importantly, teachers' active engagement in the development of an assessment leads them to accept greater responsibility for the results.

Common assessments provide teachers with a basis of comparison as they learn, skill by skill, how the performance of their students is similar to and different from that of other students who took the same assessment.

4. **Common assessments inform the practice of individual teachers:** Individual teachers' tests generate plenty of data (mean, mode, median, percentage of failing students, and so on), but they do little to inform the teachers' practice by identifying strengths and weaknesses in their teaching. Common assessments provide teachers with a basis of comparison as they learn, skill by skill, how the performance of their students is similar to and different from that of other students who took the same assessment. With this information, a teacher can seek assistance from teammates on areas of concern and can share strategies and ideas for skills in which their students excelled. For generations, teachers have been told that effective teaching is preceded by planning and followed by reflection. But the single greatest determinant of how a teacher will teach is not reflection, but rather how that teacher has taught in the past (Elmore, 2010). One of the most comprehensive studies ever conducted of factors that impact student achievement concluded that reflection enhances student learning only when it is collective—a team of teachers reflecting, rather than an individual—and based on actual evidence of student learning, rather than an appraisal of particular teaching strategies (Hattie, 2009). Team-developed common assessments are ideally suited to this collective reflection based on evidence.

5. **Common assessments build a team's capacity to achieve its goals:** When collaborative teams of teachers have the opportunity to examine achievement indicators of all students in their course or grade level and track those indicators over time, they are able to identify and address problem areas in their program. Their collective analysis can lead to new curriculum, pacing, materials, and instructional strategies designed to strengthen the academic program they offer. A longitudinal study of schools engaged in reform efforts found that for two years, those schools showed no gains despite the fact that teachers were meeting in teams. It wasn't until the collaborative teams of teachers looked at evidence of student learning from common assessments, identified the consistent problems students were experiencing, and then developed specific action plans to resolve those problems that students experienced dramatic gains in their learning (Gallimore et al., 2009).

6. **Common assessments facilitate a systematic, collective response to students who are experiencing difficulty:** Common assessments help identify a group of students who need additional time and support to ensure their learning. Because the students are identified at the same time, and because they need help with the same specific skills that have been addressed on the common assessment, the team and school are in a position to create timely, directive, and systematic interventions. We will address this topic in detail in the next chapter.

7. **Common formative assessments are the most powerful tool for changing the professional practice of educators:** The main challenge in any substantive improvement initiative is getting people to change their behavior—that is, to change what they have traditionally done (Kotter & Cohen, 2002). But what might persuade veteran educators to change their traditional practice?

> Learning new instructional strategies at workshops won't change teacher practice unless participants return to a culture where they have an opportunity for practice, feedback, and coaching. In a survey, however, only one in ten teachers reported that they have frequent opportunities for practicing new skills (The New Teacher Project, 2015).
>
> Poor student performance on assessments does not persuade teachers to explore new practices. A U.S. survey of educators revealed that 84 percent of teachers feel "very confident" that they have the knowledge and skills necessary to enable their students to succeed academically, and the remaining 16 percent are "somewhat confident." The same survey also revealed that only 36 percent of teachers believe all their students have the ability to succeed (Markow & Pieters, 2010). In another survey, more than 80 percent of teachers rated their teaching as a four or five on a five-point scale (The New Teacher Project, 2015). Thus, from the perspective of the majority of teachers, poor student performance on a test clearly reflects deficiencies in students rather than the need for educators to explore new strategies.

Learning new instructional strategies at workshops won't change teacher practice unless participants return to a culture where they have an opportunity for practice, feedback, and coaching.

Principals are being urged to devote more time to acting as *instructional leaders* by observing teachers in classrooms so they can supervise and evaluate teachers into better instructional practices. There is, however, overwhelming evidence that this strategy has little impact on either teacher practice or student achievement. A three-year study of more than one hundred principals concluded, "We find no relationship between [a principal's] overall time spent on instructional activities and schools' effectiveness or improvement trajectories" (Grissom, Loeb, & Master, 2013, p. 18). The same study found that the common principal practice of conducting brief classroom walkthroughs actually had a negative impact on student achievement.

A survey of teachers in the United States revealed that three out of four teachers feel they receive absolutely no benefit from the teacher evaluation process in their school (Duffett, Farkas, Rotherham, & Silva, 2008). Another study concluded that most teacher evaluation does not recognize good teaching, it leaves poor teaching unaddressed, and it does not "inform decision-making in any meaningful way" (Weisberg, Sexton, Mulhern, & Keeling, 2009, p. 3).

A longitudinal study of effective school leadership describes the premise of instructional leadership as "an idea that refuses to go away." As that study concludes:

> Policy makers and practitioners should avoid promoting, endorsing, or being unduly influenced by conceptions of instructional leadership which adopt an excessively narrow focus on classroom instruction. Classroom practices occur within larger organizational systems which can vary enormously in the extent to which they support, reward, and nurture good instruction. School leaders who ignore or neglect the state of this larger context can easily find their direct efforts to improve instruction substantially frustrated. (Louis, Leithwood, Wahlstrom, & Anderson, 2010, p. 76)

Robert J. Marzano (2009), one of the United States' leading researchers on effective teaching, agrees that focusing on the instructional practices of teachers is ineffective because none of those practices is guaranteed to work in all situations. He contends the checklist approach to providing teachers with feedback that is often used in teacher evaluation "probably doesn't enhance instructional expertise . . . [and] in fact, such practice is antithetical to true reflective practice" (Marzano, 2009, p. 37).

A joint study from the National Commission on Teaching and America's Future and WestEd warns that using evaluation and compensation systems in an attempt to improve schools by improving individual teachers would not result in effective schools (Fulton & Britton, 2011). As that study concludes, "Performance appraisal, compensation, and incentive systems that focus on individual teacher efforts at the expense of collaborative professional capacity building could seriously undermine our ability to prepare today's students for 21st century college and career success" (Fulton & Britton, 2011, p. 4).

Michael Fullan (2014) has predicted that this individualistic strategy of improving schools one teacher at a time through supervising their instruction will be a "bloody disaster" (p. 84), and W. James Popham (2009) considers the attempt to improve schools by focusing on instruction one of the biggest mistakes in education since the 1960s. We concur. It should be evident that a secondary principal lacks the content expertise to provide meaningful feedback to teachers in all the various disciplines taught in the school. As Rick and Mike write:

> As former social studies teachers, we were not prepared to help a Spanish teacher improve when we couldn't understand what [they were] saying. We were ill-equipped to enhance the pedagogy of an industrial arts teacher when we were mechanically inept. Because we frequently were unable to determine the appropriateness of either the content or the level of its rigor, we had to resort to generic observations about teaching and apply what we knew about effective questioning strategies, student engagement, classroom management, and so on. . . . If principals want to improve student achievement in their school, rather than focus on the individual inspection of *teaching*, they must focus on the collective analysis of evidence of student *learning*. (DuFour & Mattos, 2013, pp. 36–37)

So we return to the question, "What might persuade veteran educators to change their practice?" There are two powerful levers to bring about this change. The first is concrete evidence of irrefutably better results. If a teacher discovers that students in the next room are consistently demonstrating higher levels of learning on an agreed-on essential skill or concept than their students are—and they are demonstrating that learning on an assessment that the teacher helped create and agreed was a valid assessment of student learning—the teacher will become curious as to how their colleague is getting better results. In a study of how to influence people to change their behavior, Kerry Patterson and his colleagues (2008) concluded that "the great persuader is personal experience . . . the mother of all cognitive map changes. . . . Nothing changes the mind like the hard cold world hitting it with actual real-life data" (p. 51). Richard F.

Elmore (2003) came to a similar conclusion, writing, "Teachers have to believe there is some compelling reason for them to change practice, with the best direct evidence being that students learn better" (p. 38). Additionally, Elmore (2010) writes, "Adult beliefs about what children can learn are changed by watching students do things that the adults didn't believe that they—the students—could do" (p. 8). Concrete evidence of irrefutably better results is a powerful persuader.

The second powerful lever for changing behavior is the positive peer pressure and support that comes with being a team member. When people work in isolation, their success or failure has little to no direct and immediate bearing on others. When people work interdependently to achieve a common goal for which all members are mutually accountable, the performance of each individual directly impacts the ability of the team to achieve its goal. This interdependence and reluctance to let colleagues down can be an effective catalyst for changing behavior (Blanchard, 2007, 2019; Fullan, 2008; Lencioni, 2005; Patterson et al., 2008).

When people work interdependently to achieve a common goal for which all members are mutually accountable, the performance of each individual directly impacts the ability of the team to achieve its goal.

The collective analysis of evidence of student learning from multiple common assessments is ideally suited to utilize the power of positive peer pressure and support. Transparent results make it very difficult for people to hide from their students or teammates or to duck their responsibility (Chenoweth, 2009; Kanter, 2004). An educator who can feign compliance or find excuses for poor results in a hierarchical system will find it increasingly problematic to remain disengaged or ignore results when the achievement of their students routinely prevents the team from accomplishing its goal. Transparency of results and openness about practice create a peer-based accountability system that becomes part of the culture (Fullan, 2011).

In Summary, Consider This Series of Assertions

1. The key to the ability of schools to impact student learning is the collective expertise of the educators within the schools or district.
2. Improved student learning will require improved professional practice.
3. Improved professional practice will require educators to change many of their traditional practices.
4. Two of the most powerful motivators for persuading educators to change their practice are (a) concrete evidence of irrefutably better results and (b) the positive peer pressure and support inherent in working interdependently to achieve a common goal.
5. The best strategy for utilizing these motivators and improving professional practice is engaging collaborative team members in the individual and collective analysis of team-developed common formative assessments on a regular basis as part of the teaching and learning process.

The reason that PLCs improve teaching is, paradoxically, because they focus on learning. Educators in a PLC collaborate in constant, deep collective inquiry into the questions, "What is it our students must learn?" and "How will we know when they have learned it?" The dialogue generated from these questions results in the academic focus, collective commitments, and productive professional relationships that enhance learning for teachers and students alike. School leaders cannot waffle on this issue. Working with colleagues on these questions is an ongoing professional responsibility from which no teacher should be exempt.

Common Formative Assessments . . .

- Promote efficiency for teachers
- Promote equity for students
- Provide an effective strategy for determining whether the guaranteed curriculum is being taught and, more importantly, learned
- Inform the practice of individual teachers
- Build a team's capacity to improve its program
- Facilitate a systematic, collective response to students who are experiencing difficulty
- Offer the most powerful tool for changing adult behavior and practice

Part Four

Assessing Your Place on the PLC Journey

It is important to help your staff build shared knowledge regarding your school's current status in addressing the critical step on the PLC journey of creating common formative assessments. We have created a tool to assist you in that effort. "The Professional Learning Communities at Work® Continuum: Turning Data Into Information" and "The Professional Learning Communities at Work® Continuum: Monitoring Each Student's Learning" are on pages 185 and 187–188 and available at **go.SolutionTree.com/PLCbooks** as free reproducibles. Once your staff have established greater clarity regarding the current status of the use of and commitment to common formative assessments, we urge you to turn your attention to the "Where Do We Go From Here?" worksheets that accompany the continua (on pages 186 and 189 and also available for free download at **go.SolutionTree.com/PLCbooks**). They will prompt you to take the action necessary to close the knowing-doing gap.

The Professional Learning Communities at Work® Continuum: Turning Data Into Information

DIRECTIONS: Individually, silently, and *honestly* assess the current reality of your school's implementation of each indicator listed in the left column. Consider what evidence or anecdotes support your assessment. This form may also be used to assess district or team implementation.

Individuals, teams, and schools seek relevant data and information and use them to promote continuous improvement.

Indicator	Pre-Initiating	Initiating	Implementing	Developing	Sustaining
Collaborative teams of teachers regard ongoing analysis of evidence of student learning as a critical element in the teaching and learning process. Teachers are provided with frequent and timely information regarding the achievement of their students. They use that information to: • Respond to students who are experiencing difficulty • Enrich and extend the learning of students who are proficient • Inform and improve the individual and collective practice of members • Identify team professional development needs • Measure progress toward team goals	The only process for monitoring student learning is the individual classroom teacher and annual state, provincial, or national assessments. Assessment results are used primarily to report on student progress rather than to improve professional practice. Teachers fall into a predictable pattern: they teach, they test, they hope for the best, and then they move on to the next unit.	The district has created benchmark assessments that are administered several times throughout the year. There is often considerable lag time before teachers receive the results. Most teachers pay little attention to the results. They regard the assessment as perhaps beneficial to the district but of little use to them. Principals are encouraged to review the results of state assessments with staff, but the fact that the results aren't available until months after the assessment and the lack of specificity mean they are of little use in helping teachers improve their practice.	Teams have been asked to create and administer common formative assessments and to analyze the results together. Many teachers are reluctant to share individual teacher results and want the analysis to focus on the aggregate performance of the group. Some use the results to identify questions that caused students difficulty so they can eliminate the questions. Many teams are not yet using the analysis of results to inform or improve professional practice.	The school has created a specific process to bring teachers together multiple times throughout the year to analyze results from team-developed common assessments, district assessments, and state or provincial and national assessments. Teams use the results to identify areas of concern and to discuss strategies for improving the results.	Teachers are hungry for information on student learning. All throughout the year, each member of a collaborative team receives information that illustrates the success of his or her students in achieving an agreed-upon essential standard on team-developed common assessments he or she helped create, in comparison to all the students attempting to achieve that same standard. Teachers use the results to identify the strengths and weaknesses in their individual practice, to learn from one another, to identify areas of curriculum proving problematic for students, to improve their collective capacity to help all students learn, and to identify students in need of intervention or enrichment. They also analyze results from district, state or provincial, and national assessments and use them to validate their team assessments.

Where Do We Go From Here? Worksheet
Turning Data Into Information

Indicator of a PLC at Work	What steps or activities must be initiated to create this condition in your school?	Who will be responsible for initiating or sustaining these steps or activities?	What is a realistic timeline for each step or phase of the activity?	What will you use to assess the effectiveness of your initiative?
Collaborative teams of teachers regard ongoing analysis of evidence of student learning as a critical element in the teaching and learning process. Teachers are provided with frequent and timely information regarding the achievement of their students. They use that information to: • Respond to students who are experiencing difficulty • Enrich and extend the learning of students who are proficient • Inform and improve the individual and collective practice of members • Identify team professional development needs • Measure progress toward team goals				

The Professional Learning Communities at Work® Continuum: Monitoring Each Student's Learning

DIRECTIONS: Individually, silently, and *honestly* assess the current reality of your school's implementation of each indicator listed in the left column. Consider what evidence or anecdotes support your assessment. This form may also be used to assess district or team implementation.

We acknowledge that the fundamental purpose of our school is to help all students achieve high levels of learning, and therefore collaboratively we will monitor each student's learning.

Indicator	Pre-Initiating	Initiating	Implementing	Developing	Sustaining
We work with colleagues on our team to clarify the criteria by which we will judge the quality of student work, and we practice applying those criteria until we can do so consistently.	Each teacher establishes his or her own criteria for assessing the quality of student work.	Teachers have been provided with sample rubrics for assessing the quality of student work.	Teachers working in collaborative teams are attempting to assess student work according to common criteria. They are practicing applying the criteria to examples of student work, but they are not yet consistent. The discrepancy is causing some tension on the team.	Teachers working in collaborative teams are clear on the criteria they will use in assessing the quality of student work and can apply the criteria consistently.	Collaborative teams of teachers frequently use performance-based assessments to gather evidence of student learning. Members have established strong inter-rater reliability and use the results from these assessments to inform and improve their individual and collective practice. The team's clarity also helps members teach the criteria to students, who can then assess the quality of their own work and become more actively engaged in their learning.

Indicator	Pre-Initiating	Initiating	Implementing	Developing	Sustaining
We monitor the learning of each student's attainment of all essential outcomes on a timely basis through a series of frequent, team-developed common formative assessments that are aligned with high-stakes assessments students will be required to take.	Each teacher creates his or her own assessments to monitor student learning. Assessments are typically summative rather than formative. A teacher can teach an entire career and not know if he or she teaches a particular skill or concept better or worse than the colleague in the next room.	The district has established benchmark assessments that are administered several times throughout the year. Teachers pay little attention to the results and would have a difficult time explaining the purpose of the benchmark assessments.	Teachers working in collaborative teams have begun to create common assessments. Some attempt to circumvent the collaborative process by proposing the team merely use the quizzes and tests that are available in the textbook as their common assessments. Some administrators question the ability of teachers to create good assessments and argue that the district should purchase commercially developed tests.	Teachers working in collaborative teams have created a series of common assessments and agreed on the specific standard students must achieve to be deemed proficient. The user-friendly results of common assessments are providing each member of the team with timely evidence of student learning. Members are using that evidence to improve their assessments and to develop more effective instructional strategies.	Collaborative teams of teachers gather evidence of student learning on a regular basis through frequent common formative assessments. The team analysis of results drives the continuous improvement process of the school. Members determine the effectiveness of instructional strategies based on evidence of student learning rather than teacher preference or precedent. Members who struggle to teach a skill are learning from those who are getting the best results. The frequent common formative assessments provide the vital information that fuels the school's system of interventions and extensions. The assessments are formative because (1) they are used to identify students who need additional time and support for learning, (2) the students receive the additional time and support for learning, and (3) students are given another opportunity to demonstrate that they have learned.

Where Do We Go From Here? Worksheet
Monitoring Each Student's Learning

Indicator of a PLC at Work	What steps or activities must be initiated to create this condition in your school?	Who will be responsible for initiating or sustaining these steps or activities?	What is a realistic timeline for each step or phase of the activity?	What will you use to assess the effectiveness of your initiative?
We work with colleagues on our team to clarify the criteria by which we will judge the quality of student work, and we practice applying those criteria until we can do so consistently. We monitor the learning of each student's attainment of all essential outcomes on a timely basis through a series of frequent, team-developed common formative assessments that are aligned with high-stakes assessments students will be required to take.				

Part Five

Tips for Moving Forward: Using Common Formative Assessments

1 **Recognize that common assessments might create teacher anxiety:** Common assessments are likely to create anxiety among teachers who are concerned that the results from these assessments could be used to expose weaknesses in their instruction. Teachers' inner voice may very well say, "What if I am the weakest teacher on my team? My teammates will lose respect for me. The principal may use the results in my evaluation. If the results become public, parents may demand that their children be removed from my class. I don't want to participate in a process that can be used to humiliate or punish me. I would rather work in blissful ignorance than become aware that I may be ineffective."

These very real and understandable human emotions should be acknowledged but should not be allowed to derail the effort to create a common curriculum and common assessments. For example, principals can promise teachers that the results will not leave the building, appear in board of education reports, or show up in district newsletters.

Principals can and should assure staff that student performance on common assessments will not be a factor in teacher evaluation. The process to assess student learning should be distinct from the process to evaluate teachers. In fact, common formative assessments are an ineffective tool for evaluating teachers. If a team with four members administers a common assessment, one member will inevitably be fourth in terms of results. This inevitability does not speak to the teacher's effectiveness. The team could have four outstanding teachers. Conversely, if a team with four inept teachers gives a common assessment, one member will have the best of the terrible results. Common assessments are worthless in terms of ranking and rating teachers, but they are powerful in terms of giving each teacher the feedback and information necessary to improve.

Certainly, a teacher evaluation can address a teacher's failure to contribute to the team process or their unwillingness to change practices to improve results when students are not being successful; however, it should not address scores from common assessments.

2 **Remember that common formative assessments are only one element of an effective and balanced assessment process for monitoring student learning:** That process will continue to rely on individual teachers' assessments within the classroom on a day-to-day basis, assessments individual teachers create for their own students, occasional district benchmark assessments, summative assessments that the team or district creates, and state or provincial assessments. All can play a role in improving schools.

3 **Remember districts can play a role:** Districts make a mistake when they create common assessments as a substitute for teacher-developed assessments at the team level. Districts can create their own assessments to monitor student learning throughout the entire district, but these assessments should supplement rather than replace team-level assessments and should be administered much less frequently (for example, two or three times each year). Districts can also create test-item banks as a resource for teachers, but teams should be expected to engage in the process of developing their own tools to answer the question, "How do we know our students are learning?"

4 **Create a shared understanding of the term *common formative assessment*:** Once again, we have discovered that people who use the same terms do not necessarily assign them the same meanings. For example, a team of teachers who agree to use the quiz provided at the end of each chapter of the textbook could claim they are using common assessments, but they will not experience the benefits we have outlined. Common assessments in the PLC context "are developed *collaboratively* in grade-level and departmental teams and incorporate each team's collective wisdom (professional knowledge and experience) in determining the selection, design, and administration of those assessments" (Ainsworth & Viegut, 2006, p. 13). Effective team-developed common assessments provide three forms of feedback: (a) "information about important learning targets that are clear to students and teacher teams," (b) "timely information for both students and teacher teams," and (c) "information that tells students and teacher teams what to do next" (Bailey & Jakicic, 2012, p. 49).

5 **Embrace the regular and routine use of protocols and team tools:** When teacher teams use protocols and tools to help structure their conversations about student learning, they sharpen their pedagogy and deepen their content knowledge. According to the National Turning Points Center (2001), teachers who use protocols have a more complete and comprehensive understanding of what students know and are able to do. The regular use of protocols also helps teachers develop a shared language for assessing student work and promotes the creation of a common understanding of what quality student work looks like.

Initially, many teachers may feel protocols are a waste of time, but effective principals encourage teachers to try them anyway. Educators who are accustomed to norms of private practice and inattention to the link between instructional strategies and learning may initially balk at the idea of using protocols; however, as they witness the benefits of protocols, those same educators typically become more supportive of making protocol use part of the organizational routine (McDonald et al., 2007).

6 **Use assessments as a means rather than an end:** In too many U.S. schools, faculties have become preoccupied with the pursuit of higher test scores. Test scores should be an indicator of our effectiveness in helping all students learn rather than the primary focus of the institution. They should be viewed as a means rather than an end. Douglas Reeves (2004) does a wonderful job of providing schools with fail-safe strategies to improve test scores: increase the dropout rate, assign higher percentages of students to special education, warehouse low-performing students in one school, create magnet programs to attract enough high-performing students to a low-performing school to raise its average, eliminate electives to devote more time to areas of the curriculum that are tested, and so on. Sadly, these strategies are still routinely being used in schools that are attempting to increase scores without improving learning.

Educators will not be driven to extraordinary effort and relentless commitment because of a goal to increase student performance on the state test by five points. Most entered the profession because they felt they could make a significant difference in students' lives, and appealing to that moral purpose is what will allow school leaders to marshal and motivate faculty efforts with more effectiveness. Test scores will take care of themselves when schools and the people within them are passionately committed to helping each student develop the knowledge, skills, and dispositions essential to their success.

Part Six

Questions to Guide the Work of Your Professional Learning Community

To clarify the importance of creating common formative assessments, ask:

1. How will we monitor each student's learning of each essential skill on a timely basis?

2. Have we agreed on what proficient student work looks like?

3. What are the criteria we will use in judging the quality of student work?

4. What evidence do we have that suggests we apply the criteria consistently?

5. What evidence do we have that suggests we are using the results of common assessments to identify students who require additional time and support for learning?

6. What evidence do we have that suggests we are using the results of common assessments to extend the learning for students who demonstrate they are highly proficient?

7. What evidence do we have that suggests we are using the results from common assessments to identify strengths and weaknesses in our individual teaching?

8. What evidence do we have that suggests we are using common assessment results as part of a continuous improvement process that is helping our team get better results?

9. Does student performance on our team assessments correlate with their achievement on other assessments at the district, state, provincial, or national level?

10. Does student performance on our assessments correlate with the grades students are earning in my course or grade level? Do our assessment practices encourage or discourage learning on the part of our students?

page 2 of 2

Part Seven

Dangerous Detours and Seductive Shortcuts

It is the *process* of team members collaboratively building shared knowledge and collectively making decisions about assessment that results in adult learning and improved professional practice. Beware of any action that removes teachers from the process because doing so minimizes their role, limits their learning, and diminishes the impact of common formative assessments. Do not substitute district benchmark assessments, textbook assessments, or commercially prepared assessments for team-developed common formative assessments.

It is the process of team members collaboratively building shared knowledge and collectively making decisions about assessment that results in adult learning and improved professional practice.

Remember that common assessments are formative only if educators use the results to better meet individual students' needs through intervention and enrichment *and* if educators use the assessment results to inform and improve their individual and collective instructional practice.

Part Eight

Digging Deeper—Recommended Resources

The following resources delve deeper into the topic of creating team-developed common formative assessments.

- *Common Formative Assessment: A Toolkit for Professional Learning Communities at Work, Second Edition* by Kim Bailey and Chris Jakicic (2023)
- *Proficiency-Based Assessment: Process, Not Product* by Troy Gobble, Mark Onuscheck, Anthony R. Reibel, and Eric Twadell (2016)
- *Collaborative Common Assessments: Teamwork. Instruction. Results.* by Cassandra Erkens (2016)
- *Mathematics Assessment and Intervention in a PLC at Work, Second Edition* by Sarah Schuhl, Timothy D. Kanold, Mona Toncheff, Bill Barnes, Jessica Kanold-McIntyre, Matthew R. Larson, and Georgina Rivera (2024)
- *Unpacking the Competency-Based Classroom: Equitable, Individualized Learning in a PLC at Work* by Jonathan G. Vander Els and Brian M. Stack (2022)

Final Thoughts

The question, "How do we know our students are learning?" is the cornerstone of the PLC process. Before a team can answer that question, members must reach agreement on what knowledge, skills, and dispositions their students should acquire as a result of the unit they are about to teach. After the assessment is administered, team members will face the challenge of "How can we intervene for students who need additional time and support and extend the learning for students who are highly proficient?" The results from common formative assessments provide teams with the information and feedback they need to improve their professional practice. So the critical questions of the PLC process flow up and down from common formative assessments. If, however, the school does nothing to assist individual students who struggle to demonstrate proficiency on the assessments, little is accomplished. The next chapter explores the critical questions, "How will we respond when some students don't learn?" and "How do we extend the learning for highly proficient students?"

CHAPTER 8
Responding When Some Students Don't Learn

Part One

The Case Study: Systematic Interventions Versus an Educational Lottery

Marty Mathers, principal of Taylor High School (home of the "Mighty Swifties"), knew that his ninth-grade algebra teachers were his most challenging team on the faculty. The team was composed of four teachers: (1) Peter Pilate, (2) Alan "Cubby" Sandler, (3) Charlotte Darwin, and (4) Henrietta Higgins. All of them had years of teaching experience, very strong personalities, and markedly different classroom approaches, making it difficult for them to find common ground during their weekly collaborative team meetings.

Peter Pilate was the most challenging member of the team from Principal Mathers's perspective. The failure rate in his classes was three times higher than those in his team members' classes, and parents routinely demanded that their children be assigned to a different teacher. However, many of the students who failed Mr. Pilate's class demonstrated proficiency on the state mathematics test; the primary reason students failed his course was they did not complete their daily homework assignments in a timely manner. He refused to accept late work, stating that doing so would not teach his students responsibility or properly prepare them for the sink-or-swim environment of college and beyond. When Principal Mathers expressed his concerns to Mr. Pilate about his high failure rate, Mr. Pilate's reply was always the same: "It is my job to teach and a student's job to learn. I have told my students that I am willing to provide additional help after school for any student who schedules a time with me. But unless students choose to take advantage of this opportunity, and give the effort necessary to succeed, there is nothing I can do. That's how it is in the real world."

The students knew Alan Sandler as the "cool" teacher. He had an excellent rapport with his students and a great sense of humor. Unlike Mr. Pilate, Mr. Sandler accepted late work for full credit and offered many opportunities for extra credit, including bonus test points for bringing in boxes of tissues, whiteboard pens, and cans of food during the school's yearly food drive. Most of his students earned As and Bs in his course, and failing grades were rare. Unfortunately, each spring, almost half of Mr. Sandler's students failed to meet the proficiency standard on the state algebra exam.

Principal Mathers was aware of yet another disturbing trend in Charlotte Darwin's mathematics class. He knew that although her algebra sections had started out with a similar number of students to her peers' sections, by early October, she had requested transfers for most of her failing students to the school's remedial mathematics track. She felt that the struggling students were slowing down the class and hurting the progress of the other students. It was obvious to her that the failing students lacked innate cognitive ability, a strong mathematical aptitude, and the prerequisite skills needed to succeed in algebra. Ms. Darwin believed that the best solution for students failing her class was to place them in a lower track of mathematics that would better match each student's ability. The students who remained in her algebra class usually scored above the state average on their proficiency examination—hardly a surprise since the low-achieving students were removed from her class long before the state test was administered in the spring.

Henrietta Higgins was a true joy to have on the faculty. She believed that every student was capable of mastering algebra when given effective instruction and additional support. To ensure every student's success, she frequently monitored student progress, and when students began to fall behind, she required them to meet with her before or after school for tutoring. Likewise, she would not allow her students to choose to fail, but instead required students who were missing assignments to come to her classroom during lunch to make up the work. A vast majority of her students consistently exceeded the proficiency standard on the state assessment and excelled in their future mathematics classes. Personally, Mrs. Higgins had recently given birth to a daughter, and Principal Mathers was concerned that all her extra hours at school and the new demands at home were taking a toll on her.

Principal Mathers was increasingly uneasy about a mathematics department that he perceived as inherently unfair to students, especially considering that algebra is often referred to as the "gatekeeper to college." An honest look at the school's current reality showed that Taylor High School was playing an "educational lottery" with the lives of students, with the random placement of students into the algebra classes being the biggest determinant of whether the students would receive additional opportunities to succeed. Worst of all, the faculty knew it. Staff members whose own children attended the school often went to the counseling office to secretly request that Mrs. Higgins be their child's algebra teacher. Principal Mathers was determined to address this inequity, but he was not sure how to.

Reflection

Consider the dilemma presented in this case study—that leaving the question of how to respond when students don't learn to each teacher's discretion inevitably results in profound inequities. How closely does this story simulate conditions in your school or district? Assuming that Principal Mathers has no additional resources to hire additional interventionist staff, and no way to lengthen the school day to offer extra help, how could he best address this problem?

Part Two

Here's How

Principal Mathers and the faculty at Taylor High School need to confront the third and fourth critical questions of the PLC at Work process.

- How will we respond when our students don't learn?
- How will we respond when our students do learn?

Up to this point, each teacher has been left to resolve these questions, based on their own assumptions, educational philosophies, and availability. The result is that students who experience difficulty in learning are subject to very different experiences. Any school dedicated to a mission of high levels of learning for all students must acknowledge the inherent limitations to this traditional approach and instead create a collaborative, systematic process for interventions and extensions.

To address the issue, Principal Mathers and the school's guiding coalition might ask the faculty to assess their current reality through the lenses of the three big ideas of a PLC at Work.

1. **A focus on learning:** "As a faculty, we agreed that our shared mission—the fundamental purpose of our school—is to ensure every student learns at high levels. Not *some* students or *most* students—we had the courage to commit to *all*. And as sure as the sun will rise each day, we know that some of our students will need additional time and support to succeed."
2. **A collaborative culture and collective responsibility:** "We know that none of us possesses all the skills and knowledge required to achieve our mission to meet the diverse needs of our students. This is why we work collaboratively and take collective responsibility for student learning. Our collaboration must include how we systematically intervene; our students must benefit from our collective expertise and efforts."

3. **A results orientation:** "In a PLC, good intentions and hard work are not enough. We must be willing to evaluate every practice, policy, and procedure in our school by asking the question, 'Are all students learning at higher levels?' If we are honest, our current intervention process—leaving the decision of how to respond up to each teacher—is not aligned to our commitment of collaboration, not based on research-based practices, and not significantly increasing the learning of all students. Unless we create a more effective process to intervene when students struggle, there is no way we can achieve our school's mission."

By referencing the school's mission and collective commitments, Principal Mathers and the guiding coalition are creating context, urgency, and a call to action.

Building Shared Knowledge

Whenever a PLC wants to improve its efforts on behalf of its students, the first step is always to build shared knowledge about professional best practice. To this end, the guiding coalition of Taylor High School might create a task force—comprised of teachers, administrators, key support staff, and representation from the teachers union—to study more effective ways to systematically intervene and extend student learning within the contractual school day. The task force would review current research on creating an effective system of interventions, as well as contact similar schools that are successfully responding when their students struggle. Based on this shared learning, the faculty would create a systematic intervention process, monitor its impact, and make adjustments and improvements based on evidence of increased student and adult learning.

We have repeatedly stressed in this book that being a PLC is a never-ending process in which educators work collaboratively in *recurring* cycles of collective inquiry and action research. The perpetual nature of the work is driven by two undeniable realities. First, the very purpose of the school's collaboration is to ensure all students learn at high levels. Until this outcome is achieved—*every* student is succeeding—more collective learning by the educators is required. Unless the adults continue to improve their practices, it is unlikely that student achievement will improve.

The second reality is the collective knowledge of a profession is not stagnant. As new research is conducted—both clinical studies and action research on campuses across the world—the collective wisdom of our profession evolves and improves. What was viewed as best practice yesterday might not reach the same level of validity tomorrow. This is especially true regarding how to successfully respond when students don't learn. Since the publication of the first edition of this book, there have been many outstanding research-based resources that clearly describe how a PLC can schedule time for interventions, define staff responsibilities, and target individual student needs (Buffum et al., in press). In the Digging Deeper section of this chapter (page 221), we provide a list of these additional resources.

Equally important, the AllThingsPLC website (https://allthingsplc.info) features hundreds of Model PLC schools and districts from across the world. Collectively, these schools represent:

- PreK schools, elementary schools, middle and junior high schools, and high schools
- Large schools with thousands of students and small schools with fewer than one teacher per grade or course
- Large districts with dozens of schools and small districts comprised of a single school
- Secondary schools that have block schedules and five-period, six-period, seven-period, eight-period, nine-period, and ten-period schedules
- Traditional, dual language, alternative, public, private, charter, and virtual schools
- Schools that serve only students who come from homes of poverty and schools that serve communities of significant wealth
- Schools that represent tremendous variance in local, state, provincial, and national regulations, mandates, and assessment systems
- Schools with active teachers unions and schools with no unions
- Schools with strong parental support and schools in which most parents lack the time and resources to be active partners in their children's education
- Schools with significant supplemental funding and interventionist staff and schools with almost no supplemental resources
- Schools with average class sizes in the single digits and schools with student-to-teacher ratios of over thirty to one

Despite these tremendous differences, all these Model PLCs have developed effective systematic processes to intervene and extend student learning. In each case, these schools and districts created their systems of support and extension using their existing resources, but it was imperative that the staff agreed to modify the schedule and assume new roles and responsibilities. And, most importantly, these Model PLCs will gladly share what they are doing.

While no two Model PLC schools have absolutely identical intervention processes, there are research-based characteristics that are critical to creating an effective systematic intervention process. These traits—which are replicable at any school—should serve as a starting point for the faculty at Taylor High School. We explore these traits in the following sections.

Access to Essential Grade-Level Curriculum or Higher

When teams in a PLC answer critical question one—What do we want students to know and be able to do?—members are collectively identifying the absolutely vital skills, knowledge, behaviors, and dispositions that all students must learn to be prepared to succeed in the future. If students miss instruction on new essential curriculum to receive interventions, or are tragically deemed "too low" and placed in below-grade-level remedial coursework for their core instruction, then the school is most assuredly setting these students up to struggle the next year. Because the ultimate goal of a PLC is to ensure all students learn at grade level or higher every year, *all* students must have access to the critical learning outcomes required for success in the next grade or course. No system of interventions can make up for teaching a student below-grade-level curriculum. Additional time and support must be provided in addition to—and not in place of—access to new essential standards.

Additional time and support must be provided in addition to—and not in place of—access to new essential standards.

The essential curriculum represents the *minimum* that all students must learn in each grade or course to be prepared for the next grade level or course. As students demonstrate mastery of the essential curriculum, teams in a PLC consider critical question four: How do we respond when students have already learned? The idea of extending student learning is certainly not a new concept at most schools. Schools often refer to these programs as *advanced*, *honors*, *accelerated*, *gifted and talented*, *Advanced Placement*, and *International Baccalaureate* (*IB*). Unfortunately, many schools limit access to this more rigorous curriculum by setting predetermined limits on the percentage of students who can participate, creating restrictive prerequisite requirements, or acquiescing to parental concerns that allowing too many students into these programs will dilute their rigor. Educators in a PLC would not view student ability with a fixed mindset, nor would they restrict answering critical question four for only a select few students. Instead, educators in a PLC create a system of interventions that guarantees extra support for students who have not mastered essential grade-level curriculum, and that can also provide assistance for more and more students to excel in the school's most rigorous coursework.

Intervention and Extension Time Embedded in the Master Schedule

To guarantee that every student who needs extra help can receive it, dedicated intervention time must be embedded within the school's master schedule. There are two main reasons for this. First, students legally must be in attendance during the official school day. Therefore, educators can require students to receive additional help during this time when the school has access to all students. Second, during the faculty's contractual teaching day, staff are already being paid to help students learn. When intervention time is embedded in the master schedule, the school leadership does not have to hope that teachers might volunteer their time before or after school or at lunch to help their students—or have to secure additional funding to pay teachers or interventionist staff to provide interventions and extensions.

A Multitiered System of Support

A multitiered system of interventions is designed to address four essential outcomes needed to ensure all students learn at high levels (Buffum et al., in press).

1. As mentioned previously, if the ultimate goal of a learning-focused school is to ensure that every student ends each year having acquired the essential skills, knowledge, and behaviors required for success at the next grade level, then all students must have access to essential grade-level curriculum as part of their core instruction.
2. At the end of every unit of study, some students will need some additional time and support to master this essential grade-level or course-specific curriculum.
3. Each school year, some students will enter lacking foundational skills that should have been mastered in prior years—skills such as foundational reading, writing, number sense, and English language. These students will require intensive interventions in these areas to succeed.
4. Some students will require all three of the preceding outcomes to learn at high levels.

A multitiered system of interventions, also commonly referred to as a *multitiered system of support* or *response to intervention*, is designed to address these four realities. Buffum and colleagues (in press) capture this system visually with the shape of an inverted pyramid, with the top level representing the school's core instruction program. The purpose of this tier—Tier 1—is to provide *all* students access to essential grade-level curriculum and effective initial teaching. When the core is taught well, most students should succeed most of the time without the need for additional help.

There will be a point in every unit of study when most students have demonstrated mastery of the unit's essential learning outcomes, and the teacher will need to proceed to the next topic. But because some students may not master the essential curriculum by the end of the unit, the school must dedicate time to provide these students additional support to master this essential grade-level curriculum without missing critical new core instruction. This supplemental help to master grade-level curriculum is the second tier—Tier 2—in a multitiered system of support. Because this support is focused on very specific essential standards and learning targets, placement into Tier 2 interventions must be timely, targeted, flexible, and fluid.

At Tier 2, schools should dedicate a block of time at least twice a week—but preferably more frequently—for students to receive additional time and support to master essential grade-level curriculum. Each session should be around thirty minutes—sufficient time for targeted reteaching. The characteristics of effective Tier 2 interventions include the following (Buffum et al., in press).

- Ensure all students master the specific skills, knowledge, and behaviors identified at Tier 1 to be absolutely essential for a student's future success.
- Provide Tier 2 support in addition to Tier 1 (access to new essential grade-level curriculum), not in place of it.

- Make additional support systematic—all students can receive this targeted help as needed.
- Provide Tier 2 support collaboratively, leveraging the expertise on campus that is best trained to meet the outcomes of each intervention. It is unrealistic to expect individual teachers to effectively provide Tier 2 support solely through classroom differentiation.

And for students who need intensive reinforcement in foundational skills, the school must have a plan to provide this level of assistance too. Intensive reinforcement is the purpose of the third tier of interventions—Tier 3. The characteristics of effective Tier 3 interventions include the following (Buffum et al., in press).

- Tier 3 is not regular education or special education—it must be available for *any* student who demonstrates the need.
- Like Tier 2, Tier 3 is provided collaboratively, leveraging the expertise on campus that is best trained to meet the outcomes of each intervention.
- This intensive help must be in addition to Tier 1—access to new essential grade-level curriculum. It must also be in addition to Tier 2—extra support to learn essential grade-level standards.

Because Tier 3 addresses significant gaps in foundational skills, schools should provide these interventions daily by embedding them into a student's individualized daily instructional program. At the elementary level, this is usually accomplished by extra support "pushing into" classrooms during guided or independent practice activities or "pulling" students during those times when new direct instruction on essential standards is not occurring. At the secondary level, intensive interventions are most commonly provided through designed courses. Again, the key is that schools must provide these services *in addition to* a student's access to essential grade-level curriculum, not as a replacement.

This approach is called a multitiered system of interventions because students are not moved from tier to tier; instead, the tiers are cumulative. All students need effective initial teaching on essential grade-level standards at Tier 1. In addition to Tier 1, some students will need additional time and support in meeting essential grade-level standards at Tier 2. And in addition to Tier 1 and Tier 2, some students will need intensive help in learning essential outcomes from previous years. This level of support cannot effectively be created by an individual teacher in their own classroom. Instead, it requires a schoolwide collective effort, utilizing the specialized training and unique talents of each staff member. This collaborative approach to ensure learning for all is essential to the PLC process.

A Systematic and Timely Identification Process

A school's intervention process is *systematic* when it can guarantee all students in need of additional support actually receive it, regardless of which teacher or teachers they are assigned to for core instruction. To achieve this outcome, the school must create a fail-safe process to identify every student who needs interventions or extensions, and then ensure that each student receives the appropriate help in a timely manner. While a systematic identification process will likely look different from school to school, two essential characteristics must be present for the process to be effective.

First, every faculty member must participate. The people best positioned to identify students in need of additional help at school are the adults who work with them every day—teachers and support staff. Because teacher teams in a PLC take primary responsibility in determining essential standards for each unit of study, teaching the curriculum, and assessing student progress, they are in the best position to identify, by student and by standard, who needs additional help. Equally important, teachers and support staff get to know the student behind the assessment score, and they can glean the subjective information also required to identify students in need of help in the areas of behavior, attendance, and social skills. Just as every school has a clearly defined and mandatory process for teachers to submit student progress information for report cards, each school should use a similar timely, mandatory process for staff members to identify students for interventions. If a single teacher is allowed to opt out of this process, then the school is allowing the educational lottery to persist.

Second, the identification process must be timely. Our experience is that schools often use report card grades, district benchmark testing, universal screeners, and state or provincial assessment data to identify students who are at risk and in need of extra help. Unfortunately, these assessments usually happen every five to six weeks at the minimum, which allows students to fail too long before receiving help. We recommend that a school reassess which students are in need of interventions and extensions at least every three weeks. Furthermore, the process should not be unfairly laborious for the staff. We find that when teachers have a voice in creating the process, it will be fair and respectful of teacher time.

Interventions Targeted to Individual Student Needs

To target interventions effectively, we recommend a school consider two criteria. First, a school must target interventions *by student, by standard*. Students in the same intervention should need assistance on the exact same essential standard, learning target, or behavior. This level of intervention specificity is why identifying essential standards is so vital to effective interventions. Unless a school has clearly identified the essential standards that every student must master—unit by unit—it will be nearly impossible to have the curricular focus and specific assessment data necessary to target interventions to this level.

The second targeting criterion is *by kid, by cause*. We must address the cause of a student's struggles, not merely the symptoms. Failing grades, low test scores, disruptive behavior, and poor attendance are all symptoms that demonstrate the student is struggling, but there are often multiple reasons why the student is demonstrating these outcomes. The more important questions are, Why is this student failing a class? Why did this student fail the exam? Why is this student demonstrating disruptive behavior? And, Why is this student chronically absent? If a school staff can eliminate the cause of a student's struggles, they will solve the problem.

Required, Not Optional, Student Participation

Interventions must be directive. When interventions are optional, the students most likely to take advantage of the offer are the ones already succeeding, while the students least likely to are those most in need of help. If a school is dedicated to ensuring the success of every student, then allowing a student to take the misguided path of choosing failure is unacceptable.

Making interventions mandatory should not be too difficult if a school places the same priority on requiring students to attend interventions as it does on requiring students to attend core instruction. For regular classroom instruction, virtually every school has a schoolwide attendance process that requires students to be in specific places throughout the day. This process includes steps to monitor student attendance, recognize positive attendance, and systematically respond when students fail to meet these expectations. If a school applied these same attendance procedures to intervention attendance, the vast majority of students would be where they need to be most of the time.

Collective Responsibility for Student Learning

And finally, the most important trait of any effective system of interventions is also an essential characteristic of being a PLC: the staff must take collective responsibility for student learning. The biggest problem with Taylor High School's traditional intervention approach was that, while the faculty did work in collaborative teams, each teacher was responsible for their own students when it came to providing students with extra help. In a PLC, we do not view students as "my kids" and "your kids." We view every student as a capable scholar who can excel if they receive the benefits of the collective knowledge and skills of the entire staff. Instead of grouping students for interventions and assigning staff by generic labels—such as *SPED*, *ELL*, and *Title I*—we instead target students together when they have the same need, and staff are assigned by who is best trained to meet that need.

For example, which team is best trained to help eighth-grade students struggling to understand the essential standard of the right of peaceful assembly as defined in the First Amendment of the U.S. Constitution? The eighth-grade U.S. history team, of course! Any student—regardless of label—should receive this targeted intervention provided collaboratively by the U.S. history experts on campus. But would the U.S. history team be the best faculty members to help an eighth-grade student who needs Tier 3 reading support because he currently reads at a fourth-grade level? Of course not. The most highly trained teacher or teachers of reading should take the lead on planning those interventions. Not only is this approach the best way to ensure student learning, but this collective division of labor is what makes implementing intervention possible within a school's limited time and resources.

Using Your Existing Resources

A school-improvement initiative that requires significant increases in expenditures—such as lengthening the school day or hiring additional staff—is not realistic for many schools. While extra resources are helpful, creating an effective system of interventions does not require increased funding, additional staffing, or a longer school day. Instead, it requires schools to use their existing resources differently and more effectively. Specifically, the hundreds of Model PLC schools and districts featured on AllThingsPLC (https://allthingsplc.info) have addressed their limited resource concerns in three ways.

A school-improvement initiative that requires significant increases in expenditures . . . is not realistic for many schools.

1. **Repurposing existing intervention resources:** Many schools have implemented the same interventions for years—interventions that don't work, have never worked, and predictably won't work in the future. A school should assess the effectiveness of all its current site interventions, including special education, its use of instructional aides, push-in support, and remedial classes. For each intervention, ask this question: "Are a vast majority of students excelling in this intervention?" If the answer is "No," then stop the intervention and repurpose those resources toward better solutions.
2. **Targeting students by need, not by label:** If there were no labels on students at your school—such as *regular ed*, *special ed*, *Title I*, *EL*, *honors*, and *gifted*—how would you target students for interventions? Wouldn't you group together students who have the same learning need? For example, students who need additional help mastering single-digit subtraction would be grouped together for reteaching. Within any elementary school, there will likely be students from different grade levels, and with different labels, who need help with this foundational mathematics skill. Unfortunately, many schools group students for interventions by their label, which means the same skill might be taught multiple times—in one group for the special education students, in another for first graders who need help with the skill, and in another again for the second graders. Obviously, this is not very efficient. When possible, schools should group students by need.
3. **Staying focused:** A school can't intervene on everything; there is just too much curriculum. Effective interventions and resource allocation begin with identifying a limited, realistic number of absolutely essential academic skills and behaviors that all students *must* learn. These standards are not all that your school will teach, but the minimum that all students must learn in a particular unit, term, grade level, or course. When the targeted outcomes are reasonable and achievable, securing sufficient time and resources becomes possible.

Faculties that place a higher value on protecting their traditional culture, structures, and schedules will find every excuse to believe systematic interventions are impossible to achieve at their school.

We offer the following observation gleaned from our work with schools and districts throughout North America: faculties that are truly committed to ensuring every student learns at high levels will work through the scheduling and resource obstacles and create a systematic process that ensures students will receive extra time and support for learning in a timely, directive, and systematic way. Conversely, faculties that place a higher value on protecting their traditional culture, structures, and schedules will find every excuse to believe systematic interventions are impossible to achieve at their school.

Addressing Extension as Well as Intervention

We believe there is an important difference between enrichment and extension. We define *enrichment* as when students have access to the subjects traditionally taught by teachers of specials or electives, such as music, art, drama, applied technology, and physical education. We strongly believe that this curriculum is essential. These subjects often teach essential core curriculum through different modalities. Also, students usually view these subjects as the fun part of school. When students are pulled from enrichment to receive extra help in core curriculum, interventions turn into a punishment. Consequently, students' motivation and attitude can suffer. Finally, enrichment is an equity issue. Often, students who need interventions come from economically disadvantaged homes, and the only way these students will learn a musical instrument or use advanced technology is at school. For these reasons, students should not be denied access to enrichment because they need additional time and support in core subjects.

Extension is when students are stretched beyond essential grade-level curriculum or levels of proficiency. This outcome can be achieved in multiple ways, including the following.

- Students can be asked to demonstrate mastery of essential standards at a level beyond what is deemed grade-level proficient. For example, many schools applying a four-point rubric to a grade-level writing prompt will deem a score of three as grade-level proficient. Stretching students beyond to a score of four would be an example of extended learning. For specific examples of this extended learning on a four-point scale for different subject areas, see Marzano Resources' Critical Concepts proficiency scales (www.marzanoresources.com/educational-services/critical-concepts).
- Students can have access to more of the required grade-level curriculum that is deemed important but not essential.
- Students can be taught above-grade-level curriculum. An example might be AP classes.

If a school is going to embed flexible time into its master schedule so it can provide targeted students with additional time and support in learning essential grade-level standards, then there is no reason why it could not also use this time to extend students who have already learned these outcomes.

This is easier to achieve if teacher teams consider extension opportunities when answering PLC critical question one, "What is it we want students to know and be able to do?" As team members determine the essential learning outcomes within a particular unit of study, they should expect that some students might have already learned the standards, while others will learn them during initial instruction. So even before the unit starts, the team can discuss and identify what they can do to extend learning for the students, and then use the school's dedicated intervention time to extend these students.

Part Three

Here's Why

We have known for more than forty years that effective schools create a climate of high expectations for student learning; that is, such schools are driven by the assumption that all students are able to achieve the essential learning of their course or grade level (Cotton, 2000; Georgiades, Fuentes, & Snyder, 1983; Good & Brophy, 2002; Lezotte, 1991; Newmann & Wehlage, 1996; Purkey & Smith, 1983). An authentic way to assess the degree to which a school is characterized by "high expectations" is to examine how the organization responds "when some students do not learn" (Lezotte, 1991, p. 2).

We have known for more than forty years that effective schools create a climate of high expectations for student learning.

Key to an effective response for students who struggle is the provision of additional time and support for learning. Benjamin Bloom's research on mastery learning in the 1960s established that if all students are to learn, some students will need additional time and support for learning. Bob Marzano's (2003) meta-analysis of research on school-level factors that impact student learning revealed the schools that have a profound impact on student achievement "provide interventions that are designed to overcome student background characteristics" (p. 8). Douglas Reeves (2006), in his studies of high-poverty, high-minority, high-achieving schools, has found that those schools implement a plan for "immediate and decisive intervention" when students don't learn (p. 87). In their study of school districts that were able to double student achievement, Allan R. Odden and Sarah J. Archibald (2009) found that those districts extended learning time for struggling students. A decade of research by the Southern Regional Education Board (1998) into "things that matter most in student achievement" concluded that "extra help and time are important if they are designed to help students meet the standards of higher-level academic courses" (p. 8). Schools that improved most required students to get extra help when they performed poorly on tests. The message is clear: some students will require a greater opportunity to learn—they will need more time and support than others—and the most effective schools ensure that they receive it. (See page 210, "Why Should We Implement Systematic Interventions?" for expert commentary on this issue.)

John Hattie's (2012) comprehensive study of what most impacts student learning found that education's powerful leverage points hinge on features *within* the school, rather than outside factors like home, environmental, and economic conditions. Specially, he found that creating an effective MTSS is proven to accelerate student learning and close achievement gaps.

Another reason to create a timely, multitiered system of interventions for any student who experiences difficulty is because that is exactly what the Individuals with Disabilities Education Improvement Act (IDEA) of 2004 requires schools to do. That law discouraged the continued use of discrepancy models that required students to fail for an extended period of time before becoming eligible for additional support, and promoted an end to a focus on compliance with special education regulations in favor of a focus on results (IDEA, 2004). Schools are now asked to implement a systematic RTI process "to integrate assessment and intervention within a multi-level prevention system to maximize student achievement and reduce behavior problems" (National Center on

Why Should We Implement Systematic Interventions?

Characteristics of high-performing schools include setting high expectations for all students, using assessment data to support student success, and employing systems for identifying intervention (Ragland, Clubine, Constable, & Smith, 2002).

"Reforms must move the system toward early identification and swift intervention, using scientifically based instruction and teaching methods" (President's Commission on Excellence in Special Education, 2002, p. 9).

"[A criterion] for schools that have made great strides in achievement and equity is immediate and decisive intervention. . . . Successful schools do not give a second thought to . . . providing preventive assistance for students in need" (Reeves, 2006, p. 87).

"The most significant factor in providing appropriate interventions for students was the development of layers of support. Systems of support specifically addressed the needs of students who were 'stretching' to take more rigorous coursework" (Dolejs, 2006, p. 3).

"High-performing school systems . . . set high expectations for what each and every child should achieve, and then monitor performance against the expectations, intervening whenever they are not met. . . . The very best systems intervene at the level of the individual student, developing processes and structures within schools that are able to identify whenever a student is starting to fall behind, and then intervening to improve that child's performance" (Barber & Mourshed, 2007, p. 34).

In order to raise student achievement, schools must use diagnostic assessments to measure students' knowledge and skills at the beginning of each curriculum unit, on-the-spot assessments to check for understanding during instruction, and end-of-unit assessments and interim assessments to see how well students learned. "All of these enable teachers to make mid-course corrections and to get students into intervention earlier" (Odden & Archibald, 2009, p. 23).

In high-performing school systems, "teachers identify struggling students as early as possible, and direct them towards a variety of proven intervention strategies, developed at both the school and district level, that assist all students in mastering grade-level academic objectives" (National Center for Educational Achievement, 2009, p. 34).

"One of the most productive ways for districts to facilitate continual improvement is to develop teachers' capacity to use formative assessments of student progress aligned with district expectations for student learning, and to use formative data in devising and implementing interventions during the school year" (Louis et al., 2010, p. 214).

"The PLC process and MTSS practices are the proven 'recipes' needed to ensure all students learn at high levels—but to reap these powerful results, schools must implement these practices at a very high level" (Buffum et al., in press).

Response to Intervention, 2008). In short, MTSS aligns perfectly with the timely, directive, systematic process to provide students with additional time and support for learning that constitutes such a vital element of a PLC (Buffum et al., in press).

But most importantly, schools must create a highly effective system of interventions because failure in the K–12 system is arguably a death knell to a student's chances to live a successful adult life. In chapter 1 of this book (page 13), we included the compelling statistics of what happens to students who don't succeed in school. It is naive and profoundly unprofessional to expect individual teachers, working in isolation, to provide each of their students with the time and support needed to succeed.

There is nothing counterintuitive in what we are proposing regarding systematic intervention, and it represents nothing less than what educators would want for their own children. Whenever a school makes time and support for learning a fixed constant, the variable will always be student learning. Some students, probably most students, will learn the intended skill or concept in the given time and with the given support. Some students will not. PLCs make a conscious and sustained effort to reverse this equation. They advise students that learning is the constant—"All of you will learn this essential skill"—and then recognize that if they are to keep that commitment, they must create processes to ensure that students who need additional time and support for learning will receive them.

There is nothing counterintuitive in what we are proposing regarding systematic intervention, and it represents nothing less than what educators would want for their own children.

"Opportunity to learn" has been recognized as a powerful variable in student achievement for more than thirty-five years (Lezotte, 2005). In fact, Marzano (2003) has concluded that "opportunity to learn has the strongest relationship with student achievement of all school-level factors" (p. 22). Research on the topic has typically focused on whether the intended curriculum was actually implemented in the classroom; that is, were the essential skills actually taught? We are arguing that opportunity to learn must move beyond the question, "Was it taught?" to the far more important question, "Was it learned?" If the answer is "No" for some students, then the school must be prepared to provide additional opportunities to learn during the regular school day in ways that students perceive as helpful rather than punitive.

In the previous chapter (page 167), we made the case for the use of team-developed common formative assessments as a powerful tool for school improvement. These assessments help collaborative teams of teachers answer the question, "How do we know if our students are learning?" Raising this question is pointless, however, if the school is unprepared to intervene when it discovers that some students are not learning. The lack of a systematic response to ensure that students receive additional learning opportunities reduces the assessment to yet another summative test administered solely to assign a grade. Once again, the response that occurs after the test has been given will truly determine whether the test is being used as a formative assessment. If it is used to ensure students who experience difficulty receive additional time and support as well as additional opportunities to demonstrate their learning, it is formative; if additional support is not forthcoming, it is summative.

Many teachers have come to the conclusion that their job is not just difficult—it is impossible. If schools continue to operate according to traditional assumptions and practices, we would concur with that conclusion. Individual teachers working in isolation as they attempt to help all their students achieve at high levels will eventually be overwhelmed by the tension between covering the content and responding to students' diverse needs in a fixed amount of time with virtually no external support.

It is disingenuous for any school to claim its purpose is to help all students learn at high levels and then fail to create a system of interventions.

We cannot make this point emphatically enough: it is disingenuous for any school to claim its purpose is to help all students learn at high levels and then fail to create a system of interventions to give struggling learners additional time and support for learning. If time and support remain constant in schools, learning will always be the variable.

Furthermore, we cannot meet our students' needs unless we assume collective responsibility for their well-being. Seymour Sarason (1996) described schools as a "culture of individuals, not a group . . . [with] each concerned about [themselves]" (p. 367), a place in which "each teacher dealt alone with [their] problems" (p. 321), and an environment in which teachers "are only interested in what they do and are confronted within their encapsulated classrooms" (p. 329). The idea so frequently heard in schools—"These are *my* students, *my* room, and *my* materials"—must give way to a new paradigm of "These are *our* students, and we cannot help all of them learn what they must learn without a collective effort." As the former president of the National Commission on Teaching and America's Future notes:

> The idea that a single teacher, working alone, can know and do everything to meet the diverse learning needs of 30 students every day throughout the school year has rarely worked, and it certainly won't meet the needs of learners in years to come. (Carroll, 2009, p. 13)

Jon Saphier (2005) was exactly correct when he said, "The success of our students is our joint responsibility, and when they succeed, it is to our joint credit and cumulative accomplishment" (p. 28).

Part Four

Assessing Your Place on the PLC Journey

It is important to help your staff build shared knowledge regarding your school's current status in addressing the critical step on the PLC journey of creating systematic interventions. We have created a tool to assist you in that effort. "The Professional Learning Communities at Work® Continuum: Providing Students With Systematic Interventions and Extensions" is on page 213 and available at **go.SolutionTree.com/PLCbooks** as a free reproducible. Once your staff have established greater clarity regarding the current status of your collaborative teams, we urge you to turn your attention to the "Where Do We Go From Here?" worksheet that accompanies the continuum (on page 214 and also available for free download at **go.SolutionTree.com/PLCbooks**). It will prompt you to take the action necessary to close the knowing-doing gap.

The Professional Learning Communities at Work® Continuum: Providing Students With Systematic Interventions and Extensions

DIRECTIONS: Individually, silently, and *honestly* assess the current reality of your school's implementation of each indicator listed in the left column. Consider what evidence or anecdotes support your assessment. This form may also be used to assess district or team implementation.

We acknowledge that the fundamental purpose of our school is to help all students achieve high levels of learning, and therefore, we provide students with systematic interventions when they struggle and extensions when they are proficient.

Indicator	Pre-Initiating	Initiating	Implementing	Developing	Sustaining
We provide a system of interventions that guarantees each student will receive additional time and support for learning if he or she experiences initial difficulty. Students who are proficient have access to enriched and extended learning opportunities.	What happens when a student does not learn will depend almost exclusively on the teacher to whom the student is assigned. There is no coordinated school response to students who experience difficulty. Some teachers allow students to turn in late work; some do not. Some teachers allow students to retake a test; some do not. The tension that occurs at the conclusion of each unit when some students are proficient and ready to move forward and others are failing to demonstrate proficiency is left to each teacher to resolve.	The school has attempted to establish specific policies and procedures regarding homework, grading, parent notification of student progress, and referral of students to child study teams to assess their eligibility for special education services. If the school provides any additional support for students, it is either a "pull-out" program that removes students from new direct instruction or an optional after-school program. Policies are established for identifying students who are eligible for more advanced learning.	The school has taken steps to provide students with additional time and support when they experience difficulty. The staff is grappling with structural issues such as how to provide time for intervention during the school day in ways that do not remove the student from new direct instruction. The school schedule is regarded as a major impediment to intervention and extension, and staff members are unwilling to change it. Some are concerned that providing students with additional time and support is not holding them responsible for their own learning.	The school has developed a schoolwide plan to provide students who experience difficulty with additional time and support for learning in a way that is timely, directive, and systematic. It has made structural changes such as modifications in the daily schedule to support this system of interventions. Staff members have been assigned new roles and responsibilities to assist with the interventions. The faculty is looking for ways to make the system of interventions more effective.	The school has a highly coordinated system of interventions and extensions in place. The system is very proactive. Coordination with sender schools enables the staff to identify students who will benefit from additional time and support for learning even before they arrive at the school. The system is very fluid. Students move into intervention and extension easily and remain only as long as they benefit from it. The achievement of each student is monitored on a timely basis. Students who experience difficulty are required, rather than invited, to utilize the system of support. The plan is multilayered. If the current level of time and support is not sufficient to help a student become proficient, he or she is moved to the next level and receives increased time and support. All students are guaranteed access to this system of interventions regardless of the teacher to whom they are assigned. The *school* responds to students and views those who are failing to learn as "undersupported" rather than "at risk."

Where Do We Go From Here? Worksheet
Providing Students With Systematic Interventions and Extensions

Indicator of a PLC at Work	What steps or activities must be initiated to create this condition in your school?	Who will be responsible for initiating or sustaining these steps or activities?	What is a realistic timeline for each step or phase of the activity?	What will you use to assess the effectiveness of your initiative?
We provide a system of interventions that guarantees each student will receive additional time and support for learning if he or she experiences initial difficulty. Students who are proficient have access to enriched and extended learning opportunities.				

Part Five

Tips for Moving Forward: Creating Systematic Interventions and Extensions to Ensure Students Receive Additional Time and Support for Learning

1 **Start with PLC critical questions one and two:** Most schools don't have a scheduling problem; they have a targeting problem. This reality is best captured when we hear educators say, "We would like to revise our schedule and provide students additional time to learn, but we can't because we have too much to cover." This claim demonstrates that the school still embraces a mission of teaching, not learning. The goal of a learning-focused school is not to cover curriculum but to ensure students actually learn the skills, content, and behaviors that are critical to their future success. The four critical questions of the PLC process not only focus the collaboration of a team, but also provide a logical sequence to the work. When teams skip the first two questions ("Learn what?" and "How will we know?"), responding effectively when students don't learn is impossible.

2 **Beware of appeals to mindless precedent:** Appeals to mindless precedent include the phrases, "But we have always done it this way," "We have never done it that way," and the ever-popular, "The schedule won't let us." These appeals pose a formidable barrier to the creation of a PLC.

We have carefully perused both the Old and New Testaments and can find no evidence that any school schedule was carved into stone tablets and brought down from Mount Sinai. Yet in schools throughout North America, the schedule is regarded as an unalterable, sacrosanct part of the school not to be tampered with in any way. The reverence afforded the schedule is puzzling. Mere mortals created it, and educators should regard it as a tool to further priorities rather than as an impediment to change.

3 **Acknowledge that traditional special education is not the answer:** For most of the past half century, the only systematic intervention process that every school was mandated to provide was special education. Objective analysis of the results would conclude that special education not only has failed to close student achievement gaps, but has actually been detrimental to achieving this outcome. The graduation rate for students with special needs was 71 percent in 2019—14 percent lower than for students in regular education (NCES, 2019). Students who are male, minority, and economically disadvantaged are much more likely to be

identified as special needs. Male students are almost twice as likely as female students to be identified for special education (NCES, 2019). African American students make up 15 percent of public school enrollment but make up the highest percentage of students in special education. This trend is similar for Hispanic and Native American students (NCES, 2019). Based on these results, it would be hard to justify perpetuating traditional special education services for our youth most at risk.

We are not suggesting that special education services should be discontinued altogether, or that educators should disregard student IEPs. What we are suggesting is that federal law now advocates for giving schools much more flexibility to meet all students' needs. But taking advantage of this power requires schools to rethink the way regular and special education have worked for years.

4 **Focus on what you can control:** We find many schools, when planning interventions for struggling students, spend an inordinate amount of time identifying and discussing factors that they cannot directly change. These topics include a student's home environment, a lack of district support, the pressure of preparing students for high-stakes state or provincial assessments, and ill-conceived state or provincial and federal educational policies. While these concerns are real and might be impacting both the student and the site educators, they are rarely the primary reason why a student has not learned a specific essential learning outcome. Instead of spending precious intervention-planning time focusing on factors that cannot immediately change, a school staff should focus on what lies within their sphere of influence, like providing students with time and targeted instruction during the school day to master essential standards. In the end, schools have a significant amount of control over the instructional decisions made on behalf of their students every day.

5 **Remember more of the same is not effective intervention:** Effective intervention is characterized by differentiation and precision; it offers a setting and strategies that are different from those that have already proven to be ineffective for the student. For example, a student who failed to grasp a concept that a teacher taught in a large-group setting using a particular strategy is unlikely to learn the concept if the intervention takes place in another large-group setting and replicates the same instructional strategy. Furthermore, an intervention system that merely reports a student is failing mathematics will not be as effective as a system that can identify the precise skill or skills that are causing the student's difficulty.

6 **Align your school's grading practices to promote, celebrate, and reward students for effort, improvement, and learning:** Many school intervention programs are undermined by traditional grading practices designed to rank student achievement, punish students for initial failure, deny students opportunities to fix mistakes, value promptness over learning, and demotivate struggling students. Examples include the following.

- Establishing a "no late work accepted" policy, where once a deadline has passed, there is no reason for the struggling student to complete the assignment
- Giving half credit for late work, which guarantees the student will fail the assignment whether they make it up or not
- Averaging grades so that first attempts will always affect a grade, regardless of how much the student improves
- Not giving makeup tests, so once a student is assessed at the end of a unit, they have no way to improve their grade even if they attend interventions
- Grading on a curve, so a student's grade is based not on if they met the standard, but instead on how they did in comparison to their peers

All these traditional grading policies, which are prevalent in most schools, discourage students from fixing mistakes or deny them the opportunity to improve.

7 **Celebrate with students *how* they overcame their initial struggles:** The goal of any intervention is to have students learn a specific academic standard, and also to teach students how to learn. We want students to develop what Carol Dweck (2016) refers to as a *growth mindset*—that one's abilities are not based on innate talents, but can be developed through one's dedication and effort. We can foster this attitude when we have students reflect on how they ultimately succeeded—by getting a little extra help, giving a little extra effort, and sticking with it until they learned the concept. Helping students adopt a growth mindset will improve their self-efficacy and ultimately teach them to self-advocate once they enter more sink-or-swim environments.

8 **Realize that no support system will compensate for ineffective teaching:** A school characterized by weak and ineffective teaching will not solve its problems by creating a system of timely interventions for students. Eventually, that system will be crushed by the mass of students it is attempting to support. At the same time that the school is creating its system of interventions, it must also take steps to build every teacher's capacity to effectively meet students' needs. The battle to help all students learn must be fought on both fronts: support for the students and support for the professional staff. To focus on one and exclude the other will never result in victory. Principals and teachers must engage in a process of continuous improvement, constantly examining their practices and expanding their repertoire of skills. But no matter how skillful the professional, it is likely that some students will not master the intended learning by the end of the unit of instruction. At that point, the system of interventions comes to the aid of both students and teachers. Schools need both skillful teachers and effective schoolwide interventions.

Part Six

Questions to Guide the Work of Your Professional Learning Community

To develop systematic interventions that ensure students receive additional time and support for learning on a timely and directive basis, ask:

1. Which areas of student need should we address first?

2. How will we identify students who need additional time and support so that no student will slip through the cracks?

3. How often will we identify students so that they do not drop too far behind before receiving assistance?

4. How proactive are we? What steps do we take to identify the students who will need us most before they come to our school?

5. How will we determine which staff members will take the lead for each intervention?

6. How will we schedule time for each intervention so that identified students will not miss new essential instruction?

7. How will we ensure that targeted students attend their assigned intervention?

8. How will we monitor student progress and the effectiveness of our efforts?

9. How fluid is our system of interventions? Are students assigned to intervention for a fixed period of time, or can they move in and out of intervention based on evidence of their proficiency?

10. How can we use flexible time and targeted instruction to provide students with assistance in extending their learning?

page 2 of 2

Part Seven

Dangerous Detours and Seductive Shortcuts

Beware of pseudo plans of intervention. For example, an after-school tutoring program for students who elect to seek help is not systematic intervention. The students who need help most are typically the least likely to seek it. Furthermore, it is difficult for educators to insist that students remain after school given the after-school obligations that make it impossible for some students to stay—busing, family requirements, jobs, and so on. An intervention plan that is directive will occur during the school day, when educators serve in loco parentis.

Resist the temptation to purchase a "silver bullet" intervention program—a program that claims to remediate every struggling reader, or software that will identify and target the mathematics needs of each student. There are some effective intervention programs available, but they should not replace the ongoing processes described in this chapter. No program can or should replace a systematic process of intervention.

Beware of attempts to use intervention to further exonerate educators from responsibility for student learning. In the wrong school culture, a system of interventions could be viewed as yet another reason the teacher is not responsible for student learning: "I taught it, they didn't get it, so let the intervention people deal with it." To be effective, the program must be just one part of an explicit schoolwide commitment to help all students learn by providing those who struggle with additional time and support; at the same time, the school establishes a process to inform and improve the professional practice of every teacher and every team.

***Any school dedicated to ensuring all students learn at high levels must stop debating what they* think *students can or can't do, and instead change the question to this:* How will we get every student there?**

But perhaps most importantly, we must stop judging a student's ability to learn at high levels based on their demographic characteristics. We know that a student's ethnicity, native language, and economic status do not determine the student's innate capacity to learn. Yet, many schools make assumptions about what their students are capable of learning based on these demographic factors. Any school dedicated to ensuring all students learn at high levels must stop debating what they *think* students can or can't do, and instead change the question to this: *How will we get every student there?* It is unlikely an intervention will be effective when educators begin with the assumption that some students can't learn in the first place.

Part Eight

Digging Deeper—Recommended Resources

The following resources delve deeper into the topic of responding when some students don't learn and extending learning when students are proficient.

- *Taking Action: A Handbook for RTI at Work, Second Edition* by Austin Buffum, Mike Mattos, Janet Malone, Luis F. Cruz, Nicole Dimich, and Sarah Schuhl (in press)
- *Behavior Solutions: Teaching Academic and Social Skills Through RTI at Work* by John Hannigan, Jessica Djabrayan Hannigan, Mike Mattos, and Austin Buffum (2021)
- *It's About Time: Planning Interventions and Extensions in Elementary School* edited by Austin Buffum and Mike Mattos (2015)
- *It's About Time: Planning Interventions and Extensions in Secondary School* edited by Mike Mattos and Austin Buffum (2015)
- *When They Already Know It: How to Extend and Personalize Student Learning in a PLC at Work* by Mark Weichel, Blane McCann, and Tami Williams (2018)
- *Enriching the Learning: Meaningful Extensions for Proficient Students in a PLC at Work* by Michael Roberts (2019)
- *Parentships in a PLC at Work: Forming and Sustaining School-Home Relationships With Families* by Kyle Palmer (2022)
- *Community Connections and Your PLC at Work: A Guide to Engaging Families* by Nathaniel Provencio (2021)

Final Thoughts

A major obstacle to creating an effective system of interventions is the long-standing assumption that it is the teacher's job to teach and the student's job to learn. Educators who operate under this assumption assert that students who do not put forth sufficient effort to learn should suffer the logical consequence of their decision: failure. To provide these students with additional time and support, the educators argue, is to ensure their learning simply enables them and does not prepare them for the harsh realities of the real world. If this assumption prevails in the 21st century, schools can anticipate the same results that they experienced throughout the 20th century: high levels of failure, particularly among the most disadvantaged students. As we have stressed, however, the consequences of student failure today are much more dire than they have been in the past. Educators must not ignore those consequences.

We return to the first and biggest of the big ideas that drive the PLC process: *the fundamental purpose of the school is to ensure that all students learn at high levels (grade level or higher)*. Variations on this assertion dominate school mission statements throughout North America. Educators who align their behavior with this mission will create multitiered systems of interventions, because without those systems, it is impossible to help all students learn at high levels. Those who continue to insist that they have fulfilled their responsibility by merely teaching a lesson should feel compelled to amend their mission statements to reflect their beliefs and practices.

A common concern of schools is that just as their teams are starting to function well, new members come on board and disrupt the forward momentum the team has created. We address the challenge of selecting, training, and retaining staff in the next chapter.

CHAPTER 9 Hiring, Orienting, and Retaining New Staff

Part One

The Case Study: The Disruption of Adding New Staff

Principal Larry Geterdone took pride in his reputation for running a well-maintained and efficient school (Howard Johnson High; mascot, the Roadrunners). Discipline issues were dealt with promptly, and district paperwork was completed prior to deadlines. But the fact that he was consistently the first principal in the district to fill school teaching vacancies was particularly gratifying. This achievement was even more remarkable in his mind because the combination of increasing enrollment in his school zone and the state's early retirement incentive meant he had multiple vacancies to fill each year.

He attacked the issue with zeal every spring. He was the first principal to ask the personnel office to select two strong candidates for each position and forward him their information. During his interviews with the finalists, he stressed that the school was committed to the professional learning community process. He quizzed each candidate on whether they would be comfortable working on a collaborative team, presenting students with a guaranteed and viable curriculum for each unit, monitoring student learning through common formative assessments, and using transparent evidence of student learning to inform and improve their instructional practice. Virtually every candidate offered assurances that they would be happy to contribute to the school's PLC and the team's collaborative process.

When new teachers arrived at the beginning of the academic year, Principal Geterdone would meet with the group on its first day to distribute copies of the district and school policy manuals, copies of the state standards for each teacher's grade or course, class rolls, and room keys. He stressed that it was his philosophy to hire good teachers and then let them teach but that they should feel free to come see him if they needed anything.

Yet every fall, his veteran teachers complained that the new staff members either didn't understand the PLC process or showed little evidence of being committed to it. Teams complained that the new staff members were disrupting their established collaborative processes and making few to no team contributions. It was evident that this repeated disruption to the continuity of the school's PLC journey was increasingly frustrating for many of the key teacher leaders. Principal Geterdone was concerned that he could lose some of his most effective teachers if he didn't discover a better way to address the issue of hiring and orienting new teachers. He was uncertain, however, about what steps to take. After all, he personally interviewed each new employee and solicited their commitment to the PLC process and their grade-level team. What more could he do?

Equally troubling was the fact that many of his new staff members were electing to leave the school within a year or two of joining the faculty. Their exodus only magnified the problem of bringing in new hires every year. How could the school avoid this annual frustration?

Reflection

Consider the multiple problems the principal is facing. Newly hired staff members do not seem to be honoring commitments they made in the interview process, and they are not contributing as active members of their teams. The disruption that new staff are causing to their collaborative teams is interfering with attempts to bring the PLC process to life in the school. The fact that many new teachers are opting to leave the school is adding to the constant churn of personnel that is making it difficult for the PLC process to take hold. The growing sense of frustration may lead to the loss of key teacher leaders. How should the principal resolve these problems?

Part Two

Here's How

The issues of teacher resignation, discontentment, and labor shortages have long been challenges related to hiring and retaining staff in the field of education (Sutcher, Darling-Hammond, & Carver-Thomas, 2016), but the evidence is clear that the strain of the COVID-19 pandemic has made a dire situation turn from bad to worse. COVID-19 caused an exodus of workers that has affected nearly every field. The field of education also simultaneously experienced a massive decrease in the supply of new teachers preparing to enter the profession. According to one report, the number of new teachers being prepared in traditional four-year university credentialing programs decreased nearly 30 percent from 2010 to 2020 (Goldhaber & Holden, 2020). There was a slight uptick in new teacher preparation in 2019, compared to the previous nine years, but that uptick immediately vanished after the onset of the pandemic in 2020, primarily because many college students had to complete their student teaching requirements virtually or finish their college coursework online (Goldhaber & Holden, 2020). Many students in teacher education programs did not find these options professionally or financially advantageous, and dropped out or delayed their certification completion. The following reasons have also contributed to a massive decline in university students' interest in becoming traditionally certified teachers (Aldeman, 2022).

- COVID-related changes have made teaching less enjoyable.
- Culture wars have made teaching more political.
- Respect for teachers has declined.
- Starting salaries are too low.
- Increased certification and licensing requirements have made the profession less attractive to potential teachers.
- There are broader economic opportunities and more potential career choices.

The combination of these realities has been the catalyst to an alarming shortage of licensed teachers, and this issue appears to affect the students who have traditionally been disadvantaged most: students in urban and rural communities (Aldeman, 2022). Given these challenges of the modern educational landscape, it would be wise for leaders to be extra diligent when hiring new teachers if they want their culture to function as a PLC at Work.

Let's begin with the assumption that teaching candidates do not deliberately misrepresent their views and feelings during interviews. If that is true, the problem of the disconnect between what candidates say in an interview and their subsequent actions as employees is most likely the result of the following factors.

The Need for an Expanded Selection Process

The goal of the hiring process in a PLC is not to quickly complete the process but to ensure that the candidate will be an asset to the school because they are a good fit for the culture. Rather than hiring capable people and attempting to persuade them to embrace the culture, effective leaders "hire people who already have a predisposition to your core values and hang onto them" (Collins, 2009, p. 159).

It is certainly a mistake for schools or districts to delay the hiring process until a few weeks or days before the school year begins.

It is certainly a mistake for schools or districts to delay the hiring process until a few weeks or days before the school year begins. This approach most often results in a sense of urgency that leads to "any warm body will do" syndrome. Principal Geterdone has put too much emphasis on completing the process efficiently and not nearly enough on its effectiveness in bringing the right people into the school and ensuring they are clear on what will be expected of them.

One way Principal Geterdone could improve the process would be to contact the principal of a candidate's former school (or a cooperating teacher if the candidate has not had a previous position) to ask for a candid assessment of past performance. Reviewing written references serves a purpose, but directing pointed questions about a candidate's past effectiveness to knowledgeable people is a step that should never be skipped in the hiring process. As former principal and author Kim Marshall (2015) admits:

> My biggest regret from my years as a principal was when I rushed to make a last-minute hiring decision rather than persisting until we found the right person—and when I cut corners on calling references or didn't push previous employers to give the full story. (p. 37)

Principal Geterdone could also improve the hiring process by giving the team a role to play in selecting its new colleague. For example, the principal and assistant principal or the principal and department chair could complete an initial round of interviews and reference checks and narrow the choices to two or three candidates. The team could then interview each finalist, during which time members could ensure the candidates each become well versed in the team's norms, protocols, essential standards, and common assessments.

The hiring process should also include having finalists demonstrate their skill in the classroom. Principal Geterdone could ask the candidates to prepare and present a lesson on an appropriate essential standard while he and team members observe. As the final step in the process, the team could offer the principal an assessment of each candidate's strengths and weaknesses before Principal Geterdone extends a job offer.

Such an expanded selection process will certainly require more time than Principal Geterdone has devoted to hiring in the past. It will, however, reap several benefits. Teams will feel a greater sense of ownership of their new colleague's success if members contribute to the selection process. The candidate will have a better sense of what it will be like to work with the team when they hear firsthand from its members about their collaborative process and their expectations for new members. The opportunity to observe the candidate teaching an essential skill will provide greater insight into their instructional ability and whether it's a match with the PLC process.

The Need for Relevant Questions

Another problem with Principal Geterdone's interview process is that he uses questions that are unlikely to elicit extended responses or differentiate among candidates. A question such as, "Will you support our PLC process?" allows candidates to answer with a one-word response. Furthermore, that response is likely to be essentially the same—a variation on "Absolutely!" Such a question does not reveal the candidate's thinking and values, does not distinguish between different candidates, and is essentially a waste of time. The best questions are presented as scenarios that call on candidates to explain how they would respond to given situations, the thinking that would guide their decisions, and how they have dealt with specific situations in the past. Questions could be organized to gain insight into the candidates' thinking about the three big ideas that drive the PLC process. See pages 228–229, "Is This Candidate a Good Fit for Our PLC?" for sample questions.

The Need for a Common Vocabulary

It is probable that someone new to the organization will not understand the established common vocabulary. Terms such as *professional learning community*, *collaborative team*, *guaranteed and viable curriculum*, *common formative assessment*, and *transparent evidence of student learning* can certainly mean different things to different people. Candidates can't be held accountable for honoring a commitment if they are unclear as to what they are committing to.

To address this problem, the principal should take the necessary time during the interview to explain key terms that capture the culture and processes of the school. An excellent way to accomplish this is to review the very foundation of the school—its written mission, vision, collective commitments, and goals. The principal could ask the candidate to read through the document and react to its contents, or could check for understanding of key terms by asking questions such as:

- "What is your understanding of the term *professional learning community*?"
- "How would you explain the PLC process to someone completely unfamiliar with it?"
- "In what ways, if any, is the PLC process different from traditional schooling?"
- "How would you distinguish between a group and a team?"
- "How familiar are you with the use of team-developed common formative assessments?"
- "What do you see as the advantages or disadvantages of teams' using common formative assessments?"

Once the school year begins, engage the entire staff in reviewing the school's mission, vision, values, and goals. This helps the staff refocus and recommit their collective efforts, while also allowing new staff members to be part of the process.

We have provided a "Glossary of Key Terms and Concepts" reproducible to assist you in building a shared understanding of a common vocabulary. You can access the glossary at **go.SolutionTree.com/PLCbooks**. It is also available in the Tools and Resources section of AllThingsPLC (https://allthingsplc.info/wp-content/uploads/2023/10/Terms.pdf).

We have provided a "Glossary of Key Terms and Concepts" reproducible to assist you in building a shared understanding of a common vocabulary.

Is This Candidate a Good Fit for Our PLC?

Questions to assess if the candidate is a good fit with the big ideas of a PLC:

1. The purpose of our school is to ensure that all students learn, rather than to make sure they are taught. I'm going to present you with four statements. Please tell me which statement is closest to your personal philosophy and elaborate on your thinking.
    a. "I believe all students can learn based on their ability."
    b. "I believe all students can learn if they take advantage of the opportunities we give them to learn."
    c. "I believe all students can learn something, but it is more important that we create a warm and caring environment than fixating on academic achievement."
    d. "I believe all students can learn and we should be committed to doing whatever it takes to ensure all students learn at high levels."
2. If, at the end of the first semester, you discovered that 50 percent of your students were failing, would it trouble you? (*Then drop the percentage:* How about 25 percent? 15 percent? 10 percent?)
3. We have all encountered a student who simply does not want to work, but is not a behavior problem and is not interfering with the learning of others. How have you responded to such a student?
4. One of your colleagues states that there is little a teacher can do to help a student who is just not interested in learning. Would you respond, and if so, how would you respond?
5. How would you respond to this assertion: "The major causes of learning do not fall within the teacher's sphere of influence. Student learning will be determined primarily by factors such as innate ability, parental support, the socioeconomic conditions in which the student lives, and the beliefs and behaviors of the student's peer group."
6. If we are to help all students learn, we must work collaboratively and collectively. How would you respond to the following statement:

    "A teacher is a professional who deserves wide-ranging autonomy regarding what to teach, how to teach, how to assess, and how to run his or her classroom. I would not presume to advise another teacher how to run his or her classroom, and I would not be receptive to a teacher offering unsolicited advice to me."
7. Think of a time when you were part of a group or team that led to better results for its members and a more satisfying professional experience. Think of another time when you were part of a group or team and it was a negative experience. What factors contributed to the difference?
8. Imagine you are on a team that is experiencing significant conflict. How would you respond?

page 1 of 2

9. If you were assigned to a teaching team and encouraged to collaborate, on what questions or issues do you believe the team should focus its efforts?

10. "Do you want to be the teacher with the highest student achievement at our school or a member of a team whose students all achieve at high levels?" (Smith, 2015, p. 6).

11. We say in our vision statement that we will work collaboratively and take collective responsibility for the success of our students. What does that phrase mean to you? Can you give me examples of how a staff might take collective responsibility for student success?

12. It is important to focus on results, rather than intentions. What is your understanding of the terms *formative assessment* and *summative assessment*? Can you cite examples of when and how you have used each of these assessments in your teaching experience? What do you feel is the primary purpose of assessing students?

13. What is your reaction to this statement: "Teachers of the same course or grade level should use common assessments so each member of the team can determine the achievement of his or her students compared to other students attempting to acquire the same knowledge and skills."

14. What is your reaction to this statement: "Teachers and students benefit when evidence of student learning is easily accessible and openly shared among members of the teaching team."

15. It has been said that in most schools the quality of a student's work is assessed primarily upon the idiosyncrasies of the teacher to whom that student is assigned. What is your reaction to that statement? Can you think of steps a school might take to provide more consistent feedback to students?

16. It's the end of your first year. I ask you to provide me with evidence you have been an effective teacher. What will you give me?

Other important questions to explore:

1. What is your understanding of the term *professional learning community*? How would you explain that term to someone completely unfamiliar with it? In what ways, if any, is the PLC process different from traditional schooling?

2. I'm a student in your class the first day. Help me understand your expectations regarding the classroom environment.

3. I'm one of your students. Help me understand the essential knowledge, skills, and dispositions I will acquire as a result of being in your classroom.

4. What does the research tell us about effective teaching strategies?

5. What should I have asked you that I didn't, a question you would want to ask a teaching candidate?

6. If you are offered this position, what could we do to make this a great school year for you?

7. What questions do you have for me?

page 2 of 2

The Need for a More Thoughtful Orientation Program

In the traditional way of entering the profession, teachers are pointed to their classrooms and wished good luck. Research has revealed the most common issues new teachers face: struggles with classroom management, a lack of instructional resources or guidance to assist in their planning, and unsupportive environments in which they are left to fend for themselves (Goodwin, 2012). Too often, new teachers are ill prepared to cope with these challenges along with instructional failures, student boredom, and the crushing sense of loneliness and isolation they are likely to encounter. As a result, for too many new teachers, their good intentions give way to a diminishing sense of self-efficacy and job satisfaction. Unfortunately, school leadership has not effectively responded to these challenges, and teacher stressors have increased significantly since 2020. A Merrimack College report found that as of April 2022, only 12 percent of American teachers reported being satisfied with their jobs (Will, 2022). The primary reasons for this historically low rating include poor and inadequate compensation, increased social and emotional needs of students, public ridicule and vilification, and being stretched too thin. This report affirmed that the COVID-19 pandemic greatly impacted teachers' responses, but many of the challenges teachers shared predated the pandemic.

Doing a better job of clarifying expectations is an important step to address the problem of teacher turnover. But if new teachers are to meet those expectations, the school must provide a much more systematic and effective system of support—a system in which people throughout the school work together in an intentional, coordinated way to achieve the goal of greater teacher retention.

Anthony Muhammad (2018) found that new teacher development is pivotal to the development of a healthy school culture. In healthy school cultures, effective school leaders create systems that intensely develop new teachers' skill level in ways that limit their struggles in the classroom and in the school in general. According to Muhammad (2018):

> [Effective school leaders] felt that if they could shorten the learning curve for their new teachers and help them experience success in the classroom, these teachers would be less likely to suffer from many of the hardships that most new teachers experience. (p. 130)

A coordinated induction system should include the following five characteristics.

1. **A mentor from the same field:** There is mixed evidence on the benefits of providing a new teacher with a mentor. A study of teacher retention found that schools that assigned teachers an individual mentor did no better at improving the teachers' job satisfaction or retention rate (Johnson & Kardos, 2004). The National Commission on Teaching and America's Future (Carroll, 2007), the Alliance for Excellent Education (Haynes, 2014), and the National Center for Education Statistics (Raue & Gray, 2015) all conclude that having a mentor can improve teacher retention and providing a mentor from the same field should be part of a comprehensive induction program.

It is evident that mentoring programs can differ greatly in terms of the frequency and the quality of the interactions between the two teachers. To increase the likelihood of a positive impact on retention, the elements of the mentoring process should be clearly defined and closely monitored, and mentors should embrace their responsibilities rather than view mentoring as an imposition.

2. **A common planning team with members of a grade-level or course-specific collaborative team:** The key factor in teacher retention is the school's culture. Schools that operate as true PLCs foster collaboration, collective responsibility, and commitment to supporting the ongoing learning of their members. These are the cultural characteristics that have proven most effective in cultivating teacher satisfaction and retention (Johnson & Kardos, 2004).

Responsibility for a new teacher's success should not fall solely to a mentor; rather, every collaborative team member and the principal should share the responsibility. When new teachers are clear on the essential learning for each unit of instruction, they know how students will be called on to demonstrate proficiency, they are clear on the criteria students must meet to be deemed proficient, and they know they have colleagues to turn to and talk to when they struggle, they are positioned to be successful. There is no better way to provide ongoing support for new teachers than to engage them in the work of a high-performing teacher team.

Responsibility for a new teacher's success should not fall solely to a mentor; rather, every collaborative team member and the principal should share the responsibility.

To address the concern that new staff members often attend team meetings but fail to contribute, each team should review and revise its team commitments. Sample norms include the following.

- We will share teamwork equally.
- Everyone must be a contributing team member.
- We will elicit all points of view before making decisions.

These norms create an expectation that every team member contributes. Even if a new teacher might not yet have the content expertise to take the lead on creating a team common assessment, for example, the teacher can assist in the process by offering to type up the final product. This division of labor will help new team members feel that they are contributing, and veteran teachers will see the benefits of the new members.

3. **Ongoing supportive communication from the principal:** Principal Geterdone must do far more than invite new teachers to drop by and see him if they need anything. He should schedule weekly individual meetings with new teachers during the first month of the year and monthly meetings during the remainder of the year. These meetings should focus on gaining insights into each teacher's perceptions, experiences, and concerns;

celebrating progress; identifying problems; and offering support. Sample questions to ask include—

- "Is teaching here different from what you expected it would be?"
- "What has gone well for you so far?"
- "What questions or concerns do you have?"
- "Tell me about the next unit you are going to teach. What student outcomes do you anticipate?"
- "What more can we do to help you have a great year?"

This attention to new teachers' well-being should extend to such mundane issues as ensuring every new teacher has at least one person from their team with whom to eat lunch for the first few weeks of school. Each year, the number-one concern of new students at Rick's former high school, Adlai E. Stevenson, was the fear that they would enter the cafeteria and not have any friends to sit with at lunch. That concern is still present for adults, and a school with a supportive environment would eliminate the worry for teachers and students alike.

4. **A reduced course load or the support of a teacher aide:** In most schools, the responsibilities of first-year teachers are indistinguishable from those of a twenty-year veteran. Each will have the same preparation time, be assigned a similar number of students, and confront similar managerial responsibilities, such as communicating with parents, completing report cards, and responding to central office requests.

An environment that is supportive of new teachers recognizes that new teachers benefit from a lighter load in their first year of teaching.

An environment that is supportive of new teachers recognizes that new teachers benefit from a lighter load in their first year of teaching. At the secondary level, new teachers might be assigned a single preparation rather than multiple preparations. At the elementary level, new teachers could have the benefit of a teacher aide each day. At all levels, the school might consider a job-share arrangement in which two new teachers divide their teaching load and are assigned to assist with interventions when not teaching their classes. This arrangement not only reduces their classroom responsibilities but also gives them greater insight into the problems students are experiencing in mastering content.

Lightening a new teacher's responsibilities also includes not assigning them an unusually high number of students with potentially significant behavior problems. Unfortunately, it is common for a new faculty member to inherit the most demanding classes, as most schools determine teacher assignments by seniority. The veteran teachers claim the classes with the most traditionally successful students, leaving the most challenging assignments to the new hires. This practice not only sets new staff members up to fail but also provides the students most at risk with the teachers who are least prepared to meet their needs and ensure their success.

5. **Ongoing professional development geared specifically toward new teachers' needs:** In addition to the other supports for new teachers, schools should provide their newest members with an ongoing professional development program focused on the issues and challenges they are likely to encounter. We recommend a monthly program that teacher leaders and the principal jointly lead. Initial training follows a predetermined curriculum but also provides time for questions at each session. Topics for later sessions could be based on the results of surveys of the new teachers. Sample topics include the following. Notice how March and April will be determined based on the new teachers' input.

    - *August*—Keys to establishing effective classroom management
    - *September*—Effective grading practices
    - *October*—How to engage the unmotivated student
    - *November*—Effective questioning in the classroom
    - *December*—Evidence of student learning to inform instructional practice
    - *January*—Strategies to promote higher-level thinking
    - *February*—Effective cooperative learning structures for the classroom
    - *March*—Topic to be determined based on new teacher input
    - *April*—Topic to be determined based on new teacher input
    - *May*—A great close to the school year

Schools should provide their newest members with an ongoing professional development program focused on the issues and challenges they are likely to encounter.

The Need to Address the Concerns of Veteran Staff Members

To improve retention, Principal Geterdone also needs to address any concerns and dissatisfaction among veteran staff members. Losing them before the PLC process is deeply embedded in the school's culture could represent a major setback. In many organizations, managers only become aware of an employee's level of dissatisfaction during an exit interview, when it is too late to solve the problem. We endorse the strategy of conducting *stay interviews* with staff to express appreciation, discover concerns, and jointly plan how to enrich their jobs and improve their satisfaction (Kaye & Jordan-Evans, 2014, 2021).

Principal Geterdone could meet with key staff members individually and ask questions such as (Kaye & Jordan-Evans, 2014):

- "I want you to know how much I value your contribution to our school. Is there anything you can think of that I could do to enrich your work and improve your satisfaction?"

- "What is the most satisfying aspect of your work? How can we build on that?"
- "Is there something you would like to do or learn to do that will energize your work?"
- "Can you identify specific problems that are getting in the way of your success and satisfaction?"
- "I know you and I are both concerned about the disruption new staff members create when they join a team. Do you have some ideas about how we might address this problem?"
- "What can I do differently to make your experience here better?"

A principal may be reluctant to conduct stay interviews because of a fear that teachers will ask for things that are impossible to provide. There are, however, ways to address this possibility that can make the teacher feel both heard and valued. Consider the following dialogue between Principal Geterdone and one of his key teachers during a stay interview.

> **Principal Geterdone:** *I want you to know how much I value your contributions to your students, your team, and our school. I want you to spend your career here. Can you think of anything I might do to make your experience here more satisfying for you?*
>
> **Ms. Wantmore:** *Well, a $20,000 raise would certainly make me feel better.*
>
> **Principal Geterdone:** *In my mind, you are worth that and more. In fact, I wish all of our teachers could be better compensated for the important work they are doing. But as you know, the district salary schedule determines individual salaries, and we are both bound to honor it. There are, however, some ways that we might be able to increase your income. For example—*
>
> - *If there is a curriculum project you want to work on this summer, I could recommend to the district office that you be approved for compensation from our district's curriculum development fund.*
> - *If you have an interest in teaching summer school, I could give you that assignment.*
> - *We all know you are an expert in integrating technology into the curriculum. I could recommend your approval to teach a course in that subject to interested teachers in the district's after-school professional development program.*
> - *If you have an interest in starting a cocurricular club, and generate student interest in that club, I could seek approval for you to receive a cocurricular stipend.*

- *We are planning to introduce a yearlong new teacher induction program next year, and I would love to have a veteran teacher like you play a role in creating and presenting that program. If the program and stipend are approved, would you be interested?*

These are some initial ideas we might explore. If you have other ideas, I would welcome hearing them, so give it some thought. In the meantime, what else can I do for you other than considering ideas for additional compensation?

The *What else?* question is an effort to help the teacher focus on things that are within the principal's sphere of influence. It won't take long to establish that different teachers are interested in different things. For example, imagine different teachers asking the following questions.

- "I have been thinking about becoming a (counselor, dean, assistant principal). Could you give me an opportunity to job-shadow a person in that position for a semester?"
- "I would love to attend the national conference in my subject area. If I am approved to make a presentation there, will you help fund my participation?"
- "I am trying to finish my dissertation. Would you explore the possibility of me job-sharing with a colleague next year?"
- "My commute is killing me. Would you support my transferring to another school in the district closer to my home?"
- "I feel we may be too focused on academic indicators to monitor student success and not focused enough on other important indicators we should be instilling in our students. I would like to lead a task force to explore what more we could be doing. Would you be willing to endorse such a task force and have me lead it?"
- "I feel I have a lot to offer new teachers. I would like to help with the new teacher induction program next year."
- "I would love to attend a workshop on how to make cooperative learning more effective."
- "I know some of the schools in our district have mathematics coaches to support classroom teachers. Would you consider me for that position in our school?"

Reasonable educators won't expect the principal to provide all the answers, particularly if their requests lie outside the principal's sphere of influence. But a stay interview gives the principal a chance to express admiration and appreciation, demonstrate an interest in the teacher as an individual, help the teacher identify and explore choices, and show a willingness to listen to the teacher's concerns and ideas. Most teachers will welcome this opportunity for dialogue.

Creating an effective recruitment and selection process to ensure candidates are a good fit for both the PLC process and their collaborative team should be a high priority on every principal's agenda.

Creating an effective recruitment and selection process to ensure candidates are a good fit for both the PLC process and their collaborative team should be a high priority on every principal's agenda. But "re-recruiting" key individuals is an equally important step in sustaining the PLC process over time.

Part Three

Here's Why

If a school can only be as good as the educators within it, it makes sense that schools would be intentional in recruiting, hiring, and retaining the very best people. The American public has long recognized this fact. In the forty-seventh annual *Phi Delta Kappan*/Gallup Poll (2015) on schooling, at least 94 percent of members of every subgroup and both political parties identified the quality of teachers as "very important" for improving their schools. It was, by far, the factor most frequently cited as key to school improvement.

Skeptical administrators may object that teacher shortages prevent them from being selective when hiring new staff. There is some truth to that, because the United States is facing a teacher shortage, which was made worse by the COVID-19 pandemic. According to a 2023 report, all fifty U.S. states reported a teacher shortage in at least one content area to start the 2022–2023 school year, and 34 percent of all new teachers in 2021 were not fully certified in the subject they were hired to teach (Darling-Hammond, DiNapoli, & Kini, 2023).

The problem in this hiring environment is twofold: there are fewer teachers entering the profession and more teachers leaving the profession (Baker, 2022). Unlike in the past, leaders do not have the luxury of choosing from a large pool of qualified candidates, so hiring, developing, and retaining new talent is more important than ever. It is safe to say that it is very difficult for a school to function as a high-performing PLC without teachers. It also appears that we cannot rely on government to find the answer for our teacher shortage. States like Arizona have passed laws waiving the bachelor's-degree requirement for teaching in their state, opening up the profession to nearly anyone with a slight interest (Joyce, 2022).

In 2023, the mode years of experience for the United States' teaching force was fifteen years in the profession, according to labor and workforce organization Zippia (McCain, 2023). This same report warns that by 2025, the supply of U.S. teachers will fall short of the demand by more than one hundred thousand people, primarily related to the impact of the COVID-19 pandemic and teacher burnout. These statistics are alarming and validate why development, retention, and improvement of our current teacher workforce is so important to improving school quality and student learning.

Teacher turnover also carries significant *productivity costs*, which in education translate to lower student achievement. Several studies have found that student achievement declines when a succession of new teachers teach students, and students in high-poverty, high-minority schools are far more likely to be regularly assigned to new teachers (Darling-Hammond, 2010; Hargreaves & Fullan, 2012; Mehta, 2014; Rice, 2010). As an analysis of those studies concludes, "Students in high-poverty or high-minority schools are in desperate need of expert, high-quality teachers if their achievement and attainment levels are to improve, yet they are almost twice as likely as other students to have novice teachers" (Watlington, Shockley, Guglielmino, & Felsher, 2010, p. 26). Another study found that the educational achievement of students in historically underserved schools is further jeopardized by chronic teacher turnover, as teachers disproportionately leave schools with high-minority, low-performing student populations. Inexperienced new teachers who quickly turn over more frequently teach students in these schools, and thus, these historically underserved schools spend a larger portion of their resources replacing teachers. In fact, in many of these schools, the teacher dropout rate is higher than the student dropout rate (Carroll, 2007).

As the National Commission on Teaching and America's Future (Carroll, 2007) concludes:

> Until we recognize that we have a retention problem we will continue to engage in a costly annual recruitment and hiring cycle, pouring more and more teachers into our nation's classrooms only to lose them at a faster and faster rate. This will continue to drain our public tax dollars, it will undermine teaching quality, and it will most certainly hinder our ability to close student achievement gaps. (p. 1)

See page 239, "Why Should We Address the Quality of Teachers?" for some further evidence of why schools should be intentional in recruiting and hiring the very best teachers.

Don't Forget the Veterans

Principal Geterdone cannot focus solely on the needs of new teachers entering the school. It is imperative that he also address veteran staff members' needs and concerns. The relationship between an employee and their immediate supervisor is "the prime predictor of both daily productivity and the length of time people stay at their jobs" (Achor, 2010, p. 187). A study of twelve thousand white-collar workers found that employees who felt that their supervisor cared about them and believed their work served an important purpose were three times more likely to stay with their organizations (Schwartz & Porath, 2014). Another study of knowledge workers' satisfaction levels found that the two most important things a leader can do to foster high morale are (1) to create the conditions that allow people to succeed at what they are being asked to do and (2) to recognize progress when it occurs (Amabile & Kramer, 2011).

Attention to re-recruiting veterans, as we have stressed in this chapter, addresses the fundamental needs of feeling valued and appreciated.

Attention to re-recruiting veterans, as we have stressed in this chapter, addresses the fundamental needs of feeling valued and appreciated. After three decades of studying the keys to effective organizations, Jim Kouzes and Barry Posner (2006) concluded, "There are few if any needs more basic than to be noticed, recognized, and appreciated for our efforts. . . . Extraordinary achievements never bloom in barren and unappreciative settings" (p. 44).

The stay-interview format also provides an opportunity to connect the daily work of educators to a larger purpose: making the world a better place by developing the full potential of every student. The one great advantage of a career in education is that it serves an unquestionably moral purpose. It is easy, however, for educators to lose sight of that fact when immersed in their day-to-day activities. The stay interview gives the principal an opportunity to reconnect the work of the school to its fundamental mission. As Daniel Pink (2011) notes, "Nothing bonds a team like a shared mission. The more that people share a common cause . . . the more your group will do deeply satisfying and outstanding work" (p. 174).

Finally, although the principal is a critical figure in initiating the PLC process, that process will not be sustained unless the principal fosters shared leadership of and a strong commitment to that process. Principals need the support of key teachers if their schools are to develop a new culture. Therefore, the best systems are constantly developing widespread leadership to sustain improvement efforts (Mourshed et al., 2010). Principal Geterdone must cultivate that leadership among his veteran teachers.

Why Should We Address the Quality of Teachers?

"Regardless of the research basis, it is clear that effective teachers have a profound influence on student achievement and ineffective teachers do not. In fact, ineffective teachers might actually impede the learning of their students" (Marzano, 2003, p. 75).

"Teachers matter to student achievement more than any other aspect of schooling" (RAND Corporation, 2012, p. 1).

"The quality of an education system cannot exceed the quality of its teachers. The only way to improve outcomes is to improve instruction. High performance requires every child to succeed" (Barber & Mourshed, 2007, p. 4).

"Nationally and internationally, there is unequivocal evidence that the quality of teaching is the most significant in-school factor affecting student outcomes" (Australian Institute for Teaching and School Leadership, 2012, p. 3).

"The most abused educational research finding these days is this: 'the quality of the teacher is the single most important determinant in the learning of the student.' . . . Therefore, reward the best teachers and get rid of the bottom performers. But the highest performing countries realize the main point is not the effect of the individual teacher, for better or for worse, here and there that counts, but rather how you maximize the cumulative effect of many, many teachers over time for each and every student. Students do very well because they have a series of good teachers—not by chance, but by design" (Hargreaves & Fullan, 2012, p. 16).

"There is a constant clamor to emphasize the teacher is the key, with claims that the system is only as good as the teacher and that teacher standards must be raised. In many ways this is correct, except that teachers cannot do it on their own: they need support, they need to collaborate with others in and across schools, they need to develop expertise, and they need excellent school leaders" (Hattie, 2015b, p. 29).

"Teaching is a multifaceted human endeavor, involving a complex, moment-by-moment interplay of different categories of knowledge. Teachers' knowledge, pedagogical competence, and reasoning are keys to improving student learning achievement" (Jacob, John, & Gwany, 2020, p. 14).

"Hiring is a complex process involving several often-overlapping phases and influencers. Rigorous research is needed to inform each hiring phase, but what has been conducted to date is woefully inadequate in certain areas, such as the teacher job search process. Understanding teacher candidates' experiences and perspectives seems especially key, given that hirers often already demonstrate that they know their own preferences" (Perrone & Meyers, 2021, pp. 43–44).

Good News: Consensus on the Solution

The single most significant factor in whether new teachers have a positive or negative experience is the culture of the school in which they work.

Given the costs and negative consequences of high teacher turnover and the need for widespread leadership to sustain an improvement process, educators can take heart in the fact that there is widespread consensus among researchers regarding how to address both issues. The single most significant factor in whether new teachers have a positive or negative experience is the culture of the school in which they work. (See page 241, "Why Is a Focus on Hiring and Retaining Practices Important?") When teachers have positive perceptions of their work environment, their principal, and the cohesion and support of their colleagues, they are more likely to remain in their school because of their high level of satisfaction with their work. These positive relationships have a more significant impact on teacher retention than student demographics or teacher salaries, even under the weight of teaching during a global pandemic (Almy & Tooley, 2012; Camp, Zamarro, & McGee, 2022). The researchers consistently describe the very conditions that characterize a PLC.

Part Four

Assessing Your Place on the PLC Journey

It is important to help your staff build shared knowledge regarding your school's current status in addressing the critical step on the PLC journey of selecting, orienting, and retaining staff. We have created a tool to assist you in that effort. "The Professional Learning Communities at Work® Continuum: Selecting and Retaining New Instructional Staff Members" and "The Professional Learning Communities at Work® Continuum: Retaining Veteran Staff Members" on pages 242 and 244 are also available at **go.SolutionTree.com/PLCbooks** as free reproducibles. Once your staff have established greater clarity regarding the current status of your collaborative teams, we urge you to turn your attention to the "Where Do We Go From Here?" worksheets that accompany the continua (on pages 243 and 245 and also available for free download at **go.SolutionTree.com/PLCbooks**). They will prompt you to take the action necessary to close the knowing-doing gap.

Why Is a Focus on Hiring and Retaining Practices Important?

"Almost every other profession has a better system of induction for new members than teachers . . . beginning teachers need a chance to learn what constitutes good practice with the help of accomplished colleagues instead of being forced to figure everything out for themselves" (Shanker, 1995, as cited in Consortium on Productivity in the Schools, 1995, p. 53).

"Schools with greater staffing stability are more interdependent organizations. These schools have strong leaders, and the teachers work together in professional communities" (Johnson, 2011, p. 24).

"Teachers who work in supportive contexts stay in the classroom longer, and improve at faster rates, than their peers in less-supportive environments" (Papay & Kraft, 2015).

"The need to hire and support well-prepared teachers is clear. But to sustain the growth of those teachers over time, they should be inducted into a genuine learning organization. In such an organization, the expectation is that all members of the school's community share responsibility for each other's continued growth and success, as well as for the success of all students in the school. Transforming a school into a genuine learning organization calls for the creation of a school culture in which novice and experienced teachers work together to improve student achievement" (Carroll, 2007, p. 8).

"Schools with high stability cultivate a strong sense of collaboration among teachers and their principal. Teachers are likely to stay in schools where they view their colleagues as partners with them in the work of improving the whole school and the conditions are well-suited for them to have the potential to be effective" (Allensworth, Ponisciak, & Mazzeo, 2009, as cited in Haynes, 2014, p. 4).

"The key difference between [teachers] who have good beginnings and those who have painful ones, between those who feel like they are getting better and those who are not, is the quality of the school's culture and level of support" (Hargreaves & Fullan, 2012, p. 69).

"Teachers' learning opportunities influence the degree to which teachers develop a sense of collective efficacy. Teachers from low-poverty schools were more likely to describe how collaborative learning occurred in their schools, often by a school's expert teachers having time to work closely with novices, constructing joint lessons, assessing each other's student work, and seeing each other teach" (Berry, Bastian, Darling-Hammond, & Kini, 2021).

"Teacher stress has been linked to turnover (i.e., mobility and attrition), which is critical given concerns about teacher shortages and the links between turnover and student achievement" (Steiner & Woo, 2021, p. 2).

The Professional Learning Communities at Work® Continuum: Selecting and Retaining New Instructional Staff Members

DIRECTIONS: Individually, silently, and *honestly* assess the current reality of your school's implementation of each indicator listed in the left column. Consider what evidence or anecdotes support your assessment. This form may also be used to assess district or team implementation.

Our school has a thorough process for selecting new instructional staff that includes input from several sources and evidence of the candidate's teaching effectiveness. Once a new staff member is hired, we have an ongoing process of orientation that ensures the teacher has the benefit of a collaborative culture, the wisdom of his or her colleagues, and ongoing monitoring and support.

Indicator	Pre-Initiating	Initiating	Implementing	Developing	Sustaining
Our instructional staff selection process includes input from several sources and evidence of the candidate's teaching effectiveness. We have an intentional orientation program that ensures new staff members have the ongoing support of both their teammates and the administration.	Hiring decisions are made by the personnel office. The school site has little or no say regarding who will be assigned to the school. The orientation for new staff members is limited to the first week of school and focuses on helping new staff members learn about policies and procedures.	The principal has the major responsibility for hiring decisions. The principal makes those decisions primarily based on his or her perceptions of candidates during the interview process. New staff members may be assigned a mentor.	The principal solicits the opinion of others in making hiring decisions. The assistant principal, department chairperson, or team leaders are included in the interview process. They have worked together to create interview questions that present the candidates with scenarios to determine if they will be a good fit for the PLC process and for their potential team. The collaborative team process is considered the primary strategy for supporting new staff members as they make their transition into the school.	Because the collaborative team is primarily responsible for ensuring new staff members have a positive experience in the school, team members participate in the interview and selection process. In addition to scenario-based questions, the process includes a thorough review with each finalist of the team's norms, essential outcomes, common assessments, and protocols for analyzing data. The principal and team also observe finalists teach an essential skill. Once a candidate is hired, every team member accepts responsibility for his or her success. The principal continues to meet with the new staff members on a regular basis. Teacher leaders have created an ongoing professional development program based on the needs of new teachers. The program is presented each month.	Selection and orientation of new staff members are recognized as a joint responsibility of teachers and administrators. Members of a teaching team are fully engaged in the selection process, and their perceptions and preferences play a major role in hiring. Teachers have assumed the leadership role in the monthly orientation program. Every new staff member recognizes that there are many people to turn to and talk to for assistance who are interested in their success. The comprehensive orientation process is so much a part of the school's culture that it continues without interruption even when the principal and key teacher leaders are no longer at the school.

Where Do We Go From Here? Worksheet
Selecting and Retaining New Instructional Staff Members

Indicator of a PLC at Work	What steps or activities must be initiated to create this condition in your school?	Who will be responsible for initiating or sustaining these steps or activities?	What is a realistic timeline for each step or phase of the activity?	What will you use to assess the effectiveness of your initiative?
Our instructional staff selection process includes input from several sources and evidence of the candidate's teaching effectiveness. We have an intentional orientation program that ensures new staff members have the ongoing support of both their teammates and the administration.				

The Professional Learning Communities at Work® Continuum: Retaining Veteran Staff Members

DIRECTIONS: Individually, silently, and *honestly* assess the current reality of your school's implementation of each indicator listed in the left column. Consider what evidence or anecdotes support your assessment. This form may also be used to assess district or team implementation.

Our school has a process to identify and seek to remove obstacles to teacher satisfaction and our school's progress on the PLC journey. Expressions of appreciation and admiration are commonplace throughout the school. The leadership team conducts stay interviews with key staff to explore ways to enrich their jobs.

Indicator	Pre-Initiating	Initiating	Implementing	Developing	Sustaining
Our school has a low rate of teacher turnover because of an ongoing process to create the conditions that lead to high levels of teacher satisfaction. We recognize that working together to make our school a high-performing PLC is a key factor in creating the satisfaction and sense of accomplishment that lead to high teacher retention rates.	There is no process for gathering information about the concerns and hopes of veteran staff members outside of the negotiation process. Administrators are often surprised to hear the concerns and question how widespread they might be.	The personnel office administers teacher satisfaction surveys each year and conducts exit interviews when staff members leave the district to find out why they are leaving.	The principal meets with a representative group of teachers on a quarterly basis to identify and address issues that are of concern to the faculty.	The principal makes a point to express appreciation to staff members individually and collectively. The principal sends personal notes of appreciation to individual members of the staff on a regular basis. The school's progress on the PLC journey is noted and celebrated.	The leadership team recognizes that one of its primary responsibilities is to identify and remove obstacles and impediments so that educators can succeed at what they are being asked to do. The principal conducts stay interviews with key individual staff members to express appreciation and explore strategies for enriching their jobs.

Where Do We Go From Here? Worksheet
Retaining Veteran Staff Members

Indicator of a PLC at Work	What steps or activities must be initiated to create this condition in your school?	Who will be responsible for initiating or sustaining these steps or activities?	What is a realistic timeline for each step or phase of the activity?	What will you use to assess the effectiveness of your initiative?
Our school has a low rate of teacher turnover because of an ongoing process to create the conditions that lead to high levels of teacher satisfaction. We recognize that working together to make our school a high-performing PLC is a key factor in creating the satisfaction and sense of accomplishment that lead to high teacher retention rates.				

Part Five

Tips for Moving Forward: Selecting and Retaining Staff

1. **Solicit input from veterans:** Ask current teachers to reflect on their own orientation to the school and how the process can be improved, the skills and traits they feel are most important for new teachers to bring to the school and team, and the questions they feel will be most helpful in assessing a candidate's fit for the school.

2. **Determine what is essential to know about your school:** Clarify the most important aspects of the school culture that each candidate should be made aware of as a result of the interview process.

3. **Engage the prospective team in the selection:** Facilitate a process to help each team prepare to interview finalists and observe them in the classroom.

4. **Include staff members in orientation and ongoing professional development:** Solicit teacher leaders to help create the different elements of the curriculum for the monthly new-teacher professional development program.

5. **Conduct follow-up contact for new hires:** Require team leaders or mentors to contact new hires after the board of education has approved them and before the school year starts to welcome them to the team, answer any questions, and offer assistance in helping the new teachers make the transition to the school.

6. **Respond to stay-interview discussions:** Be certain to have a follow-up discussion after the stay interview with veteran staff. Let staff members know what actions you have taken as a result of the conversation.

Part Six

Questions to Guide the Work of Your Professional Learning Community

To promote the importance of selecting, orienting, and retaining staff for work in a PLC, ask:

1. If a candidate were to ask how working in a PLC is different from working in the traditional school setting, how would we respond?

2. What are the personal skills and traits that we hope our new colleagues will bring to our school?

3. How can we best determine who has those skills and traits?

4. How invested are we in the success of our new colleagues? How do we demonstrate our investment?

5. How would we like the orientation we provide our new colleagues to be similar to or different from our own orientation to the profession?

6. What steps can the administration take (that are within its sphere of influence) to help us succeed at what we are being asked to do?

7. How do we express appreciation and admiration to one another in our school? Can we do a better job in this area?

Part Seven

Dangerous Detours and Seductive Shortcuts

Selecting the right people for the PLC process is vitally important.

Stephen Covey (1989, 2013) points out that there is a difference between *urgent* and *important.* Urgent matters demand immediate attention and quick steps. Selecting the right people for the PLC process is vitally important. Every vacancy presents an opportunity to improve the school and improve a collaborative team. But if the vacancy remains unfilled the week before school opens, *urgent* will trump *important.* The priority becomes finding someone to assign to the classroom regardless of the fit. Avoid the temptation to procrastinate when it comes to hiring. Enter the market early and be thorough and thoughtful in the selection process. Attention paid to the front end of the hiring process can save hours of future grief caused by the prospect of removing a bad hire. More importantly, students deserve the very best teacher a principal can find.

Particularly at the secondary level, principals are tempted to hire the candidate who helps plug the most holes. So the candidate who has minimum certification in science and social studies but is willing to be an assistant football coach gets priority over a candidate with a stronger academic background who teachers feel is a better fit for their team and the school. Principals must remember that every hiring decision conveys their priorities and values to the staff. Administrative appeals for excellence will be muted if expediency is consistently the driving force in decisions.

Part Eight

Digging Deeper—Recommended Resources

The following resource delves deeper into the topic of hiring, orienting, and retaining new staff.

- *Building Your Building: How to Hire and Keep Great Teachers* by Jasmine K. Kullar and Scott A. Cunningham (2020)

Final Thoughts

Regardless of how carefully a school hires and supports new faculty, it is possible that a new hire might prove to be the wrong fit for the school or might not possess the innate qualities needed to be an exceptional teacher and teammate. When this is the case, it is critical that the principal have the courage to dismiss the teacher. Undoubtedly, taking this step can be uncomfortable and difficult. But if a school is committed to ensuring every student's success, then it must hire and retain exceptional educators. A weak link in the chain can break the progress of the entire team.

School leaders communicate most powerfully by what they do and what they say. In the next chapter, we consider two important forms of communicating what is important: (1) confrontation and (2) celebration.

CHAPTER 10

Addressing Conflict and Celebrating

Part One

The Case Study: Responding to Resistance

David C. Roth, the principal of Van Halen High School (mascot: the Rockers), was annoyed. He knew how hard he had worked to build consensus for moving forward with the professional learning community concept. He provided the entire staff with research and readings on the benefits of PLCs. He sent key teacher leaders to conferences on PLCs and used those staff members as a guiding coalition to promote the concept. He encouraged interested staff to visit schools that had successfully implemented the PLC process. He met with the entire faculty in small groups to listen to their concerns and answer their questions. Finally, at the end of this painstaking effort to build shared knowledge, he used the fist to five technique, which revealed an overwhelming majority of the faculty was ready to move forward. He assigned teachers to subject-area teams and asked each team to work collaboratively to establish its norms, clarify the essential outcomes of its courses, and develop common assessments to monitor student proficiency.

Within a month, the sophomore English team met with Principal Roth to ask if the team could exempt one of its members from meetings. The team explained that Fred made it evident he was opposed to the entire idea of collaborative teams and common assessments. Fred made no effort to contribute, and his ridicule and sarcasm were undermining the team. Principal Roth assured the team that he would look into the situation and attempt to remedy it.

The next day, Principal Roth called Fred to his office to discuss Fred's attitude toward his colleagues and the collaborative team process. After listening to the principal's concerns, Fred expressed his unhappiness with what he felt was a heavy-handed, top-down dictate to work in teams. He argued that many staff members had voted to support the process only because they were afraid of repercussions from the principal if they opposed it. He pointed out that he had been a "fist" when the vote was taken, and that he remained convinced the PLC process was just the latest fad the administration had cooked up. It was fine with him if the team did not want him to participate, because he had no interest in participating. He had always been an effective teacher, and he did not need some artificial process of working with colleagues to become effective.

Principal Roth resented Fred's characterization of the decision-making process. As he expressed that resentment, it became evident that the emotions of both men were becoming more heated. Principal Roth decided the prudent course would be to adjourn the meeting.

Throughout the day, the principal struggled with his dilemma. On the one hand, he was not amenable to exempting Fred from the PLC process. He was wary of establishing a precedent that released overt resisters from the obligation to contribute to their collaborative teams. He was concerned that others on staff would resent devoting time and energy to collaboration if their colleagues were able to opt out of the process. On the other hand, he knew Fred could be difficult, and he considered it unlikely that Fred could be persuaded to change his attitude.

After much deliberation, Principal Roth decided to ask the English team to continue working with Fred in the hope that his attitude would improve over time.

Reflection

Consider Principal Roth's approach to dealing with a staff member who was unwilling to support the process. What is your reaction? Can you identify alternative strategies the principal might have used that would have been more effective?

Part Two

Here's How

In chapter 2 (page 33), we offered suggestions for developing consensus: create a guiding coalition, build shared knowledge, and dialogue with staff members in small groups to listen to and address concerns. Principal Roth was attentive to each of these suggestions, yet he still encountered difficulties. Let's examine some next steps he might take.

Recognize the Need to Confront

A staff that have built a solid foundation for a PLC by carefully crafting consensus regarding their purpose, the school they seek to create, their collective commitments, the specific goals they will use to monitor their progress, and the strategies for achieving those goals have not eliminated the possibility of conflict. The response to the disagreements that inevitably occur determines the real strength of a school committed to the PLC process. Every organization will experience conflict, particularly when the organization is engaged in significant change. Every collective endeavor will include instances when people fail to honor agreed-on priorities and collective commitments. The ultimate goal, of course, is to create a culture that is so strong and so open that members throughout the organization will use the violation as an opportunity to reinforce what is valued by bringing peer pressure to bear on the offender, saying, in effect, "That is not how we do it here." In the interim, however, it typically will be the responsibility of the leader (that is, the principal or administrator) to communicate what is important and valued by demonstrating a willingness to confront when appropriate. Nothing will destroy a leader's credibility faster than an unwillingness to address an obvious violation of what the organization contends is vital. Leaders must not remain silent; they must be willing to act when people disregard the purpose and priorities of the organization.

Leaders must not remain silent; they must be willing to act when people disregard the purpose and priorities of the organization.

Confrontation does not, however, involve screaming, demeaning, or vilifying. It is possible to be tough-minded and adamant about protecting purpose and priorities while also being tender with people. Kerry Patterson and his colleagues (2002) study the challenge of conducting difficult conversations. They contend that skillful communicators reject the false dichotomy of the "sucker's choice": "I can either be honest and hurtful *or* be kind and withhold the truth." Instead, they search for the Genius of And—a way to be both honest *and* respectful and say what needs to be said to the people who need to hear it without brutalizing them or causing undue offense (Patterson et al., 2002).

Ten strategies Patterson and colleagues (2002) offer for engaging in honest and respectful dialogue include the following.

1. Clarify what you want and what you do not want to result from the conversation—for yourself, for the other person, and for the relationship—before initiating it.
2. Create a safe environment for honest dialogue.
3. Clarify if you will be addressing a specific incident of behavior, a pattern of repeated behavior, or the impact the behavior is having on the individual's relationships with others.
4. Be concise when presenting the problem. Frame the conversation in terms of a gap between expectations and actions.
5. Attempt to find mutual purpose.
6. Use facts because "gathering facts is the homework required for holding an accountability discussion" (Patterson, Grenny, Maxfield, McMillan, & Switzler, 2013, p. 95).
7. Share your thought process that has led you to engage in the conversation.
8. Encourage recipients to share their facts and thought process.

9. Explain both the natural consequences and the potential for disciplinary action if the behavior continues.

10. Clarify the specific behavior that must be demonstrated and the process to be used both for monitoring and for following up.

Understand Cultural Change Versus Technical Change

Though we respect and honor the work of researchers like Kerry Patterson who have advanced the literature on organizational change, change in schools is unique. In 1932, sociologist Willard Waller wrote:

> Schools have a culture that is definitely their own. There are, in the school, complex rituals of personal relationships, a set of folkways, mores, and irrational sanctions, a moral code based upon them. There are games, which are sublimated wars, teams, and an elaborate set of ceremonies concerning them. There are traditions and traditionalists waging their world-old battles against innovators. (p. 96)

School change is multidimensional. It happens at two levels: (1) technical change and (2) cultural change (Muhammad, 2018). Effective change in schools requires a strategic focus on both dimensions of change.

"Technical changes are changes to the tools or mechanisms professionals use to do their jobs effectively" (Muhammad, 2018, p. 22).

"*Technical changes* are changes to the tools or mechanisms professionals use to do their jobs effectively" (Muhammad, 2018, p. 22). Technical changes are important. Effective improvement requires consistent analysis and action in relationship to curriculum, time for tasks (like collaboration), protocols, policies, and technology. Technical change will always be necessary because systemic challenges will always change and evolve, and the tools needed to respond will have to change as well. Leaders are constantly exposed to innovations, and it can be tempting to embrace each one. Leaders should resist this temptation because too much technical change can have an adverse effect on the culture. Douglas Reeves (2021) refers to the crush of implementing too many changes as *innovation fatigue*. Leaders must consider the number of proposed technical changes they place on the shoulders of educators as a school plans its improvement journey. Robert J. Marzano and Timothy Waters (2009) have found that when school systems institute too many technical changes simultaneously, the sheer scope can overwhelm practitioners and create an aversion toward change itself.

Cultural change involves active influence on a school's "norms, values and beliefs, rituals and ceremonies, symbols and stories that make up the 'persona' of the school," according to Kent D. Peterson (as cited in Education World, n.d.). Even a cursory review of literature on the change process indicates that meaningful, substantive, sustainable improvements can occur in an organization only if those improvements become anchored in the organization's culture: *the assumptions, beliefs, values, expectations, and habits that constitute the norm for that organization.* Some refer to school culture as the *hidden curriculum*, or the deeply held assumptions that propel a school to success or anchor it in stagnation (Wren, 1999). A 2019 study of 156 California schools with student test proficiency in mathematics and reading ranking at or above the state performance average despite student poverty rates above 50 percent found that the only factor all 156 schools had in common was a positive school culture (Podolsky, Darling-Hammond, Doss, & Reardon, 2019).

Cultural change *involves active influence on a school's "norms, values and beliefs, rituals and ceremonies, symbols and stories that make up the 'persona' of the school" (Kent D. Peterson as cited in Education World, n.d.).*

Leaders often use the terms *culture* and *climate* interchangeably. These two concepts, however, are profoundly different. To put it simply, climate is how we feel and culture is how we behave; culture is "the way we do things around here" and climate is "the way we feel around here" (Gruenert & Whitaker, 2015, p. 10). It is not unreasonable that a group of educators might feel good about themselves and their school community but still behave in unproductive ways. It is important for Principal Roth to consider whether his uneasiness with Fred's resistance to the PLC process is rooted in a concern for the school's climate or the school's culture.

Consider both forms of change in the following context: If a person desires to cultivate a productive garden, they need to prepare the garden's soil so planted seeds will germinate and blossom. When considering organizational change, think of technical change as gathering the right *seeds* and cultural change as preparing the right *soil* conditions. Both are essential to achieve a bountiful harvest, but one task is much more difficult than the other. It takes a lot of sweat equity, strenuous labor, and patience to till, fertilize, and hydrate soil. If a gardener is not willing to commit to this work, and places seeds in bad soil, the likelihood of reaping a good harvest will be very low. Schools often think they can cheat the change process and compensate for their unwillingness to cultivate culture by seeking technical changes that can provide them with a shortcut. Principal Roth needs to consider whether he has created the culture (soil) that the staff, including Fred, need to thrive in the PLC at Work process.

The by-product of this sustained effort to improve culture is a *positive school culture*. According to Muhammad (2018), a positive school culture is a place where:

> 1. Educators have an unwavering belief in the ability of all their students to achieve success, and they pass that belief on to others in overt and covert ways.
>
> 2. Educators create policies and procedures and adopt practices that support their belief in every student's ability. (p. 20)

Creating this type of environment greatly enhances the improvement process. The impatience with cultural change and the haste to mandate technical changes have doomed many schools in their PLC at Work journeys.

Courageous, moral leadership presents our best chance to change culture. Principal Roth cannot allow Fred to stubbornly subvert the will of the masses. If he is allowed to simply opt out of the essential function of being a contributor to a high-performing team, sustained schoolwide implementation will be nearly impossible. Plainly put, if you let one person exit the bus, you give permission for everyone else to exit the bus.

Use the *Time for Change* Framework for Building Consensus

The human component of systemic change and improvement is infinitely more complex than the structural component. Professor Zhouying Jin (2011) describes this challenge as the conflict between *soft technology* (human beings) and *hard technology* (structures and inanimate objects). Jin (2011) states that soft technology change challenges "the realm of ideology, emotion, values, worldview, individual and organizational behaviors, as well as human society" (p. 11). In essence, changes in practice or structure do not implement themselves; they require the cooperation of human beings.

Recognition of the human being as the center of the cultural change process is paramount in successful cultural change. University of Michigan professor Robert E. Quinn (1996) notes:

> There is an important link between deep change at a personal level and deep change at an organizational level. To make deep change is to develop a new paradigm, a new self, one that is more effectively aligned with today's realities. This can happen only if we are willing to journey into unknown territory and confront the wicked problems we encounter. (p. 9)

So what are the challenges we face—the deep challenges that make creating a PLC culture more difficult? What are the paradigm shifts that have to occur personally, organizationally, and socially for us to create a culture in which all students can learn at high levels? Perhaps Fred's needs have not been met and his hesitance is symptomatic of a deeper, more personal issue that Principal Roth could meet if he truly understood the change process. Resistance to change is usually less about a person's desire to be difficult and more about unmet needs. As we outlined previously, the COVID-19 pandemic has caused unprecedented physical and emotional strain on teachers. Combine that with an unprecedented teacher shortage, and it is more important than ever before that Principal Roth gain Fred's commitment rather than simply discard him.

What exactly is it that effective leaders do when transforming the culture of their organization? Do they resort to tight leadership—imposing a new regimen and demanding employees adhere to the direction established from the top? Or do effective leaders change their organization's culture by using a loose approach to leadership that encourages those within the organization to pursue their own independent interests and initiatives in the belief that such freedom and autonomy will spark the energy and enthusiasm necessary for significant change?

DuFour and Fullan (2013) argue that this question of loose versus tight leadership represents the essential dilemma of large-scale school reform:

> How should leaders engage people in the complex process of cultural change? Should they be tight—assertive, issuing top-down directives that mandate change? Or should they be loose—merely encouraging people to engage in the change process, but leaving participation optional? The challenge at all levels of the system is

> to navigate this apparent dichotomy and find the appropriate balance between tight and loose, between assertiveness and autonomy. If we know anything about change, it is that ordering people to change doesn't work, nor does leaving them alone. (p. 33)

We argue that change requires *both* loose and tight conditions. It would not be wise to address Fred's resistance from a singular perspective. As Quinn (1996) notes, people are not simple beings. Finding the proper balance in leadership can be a challenge. If the goal of change is improvement, then leaders must be skilled in influencing others to improve their practice. A leader's success is measured by their ability to positively influence others.

In *Time for Change: Four Essential Skills for Transformational School and District Leaders*, coauthors Anthony Muhammad and Luis F. Cruz (2019) assert that the ability to influence others lies in the leader's ability to understand and meet the needs of those they lead. When a person is not changing, it means that a need has not been met, and resistance is a symptom of that unmet need. Principal Roth should view Fred not as a problem, but as a victim of a need still unmet. Four basic human needs must be satisfied in order for change to occur (Muhammad & Cruz, 2019).

1. **Cognitive need:** "Why is change necessary, and why is your vision best suited to meet this need?"
2. **Emotional need:** "Why should I trust you to lead me in this process?"
3. **Professional capacity need:** "Am I equipped to meet this new requirement?"
4. **Need for accountability:** "Will I be required to participate, even if I don't want to?"

Instead of using the terms *loose* and *tight*, Muhammad and Cruz (2019) use the terms *support* and *accountability*. Most professionals respond to the complexity of cultural change when they receive adequate support, and some change simply because there is a demand for performance. No one strategy alone garners systemic change, but a combination of these loose and tight strategies can create the right atmospheric conditions for substantive change.

Support must precede accountability because it is unfair to hold someone accountable for a task they have not had preparation to implement (Muhammad & Cruz, 2019). It is unreasonable to expect a school leader to naturally embody all the characteristics associated with change leadership because of the complexity of the human condition. Instead, Muhammad and Cruz (2019) suggest that filling staff's needs should be the responsibility of a leadership team whose members have diverse skill sets. Principal Roth should not have to tackle this task alone. To meet their staff's basic needs, or confront Fred's resistance to the PLC at Work process, a leadership team should become adept at an approach that includes four critical leadership skills: (1) communicating the rationale (fulfilling the cognitive need), (2) establishing trust (fulfilling the emotional need), (3) building capacity (fulfilling the professional capacity need), and (4) getting results (fulfilling the need for accountability).

Communicate the Rationale

People tend to resist change to practice and lack motivation to improve when leaders have not skillfully communicated the rationale or case for improvement. To embrace a vision, people have to clearly understand the vision and feel personally compelled to contribute to the vision. Perhaps Principal Roth did not communicate the change's urgency through compelling data or evidence and artifacts that validate a need to change the status quo. Perhaps Principal Roth assumed that Fred had the same understanding of the PLC at Work process that he possesses, and Fred's apprehension is based on a misunderstanding of the potential power of the process. Maybe Fred would be more agreeable if he had a deeper understanding of the PLC at Work process and its profound potential benefit for students and teachers.

Establish Trust

A leader needs the very essential ability to connect with others' emotions. Facts and objective evidence alone do not inspire people; people need to connect with their leader on a personal level and know that their leader has not just an intellectual connection but an ethical connection to their purpose. Perhaps Fred has unhealed wounds from mistreatment by a school leader who served before Principal Roth. A sincere and empathetic conversation focusing on his emotional well-being may be all that Fred needs to cooperate.

Build Capacity

People will more willingly take a risk and try a new idea if leaders have prepared them professionally. Leaders must invest in training, resources, and time if they want educators to enthusiastically embrace new ideas and practices. Perhaps Fred is insecure about his ability to perform with such a seismic shift in professional practice. It can be scary to move from isolation to collaboration, clarify essential standards, create and analyze the results of common assessments used formatively, and help or extend students based on their evidence of learning. It may be wise for Principal Roth to engage Fred in a dialogue about his readiness and confidence in the skills that are required of a teacher to be successful in a PLC at Work.

Get Results

Ultimately, improvement cannot be optional. Effective leaders must skillfully assess and meet the needs of those they lead, but eventually, they have to demand full participation in the change and improvement process. After Principal Roth and his leadership team have done an honest assessment of their support for Fred and the rest of the faculty, and they have effectively provided for the first three needs, all that remains is a demand for performance through the use of authority. Principal Roth should consider an open, frank dialogue with Fred concerning communication of purpose, issues of trust, and professional support. If Fred cannot provide a valid reason why these needs are still unmet, Principal Roth has no choice but to use the power of his office to create labor parameters that closely monitor Fred's collaborative behaviors without consideration for how he feels. If Fred's position is that Principal Roth cannot make him change, all that Principal Roth can do is use the means at his disposal to prove to him that he can. This course of action will lead to a reluctant change of behavior or create the right conditions for Fred to leave the faculty and the school (Muhammad & Cruz, 2019).

Part Three

Here's Why

As we emphasized in chapter 2 (page 33), research consistently concludes that effective leaders build a shared vision and purpose that bind people together. But unless the vision and purpose result in the desired action, nothing is accomplished. So what are leaders to do when some members of the organization are opposed to taking action that is critical to moving forward? Effective leaders do not wait for unanimity, but instead build shared knowledge until they have created a critical mass of those willing to act—and then they move the organization forward without expecting universal support. When they do move forward, they can expect conflict.

Managing Conflict

Transforming traditional schools and districts into PLCs requires that people "do things that they have never done before—not just to get better at what they have always done" (Schlechty, 2009, p. 4). Those leading the PLC process at any level must recognize that conflict is an inevitable by-product of this substantive change process (Evans, 1996; Lieberman, 1995; Louis, Kruse, & Marks, 1996). In fact, an absence of conflict suggests the changes are only superficial because "conflict and disagreements are not only inevitable but fundamental to successful change" (Fullan, 2007, p. 21).

The challenge, then, is not to eliminate or avoid conflict. The challenge is to learn how to manage conflict productively.

The challenge, then, is not to eliminate or avoid conflict. The challenge is to learn how to manage conflict productively. Effective leaders will surface the conflict, draw out and acknowledge the varying perspectives, and search for common ground that everyone can endorse (Goleman et al., 2004). When managed well, conflict can serve as an engine of creativity and energy (Saphier, 2005), clarify priorities (Bossidy & Charan, 2002), and develop stronger teams (Lencioni, 2005).

Because conflict should be not only expected but desired in a PLC, it is critical to plan for this reality when creating a school mission and collective commitments. Members should agree that decisions in a learning-focused school must be based on what research and evidence have proven to best improve student learning. Subsequently, when disagreements arise regarding the specific actions the school or team should take, team members should not argue their individual opinions but instead share research and evidence to advocate for their positions.

Repeated conflict over the same issues can certainly represent a drain on an organization's time and energy, and at some point, there is a need for closure. But when educational leaders at the district or school level avoid confrontation because they favor keeping the peace over productive conflict, they can do tremendous damage to any improvement process.

Celebrating

When celebrations continually remind people of the purpose and priorities of their organization, members are more likely to embrace the purpose and work toward agreed-on priorities.

For the purposes of communicating what is important, the flip side of confrontation is celebration (Amabile & Kramer, 2010; Kanold, 2011; Kouzes & Posner, 2006). When celebrations continually remind people of the purpose and priorities of their organization, members are more likely to embrace the purpose and work toward agreed-on priorities. Regular public recognition of specific collaborative efforts, accomplished tasks, achieved goals, team learning, continuous improvement, and support for student learning reminds staff of the collective commitment to create a PLC. The word *recognize* comes from the Latin word for "to know again." Recognition provides opportunities to say, "Let us all be reminded and let us all know again what is important, what we value, and what we are committed to do. Now let's all pay tribute to someone in the organization who is living that commitment."

Most schools and districts, however, will face a significant challenge as they attempt to integrate meaningful celebration into their cultures. The excessively egalitarian culture of schools makes it difficult to publicly recognize either individuals or teams. In most schools and districts, generic praise ("You are the best darn faculty in the state!") and private praise ("I want to send you a personal note of commendation") are acceptable—public recognition is not. Generic praise and private praise are ineffective in communicating priorities because neither conveys to the members at large what specific actions and commitments are valued, and therefore, neither is effective in shaping behavior or beliefs. As Peter F. Drucker (1992) advises, "Changing habits and behavior requires changing recognition and rewards . . . [because] people in organizations tend to act in response to being recognized and rewarded" (p. 195). Tom Peters (1987) puts it this way: "Well-constructed recognition settings provide the single most important opportunity to parade and reinforce the specific kinds of new behaviors one hopes others will emulate" (p. 307).

We offer the following four suggestions to those who face the challenge of incorporating celebration into the culture of their school or district.

1. **Explicitly state the purpose of celebration:** The rationale for public celebration should be carefully explained at the outset of every celebration. Staff members should be continually reminded that celebration represents—
    - An important strategy for reinforcing the school's or district's shared purpose, vision, collective commitments, and goals
    - The most powerful tool for sustaining the improvement initiative
2. **Make celebration everyone's responsibility:** Recognizing extraordinary commitment should be the responsibility of everyone in the organization, and each individual should be called on to contribute to the effort. If the formal leader is the sole arbiter of who will be recognized, the rest of the staff can merely sit back and critique the choices. All staff members should have the opportunity to publicly report when they appreciate and admire the work of a colleague.
3. **Establish a clear link between the recognition and the behavior or commitment you are attempting to encourage and reinforce:** Recognition must be specifically linked to the organization's purpose, vision, collective

commitments, and goals if it is to play a role in shaping culture. As Rick and Bob write—

> Recognition will have little impact if a staff believes [the] recognition is presented randomly, that each person deserves to be honored regardless of [their] contribution to the improvement effort, or that rewards are given for factors unrelated to the goal of creating a learning community. (DuFour & Eaker, 1998, p. 145)

It is imperative, therefore, to establish clear parameters for recognition and rewards. The answer to the question, "What behavior or commitment are we attempting to encourage with this recognition?" should be readily apparent. Recognition should always be accompanied with a story relating the efforts of the team or individual back to the core foundation of the school or district. It should not only express appreciation and admiration but also provide others with an example they can emulate.

4. **Create opportunities to have many winners:** Celebration will not have a significant effect on the culture of a school if most people in the organization feel they have no opportunity to be recognized. In fact, celebration can be disruptive and detrimental if there is a perception that recognition and reward are reserved for an exclusive few. Establishing artificial limits on appreciation—such as, "We honor no more than five individuals per meeting," or "Only those with five or more years of experience are eligible"—lessens the impact celebration can have on a school or district. Developing a PLC requires creating systems specifically designed not only to provide celebrations but also to ensure that there are many winners.

Frequent public acknowledgments of jobs well done and a wide distribution of small symbolic gestures of appreciation and admiration are far more powerful tools for communicating priorities than infrequent grand prizes that create a few winners and many losers. An effective celebration program will convince every staff member that they can be a winner and that their efforts can be noted and appreciated.

An effective celebration program will convince every staff member that they can be a winner and that their efforts can be noted and appreciated.

Four Keys for Incorporating Celebration Into School or District Culture

1. Explicitly state the purpose of celebration.
2. Make celebration everyone's responsibility.
3. Establish a clear link between the recognition and the behavior or commitment you are attempting to encourage and reinforce.
4. Create opportunities to have many winners.

Adlai E. Stevenson High School in Lincolnshire, Illinois, is often cited as a school that has used celebration to communicate purpose and priorities and to shape culture (Deal & Peterson, 1999; DuFour & Eaker, 1998; Kanold, 2006; Schmoker,

2006). Stevenson does not offer a Teacher of the Year program, but over several decades, it has distributed thousands of Super Pat awards (small tokens of appreciation that represent a pat on the back for a job well done) to hundreds of teachers. In fact, since 1995, Stevenson has *never* had a faculty meeting without celebrating the effort and commitment of individuals and teams. Stevenson also surveys its seniors each year to ask, "Which staff member has had the most profound impact on your life and why?" The students' heartfelt responses are then published in an internal kudos memorandum and distributed to the entire staff each quarter. Staff members have read thousands of testimonials citing specific examples of how they and their colleagues are making a difference in the lives of students. Stevenson employees receive ongoing reminders of the school's priorities and the commitments to those priorities that are honored, and every staff member feels they have the opportunity to be recognized and celebrated as a winner.

When educators are wary of making celebration part of their school or district, they frequently raise a concern that frequent celebration will lose its impact to motivate. Yet research has drawn the opposite conclusion; it reaffirms that frequent celebration communicates priorities, connects people to the organization and to each other, and sustains improvement initiatives (Amabile & Kramer, 2011; Kegan & Lahey, 2001; Kouzes & Posner, 2003; Peters, 1987).

A commendation should represent genuine and heartfelt appreciation and admiration. If that sincerity is lacking, celebration can be counterproductive.

Can celebration be overdone? Absolutely. The criterion for assessing the appropriateness of a team or individual recognition should be the sincerity with which the recognition is given. A commendation should represent genuine and heartfelt appreciation and admiration. If that sincerity is lacking, celebration can be counterproductive.

Celebrations allow for expressions of both appreciation and admiration. Appreciation lets others know we have received something we value, something we are happy to have. Admiration conveys the message that we have been inspired or instructed by observing others' work and commitments. When admiration and appreciation are repeatedly expressed, organizations create a culture of ongoing regard that sustains effort because such language is "like pumping oxygen into the system" (Kegan & Lahey, 2001, p. 102).

Celebrations also provide an opportunity to use one of the oldest ways in the world to convey the values and ideals of a community: telling stories. As Kouzes and Posner (2003) write, "The intention of stories is not just to entertain. . . . They're also intended to teach. . . . Good stories move us. They touch us, they teach us, and they cause us to remember" (p. 25). Good stories appeal to both the head and the heart and are more compelling and convincing than data alone. They bring data and evidence to life and persuade people to act in new ways (Pfeffer & Sutton, 2006). Good stories personify purpose and priorities. They put a human face on success by providing examples and role models that can clarify for others what is noted, appreciated, and valued. They represent one of the most powerful tools for shaping others' thinking and feelings (Grenny, Patterson, Maxfield, McMillan, & Switzler, 2013).

Finally, a multiyear study of what motivates knowledge workers concludes that the best motivator is celebration of progress (Amabile & Kramer, 2010). The study advises leaders to set clear overall goals, sustain the commitment to the pursuit of those goals, proactively create both the reality and the perception of progress, and celebrate even incremental progress (Amabile & Kramer, 2010).

An excellent way to predict any organization's future behavior is to examine the people and events the organization elects to honor (Buckingham, 2005). This is true of schools in particular. In his study of school culture, organizational psychologist Robert Evans (1996) concludes, "The single best low-cost, high-leverage way to improve performance, morale, and the climate for change is to dramatically increase the levels of meaningful recognition for—and among—educators" (p. 254).

Study after study of what workers want in their jobs offers the same conclusion: they want to feel appreciated (Kouzes & Posner, 2003). Yet Robert Kegan and Lisa Laskow Lahey (2001) concluded that almost every organization or work team they've spent time with "astonishingly undercommunicates the genuinely positive, appreciative, and admiring experiences of its members" (p. 92).

One challenge every organization will face in implementing a comprehensive improvement effort is how to sustain the momentum of that effort over time. Experts on the process of organizational change offer very consistent advice regarding that question (see page 262, "Why Should Celebration Be Part of Our Culture?").

Part Four

Assessing Your Place on the PLC Journey

It is important to help your staff build shared knowledge regarding your school's current status in addressing the critical step on the PLC journey of responding to conflict and celebration. We have created a tool to assist you in that effort. "The Professional Learning Communities at Work® Continuum: Responding to Conflict" on page 263 is also available at **go.SolutionTree.com/PLCbooks** as a free reproducible. Once your staff have established greater clarity regarding the current status of your collaborative teams, we urge you to turn your attention to the "Where Do We Go From Here?" worksheet that accompanies the continuum (on page 264 and also available for free download at **go.SolutionTree.com/PLCbooks**). It will prompt you to take the action necessary to close the knowing-doing gap.

Why Should Celebration Be Part of Our Culture?

"In successful change efforts, empowered people create short-term wins—victories that nourish faith in the change effort, emotionally reward the hard workers, keep the critics at bay, and build momentum. Without sufficient wins that are visible, timely, unambiguous, and meaningful to others, change efforts inevitably run into serious problems" (Kotter & Cohen, 2002, p. 125).

Milestones that are "identified, achieved, and celebrated" represent an essential condition "for building a learning organization" (Thompson, 1995, p. 96).

"Remembering to recognize, reward, and celebrate accomplishments is a critical leadership skill. And it is probably the most underutilized motivational tool in organizations" (Kanter, 1999, p. 20).

"Win small. Win early. Win often" (Hamel, 2002, p. 202).

"The most effective change processes are incremental—they break down big problems into small, doable steps and get a person to say 'yes' numerous times, not just once. They plan for small wins that form the basis for a consistent pattern of winning that appeals to people's desire to belong to a successful venture. A series of small wins provides a foundation of stable building blocks for change" (Kouzes & Posner, 1987, p. 210).

"Specific goals should be designed to allow teams to achieve small wins as they pursue their common purpose. Small wins are invaluable to building members' commitment and overcoming the obstacles that get in the way of achieving a meaningful, long-term purpose" (Katzenbach & Smith, 1993, p. 54).

"When people see tangible results, however incremental at first, and see how the results flow from the overall concept, they will line up with enthusiasm. People want to be a part of a winning team. They want to contribute to producing visible, tangible results. When they feel the magic of momentum, when they can begin to see tangible results—that's when they get on board" (Collins, 2001, p. 178).

"Reward small improvements in behavior along the way. Don't wait until people achieve phenomenal results" (Patterson et al., 2008, p. 205).

"Small successes stimulate individuals to make further commitments to change. Staffs need tangible results in order to continue the development of their commitment to the change program and small steps engender understanding as well" (Eastwood & Louis, 1992, p. 219).

"Celebration in school provides consistent reinforcement about what is important. People often celebrate what they value, such as holidays and birthdays, for example. How schools celebrate learning and those who help students learn says a lot about how much the school values learning" (Muhammad, 2018, p. 126).

"The results of the study indicated that the dimension of the social need has the highest mean score than other dimensions. Hence, teachers' well-being in terms of social needs is very essential for school organizations, especially regarding the social relationships between teachers and colleagues, and the social responsibility of a teacher" (Zakaria, Don, & Yaakob, 2021, p. 644).

The Professional Learning Communities at Work® Continuum: Responding to Conflict

DIRECTIONS: Individually, silently, and *honestly* assess the current reality of your school's implementation of each indicator listed in the left column. Consider what evidence or anecdotes support your assessment. This form may also be used to assess district or team implementation.

We have established processes for addressing conflict and use conflict as a tool for learning together in order to improve our school.

Indicator	Pre-Initiating	Initiating	Implementing	Developing	Sustaining
Members of the staff recognize that conflict is an essential and inevitable by-product of a successful substantive change effort. They have thoughtfully and purposefully created processes to help use conflict as a tool for learning together and improving the school.	People react to conflict with classic fight-or-flight responses. Most staff members withdraw from interactions in order to avoid contact with those they find disagreeable. Others are perpetually at war in acrimonious, unproductive arguments that never seem to get resolved. Groups tend to regard each other as adversaries.	Addressing conflict is viewed as an administrative responsibility. School leaders take steps to resolve conflict as quickly as possible. The primary objective in addressing disputes is to restore the peace and return to the status quo.	Teams have established norms and collective commitments in an effort both to minimize conflict and to clarify how they will address conflict at the team level. Nonetheless, many staff members are reluctant to challenge the thinking or behavior of a colleague. If the situation becomes too disturbing, they will expect the administration to intervene.	Staff members have created processes to help identify and address the underlying issues causing conflict. They are willing to practice those processes in an effort to become more skillful in engaging in crucial conversations that seek productive resolution to conflict.	Staff members view conflict as a source of creative energy and an opportunity for building shared knowledge. They have created specific strategies for exploring one another's thinking, and they make a conscious effort to understand as well as to be understood. They seek ways to test their competing assumptions through action research and are open to examining research, data, and information that support or challenge their respective positions. They approach disagreements with high levels of trust and an assumption of good intentions on the part of all members because they know they are united by a common purpose and the collective pursuit of shared goals and priorities.

Where Do We Go From Here? Worksheet Responding to Conflict

Indicator of a PLC at Work	What steps or activities must be initiated to create this condition in your school?	Who will be responsible for initiating or sustaining these steps or activities?	What is a realistic timeline for each step or phase of the activity?	What will you use to assess the effectiveness of your initiative?
Members of the staff recognize that conflict is an essential and inevitable by-product of a successful substantive change effort. They have thoughtfully and purposefully created processes to help use conflict as a tool for learning together and improving the school.				

Part Five

Tips for Moving Forward: Addressing Conflict and Celebrating

1. **Practice the skill of difficult conversations:** Teach and practice skills for dealing with conflict.

2. **Create cues you can use to refocus when participants seem to be resorting to fight or flight:** Signal time-out or simply ask, "Are we moving away from dialogue?"

3. **Remember that gathering facts is the prerequisite homework for any crucial conversation:** What are the facts you can bring to the dialogue?

4. **Build shared knowledge when faced with contrasting positions:** Seek agreement on what research or evidence could help lead to a more informed conclusion.

5. **Use action research to explore differences:** Create strategies that allow participants to put their theories to the test.

6. **Refer to your shared foundation:** Recognize that resolving conflict is more productive when members find common ground on major issues and approach one another with an assumption of good intentions.

7. **Be patient:** Remember that you are attempting to develop new skills that will require practice. Therefore, "don't expect perfection; aim for progress" (Patterson et al., 2002, p. 228). Be tender with one another.

8. **Use what you know about celebration:** Apply each of the suggestions presented earlier in the chapter when attempting to introduce celebration as part of your school culture. Explicitly state the purpose of celebration, make celebration everyone's responsibility, establish a clear link between the recognition and the behavior or commitment you are attempting to encourage and reinforce, and create opportunities to have many winners.

Part Six

Questions to Guide the Work of Your Professional Learning Community

To assess how your school addresses conflict, ask:

1. Has a conflict emerged in our school in the past? How was that conflict addressed?

2. Are we building shared knowledge and conducting action research in an effort to address conflict productively? Can we cite an example in which we resolved a difference of opinion through examining the research or conducting our own action research?

3. What is the process we currently use to resolve conflict? What skills could we identify and practice to become more effective in this important area?

4. Do we view conflict as something to be avoided?

5. Do we expect administrators to resolve conflict or do we work together to address it in ways that improve our effectiveness?

6. Are we developing our skills to hold crucial conversations?

To assess the presence of celebration in your school, ask:

7. What gets publicly celebrated in our school?

8. Do our public celebrations reinforce our purpose and priorities?

9. Have we created opportunities for lots of people in our organization to be recognized and celebrated?

Part Seven

Dangerous Detours and Seductive Shortcuts

Don't assign responsibility for confrontation to others. In *Crucial Conversations*, Patterson and his colleagues (2002) conclude what makes teams effective is not the absence of conflict but rather how the teams deal with conflict. Bad teams ignore it, letting it fester until the situation deteriorates into fight or flight—people bickering unproductively or not attending meetings. Good teams go to the boss and ask them to resolve the problem. Great teams deal with the issue themselves, recommitting to norms or establishing new norms to address the issue.

Principals cannot expect every team to start off as a great team. . . . As teams become more mature and sophisticated in the process, they should assume greater responsibility for addressing their own problems.

Principals cannot expect every team to start off as a great team. Principals will inevitably be called on to intervene when teams experience problems, and they should not shirk that responsibility. As teams become more mature and sophisticated in the process, they should assume greater responsibility for addressing their own problems.

Another example of deflecting responsibility to others is when a leader addresses an issue with a staff member but explains that they are doing someone else's bidding. For example, the principal who advises a teacher of the need for change because "the central office wants you to do this" is abdicating responsibility and undermining a systematic effort.

Don't use blanket announcements to deal with individual problems. Ineffective leaders will sometimes seek to avoid personal confrontation by sending out general admonitions regarding inappropriate behavior. Not only does this typically fail to impact the inappropriate behavior, but it also is offensive to those who are not acting in that way.

Part Eight

Digging Deeper—Recommended Resources

The following resources delve deeper into the topic of addressing conflict and celebrating.

- *Transforming School Culture: How to Overcome Staff Division, Second Edition* by Anthony Muhammad (2018)
- *Time for Change: Four Essential Skills for Transformational School and District Leaders* by Anthony Muhammad and Luis F. Cruz (2019)

- *100-Day Leaders: Turning Short-Term Wins Into Long-Term Success in Schools* by Douglas Reeves and Robert Eaker (2019)
- *Cultures Built to Last: Systemic PLCs at Work* by Richard DuFour and Michael Fullan (2013)
- *Leaders of Learning: How District, School, and Classroom Leaders Improve Student Achievement* by Richard DuFour and Robert J. Marzano (2011)
- *Leading With Intention: Eight Areas for Reflection and Planning in Your PLC at Work* by Jeanne Spiller and Karen Power (2019)
- *Leading Beyond Intention: Six Areas to Deepen Reflection and Planning in Your PLC at Work* by Jeanne Spiller and Karen Power (2022)
- *Leading by Design: An Action Framework for PLC at Work Leaders* by Cassandra Erkens and Eric Twadell (2012)

Final Thoughts

As we have stressed throughout this book, how people behave is a much more powerful way to communicate their priorities than what they say or write in documents that are too often filed away and forgotten. One way leaders best convey their priorities is by what they pay attention to. Confronting behavior that violates the purpose and priorities of the school or district and publicly celebrating behavior that reflects the purpose and priorities are very effective ways to communicate what is important. The skillful use of confrontation and celebration has not traditionally been part of the culture of most schools; however, effective leaders of PLCs will develop and model these skills if they hope to sustain the PLC process.

Although we have referenced district leadership at various points throughout the book, most of the case studies have focused on the school site. Districts can, however, play a very important role in implementing the PLC process in all their schools. We turn our attention to a district's attempt to do so in the next chapter.

CHAPTER 11

Implementing the PLC Process Districtwide

Part One

The Case Study: The High Cost of Failing to Speak With One Voice

Superintendent Matt Ditka prided himself on being a take-charge, action-oriented leader who wanted the very best for all the schools in Dunning-Kruger School District. When he identified a powerful concept or program that he felt would improve the district, he was determined to do whatever was necessary to introduce it to educators in every school.

Superintendent Ditka was particularly enthused about the professional learning community concept after attending an institute on the topic. He was convinced that it offered the most promising strategy for sustained and substantive improvement for the schools in his district, and he resolved to make implementation of the concept a districtwide initiative. He provided the board of education with information about PLCs and persuaded the board to adopt a goal to implement the concept throughout the district. He also obtained board approval for funding to train the principals and teacher leaders from every school to ensure they had the knowledge, skills, and tools to bring the PLC process to life. He purchased books on the PLC process for each member of the central office cabinet and every principal, and he encouraged them to visit schools that had been identified as Model PLCs.

Superintendent Ditka charged the district's professional development department with providing the PLC training. The department created a plan to provide six days of training for the principal and five representatives of each of the district's 150 schools. Each training session was designed to build on the knowledge and concepts presented at earlier sessions. The district's financial commitment to the initiative was extraordinary. The cost of securing 4,500 substitute teachers to cover classes for all the staff who attended the training represented a major investment in this districtwide initiative.

Superintendent Ditka directed his five area assistant superintendents to oversee implementation. Each of these administrators supervised about thirty schools, but they took very different approaches to the PLC initiative. Two of the assistant superintendents attended every day of training and huddled with principals at lunch each day to discuss their concerns and answer their questions. At the end of the training, they stipulated that all the principals in their area were expected to address certain nondiscretionary priorities, and they clarified the indicators they would monitor to assess the progress that each school was making. From that point on, all their meetings with principals focused on addressing and resolving PLC implementation questions.

Two other assistant superintendents were convinced that administrative mandates were ineffective in improving schools. They believed that their job was to provide educators with exposure to ideas and concepts, but to avoid top-down mandates. So they asked the principals and teacher leaders in their schools to attend the training in the hope that making them aware of the PLC process would motivate them to act on the concept. These assistant superintendents attended some of the training; however, they left the question of implementation to the discretion of each principal.

The last of the assistant superintendents did not attend the training, nor did she stipulate that principals were to attend. She informed her principals of the number of participants they were expected to send to each session, but she offered no other direction. Many of the principals in her area did not attend any of the training. In several instances, principals sent a different group of teachers to each of the sessions. These participants had no background on what had occurred during earlier training and no clear reason as to why they were attending.

Two years later, Superintendent Ditka had to acknowledge that the district's PLC initiative had produced very uneven results. Some of the schools had made tremendous strides, experienced significant gains in student achievement, and energized their staffs with the positive momentum they were experiencing. Other schools had dabbled in some elements of the PLC process but had little to show for their efforts. Still others had done virtually nothing. He was puzzled. He had clarified the goal of transforming all the district's schools into PLCs, secured the board's support, and publicly announced the initiative to the community and to educators throughout the district. He had asked the professional development department to create a plan to provide training to representative staff from every school. He had devoted district resources to support that extensive training. Why were there such dramatic differences in the quality of implementation when all schools had been operating under the same directive, been the beneficiaries of the same plan, and received the same level of support? Why had his effort to implement the PLC process throughout the district yielded such disappointing results?

Reflection

Can a central office successfully implement a substantive improvement initiative in schools throughout a district, or is school improvement something that must occur one building at a time?

Part Two

Here's How

Superintendent Ditka has done a lot of things right in this scenario. He made an effort to build shared knowledge about PLCs with his board and his administrators through articles, books, visitations, and dialogue. He secured the support of the board in articulating that implementation of the PLC process was a district priority. He attempted to foster a district culture that was simultaneously loose and tight by publicly articulating what was to be tight—all schools were to function as PLCs. He provided training to assist representatives from each school in implementing the process and directed resources to support the initiative. District leaders did a lot of things well, yet despite all of this, the results were disappointing. What went wrong? What more could he have done?

Before answering the questions of what went wrong and what more could have been done, the district should consider another question: What was the root cause of the disappointing results? Was it possible PLC was the wrong process to implement? Or could it be that PLC was the right process, and the disappointing results were because the right process was poorly implemented?

A growing body of scholarly research and anecdotal evidence has established the effectiveness of the PLC process. Ditka and his colleagues can be confident the decision to implement PLCs was the right choice. Therefore, it is far more likely that the reason the results were disappointing lay in how the PLC process was implemented.

Form Collaborative Teams at Every Level

Successful districtwide implementation of the PLC at Work process requires structural and cultural alignment of the work at every level, from the school board to the classroom, including the entire support staff—in other words, *everyone, every day*. Any successful organization is more than an incremental assembly of random parts resulting from years of disjointed decision making. The phrase, "That is the way we have always done it around here," rings true in many districts. Successful districtwide implementation of the PLC at Work process requires purposeful planning, aligned with the day-to-day work at every level.

Successful districtwide implementation of the PLC at Work process requires structural and cultural alignment of the work at every level.

In their book *Leading PLCs at Work Districtwide: From Boardroom to Classroom*, Robert Eaker, Mike Hagadone, Janel Keating, and Meagan Rhoades (2021) provide a detailed description of how White River School District in Buckley, Washington, aligned their PLC work in a way that was both top-down and bottom-up, doable, and most importantly, effective. Recognizing that every district is different and alignment will need to be adapted to meet individual needs, the White River approach can serve as a starting point for effective districtwide alignment. The following sections describe the alignment of work in White River (adapted from Eaker et al., 2021).

The School Board and Superintendent Team

Alignment in White River School District begins at the top with the school board and superintendent team. It is important to think of the school board and the superintendent as a *team*. The school board and superintendent team models the work that is expected of others throughout the district. As Eaker and colleagues (2021) point out:

> What would lead us to believe that other teams in a district will seek to perform at a higher level more than the team that has the primary responsibility for ensuring high levels of learning for all students throughout the district . . . ? (p. 8)

The school board and superintendent team is the model that drives the work throughout the entire district.

The District Leadership Team

This team is composed of district administrators, principals, and other key individuals from across the district, including teachers, building learning coordinators, and support staff team leaders. The teachers (and others) who attend these meetings vary depending on the topics on the agenda. For example, if the agenda topic is a review of districtwide third grade reading data school by school, principals might bring a third-grade team leader with them to the meeting. This team focuses primarily on analyzing and improving student learning data school by school, grade by grade, subject by subject, and goal by goal.

Additionally, this team anticipates issues and questions that are likely to arise and determines the most effective ways to prevent and address them. When appropriate, this team will practice and rehearse the work that is going to be expected of the teacher teams throughout the district. This makes them better prepared to assist teams with questions and issues with which they might struggle.

The Building Leadership Team

It would be virtually impossible to overstate the importance of the building leadership team. While the district leadership team is the primary link between the school board and superintendent and the schools, the building leadership team is the primary link between the school-level leadership and the teacher and support staff teams. Although others may be included, the building leadership team is composed of the principal and *each team leader* within the school. This team's members meet regularly, at least every other week, and their work mirrors the work of the district leadership team. That is, they review learning data, anticipate problems and issues, and develop strategies for how to best approach each one, and when appropriate, they practice and rehearse the work that teacher teams will be asked to engage in.

Teacher Teams

The use of teacher teams is the primary structural characteristic of schools that successfully embed the PLC at Work process. Teacher teams are composed of teachers who teach the same or similar content. Teacher teams are responsible for improving the learning of *every* student, skill by skill, as well as improving student behavior. They collaboratively plan units of instruction and focus their work around the four critical questions of learning described in chapter 2 (page 33). Like other teams, teacher teams review learning data, and using the district and school goals as a foundation, they set learning improvement goals for both students and their own work as a team.

Support Staff Teams

In a successful PLC, the district leadership organizes the support staff into teams. Since every district is different, there is no one right way to organize support staff teams, but generally, they are composed of personnel who have the same or similar jobs and responsibilities. Examples of support staff teams are clerical, maintenance, transportation, and food service teams. These teams meet regularly, following a preset agenda. Each team has a team leader and develops and utilizes team norms, sets improvement goals, and anticipates problems and issues. In short, support staff teams in a PLC operate much like other teams throughout the district, creating a system of shared leadership and collective responsibility for student learning.

The Implementation Team

There is one last team to consider—the implementation team, which is an ad hoc body charged with the task of facilitating a successful implementation process. Membership of the implementation team is diverse by design and includes representation from every role and level in the district. Whether the implementation team is created as a separate, independent body or as a subset of the district leadership team, its sole purpose is to promote the alignment of district resources by serving as the single point of contact for clarity and communication about the implementation process. (See Part Three, page 286, for more information on the benefits of implementation teams.)

Be Intentional and Systematic With Implementation

Scholars have identified hundreds of theories, models, and frameworks that describe the implementation process (Shelton & Moise, 2022). While no single theory, model, or framework has proven to be more effective than all others, researchers have identified three elements common to nearly all of them.

1. **Implementation happens over time and progresses through a series of steps, stages, or phases:** According to researchers at the National Implementation Research Network (2020), "Implementation stages do not always end as the next begins; stages often overlap, and activities can cross stages" (p. 3). Leaders should understand that there also may be times when different schools, departments, or grade levels within the same organization are in different stages at the same time.
2. **The implementation process simultaneously affects multiple audiences and levels within the organization:** There are a lot of moving parts and pieces to monitor during a districtwide implementation effort. The presence of an implementation team—charged with the responsibility of

coordinating, communicating, and aligning resources among, between, and across the different audiences and stakeholders—is critical to the success of a district's implementation effort and outcomes.

3. **There is a dynamic synergy among the culture, the context, and the evidence-based practice being implemented:** The many theories, models, and frameworks are all designed to close the gap between theory and practice. Understanding barriers and enablers of a successful implementation and applying those insights to the process itself will influence the overall effectiveness of an organization's efforts and outcomes.

Implementation proceeds in a predictable and knowable pattern. Examining the process through the lens of a stage-based framework provides the implementation team with a way to organize the process and monitor the initiative's progress. It is the implementation team's job to understand how the implementation process unfolds (by what steps or stages and in what order) and to use those insights to monitor and adjust resources in order to maximize the likelihood of success.

Here, we describe the implementation process in six stages.

1. Exploring
2. Adopting
3. Learning about the work
4. Doing the work
5. Innovating
6. Sustaining

Stage 1: Exploring

The first task during exploration is to create a team that will monitor the implementation process. Membership should include administrative and teacher leaders, including formal leaders with the authority to allocate resources as well as informal leaders with the ability to influence others. It is recommended that the implementation team "draw together multiple types of expertise and skills, from a range of different perspectives, to guide and support the implementation process" (Sharples, Albers, Fraser, & Kime, 2019, p. 10).

The consensus is organizations that invest in implementation teams are more likely to get the kind of results they seek (Fixsen, 2013). Unlike most of the teams described previously, the implementation team has the singular purpose of maintaining the focus, advocating for support, and monitoring progress of the implementation process.

Once established, the implementation team's initial undertaking is to learn as much as possible about the evidence-based practice—in this case, PLC—that is being implemented. Members explore relevant research, read articles, attend conferences, and reach out to colleagues with similar experience to ascertain how implementing the PLC process might impact teaching and learning in their district or at their school. Sharing information from a variety of sources and formats "is essential to increasing awareness of innovations and prompting professionals to consider the need to make changes in current practice" (Fixsen, Naoom, Blasé, & Wallace, 2007, p. 5). This process of collective inquiry builds a foundation of shared knowledge about PLCs.

Next, the implementation team addresses a series of important questions. First, the team should determine if the district (or school) is ready, willing, and able to prioritize the implementation of PLCs over other competing initiatives. The team's conversation should focus on what it will take to fully implement PLCs; we know from experience that when leaders are unable to resist the impulse to add more and more initiatives, the effort to implement the PLC process will certainly fail.

As the second part of this conversation, the team should begin creating a list of ineffective, outdated, and irrelevant policies, practices, and procedures that could be eliminated to make room for PLC. Creating a stop-doing list operationalizes the commitment to prioritize the implementation of PLCs over other initiatives and reinforces the message that fully implementing the PLC process is the top priority.

Finally, the team works to clearly define and disseminate expectations for the faculty and staff. According to Fullan (2007), "Leaders need to set clear and consistent expectations about implementation with frequency, consistency, and accuracy to produce intended results." To do this well, the team needs to identify what is loose and what is tight.

These initial tasks are critical and worth the investment of time. Only after learning as much as possible about the PLC process, agreeing to limit other competing initiatives, creating a stop-doing list, and identifying what is loose and tight is the team ready to begin building a rationale for why implementing the PLC process is important.

Questions to Ask After Stage 1—Exploring

- Has the district (or school) created a team to oversee the implementation of the PLC process? Is the team's charge clear, and have the team's responsibilities been shared and understood throughout the district?
- What evidence was used to determine the appropriateness of, readiness for, and rationale in support of implementing the PLC process?
- Are there any policies, practices, and procedures that can be stopped or eliminated to free up time and resources to support the implementation of PLCs?
- How will the district or school monitor the PLC initiative? What evidence will be gathered to demonstrate progress, and how often and with which audiences will that evidence be shared?
- Has the implementation team conducted a premortem exercise to identify potential stumbling blocks?
- What outcome will be considered a success? What are some short-, medium-, and long-range indicators of successful implementation?

Stage 2: Adopting

This stage begins when the decision is made to move forward with implementation of the PLC process. Adoption requires that the implementation team engage in three tasks: (1) communicate a clear and compelling vision of the PLC process, (2) seek commitment through a consensus to implement the PLC process, and (3) secure the resources necessary to support PLC implementation.

To build the rationale for why PLC matters, the implementation team gathers data and other pertinent information to establish the current reality. The goal for the team is to describe in vivid detail what PLCs will look like when fully implemented. Every effort should be made to avoid drafting an unrealistic and generic vision statement full of platitudes and educational buzzwords. An effective rationale should be aspirational, but it also must be pragmatic and attainable; otherwise, it's not worth the paper it's printed on.

To breathe life into the process of *why*, the implementation team should ask and answer a series of practical questions such as, "What milestones will we look for?" "How often will the team assess the progress of implementation?" and "What evidence of progress will we monitor?" Leaders must remember, "If you can't write it down, it doesn't exist"; thus, if the team cannot answer these kinds of questions, it is a sign the rationale is not yet clear, concise, or coherent enough to be communicated.

It is not uncommon at this stage to confuse the dissemination of information about PLCs with the understanding and implementation of PLCs. Establishing the effectiveness of an innovation is important but is not enough to guarantee that teachers will incorporate it into their regular and routine classroom practice. "What is important is that we first engage staff members in building shared knowledge of certain key assumptions and critical practices and then call upon them to act in accordance with that knowledge" (DuFour, DuFour, Eaker, & Many, 2010, p. 53). District- and building-level leaders must remember the single most important outcome of the adoption stage: ensuring everyone understands the why behind the proposal to implement PLCs.

The implementation team should leverage as many opportunities and methods as possible to communicate why the PLC process matters. It is virtually impossible to overcommunicate why the PLC process is vital to the mission, so whether the work is being done at the district or building level, every member of the team shares the responsibility to communicate. This is the first of several opportunities for the team to speak with one voice.

Leadership's next assignment is to ensure that faculty and staff have a legitimate opportunity to reach consensus on the proposal to implement PLC. Questions about how this new initiative will impact individual teachers are commonplace, and these conversations often challenge the faculty and staff to examine existing beliefs and practices. The implementation team should look to provide opportunities for dialogue while simultaneously being responsive to questions and concerns.

The goal is not total buy-in or unanimous agreement. Consensus does not suggest that everyone agrees with the idea of implementing PLCs or that anyone has changed their fundamental beliefs about teaching and learning; it simply means everyone has had a chance to say what they need to say, and the will of the group is clear even to those who most oppose the idea.

Douglas Reeves (2009) reminds leaders of an important truth: "Implementation precedes buy-in; it does not follow it" (p. 44). He points out that "most people must engage in a behavior before they accept that it is beneficial; then they see the results, and then they believe that it is the right thing to do" (Reeves, 2009, p. 44). At this stage, the goal is to reach consensus to move forward with the expectation that everyone will make an honest effort to implement the PLC process with fidelity. Once the faculty and staff reach consensus, it is critical to turn that consensus into a commitment among members of the implementation team to do whatever it takes to promote the successful implementation of the PLC process.

A lot of the work thus far has involved extensive preplanning. It is important that leadership review the plans to ensure the necessary resources (time, money, personnel) are in place before moving to the next stage. You can tell a lot about a district's or school's values, beliefs, and priorities by the way resources are allocated. Evidence of a commitment to PLCs includes things like money for training and release time earmarked in the budget, structural supports such as time for teams to meet during the regular school day codified into the master schedule, relevant policies and procedures reviewed and revised, and expectations for teachers and administrators clarified and publicly shared.

During the adoption stage, communicating with stakeholders is the priority. The guiding coalition accomplishes this important responsibility by:

- Communicating a compelling vision of why the PLC process is important
- Reaching consensus on the need for, and a commitment to, the successful implementation of the PLC process
- Ensuring that the necessary time, money, and support for the PLC process are in place

Questions to Ask After Stage 2—Adopting

- How confident are we (based on what evidence) that the rationale for why the PLC process is important has been shared with, and understood by, the faculty and staff?
- What evidence can we cite that indicates the faculty and staff have reached consensus? Have adequate opportunities been provided to ask questions, provide input, and express concerns?
- Have we clarified what is tight and what is loose? Has this information been shared with faculty and staff?
- Have adequate resources—time, money, and personnel—been allocated for a successful implementation?
- Is there a commitment to implement PLCs as the primary means of school improvement? Is there a pledge, promise, or commitment to resist initiating competing initiatives?

Stage 3: Learning About the Work

Stage 3 is where most of the formal training takes place. Implementation of any initiative benefits from high-quality professional development delivered prior to, coinciding with, and following the introduction of new policies, programs, or procedures. It is important to give teachers a variety of professional development opportunities of different formats that are offered at different times and in different settings. These may include, but are not limited to, attending workshops and conferences, engaging in book studies and relevant professional reading, visiting other classrooms or schools, altering incentive structures, or simply having time to reflect on the work as part of collaborative team meetings. At this stage of implementation, the focus is on learning, and the district must provide multiple opportunities to build shared knowledge and common vocabulary about PLCs through the process of collective inquiry.

The use of the term *PLC* has become pervasive, and many teachers have had prior experiences with a version of the PLC process—experiences that may have been good or bad. Elements of the PLC process are often misunderstood, misinterpreted, or misconstrued; therefore, the implementation team should anticipate that teachers' levels of background knowledge of PLCs will be in many different places. Whatever professional development opportunities are offered to teachers must accommodate new learning, relearning, and the recalibrating of prior learning.

The emphasis during this stage of implementation is learning. And while the need for ongoing professional development continues long after the official training is complete, Jonathan Sharples, Bianca Albers, Stephen Fraser, and Stuart Kime (2019) warn, "A common mistake in implementing new programs and practices is only providing up-front training, with little or no follow-on support" (p. 31). As the professional development needs of teachers evolve and change, so too should the response.

Clearly, completion of the formal training in stage 3 does not mark the end of learning about the PLC process; opportunities for traditional professional development should be ongoing and available long after the formal training period is over. New teachers and experienced teachers who are new to the district need access to what others have experienced; however, the most effective guiding coalitions realize that if they continue to provide *only* traditional training, they risk allowing the implementation process to lose momentum and become stagnant. Leaders must figure out ways to combine the benefits of training with the power of job-embedded coaching. The next stage of the implementation process is designed to address this need.

Questions to Ask After Stage 3—Learning About the Work

- What percentage of the faculty and staff participated in the various professional development activities?
- Have we honestly appraised our capacity to implement the PLC process with fidelity?
- Are the staff adequately trained? If not, how do we better support them so they will be successful?
- What feedback have we received from staff? What topics require additional training?
- How intentionally have we promoted the development of shared knowledge and a common vocabulary?

Stage 4: Doing the Work

In this stage, the focus shifts from learning to doing, which means the priority becomes finding ways to facilitate the transfer of what was learned during workshops to the classroom. This shift presents districts with a terrific opportunity to reposition the way professional development is delivered. Experts (Sharples et al., 2019) remind us:

> While up-front training is important in developing a conceptual understanding of a new approach, crucially, training alone is unlikely to be sufficient to yield changes in practice. Often, it is only when follow-on support is added to training, in the form of expert coaching or mentoring, that teachers are able to apply their conceptual understanding to practical classroom behaviors. (p. 33)

Effectively shifting the focus from learning new skills or strategies to doing them in the classroom means shifting the way the district supports teachers and principals. Implementation teams should ask themselves, "How do we make sure what we learned leads to action? How can we help build the capacity of our colleagues to do this work?" Unfortunately, the all-too-common answer to these questions is to offer more training, which, by default, means more workshops, seminars, and conferences. When this happens, the implementation process stalls, teachers become cynical, and learning rarely, if ever, gets to doing.

Rather than scheduling more workshops, seminars, and conferences, a better alternative is to gather evidence about the PLC initiative's progress, identify what is going well and what is not, shift the primary way professional development is delivered from generalized workshops to contextualized coaching, and tailor new learning opportunities to what individual teachers and collaborative teams need.

This is an opportune time to leverage the implementation process into a powerful professional development opportunity by developing and disseminating SIGs and pathways (see chapter 4, page 97). Creating these tools facilitates the subsequent coaching of collaborative teams while simultaneously promoting the development of a host of important elements of the PLC process, including collective inquiry, continuous improvement, shared knowledge, common vocabulary, and a standard of PLC best practice.

It is not surprising that attempting new skills will push some teachers and principals out of their comfort zones. At this stage, leadership should expect the initial efforts to operationalize the PLC process will make some uncomfortable, others impatient, and a few resistant. Some will express this discomfort and lack of confidence by asking for more training, but the response to these reactions should not be more workshops and seminars. Teachers who attended the formal training offered previously already know what to do; they just need help figuring out how to do it. What they need is coaching and technical support.

Because of the emphasis on doing, doing, doing, and the fact that teams are in the process of practicing newly acquired skills, teams will make mistakes. Rick DuFour reminds us, "Leaders should approach the change process honestly and advise staff that it is unrealistic to expect flawless execution in initial efforts to implement complex concepts" (DuFour, DuFour, Eaker, & Many, 2010, p. 260). Sharing artifacts generated by teams as they work through the PLC process, creating forums for teachers to talk with teachers, and creating a central depository for sample forms and tools have all proven to be invaluable.

Unfortunately, many well-intentioned implementation efforts end after stage 4, which makes it likely that most of these same efforts will fail to cause any lasting changes in teachers' professional practice. The next two stages of the implementation process (stage 5, innovation, and stage 6, sustainability) are critical to the long-term improvement of teaching and learning.

Questions to Ask After Stage 4—Doing the Work

- Is enough technical assistance (coaching, mentoring, and peer-to-peer collaboration) available to promote the transfer of what was learned during formal training into the classroom?
- Has the district facilitated the opportunity to develop an agreed-on standard of best practice?
- What data do we have about which elements of the PLC process are going well and which are not? What evidence can we cite to guide continued professional development offerings?
- Have we intentionally created formal and informal opportunities for teachers to learn from one another and talk about how they have applied what they learned to their professional practice?
- What systems are in place to encourage the sharing of forms, tools, and artifacts?

Stage 5: Innovating

During the innovation stage, there will be tension between fidelity and adaptation. For a long time, it was believed that for a new program to succeed, it had to be implemented with fidelity, and any adaptation or variance from the prescribed implementation process was viewed negatively. This perspective is no longer supported; in fact, researchers have acknowledged that some degree of adaptation is inevitable (Durlak & DuPre, 2008; Ringwalt et al., 2003; Shelton, 2020b).

The truth is expecting everyone to identically implement new programs, policies, or procedures is not possible or appropriate. This ignores the fact that conditions are different in every school and every classroom. Schools must have the ability to adapt programs to better align with available resources and meet the diverse needs of their students. Researchers have known for decades that to maximize success, "organizations should adapt to the innovation at the same time as the innovation is adapted to fit the organization" (Berman & McLaughlin, 1976). Rachel Shelton (2020a) acknowledges the tension between implementing a program with a high degree of fidelity and needing to adapt a program to the unique needs of different settings. She asserts that adaptation of a program may actually *increase* the program's odds of being sustained, and concedes that most researchers now believe adapting programs is beneficial, perhaps even required for success.

One of the reasons why the PLC process is so powerful is it embraces the idea that fidelity and adaptation can and do coexist. To protect fidelity, the essential elements of PLCs—including such things as membership on collaborative teams, identification of essential outcomes, use of common assessments, and the availability of interventions—are considered non-negotiable, identified as tight, and implemented with fidelity. Other elements of the PLC process are described as loose; adaptation of these is appropriate and even encouraged so long as adjustments are made carefully and based on evidence. As Joseph A. Durlak and Emily P. DuPre (2008) note, "The prime focus should be on finding the right mix of fidelity and adaptation" (p. 341) to allow for adaptation without sacrificing fidelity.

Collaborative teams are perfectly poised to embrace a culture of continuous improvement through the process of collective inquiry and action research with a focus on results. Examples where fidelity and adaptation are simultaneously present in PLCs are easy to identify. For example, all teachers are members of collaborative teams (tight), but how teams organize will look different in a large suburban high school and in a small rural elementary school (loose). It is expected that all students will master the essential outcomes (tight), but teachers have some discretion over their methodology (loose). Every student must have access to opportunities for additional time and support (tight), but the structure of those interventions may look different depending on available resources (loose).

Leaders create this balance between fidelity and adaptation by ensuring that (1) essential elements of a PLC are identified and protected and (2) any adjustments are based on evidence and experience. Leaders should encourage teachers to "first do it right, then do it differently," which means using relevant data, anecdotal evidence, and classroom experience as the basis for any modification, adaptation, or change. Experience has shown that the regular use of plan-do-study-act (PDSA) cycles is one of the best ways to ensure that adaptations meet these criteria.

Questions to Ask After Stage 5—Innovating

- Is the PLC process being implemented as intended? What evidence can we cite that the elements considered tight are being honored? Are those elements being observed as part of the faculty's practice?
- Are we able to respond to the questions about adaptation that arise during this stage of implementation?
- Are adaptations to the PLC process carefully considered and based on relevant data, anecdotal evidence, and classroom experience? Do teams use PDSA cycles to support modifications, adjustments, or changes?
- Can we use existing structures to encourage teachers to combine individual behaviors into repeatable routines that become lasting habits of professional practice?

Stage 6: Sustaining

Sustainability is the continued use of program components at sufficient intensity for the sustained achievement of program goals (Scheirer & Dearing, 2011). Sounds simple enough, but sustainability is a challenge. Even when an initiative has been implemented successfully, it can be difficult to create lasting changes in professional practice. The adoption stage is a better place to anticipate what it will take to sustain the PLC process long enough to become a habit of professional practice, but if the school or district has waited until the sustainability stage to consider how the PLC process will become part of the school's culture, it is not too late.

To ensure the work to implement the PLC process sticks, the implementation team should consider two things. First, they could revisit the premortem they may have completed during the exploration stage. This exercise provides an excellent jumping-off point for discussions about what happened and what still needs to be done to ensure the PLC process has a lasting impact. Second, this is also a great time to revisit what was identified as tight or non-negotiable and look for evidence of strengths and weaknesses in the implementation process. Both of these activities will generate valuable insights and information that the team can use to revisit or adjust any decisions made earlier in the process.

The implementation team should take great care to avoid the trap of assuming that once the process reaches this final stage, PLCs no longer need nurturing and support. Quite the contrary; if the goal is to improve teaching and learning, and the PLC process has been chosen as the best way to achieve that goal, the administrative and teacher leaders should continue to monitor it, support it, and celebrate its success.

Questions to Ask After Stage 6—Sustaining

- What evidence do we have of widespread use of the PLC process? Do results indicate the PLC process is having the intended positive impact on teaching and learning in our school?
- Is the PLC process embedded in the structure and culture of the school, the district, or both? For example, is every teacher a member of a meaningful team with time for collaboration built into the regular school day?
- Has the system created a critical mass of practitioners who have the necessary skills? How can the existing resources be used to create more capacity for our teachers to function as collaborative teams?
- Is there a plan to provide the necessary support to new teachers who enter the system? How intentionally does the school or district help new teachers understand the value placed on the PLC process?
- What gets monitored? What policies, practices, and procedures are in place to ensure that the PLC process continues to be the vehicle for improving teaching and learning?

Part Three

Here's Why

So, why should schools and districts pay more attention to implementation in general and, specifically, to the greater use of implementation science? Mountains of evidence show that the proper use of implementation science makes a new practice more likely to be successfully implemented in less time, and sustained over time (Durlak & DuPre, 2008; Fixsen & Blase, 2009; Fullan, 2007, 2016; Pustkowski, Scott, & Tesvic, 2014). These represent some of the most practical reasons why school districts should embrace the implementation process more intentionally, but perhaps the best reason is the literature shows that how an idea is implemented is just as important as the quality of the idea or innovation itself. As Sharples and colleagues (2019) say, "One of the characteristics that distinguishes effective and less-effective schools, in addition to what they implement, is how they put those new approaches into practice" (p. 3).

After a meta-analysis of more than five hundred studies, Durlak and DuPre (2008) found "strong empirical evidence to support the conclusion that the level [quality] of implementation affects outcomes" (p. 327). They summarized their findings by stating, "In sum, the results of 483 studies included in five meta-analyses . . . combined with the results of 59 additional studies with more specific findings clearly indicate that *implementation matters*" (p. 334, emphasis added).

The reason why schools and districts should pay attention to how a new idea is implemented is really quite simple: the better the implementation process, the better the results. "The success of a new school program, curriculum, or initiative depends on the quality of its implementation" (New Leaders, 2023). Experts on change implementation are consistent in their agreement that implementation matters (see page 287, "Why Does Implementation Matter?").

Experts at the Centre for Effective Services (2022) have argued that for successful implementation, developing an implementation team is a key step. Leaders must not skip this step; it is simply one of the most important things a leader can do. Whatever name the district chooses—*task force, ad hoc committee, implementation team*, or even *guiding coalition* at the district and school levels—the absence of some kind of team charged with monitoring implementation has serious implications for a successful initiative.

Wendy Hirsch (2023) argues the implementation team's role is to support the successful implementation of a new policy, program, or procedure. Whether designated as a separate entity or part of an existing structure, this team is not a steering committee or an advisory board; rather, its fundamental job is to gather data, monitor progress, anticipate barriers, and identify solutions.

Engaging members of the faculty and staff early in this effort is one of the best ways leaders can ensure the implementation process goes well. Had Ditka created and deployed an implementation team, it would have undoubtedly enhanced the chances

Why Does Implementation Matter?

"A poorly implemented program can lead to failure as easily as a poorly designed one" (Mihalic, Irwin, Fagan, Ballard, & Elliott, 2004, p. 1).

"Implementation of improvement plans is the least acknowledged, least understood, and least supported phase of the school improvement process. That doesn't mean it is the least important, however" (Jerald, 2005, p. 9).

"Effective leadership is crucial to implementation, and the existence of at least one program champion has long been recognized as a valuable resource to encourage innovation" (Durlak & DuPre, 2008, p. 338).

"The best idea is going to be only as good as its implementation" (Samit, 2016, p. 222).

"Greater use of change knowledge embedded in policy and strategy will reduce the timeline for successful initiation and implementation" (Fullan, 2016, p. 58).

"Overall, the research literature reveals a range of reasons preventing implementation from being effective, including a lack of focus on the implementation process" (Viennet & Pont, 2017, p. 13).

"One review of 25 implementation frameworks found that nearly 70% of them included the development of an implementation team as a key step" (Hirsch, 2023).

"In the education system, where resources and time are limited, strategic implementation can often be the difference between programs that fail and programs that create sustainable change" (Lyon, 2017, p. 6).

"Successful implementation happens in stages and unfolds over an extended period of time. It is not a single event that takes place when the decision to adopt a new teaching practice is made, or on the day when training begins" (Sharples et al., 2019, p. 8).

"Implementation is a process—not an event—it cannot happen instantly, despite common expectations and pressures to demonstrate rapid change and improved outcomes for the focus population" (National Implementation Research Network, 2020, p. 3).

"Implementing new initiatives gives you a great opportunity to ask yourself which of your current programs or practices should be on your 'stop it' list, or de-implemented" (New Leaders, 2023).

of success. Consider the specific benefits of deploying a dedicated team responsible for PLC implementation.

First, the team is the primary tool for monitoring the initiative's progress. Durlak and DuPre (2008) report that David L. DuBois, Bruce E. Holloway, Jeffrey C. Valentine, and Harris Cooper (2002) found districts that monitored the implementation process saw effect sizes three times larger than those of districts where no monitoring was present. Durlak and DuPre (2008) share similar findings from J. David Smith, Barry H. Schneider, Peter K. Smith, and Katerina Ananiadou (2004), who note, "Schools that monitored implementation obtained twice the mean effects as those that did not monitor implementation" (p. 30).

Second, the team acts as a clearinghouse for information about the initiative and improves clarity and communication during every aspect of the process. As the primary source for questions and answers, an implementation team in Superintendent Ditka's district could have cleared up any confusion by responding to logistic questions such as, "Are principals expected to attend all sessions as the lead learners?" or "Should the same cadre of teachers attend all training sessions, or is it better to rotate teachers so everyone has an opportunity to participate?"

Clarity precedes competence, and Ditka laid the foundation for monitoring the implementation process when he identified what was loose and tight. Had a district-level team taken the next step by publishing examples of the tight elements and creating a system to monitor those elements, there would have been more clarity around the expectations for teachers and administrators.

Third, the existence of an implementation team would have enhanced consistency and coordination of the initiative to implement PLCs. The team would have done a better job of aligning information across the district's different audiences and stakeholders about how to adapt the PLC process to the unique demographic characteristics of Dunning-Kruger School District. The team could have collected, updated, and publicized a list of common terminology; served as a clearinghouse for the sharing of artifacts; and compiled a stop-doing list. Had an implementation team existed, conversations about how to sustain the PLC process would have been ongoing, and course corrections would have been more timely, targeted, and efficient.

Fourth, an implementation team serves as a forum for public information sharing about the PLC initiative. Updates or status reports, shared publicly as a standing agenda item during monthly district and building leadership team meetings, would have provided Ditka with an opportunity to create greater awareness and accountability among the area superintendents. It would also have sent the message that the districtwide PLC initiative was a priority.

Fifth, an implementation team also introduces a degree of healthy competition. Peer pressure is powerful; there is no better way to break through barriers than to see someone like yourself, with similar resources, in a similar setting, being successful. Ideas shared by one area superintendent would undoubtedly have been considered by the others, and quarterly reports to the board of education by principals and area superintendents would have added an incentive for those who may have needed additional motivation.

Finally, an implementation team would have generated greater ownership and promoted the sustained success of PLCs. Perhaps most importantly, the existence of an implementation team would have created a group of ambassadors to champion the reasons why PLCs are so critical to accomplishing the mission of higher levels of learning for all. The simple act of having a group of people regularly gather together to monitor the implementation of the PLC process would have created opportunities for collaboration.

Implementation teams, actively involved in managing and monitoring the implementation process, are commonplace (Hirsch, 2023). Establishing some kind of structure or organization to monitor the implementation process is probably the single most important decision a leader makes and should be considered a prerequisite for a successful initiative.

The fact that implementation science can have such a positive effect on school improvement is enough to encourage most practitioners to support the concept, but some schools and districts suffer from a degree of inertia when it comes to initiating school improvement. In theory, implementing a new evidence-based practice will bring about positive and lasting changes in teaching and learning. In practice, given the uncertainty about outcomes on the front end and the high cost of a failed implementation on the back end, school leaders often prefer sticking to the status quo rather than moving forward with school-improvement initiatives.

Unfortunately, the implementation process that unfolded in Dunning-Kruger School District is not unusual, and even though the effort started off well enough, the absence of key structures meant the disappointing results were predictable. The takeaway from Ditka's effort is that, while a lot of time, money, and effort were invested with little to show for it, it didn't have to be that way.

Part Four

Assessing Your Place on the PLC Journey

It is important to help your staff build shared knowledge regarding your school's current status in addressing the critical step on the PLC journey of implementing the PLC process districtwide. We have created a tool to assist you in that effort. "The Professional Learning Communities at Work® Continuum: Implementing the PLC Process Districtwide" on page 290 is also available at **go.SolutionTree.com/PLCbooks** as a free reproducible. Once your staff have established greater clarity regarding the current status of your collaborative teams, we urge you to turn your attention to the "Where Do We Go From Here?" worksheet that accompanies the continuum (on page 291 and also available for free download at **go.SolutionTree.com/PLCbooks**). It will prompt you to take the action necessary to close the knowing-doing gap.

The Professional Learning Communities at Work® Continuum: Implementing the PLC Process Districtwide

DIRECTIONS: Individually, silently, and *honestly* assess the current reality of your school's implementation of each indicator listed in the left column. Consider what evidence or anecdotes support your assessment. This form may also be used to assess district or team implementation.

The central office leadership provides the clear parameters and priorities, ongoing support, systems for monitoring progress, and sustained focus essential to implementing the professional learning community process in schools throughout the district.

Indicator	Pre-Initiating	Initiating	Implementing	Developing	Sustaining
The district has demonstrated a sustained commitment to improving schools by developing the capacity of school personnel to function as a PLC. District leaders have been explicit about specific practices they expect to see in each school, have created processes to support principals in implementing those practices, and monitor the progress of implementation.	There is no focused and sustained districtwide process for improving schools. Improvement efforts tend to be disconnected, episodic, and piecemeal. Projects come and go, but the cultures of schools remain largely unaffected.	The district has announced that schools should operate as professional learning communities and may have articulated a rationale in support of PLCs, but the process remains ambiguous, and educators at the school site view it as just one of many initiatives raining down upon them from the central office. Little is done to monitor implementation. Some central office leaders and principals demonstrate indifference to the initiative.	Central office leaders made a concerted effort to build shared knowledge and to establish a common language regarding the PLC process throughout the district. They have called for schools to operate as PLCs and clarified some of the specific structural changes to support teacher collaboration and systems of interventions that they expect to see in each school. They monitor the implementation of the structural changes and offer assistance to schools that seek it. Some schools move forward with effective implementation, while others merely tweak their existing structures. Professional practice is impacted in some schools and not in others.	Central office leaders have put processes in place to develop the capacity of principals to lead the PLC process in their schools, monitor implementation of the PLC process, and respond to schools that are experiencing difficulty. Building-level and central office leaders have begun to function as their own collaborative team and work interdependently to achieve common goals and identify and resolve issues that are interfering with the PLC process. Individual schools are examining ways to become more effective in the PLC process.	Administrators at all levels function as coordinated, high-performing teams characterized by a deep understanding of and commitment to the PLC process. They consider that process not as one of several improvement initiatives, but rather as *the* process by which they will continuously improve student and adult learning. They are intensely focused on student learning and make student achievement data transparent among all members. They work together collaboratively to resolve problems, develop a deeper understanding of the PLC process, and learn from one another. They are committed to the collective success of the team and the individual success of each member.

Where Do We Go From Here? Worksheet
Implementing the PLC Process Districtwide

Indicator of a PLC at Work	What steps or activities must be initiated to create this condition in your school?	Who will be responsible for initiating or sustaining these steps or activities?	What is a realistic timeline for each step or phase of the activity?	What will you use to assess the effectiveness of your initiative?
The district has demonstrated a sustained commitment to improving schools by developing the capacity of school personnel to function as a PLC. District leaders have been explicit about specific practices they expect to see in each school, have created processes to support principals in implementing those practices, and monitor the progress of implementation.				

Part Five

Tips for Moving Forward: Implementing a Districtwide PLC Process

Train principals: Principals should be trained together in how to lead the PLC process. In large districts, training may take place in cohorts. As the former assistant superintendent of a districtwide Model PLC writes—

> To create collaborative districts, district leaders must provide principals with training opportunities that allow them to collaborate, learn together, and find best practices. In this way, principals have the opportunity to discuss and find meaning in the new PLC concepts presented to them. As practitioners, principals need time to collaborate to clearly see how implementation might look in their schools. They need to bounce ideas off one another and hear what others are planning. (Smith, 2015, pp. 31–32)

2

Don't assume common verbiage means common understanding: The fact that people use the same term does not mean they have a shared understanding of the term's meaning or implications. Remember the advice of Jeffrey Pfeffer and Robert Sutton (2000), based on their research on high-performing organizations—

> The use of complex language hampers implementation . . . when leaders or managers don't really understand the meaning of the language they are using and its implications for action. It is hard enough to explain what a complex idea means for action when you understand it and others don't. It is impossible when you use terms that sound impressive but you don't really understand what they mean. (p. 52)

Develop formal and informal processes to determine people's interpretations of the key terms in the PLC lexicon. "Help me understand what you mean by that term" should be a phrase you use routinely in conversations with others. A portion of district-led principals' meetings should ask members to clarify terms that are essential to the PLC process. Principals, in turn, should use the same strategies in their buildings until there is a truly common language. Remember that in high-performing PLCs, people not only "walk the talk" by acting in accordance with the process, but also can "talk the walk" by explaining what they are doing and why (Fullan, 2014).

3 **Don't assume that others share or understand your interpretation of what is tight:** Develop formal and informal processes to provide you with feedback on what people throughout the organization believe are the priorities. For example, at a principals' meeting, the superintendent could ask principals to write down the two or three things they believe are tight in the district. The responses should be gathered, read aloud, and discussed. How consistent are the responses? Principals should repeat this process in their schools.

4 **Link what is tight to board policy:** Work with the board of education to codify expectations of priorities through adoption of board policy. For example, Blue Valley School District in Kansas specifically stipulates, "We are committed to professional learning communities as the means of continuous school improvement." The board of education of Montgomery County, Maryland, adopted "guiding tenets" that specify the work of the district will be driven by the four critical questions of a PLC.

- What do students need to know and be able to do?
- How will we know when they have learned it?
- What will we do when they haven't learned it?
- What will we do when they already know it?

5 **Recognize the need for specificity regarding what people throughout the organization must do:** Telling educators to operate their schools as PLCs will almost certainly have no impact unless there is a clear understanding of the specific actions people take in a PLC. The goal is not to have educators in a district refer to their school as a PLC; the goal is to have them do what members of a PLC do. In many instances, we have seen the adoption of language substitute for meaningful action. It is far more effective to stipulate exactly what must be done and then provide some latitude regarding how it is done.

6 **Create systems to monitor conditions that are vital to the success of a PLC:** One of the most important and frequent questions effective district leaders of the PLC process ask is, "How do we know?" They identify elements they believe must be in place for the process to be effective, and then they develop specific strategies to gather ongoing evidence of the presence of those elements.

7 **Review data about the implementation frequently:** Identify, gather, and review relevant data about the implementation process on a regular basis, and set up a system to share the results of these reviews publicly. These minireviews should occur often; at a minimum, the implementation team should reflect on the data after each stage of the implementation. The data can be used to identify the status, discuss any concerns, and celebrate progress of the initiative.

8 **Conduct a premortem during the exploration stage:** During any implementation process, there will be unanticipated obstacles and opportunities. A group of researchers recommends the implementation team conduct a premortem to help identify any potential barriers that might arise and brainstorm potential solutions (Sharples et al., 2019). The results of the premortem also provide an opportunity to establish short-, medium-, and long-term indicators of success.

9 **Provide opportunities for teachers to learn and do:** Traditional training offered through workshops, seminars, and conferences serves an important purpose—it helps build the kind of shared knowledge and common vocabulary essential to success. But transferring new learning from workshops to the classroom is easier said than done.

Leaders should remember that traditional professional development opportunities represent a necessary but insufficient condition for lasting improvement in teachers' professional practice. Sharples and colleagues (2019) observe, "The application of a single strategy alone will be insufficient to successfully support the implementation of a new approach" (p. 22). Providing multiple learning opportunities is the best way to meet the diverse needs of an entire faculty.

Finding ways to give the faculty the kind of ongoing support and technical assistance that can only be provided through coaching is the key to sustaining best practice. This requires a deliberate shift in the way teachers receive professional development.

10 **Demonstrate reciprocal accountability:** Work with leaders throughout the organization to identify the specific support and resources staff will need in order to accomplish what they are being called to do, and then provide the necessary support and resources. Remember that part of the responsibility of leadership is helping others develop the capacity to succeed at what they are asked to accomplish.

Part Six

Questions to Guide the Work of Your Professional Learning Community

To implement the PLC at Work process districtwide, ask:

1. What aspects of the initiative do we monitor? What data do we collect to monitor the progress of the initiative?

2. Which policies, practices, and procedures are in place to ensure that the PLC process continues to be the vehicle for improving teaching and learning?

3. How will we know educators throughout the district understand what is loose and tight? How will we know if a common, widely understood language exists throughout the district?

4. Have we provided training that gives teachers a solid understanding of the PLC process while delivering the technical support they need to succeed?

5. Is there a plan in place to provide the necessary support to new teachers who enter the system? How intentionally does the school or district help new teachers understand the value our school places on the PLC process?

6. Does the district or school have a critical mass of practitioners with the necessary skills? Evidence of this might be that teacher teams are able to respond to the four critical questions of a PLC with fidelity.

7. Is the PLC process embedded in the structure and culture of the school or district? For example, is every teacher a member of a meaningful team? Is time for collaboration built into the regular school day?

8. How do we know what teachers feel they need to make the initiative successful?

Part Seven

Dangerous Detours and Seductive Shortcuts

No one person can lead the PLC process at the building or district level; effective leaders must delegate responsibility and authority to others. There are some things, however, that they cannot delegate. Clarifying purpose and priorities, establishing systems to monitor specific indicators of progress, ensuring steps are taken to build people's capacity to be successful, and aligning their own behavior with the priorities are among those nontransferable responsibilities.

No one person can lead the PLC process at the building or district level; effective leaders must delegate responsibility and authority to others.

Conversely, some well-intentioned districts have attempted to implement the PLC process in a way that removes educators at the building level from doing the work. Central office leaders think as follows.

- We won't ask teachers to identify essential standards. We will do it for them.
- We won't ask teachers to create assessments. We will do it for them.
- We won't ask teachers to analyze evidence of student learning. We will do it for them.
- We won't ask principals to create systems of interventions. We will buy a computer program that will provide interventions for them.

It is easy to make this mistake with implementing the PLC process. Some district leaders may feel implementation is a burden and teachers are already busy enough. Others in central office positions may believe they alone are knowledgeable enough to be successful or, even if teachers could implement PLCs, they would not be willing to do what it takes to improve. Whatever the rationale, leadership initiate the implementation process on their own.

These wrong mindsets ignore the fact that people support that which they help create and involving the faculty and staff is a crucial ingredient to success. Remember this fundamental truth about implementing the PLC process: *when you remove educators from doing the work, you remove them from the learning.* It is the process of *engaging* in this collective learning that begins to transform traditional schools into PLCs.

Part Eight

Digging Deeper—Recommended Resources

The following resources delve deeper into the topic of implementing the PLC process districtwide.

- *Every School, Every Team, Every Classroom: District Leadership for Growing Professional Learning Communities at Work* by Robert Eaker and Janel Keating (2012)
- *Leading PLCs at Work Districtwide: From Boardroom to Classroom* by Robert Eaker, Mike Hagadone, Janel Keating, and Meagan Rhoades (2021)
- *Inside PLCs at Work: Your Guided Tour Through One District's Successes, Challenges, and Celebrations* by Craig Dougherty and Casey Reason (2019)

Final Thoughts

In his research, Douglas Reeves (2009) found, "Implementation that was moderate or occasional was no better than implementation that was completely absent" (p. 44). What he is saying is that mediocre or half-hearted efforts to implement new ideas are a waste of time, yielding no better results than the complete absence of implementation. While it is true that most implementation efforts fail, it's also true that most implementation efforts are abandoned prematurely, usually about halfway through the process.

No school ever made dramatic improvements by lackadaisically implementing a new idea. So why, despite all the evidence that the proper use of implementation science dramatically enhances the chances of success, do so many schools dip their toes into the implementation waters instead of diving in headfirst? A successful implementation initiative requires courage to stay the course and complete the entire process. Improving teaching and learning is difficult enough; why make it harder by approaching it in a half-hearted fashion?

EPILOGUE

Touching the Emotions: Creating a Culture of Caring

We acknowledge that improving student and adult learning by embedding PLC at Work practices is a complex journey requiring time, patience, and above all, effective leadership—at every level. Because organizational change is difficult and time consuming, many leaders focus their efforts on making only *structural* changes—policies, procedures, schedules, organizational charts, position descriptions, and so on. Structural changes are easier and much quicker to implement than the deeper, more complex cultural changes necessary to sustain meaningful change over time. Structural changes are almost always necessary, but by themselves, they are inadequate—hence, the prevalence of PLC Lite.

Successful implementation of the PLC at Work process requires leaders to go beyond structural change and focus on the human side of schooling by developing a culture of caring, for both students and adults. Daniel Goleman, Richard Boyatzis, and Annie McKee (2002), authors of *Primal Leadership*, emphasize the importance of the emotional aspects of leadership by observing:

> Great leaders move us. They ignite our passion and inspire the best in us. When we try to explain why they are so effective, we speak of strategy, vision, or powerful ideas. But the reality is much more primal: Great leadership works through the emotions. (p. 3)

The role that feelings and emotions play in organizational improvement has not always been recognized. In the early days of industrialization, ideas about improving organizational effectiveness were based, for the most part, on the research and writings of Frederick Winslow Taylor (1911) and his principles of scientific management. Human feelings and emotions were not considered as factors for improving organizational effectiveness; rather, improvement was sought by tinkering with organizational structure and processes to improve *efficiency*. The connection between the needs of the organization and the needs of the individual was simply not considered.

Recognizing the Human Side of Organizations

That view changed in the 1920s and 1930s with what became known as the *human relations movement* (Hendry, 2013). While structural aspects of organizations could not be ignored, the needs and feelings of employees gained recognition as an essential element of organizational life.

This view was heavily influenced by the work of Elton Mayo and his colleagues, especially their studies of the Western Electric facility in Hawthorne, Illinois (Hendry, 2013). Their pioneering research uncovered the role feelings played in employee performance and, hence, productivity. The work of Mayo and his colleagues triggered a new era of research focusing on the psychological aspects of human motivation.

Researchers, theorists, and writers such as Abraham Maslow (1943; hierarchy of needs) and Douglas McGregor (1960; Theory X and Theory Y), among others, added to the rapidly growing body of research that focused on the connection between emotions and human motivation. Beginning in 1945, research studies, such as the Ohio State University leadership studies and the University of Michigan leadership studies, supported the position that effective leadership requires attention to *both* structural and psychological aspects of organizational behavior (Hersey, Blanchard, & Johnson, 2001, 2013). This assumption remains relevant for today's leaders and is essential for the successful implementation of the PLC process and, in turn, improved student and adult learning.

Creating Schools That Care

One of the most frequently asked questions we receive from teachers and administrators is, "How can I better motivate my students?" And it is not unusual for principals to ask, "How can I motivate my teachers?" Of course, superintendents ask the same question regarding principals, and so on. There is no one answer to this question since every student and adult (and by extension, each team and school) is unique and every situation is different. However, it is virtually impossible to effectively motivate students—and adults—absent a culture of caring.

Consider the quote, "No one cares how much you know until they know how much you care," which is often attributed to President Theodore Roosevelt. Regardless of the source, this observation is frequently quoted because it is so true. The secret to human motivation does not lie in high-stakes state or provincial test scores or threats of getting a low grade or of being held back; rather, it is in touching the emotions of others. Developing a culture of caring begins with understanding and communicating the connection between the why and human motivation. Simon Sinek (2009) reminds us, "Remember, people don't buy WHAT you do, they buy WHY you do it" (p. 64).

In a school seeking to function as a high-performing PLC, it is not enough to proclaim the school's core purpose, its fundamental mission of ensuring high levels of learning for all students. A school or district mission must connect to the why—why ensuring all students learn at high levels is the essential mission. Is it merely to score well on high-stakes state or provincial assessments? The answer should simply be this:

"It's because we care! We care about each student personally, and because we care so much, we—individually and collectively—are going to do everything in our power to ensure that each and every one of you learn the things that are essential for your future happiness, health, and intellectual success beyond this school."

Connecting the why to a culture of caring is reflected in multiple ways, such as these.

- **Why do we work in collaborative teams?** Because we care for you and your learning, and the evidence is clear: collaborative teaming is a powerful tool for improving learning outcomes for students.
- **Why do teams clarify the skills, knowledge, and dispositions that are essential for all students to learn?** Because we care for you and your learning! It is unreasonable to think that all students will learn the things that are essential for their future success if we have not articulated what the essential things are and what essential learning looks like in student work when students are successful.
- **Why do we monitor student learning on a frequent and timely basis through the use of collaboratively developed common formative assessments?** Because we care for you and your learning! We check the progress of student learning during the teaching and learning process, not just at the very end. Assessing student learning during the teaching and learning process is much more effective than relying only on end-of-unit or end-of-course summative assessments.
- **Why do we have a system in place to ensure every student receives additional time and support or extension for their learning within the school day, regardless of the teacher to whom they are assigned?** Because we care for you and your learning! Students learn at different rates and in different ways. Some students need more time and support, while others need to move beyond proficiency. Rather than leave additional time and support or extension of learning up to individual teachers (the luck of the teacher to whom students are assigned), we have developed a schoolwide system to ensure and insist each student receives the support they need to succeed because we care for our students and their success.

The actions educators undertake communicate what is valued—not only for students, but also for adults (administrators, faculty, support staff, parents, and the larger community)—and in a school that functions as a high-performing PLC, the message is clear: "We do what we do because we care about the physical, emotional, and intellectual success of each student, the broader adult community, and each other!"

Demonstrating Empathy and Compassion

Empathy and compassion are central to demonstrating a caring culture. For many students, the time they spend at school is the best part of their day. Adults in a PLC know their students. They learn as much about them as possible, and knowing each student is greatly enhanced by teachers' working together in collaborative teams.

Much is gained when teacher teams discuss and share knowledge about individual students—not only their attitude and behavior in school, but also their life beyond the school walls. Information about students, in and of itself, is of little value unless it impacts understanding, empathy, and compassion, and empathy and compassion will have little meaning unless they result in action.

However, empathy and compassion are not synonymous with "feeling sorry" for individual students or a group of students. Simply feeling sorry for certain students can lead to a culture of low expectations, which not only is unhelpful but also can actually hinder student learning. True empathy and compassion cause educators to act, to move forward together, and in doing so, to overcome seemingly insurmountable odds (Eaker & Keating, 2015).

Giving Feedback With Encouragement and Support

All teachers provide some form of feedback to their students. However, the quantity and quality of feedback vary greatly from teacher to teacher. Students within the same classroom might receive differing feedback.

The quantity of feedback can range from one or two major summative assessments per semester to frequent and timely formative assessments during the instructional unit. The quality of feedback for students is represented in a variety of ways, most notably through specificity. For example, some students receive feedback for test results or homework assignments in the form of a simple grade or number. While this limited feedback does inform students, especially about whether their answers are correct or incorrect, it does little to communicate to students where or why an answer is wrong or could be improved and, importantly, what they need to do to make the answer or assignment correct. Researchers often refer to this as *product feedback* (simply providing students with a grade or score) versus *process feedback* (specifying whether the student work is right or wrong, where mistakes were made, and how the work can be corrected or improved). In other words, specificity is an important aspect of feedback quality.

Providing students with specific process feedback is one way that teachers communicate to students that they care. In effect, these teachers are saying, "I took the time to provide you with this information because I care for you and your learning. You can do this, and I want to help."

It must be recognized, however, that to gain maximum impact, feedback must be coupled with encouragement and support. Feedback absent encouragement and support is simply information. It does not touch the emotions. Encouragement and support are the essential ways teachers communicate, "I care about you as a person, and you can do this. I'll show you how."

Everything concerning the quantity and quality of feedback, encouragement, and support for students is applicable to adults and teams of adults. What would lead us to believe that the quantity and quality of feedback, encouragement, and support provided to students would be better than the quantity and quality of feedback, encouragement, and support provided to adults?

Removing Communication That Says, "We Don't Care"

It might seem counterintuitive that teachers can communicate a lack of care. However, it does often, in fact, occur—usually unconsciously. When teachers express the belief, "It's my job to teach, but it's my students' job to learn, and if they choose not to learn, they must suffer the consequences of their choice," they are communicating, "I don't care whether you learn or not. It's up to you."

There are a number of ways adults communicate a culture of "We don't care." The most common are behaviors that communicate we have low expectations of certain students, and as a result, those students are treated differently. For example, if teachers have low expectations of certain students, those students may be consistently seated farther away from the teacher. Some students are rarely called on, recognized, or publicly praised. Some students receive less accurate feedback or praise when they do respond correctly, and less work is demanded from some students (Good & Brophy, 1978).

These specific classroom behaviors are part of a larger school structure and culture that send a message of "We don't care" to students. Another example is this: schools might communicate a culture of high expectations for student learning but fail to have the structure and resources in place to provide students with additional time and support when they experience difficulty with their learning. In personal conversations, Larry Lezotte frequently remarked that ultimately, schools communicate high expectations for students by how they respond when students don't learn or are experiencing difficulty with their learning.

Some schools, teams, and individual teachers have rules that forbid students from turning in work late for any reason or redoing work that is incorrect, incomplete, or lacking in quality. If assigned work is important and teachers care, then teachers must insist that students complete the work or redo the work within a framework of agreed-on, reasonable conditions and consequences.

The point is this: it is not enough to communicate a culture of caring; administrators and teachers must engage in an examination of the school's and district's policies, procedures, and day-to-day practices in order to ensure that what they are doing—how they act—is congruent with what the school proclaims.

Making Students Feel Special

How we view ourselves and the world around us is greatly influenced, both positively and negatively, by interactions we have with others—especially interactions we had with our teachers. In a PBS interview with Kelly Corrigan, best-selling author Michael Lewis observed, "When someone said something to you, it could completely change how you saw the world" (Robinson, 2023). Teachers, and the larger school culture, must be proactive in helping students feel special. Doesn't every parent want their child to feel special? Doesn't every student need to feel special? Isn't the same true for adults?

In his autobiographical book *My Reading Life*, Pat Conroy (2010) tells of how his high school English teacher, Gene Norris, had a huge influence on his life, as well as the lives of other students. Conroy recalls an encounter with a young woman at Gene Norris's funeral and uses the conversation to share how Norris made students feel special—especially students who were experiencing difficulty in their lives. Conroy (2010) writes:

> "But why are you here? Did you know Mr. Norris? You're too young to have been a student of his."
>
> "My first year at Robert Smalls," she said. "I was such a mess. In trouble. Boys. Drugs. That kind of thing. They sent me to Mr. Norris."
>
> "He was good, wasn't he?"
>
> "Mr. Norris told me to come to his office every day at lunch. We could talk and get to know each other. I went there for the next two years. Two years. Yet he didn't even know me."
>
> "You got the best of Gene," I said.
>
> "He saved my life. He literally saved my life."
>
> "Come on in," I said, putting my arm around her. "I'll introduce you to a couple of hundred people who'll tell you the same thing."
>
> "Mr. Norris acted like I was the most important girl in the world," she said.
>
> "You were. That was Gene's secret. All of us were." (pp. 70–71)

Conroy's recollections of his teacher serve as a reminder that it is not enough for a school to have only *some* teachers like Gene Norris. In schools that have only some caring teachers, luck becomes a key factor in students' attitudes, self-esteems, motivations, and successes.

Of course, adults have a need to feel special too. The importance of how one is treated forms the basis for George Bernard Shaw's (1916/2003) *Pygmalion*, upon which the popular stage musical and movie *My Fair Lady* is based. In the following dialogue, the former flower seller Eliza Doolittle explains to Colonel Pickering why his behavior was so important to her success in becoming a "lady" (Eaker & Keating, 2015):

> ***Eliza:*** But do you know what began my real education? Your calling me Miss Doolittle that day when I first came to Wimpole Street. . . . And there were a hundred little things you never

> noticed because they came naturally to you. Things about standing up and taking off your hat and opening doors—
>
> ***Pickering:*** Oh, that was nothing.
>
> ***Eliza:*** Yes. Things that showed you thought and felt about me as if I were something better than a scullery-maid, though of course I know you would have been just the same to a scullery-maid if she had been let in the drawing room. You never took off your boots in the dining room when I was there.
>
> ***Pickering:*** You mustn't mind that. Higgins takes off his boots all over the place.
>
> ***Eliza:*** I know. I am not blaming him. It is his way, isn't it? But it made such a difference to me that you didn't do it. You see, really and truly, apart from the things anyone can pick up (the dressing and the proper way of speaking, and so on), the difference between a lady and a flower girl is not how she behaves, but how she is treated. I shall always be a flower girl to Professor Higgins because he always treats me as a flower girl, and always will; but I know I can be a lady to you, because you always treat me as a lady, and always will. (Shaw, 1916/2003, pp. 94–95)

Making a student feel special is a powerful motivator—especially for students who feel inadequate in a number of ways. The illustrator Norman Rockwell often felt bad about himself due to his slim physical frame and lack of athletic skills. But, fortunately, he had a teacher, Miss Smith, who made him feel special. In her 2013 biography of Rockwell, Deborah Solomon writes:

> Miss Smith fussed over his drawings. She made him feel that he was artistic and hence special. . . . He would keep in touch with her for the rest of her life, and she is one of the few people from his childhood for whom he admitted to feeling a special fondness. Later, he would marry three times and each time he married a schoolteacher. (p. 35)

Committing to Caring

Ernest Hemingway once advised his friend Marlene Dietrich to "never mistake movement for action" (Hotchner, 1989, p. 11). Declaring a commitment to a culture of caring will simply be a public relations strategy that has little impact on either students or adults unless it causes everyone, at every level, to act.

Connecting what a school or school district declares and what actually occurs is the shared value and commitment everyone in the organization is prepared to make. The central question of a PLC focuses not on the declared beliefs, as impressive as they might sound, but ultimately on the things that collectively, at every level, a school district, school, or team is prepared to *do*. The central question is not, "What do we say?" but, "What are we prepared to do?" Are we committed, with fidelity, to touching the emotions of both students and adults at every level by embedding a culture of caring?

Developing shared commitments in order to create a caring culture also requires an analysis of our current practices. Since every policy, procedure, practice, decision, and interaction sends a message, it is essential that deep, rich conversation occurs around the question, "When it comes to caring for our students and adults in our school and school district, what messages are we sending to our students, each other, our parents, and our broader community by what we do?"

Involving Everyone, at Every Level, Every Day

Many school districts, and by extension the schools within each district, have a hierarchical, top-down structure. Successful PLCs represent a flatter leadership structure in which everyone, at every level, plays a key role. For example, while it is obvious that focus must be given to administrators and faculty in school-improvement initiatives, the support staff in schools are often overlooked. When there is a telephone call to a school district office or an individual school, the caller will most likely speak with a secretary. Imagine the goodwill or harm that can be done simply because of how telephone calls are received. Here is another example: a bus driver can undo in one afternoon what a teacher has been working on for months when it comes to improving student behaviors or attitudes.

The word *leader* is powerful, and it is essential that everyone, at every level, understand the leadership responsibilities they have every day in their decisions, their attitudes, and their interactions. Everyone must understand that what they do and say matters—a lot!

And we must remember that the adults at every level are kids who have grown up, and even though they have grown up, they retain many of the same needs they had in their youth. They still want to be in a culture that cares for them, and they want to feel special. They want the people they work for and those they work with to know them as a person, not simply as a teacher or an administrator or a staff member. Educators especially want to be recognized for doing a difficult and complex job well. In other words, like everyone, they want to feel appreciated.

Creating a caring culture for adults provides a model for students to emulate. What would lead us to think that students will believe pronouncements about how the adults care for them when they do not witness caring behaviors and attitudes among adults? James Baldwin observed, "Children have never been very good at listening to their elders, but they have never failed to imitate them" (as quoted in Hamilton, 2017, p. 13).

Leading: The Courage to Care

Developing a caring culture throughout a school or school district sounds simple. But *simple* does not mean *easy*. Creating and maintaining a culture of caring is a never-ending journey, and every journey has its detours, potholes, breakdowns, and unforeseen challenges. The journey is difficult, and success will not happen by accident. It takes strong, persistent, dedicated leaders at every level to create a districtwide, schoolwide, or classroom-wide culture of caring.

Success requires that leadership, at every level, be intentional rather than merely hopeful. To paraphrase Richard DuFour and Robert J. Marzano (2011), don't ask if you are creating a school culture. You are. Don't ask if the culture you are creating will make a difference. It will. The question is, "What kind of culture will you, as leader, create?" When reflecting on the kind of culture students and adults need, leaders would be well served to remember Maya Angelou's observation that "people will forget what you said, people will forget what you did, but people will never forget how you made them feel" (Goodreads, n.d.).

Final Thoughts

This book has attempted to address some of the challenges that prevent schools and districts from making progress as PLCs. We have attempted to draw on research from organizational development, education, leadership, psychology, and sociology to suggest alternative strategies for dealing with those challenges. We have attempted to give you the preliminary awareness, knowledge, and tools to help you begin the PLC journey—but you will only develop your skill and capacity to build a PLC by engaging in the work. You must learn by doing.

Thus, we have not presented you with a how-to book. The histories, cultures, and contexts of each school and district are unique and must be considered in the improvement process. Furthermore, in the coming years, challenges to education will arise that we could not possibly have anticipated when writing this book. We remain convinced, however, that when educators learn to clarify their priorities, to assess the current reality of their situation, to work together, and to build continuous improvement into the very fabric of their collective work, they create conditions for the ongoing learning and self-efficacy essential to solving whatever problems they confront. We hope every school and district that begins the PLC journey will come to believe deeply in and, more importantly, act on the advice attributed to Ralph Waldo Emerson: "What lies behind us and what lies ahead of us are tiny matters compared to what lies within us."

References and Resources

Achor, S. (2010). *The happiness advantage: The seven principles of positive psychology that fuel success and performance at work.* New York: Crown Business.

ACT. (2013). *2012 retention/completion summary tables.* Accessed at www.act.org/research/policymakers/pdf/12retain_trends.pdf on December 1, 2015.

Ainsworth, L. (2014). *Common formative assessments 2.0: How teacher teams intentionally align standards, instruction, and assessment.* Thousand Oaks, CA: Corwin Press.

Ainsworth, L. (2015a, February 24). Priority standards: The power of focus [Blog post]. *Education Week.* Accessed at www.edweek.org/teaching-learning/opinion-priority-standards-the-power-of-focus/2015/02 on March 15, 2024.

Ainsworth, L. (2015b, March 25). Unwrapping the standards: A simple way to deconstruct learning outcomes [Blog post]. *Education Week.* Accessed at www.edweek.org/education/opinion-unwrapping-the-standards-a-simple-way-to-deconstruct-learning-outcomes/2015/03 on March 15, 2024.

Ainsworth, L., & Viegut, D. (2006). *Common formative assessments: How to connect standards-based instruction and assessment.* Thousand Oaks, CA: Corwin Press.

Aldeman, C. (2022, September 28). Why are fewer people becoming teachers? [Blog post]. *Education Next.* Accessed at www.educationnext.org/why-are-fewer-people-becoming-teachers on November 7, 2023.

Allensworth, E., Ponisciak, S., & Mazzeo, C. (2009, June). *The schools teachers leave: Teacher mobility in Chicago Public Schools.* Chicago: Consortium on Chicago School Research.

AllThingsPLC. (2024). *See the evidence.* Accessed at https://allthingsplc.info/evidence on April 1, 2024.

Almy, S., & Tooley, M. (2012). *Building and sustaining talent: Creating conditions in high-poverty schools that support effective teaching and learning.* Washington, DC: Education Trust.

Amabile, T., & Kramer, S. (2010). What really motivates workers. *Harvard Business Review, 88*(1), 44–45.

Amabile, T., & Kramer, S. (2011). *The progress principle: Using small wins to ignite joy, engagement, and creativity at work.* Boston: Harvard Business Review Press.

American Society for Quality. (n.d.). *About ASQ.* Accessed at https://asq.org/about-asq on September 24, 2015.

Annenberg Institute for School Reform. (2004). *Professional development strategies: Professional learning communities/instructional coaching*. Providence, RI: Author.

Annenberg Institute for School Reform. (2005). *Professional learning communities: Professional development strategies that improve instruction*. Providence, RI: Author.

Anrig, G. (2013). *Beyond the education wars: Evidence that collaboration builds effective schools*. New York: Century Foundation Press.

Australian Institute for Teaching and School Leadership. (2012). *Australian teacher performance and development framework*. Melbourne: Author. Accessed at www.aitsl.edu.au/docs/default-source/national-policy-framework/australian-teacher-performance-and-development-framework.pdf on January 22, 2014.

Autry, J. A. (2001). *The servant leader: How to build a creative team, develop great morale, and improve bottom-line performance*. New York: Three Rivers Press.

Axelrod, R. H. (2002). *Terms of engagement: Changing the way we change organizations*. San Francisco: Berrett-Koehler.

Bailey, K., & Jakicic, C. (2012). *Common formative assessment: A toolkit for Professional Learning Communities at Work*. Bloomington, IN: Solution Tree Press.

Bailey, K., & Jakicic, C. (2019). *Make it happen: Coaching with the four critical questions of PLCs at Work*. Bloomington, IN: Solution Tree Press.

Bailey, K., & Jakicic, C. (2023). *Common formative assessment: A toolkit for Professional Learning Communities at Work* (2nd ed.). Bloomington, IN: Solution Tree Press.

Baker, L. (2022, April 5). Forever changed: A timeline of how COVID upended schools. *Education Week*. Accessed at www.edweek.org/leadership/forever-changed-a-timeline-of-how-covid-upended-schools/2022/04 on November 7, 2023.

Barber, M., & Mourshed, M. (2007, September). *How the world's best-performing school systems come out on top*. New York: McKinsey & Company. Accessed at www.mckinsey.com/~/media/mckinsey/industries/public%20and%20social%20sector/our%20insights/how%20the%20worlds%20best%20performing%20school%20systems%20come%20out%20on%20top/how_the_world_s_best-performing_school_systems_come_out_on_top.pdf on January 22, 2024.

Barber, M., & Mourshed, M. (2009, July). *Shaping the future: How good education systems can become great in the decade ahead*. New York: McKinsey & Company.

Basileo, L. D. (2016). *Did you know? Your school's PLCs have a major impact*. West Palm Beach, FL: Learning Sciences International. Accessed at www.hancock.stier.org/Downloads/PLC-Report.pdf on November 7, 2023.

Battelle for Kids. (2013). *Five strategies for creating a high-growth school*. Accessed at https://static.battelleforkids.org/images/eblasts/BFK_Five_Strategies_for%20Creating_High-Growth_School.pdf on March 15, 2024.

Bennis, W., & Biederman, P. W. (1997). *Organizing genius: The secrets of creative collaboration.* New York: Basic Books.

Berman, P., & McLaughlin, M. W. (1976). Implementation of educational innovation. *The Educational Forum, 40*(3), 345–370.

Berry, B., Bastian, K. C., Darling-Hammond, L., & Kini, T. (2021, January 4). *The importance of teaching and learning conditions: Influences on teacher retention and school performance in North Carolina* [Brief]. Palo Alto, CA: Learning Policy Institute. Accessed at https://learningpolicyinstitute.org/product/leandro-teaching-and-learning-conditions-brief on January 25, 2024.

Berry, L. L., & Seltman, K. D. (2008). *Management lessons from Mayo Clinic: Inside one of the world's most admired service organizations.* New York: McGraw-Hill.

Berry, L. L., & Seltman, K. D. (2017). *Management lessons from Mayo Clinic: Inside one of the world's most admired service organizations* (2nd ed.). New York: McGraw-Hill.

Black, P., Harrison, C., Lee, C., Marshall, B., & Wiliam, D. (2004). Working inside the black box: Assessment for learning in the classroom. *Phi Delta Kappan, 86*(1), 9–21.

Black, P., & Wiliam, D. (2004). The formative purpose: Assessment must first promote learning. In M. Wilson (Ed.), *Towards coherence between classroom assessment and accountability: 103rd yearbook of the National Society for the Study of Education* (pp. 20–50). Chicago: University of Chicago Press.

Black, P., & Wiliam, D. (2009). Developing the theory of formative assessment. *Educational Assessment, Evaluation and Accountability, 21*(1), 5–31.

Blackbyrn, S. (2024, January 4). *5 ensured benefits of team coaching* [Blog post]. Accessed at https://coachfoundation.com/blog/team-coaching-benefits on November 7, 2023.

Blanchard, K. (2007). *Leading at a higher level: Blanchard on leadership and creating high performing organizations.* Upper Saddle River, NJ: Prentice Hall.

Blanchard, K. (2019). *Leading at a higher level: Blanchard on leadership and creating high performing organizations* (3rd ed.). Upper Saddle River, NJ: Prentice Hall.

Block, P. (2003). *The answer to how is yes: Acting on what matters.* San Francisco: Berrett-Koehler.

Blythe, T., Allen, D., & Powell, B. S. (2015). *Looking together at student work* (3rd ed.). New York: Teachers College Press.

Bossidy, L., & Charan, R. (2002). *Execution: The discipline of getting things done.* New York: Crown Business.

Boston, R. (2014). *Team coaching: The future of leadership development—An interview with Richard Boston, managing director at LeaderSpace.* Accessed at www.leader-space.com/wp-content/uploads/2014/03/Team-coaching-the-future-of-leadership-development.pdf on November 7, 2023.

Boston Consulting Group. (2014, December). *Teachers know best: Teachers' views on professional development.* Seattle: Bill and Melinda Gates Foundation. Accessed at https://usprogram.gatesfoundation.org/-/media/dataimport/resources/pdf/2016/11/gates-pdmarketresearch-dec5.pdf?rev=f770d1b3de574f8c855c1428811ba30f&hash=991179D78E52CC037B0D0B4CA00EE9EE on January 22, 2024.

Breslow, J. M. (2012, September 21). *By the numbers: Dropping out of high school.* Accessed at www.pbs.org/wgbh/pages/frontline/education/dropout-nation/by-the-numbers-dropping-out-of-high-school on September 21, 2012.

Brown, T., & Ferriter, W. M. (2021). *You can learn! Building student ownership, motivation, and efficacy with the PLC at Work process.* Bloomington, IN: Solution Tree Press.

Bryant, A. (2014, January 4). Management be nimble. *The New York Times.* Accessed at www.nytimes.com/2014/01/05/business/management-be-nimble.html?_r=0 on September 10, 2015.

Bryk, A. S., Sebring, P. B., Allensworth, E., Luppescu, S., & Easton, J. Q. (2010). *Organizing schools for improvement: Lessons from Chicago.* Chicago: University of Chicago Press.

Buckingham, M. (2005). *The one thing you need to know . . . about great managing, great leading, and sustained individual success.* New York: Free Press.

Buckingham, M., & Goodall, A. (2019, March–April). The feedback fallacy. *Harvard Business Review.* Accessed at https://hbr.org/2019/03/the-feedback-fallacy on January 12, 2024.

Buffum, A., & Mattos, M. (Eds.). (2015). *It's about time: Planning interventions and extensions in elementary school.* Bloomington, IN: Solution Tree Press.

Buffum, A., Mattos, M., Malone, J., Cruz, L. F., Dimich, N., & Schuhl, S. (in press). *Taking action: A handbook for RTI at Work* (2nd ed.). Bloomington, IN: Solution Tree Press.

Buffum, A., Mattos, M., & Weber, C. (2009). *Pyramid response to intervention: RTI, professional learning communities, and how to respond when kids don't learn.* Bloomington, IN: Solution Tree Press.

Buffum, A., Mattos, M., & Weber, C. (2012). *Simplifying response to intervention: Four essential guiding principles.* Bloomington, IN: Solution Tree Press.

Buffum, A., Mattos, M., Weber, C., & Hierck, T. (2015). *Uniting academic and behavior interventions: Solving the skill or will dilemma.* Bloomington, IN: Solution Tree Press.

Bureau of Labor Statistics. (2019, September 11). 44.6 percent of high school dropouts and 72.3 percent of college graduates employed in August 2019. *The Economics Daily.* Accessed at www.bls.gov/opub/ted/2019/44-6-percent-of-high-school-dropouts-and-72-3-percent-of-college-graduates-employed-in-august-2019.htm on January 29, 2024.

Burns, J. M. (1979). *Leadership*. New York: Harper & Row.

Camera, L. (2021, July 27). Study confirms school-to-prison pipeline: New research found that early strict discipline causes an increase in adult crime. *U.S. News & World Report*. Accessed at www.usnews.com/news/education-news/articles/2021-07-27/study-confirms-school-to-prison-pipeline on January 26, 2024.

Camp, A., Zamarro, G., & McGee, J. B. (2022). Changes in teachers' mobility and attrition in Arkansas during the first two years of the COVID-19 pandemic. *Education Reform Faculty and Graduate Students Publications*. Accessed at https://scholarworks.uark.edu/edrepub/138 on January 26, 2024.

Carnevale, A. P., Smith, N., & Strohl, J. (2010, June). *Help wanted: Projections of jobs and education requirements through 2018*. Washington, DC: Center on Education and the Workforce. Accessed at https://cew.georgetown.edu/wp-content/uploads/2014/12/HelpWanted.ExecutiveSummary.pdf on December 17, 2015.

Carroll, T. (2007). *Policy brief: The high cost of teacher turnover*. Washington, DC: National Commission on Teaching and America's Future. Accessed at https://files.eric.ed.gov/fulltext/ED498001.pdf on January 22, 2024.

Carroll, T. (2009). The next generation of learning teams. *Phi Delta Kappan, 91*(2), 8–13.

Centre for Effective Services. (2022). *The development of an implementation team is a key step for successful implementation*. Accessed at https://implementation.effectiveservices.org/enablers/implementation-teams on January 12, 2024.

Champy, J. (1995). *Reengineering management: The mandate for new leadership*. New York: HarperBusiness.

Chenoweth, K. (2009). It can be done, it's being done, and here's how. *Phi Delta Kappan, 91*(1), 38–43.

Chenoweth, K. (2015a). How do we get there from here? *Educational Leadership, 72*(5), 16–20.

Chenoweth, K. (2015b). Teachers matter. Yes. Schools matter. Yes. Districts matter—really? *Phi Delta Kappan, 97*(2), 14–20.

Childress, S. M., Doyle, D. P., & Thomas, D. A. (2009). *Leading for equity: The pursuit of excellence in Montgomery County Public Schools*. Cambridge, MA: Harvard Education Press.

Christman, J. B., Neild, R. C., Bulkley, K., Blanc, S., Liu, R., Mitchell, C., et al. (2009, June). *Making the most of interim assessment data: Lessons from Philadelphia*. Philadelphia: Research for Action. Accessed at www.researchforaction.org/making-the-most-of-interim-assessment-data-lessons-from-philadelphia on January 10, 2010.

Collie, R. J., Shapka, J. D., & Perry, N. E. (2012). School climate and social-emotional learning: Predicting teacher stress, job satisfaction, and teaching efficacy. *Journal of Educational Psychology, 104*(4), 1189–1204.

Collins, J. (1996). Aligning action and values. *Leader to Leader, 1*, 19–24.

Collins, J. (1999). Aligning actions and values. In F. Hesselbein & P. M. Cohen (Eds.), *Leader to leader: Enduring insights on leadership from the Drucker Foundation's award-winning journal* (pp. 237–266). San Francisco: Jossey-Bass.

Collins, J. (2001). *Good to great: Why some companies make the leap . . . and others don't.* New York: HarperBusiness.

Collins, J. (2009). *How the mighty fall: And why some companies never give in.* New York: HarperBusiness.

Collins, J., & Porras, J. I. (1994). *Built to last: Successful habits of visionary companies.* New York: HarperBusiness.

Conroy, P. (2010). *My reading life.* New York: Random House.

Consortium on Productivity in the Schools. (1995). *Using what we have to get the schools we need: A productivity focus for American education.* New York: Author.

Conzemius, A. E., & O'Neill, J. (2014). *The handbook for SMART school teams: Revitalizing best practices for collaboration* (2nd ed.). Bloomington, IN: Solution Tree Press.

Cornett, J., & Knight, J. (2009). Research on coaching. In J. Knight (Ed.), *Coaching approaches and perspectives* (pp. 192–216). Thousand Oaks, CA: Corwin Press.

Cottingham, B. W., Hough, H. J., & Myung, J. (2023). *What does it take to accelerate the learning of every child? Early insights from a CCEE school-improvement pilot.* Stanford, CA: Policy Analysis for California Education. Accessed at https://edpolicyinca.org/sites/default/files/2023-12/r_cottingham-dec2023.pdf on April 1, 2024.

Cotton, K. (2000). *The schooling practices that matter most.* Alexandria, VA: ASCD.

Covey, S. R. (1989). *The seven habits of highly effective people: Powerful lessons in personal change.* New York: Fireside.

Covey, S. R. (2006). *The speed of trust: The one thing that changes everything.* New York: Free Press.

Covey, S. R. (2013). *The seven habits of highly effective people: Powerful lessons in personal change* (25th anniversary ed.). New York: Simon & Schuster.

Custable, W., & Farmer, P. C. (2020). *Collaboration for career and technical education: Teamwork beyond the core content areas in a PLC at Work.* Bloomington, IN: Solution Tree Press.

Daniels, B. L. (2020). *PLC at Work and your small school: Building, deepening, and sustaining a culture of collaboration for singletons.* Bloomington, IN: Solution Tree Press.

Darling-Hammond, L. (1996). What matters most: A competent teacher for every child. *Phi Delta Kappan, 78*(3), 193–200.

Darling-Hammond, L. (2010). *The flat world and education: How America's commitment to equity will determine our future*. New York: Teachers College Press.

Darling-Hammond, L., DiNapoli, M., Jr., & Kini, T. (2023). *The federal role in ending teacher shortages*. Palo Alto, CA: Learning Policy Institute.

D'Auria, J. (2015). Learn to avoid or overcome leadership obstacles. *Phi Delta Kappan*, *96*(5), 52–54.

David, J. L. (2008). What research says about pacing guides. *Educational Leadership*, *66*(2), 87–88.

Deal, T. E., & Peterson, K. D. (1999). *Shaping school culture: The heart of leadership*. San Francisco: Jossey-Bass.

Delehant, A. M. (2007). *Making meetings work: How to get started, get going, and get it done*. Thousand Oaks, CA: Corwin Press.

Dennison, K. (2021, September 20). Why leaders should consider shifting to a coaching leadership style now more than ever. *Forbes*. Accessed at www.forbes.com/sites/karadennison/2021/09/20/why-leaders-should-consider-shifting-to-a-coaching-leadership-style-now-more-than-ever on January 1, 2024.

Diament, M. (2014, April 29). Graduation rates fall short for students with disabilities. *Disability Scoop*. Accessed at www.disabilityscoop.com/2014/04/29/graduation-rates-disabilities/19317 on December 17, 2015.

Dimich, N. (2015). *Design in five: Essential phases to create engaging assessment practice*. Bloomington, IN: Solution Tree Press.

Dimich, N. (2024). *Design in five: Essential phases to create engaging assessment practice* (2nd ed.). Bloomington, IN: Solution Tree Press.

Dolan, W. P. (1994). *Restructuring our schools: A primer on systemic change*. Kansas City, MO: Systems and Organization.

Dolejs, C. (2006, October). *Report on key practices and policies of consistently higher performing high schools*. Washington, DC: National High School Center. Accessed at https://files.eric.ed.gov/fulltext/ED501046.pdf on January 23, 2024.

Dougherty, C., & Reason, C. (2019). *Inside PLCs at Work: Your guided tour through one district's successes, challenges, and celebrations*. Bloomington, IN: Solution Tree Press.

Drucker, P. F. (1992). *Managing for the future: The 1990s and beyond*. New York: Truman Talley Books.

Druskat, V. U., & Wolff, S. B. (2001). Group emotional intelligence and its influence on group effectiveness. In C. Cherniss & D. Goleman (Eds.), *The emotionally intelligent workplace: How to select for, measure, and improve emotional intelligence in individuals, groups, and organizations* (pp. 132–158). San Francisco: Jossey-Bass.

DuBois, D. L., Holloway, B. E., Valentine, J. C., & Cooper, H. (2002). Effectiveness of mentoring programs for youth: A meta-analytic review. *American Journal of Community Psychology*, *30*(2), 157–197.

Duffett, A., Farkas, S., Rotherham, A. J., & Silva, E. (2008, May). *Waiting to be won over: Teachers speak on the profession, unions, and reform.* Washington, DC: Education Sector.

DuFour, R. (2002). The learning-centered principal. *Educational Leadership, 59*(8), 12–15.

DuFour, R. (2003). *Through new eyes: Examining the culture of your school* [Video]. Bloomington, IN: Solution Tree Press.

DuFour, R. (2015). *In praise of American educators: And how they can become even better.* Bloomington, IN: Solution Tree Press.

DuFour, R., & DuFour, R. (2012). *The school leader's guide to Professional Learning Communities at Work.* Bloomington, IN: Solution Tree Press.

DuFour, R., DuFour, R., Brown, T., & Mattos, M. (2016). *Creating and protecting the shared foundation of a Professional Learning Community at Work* [Video and facilitator's guide]. Bloomington, IN: Solution Tree Press.

DuFour, R., DuFour, R., Eaker, R., & Karhanek, G. (2010). *Raising the bar and closing the gap: Whatever it takes.* Bloomington, IN: Solution Tree Press.

DuFour, R., DuFour, R., Eaker, R., & Many, T. W. (2010). *Learning by doing: A handbook for Professional Learning Communities at Work* (2nd ed.). Bloomington, IN: Solution Tree Press.

DuFour, R., DuFour, R., Eaker, R., Many, T. W., & Mattos, M. (2016). *Learning by doing: A handbook for Professional Learning Communities at Work* (3rd ed.). Bloomington, IN: Solution Tree Press.

DuFour, R., DuFour, R., Eaker, R., Mattos, M., & Muhammad, A. (2021). *Revisiting Professional Learning Communities at Work: Proven insights for sustained, substantive school improvement* (2nd ed.). Bloomington, IN: Solution Tree Press.

DuFour, R., & Eaker, R. (1998). *Professional Learning Communities at Work: Best practices for enhancing student achievement.* Bloomington, IN: Solution Tree Press.

DuFour, R., & Fullan, M. (2013). *Cultures built to last: Systemic PLCs at Work.* Bloomington, IN: Solution Tree Press.

DuFour, R., & Marzano, R. J. (2011). *Leaders of learning: How district, school, and classroom leaders improve student achievement.* Bloomington, IN: Solution Tree Press.

DuFour, R., & Mattos, M. (2013). How do principals really improve schools? *Educational Leadership, 70*(7), 34–40.

DuFour, R., & Reason, C. (2016). *Professional Learning Communities at Work and virtual collaboration: On the tipping point of transformation.* Bloomington, IN: Solution Tree Press.

Duhigg, C. (2016, February 25). What Google learned from its quest to build the perfect team. *The New York Times Magazine.* Accessed at www.nytimes.com/2016/02/28/magazine/what-google-learned-from-its-quest-to-build-the-perfect-team.html on March 1, 2016.

Dulaney, S. K., Hallam, P. R., & Wall, G. (2013). Superintendent perceptions of multi-tiered systems of support (MTSS): Obstacles and opportunities for school system reform. *AASA Journal of Scholarship and Practice, 10*(2), 30–45.

Durlak, J. A., & DuPre, E. P. (2008). Implementation matters: A review of research on the influence of implementation on program outcomes and the factors affecting implementation. *American Journal of Community Psychology, 41*(3–4), 327–350.

Dweck, C. S. (2006). *Mindset: The new psychology of success.* New York: Random House.

Dweck, C. S. (2007). The perils and promises of praise. *Educational Leadership, 65*(2), 34–39.

Dweck, C. S. (2016). *Mindset: The new psychology of success* (Updated ed.). New York: Random House.

Eaker, R., & Dillard, H. (2017, Fall). Why collaborate? Because it enhances student learning. *AllThingsPLC Magazine*, 46–47.

Eaker, R., Hagadone, M., Keating, J., & Rhoades, M. (2021). *Leading PLCs at Work districtwide: From boardroom to classroom.* Bloomington, IN: Solution Tree Press.

Eaker, R., & Keating, J. (2012). *Every school, every team, every classroom: District leadership for growing Professional Learning Communities at Work.* Bloomington, IN: Solution Tree Press.

Eaker, R., & Keating, J. (2015). *Kid by kid, skill by skill: Teaching in a Professional Learning Community at Work.* Bloomington, IN: Solution Tree Press.

Eaker, R., & Sells, D. (2016). *A new way: Introducing higher education to Professional Learning Communities at Work.* Bloomington, IN: Solution Tree Press.

Eastwood, K. W., & Louis, K. S. (1992). Restructuring that lasts: Managing the performance dip. *Journal of School Leadership, 2*(2), 212–224.

Edmondson, A. C. (2013, December 17). The three pillars of a teaming culture. *Harvard Business Review.* Accessed at https://hbr.org/2013/12/the-three-pillars-of-a-teaming-culture on November 11, 2015.

Education Northwest. (n.d.). *At a glance: Successfully implementing PLC at Work in Arkansas.* Accessed at https://educationnorthwest.org/sites/default/files/plc-at-work-at-a-glance.pdf on April 1, 2024.

Education World. (n.d.). *Is your school's culture toxic or positive?* Accessed at www.educationworld.com/a_admin/admin/admin275.shtml on March 26, 2024.

Ellerbeck, S. (2023, January 25). *The Great Resignation continues. Why are US workers continuing to quit their jobs?* Accessed at www.weforum.org/agenda/2023/01/us-workers-jobs-quit on January 26, 2024.

Elmore, R. F. (2000). *Building a new structure for school leadership.* Washington, DC: Albert Shanker Institute. Accessed at https://files.eric.ed.gov/fulltext/ED546618.pdf on January 23, 2024.

Elmore, R. F. (2003). *Knowing the right thing to do: School improvement and performance-based accountability*. Washington, DC: National Governors Association Center for Best Practices.

Elmore, R. F. (2004). *School reform from the inside out: Policy, practice, and performance*. Cambridge, MA: Harvard Education Press.

Elmore, R. F. (2010). "I used to think . . . and now I think . . ." *Harvard Education Letter, 26*(1), 7–8.

Elmore, R. F., & City, E. (2007, May/June). The road to school improvement. *Harvard Education Letter, 23*(3).

Erkens, C. (2016). *Collaborative common assessments: Teamwork. Instruction. Results.* Bloomington, IN: Solution Tree Press.

Erkens, C., & Twadell, E. (2012). *Leading by design: An action framework for PLC at Work leaders*. Bloomington, IN: Solution Tree Press.

Evans, N. J. (2011). The argument against coaching cultures. *International Journal of Coaching in Organizations, 30*(8), 35–48.

Evans, R. (1996). *The human side of school change: Reform, resistance, and the real-life problems of innovation*. San Francisco: Jossey-Bass.

Farbman, D. A., Goldberg, D. J., & Miller, T. D. (2014, January). *Redesigning and expanding school time to support Common Core implementation*. Washington, DC: Center for American Progress. Accessed at https://cdn.americanprogress.org/wp-content/uploads/2014/01/CommonCore-reprint.pdf on October 20, 2015.

Farhi, P. (2012, April/May). Flunking the test. *American Journalism Review*. Accessed at http://ajrarchive.org/Article.asp?id=5280 on January 26, 2016.

Farmer, P. C., & King, D. (2022). *Virtual PLCs at Work: A guide to effectively implementing online and hybrid teaching and learning*. Bloomington, IN: Solution Tree Press.

Ferlazzo, L. (2014, November 29). Response: Formative assessments are "powerful" [Blog post]. *Education Week*. Accessed at http://blogs.edweek.org/teachers/classroom_qa_with_larry_ferlazzo/2014/11/response_formative_assessments_are_powerful.html on April 11, 2015.

Ferriter, W. M. (2020). *The big book of tools for collaborative teams in a PLC at Work*. Bloomington, IN: Solution Tree Press.

Fixsen, D. L. (2013, September). *Applied implementation science* [Plenary talk]. First Global Conference on Research Integration and Implementation, Canberra, Australia.

Fixsen, D. L., & Blase, K. A. (2009, January). *Implementation: The missing link between research and practice*. Chapel Hill, NC: National Implementation Research Network.

Fixsen, D., Naoom, S., Blasé, K., & Wallace, F. (2007). Implementation: The missing link between research and practice. *APSAC Advisor, 19*(1). National Implementation Research Network, University of North Carolina at Chapel Hill.

Francis, E. M. (2022). *Deconstructing depth of knowledge: A method and model for deeper teaching and learning.* Bloomington, IN: Solution Tree Press.

Friziellie, H., Schmidt, J. A., & Spiller, J. (2016). *Yes we can! General and special educators collaborating in a professional learning community.* Bloomington, IN: Solution Tree Press.

Fullan, M. (2001). *Leading in a culture of change.* San Francisco: Jossey-Bass.

Fullan, M. (2005). *Leadership and sustainability: System thinkers in action.* Thousand Oaks, CA: Corwin Press.

Fullan, M. (2007). *The new meaning of educational change* (4th ed.). New York: Teachers College Press.

Fullan, M. (2008). *The six secrets of change: What the best leaders do to help their organizations survive and thrive.* San Francisco: Jossey-Bass.

Fullan, M. (2010). *Motion leadership: The skinny on becoming change savvy.* Thousand Oaks, CA: Corwin Press.

Fullan, M. (2011). *The moral imperative realized.* Thousand Oaks, CA: Corwin Press.

Fullan, M. (2014). *The principal: Three keys to maximizing impact.* San Francisco: Jossey-Bass.

Fullan, M. (2016). *The new meaning of educational change* (5th ed.). New York: Teachers College Press.

Fullan, M. (2020). *Leading in a culture of change* (2nd ed.). San Francisco: Jossey-Bass.

Fullan, M., & Knight, J. (2011). Coaches as system leaders. *Educational Leadership, 69*(2). Accessed at https://michaelfullan.ca/wp-content/uploads/2019/12/Fullan-Knight-2011.pdf on November 7, 2023.

Fullan, M., & Quinn, J. (2016). *Coherence: The right drivers in action for schools, districts, and systems.* Thousand Oaks, CA: Corwin Press.

Fulton, K., & Britton, T. (2011, June). *STEM teachers in professional learning communities: From good teachers to great teaching.* Washington, DC: National Commission on Teaching and America's Future.

Fulton, K., Yoon, I., & Lee, C. (2005, August). *Induction into learning communities.* Washington, DC: National Commission on Teaching and America's Future. Accessed at https://files.eric.ed.gov/fulltext/ED494581.pdf on January 23, 2024.

Gabriel, J. G., & Farmer, P. C. (2009). *How to help your school thrive without breaking the bank.* Alexandria, VA: ASCD.

Galey, S. (2016). The evolving role of instructional coaches in U.S. policy contexts. *The William and Mary Educational Review, 4*(2), 54–71.

Gallimore, R., Ermeling, B. A., Saunders, W. M., & Goldenberg, C. (2009). Moving the learning of teaching closer to practice: Teacher education implications of school-based inquiry teams. *Elementary School Journal, 109*(5), 537–553.

Gallup. (2024). *Education: Satisfaction with K–12 education in the U.S.* Accessed at https://news.gallup.com/poll/1612/education.aspx on April 1, 2024.

Gardner, H. (2004). *Changing minds: The art and science of changing our own and other people's minds.* Boston: Harvard Business School Press.

Garmston, R. J. (2007). Results-oriented agendas transform meetings into valuable collaborative events. *Journal of Staff Development, 28*(2), 55–56.

Georgiades, W., Fuentes, E., & Snyder, K. (1983). *A meta-analysis of productive school cultures.* Houston: University of Texas.

Gobble, T., Onuscheck, M., Reibel, A. R., & Twadell, E. (2016). *Proficiency-based assessment: Process, not product.* Bloomington, IN: Solution Tree Press.

Goldhaber, D., & Holden, K. (2020). *Understanding the early teacher pipeline: What we can (and, importantly, can't) learn from national data* (CALDER Policy Brief No. 21-1120). Washington, DC: National Center for Analysis of Longitudinal Data in Education Research.

Goldhaber, D., Kane, T. J., McEachin, A., Morton, E., Patterson, T., & Staiger, D. O. (2022, May). *The consequences of remote and hybrid instruction during the pandemic* (NBER Working Paper No. 30010). Cambridge, MA: National Bureau of Economic Research. Accessed at www.nber.org/system/files/working_papers/w30010/w30010.pdf on January 26, 2024.

Goldring, E., Porter, A. C., Murphy, J., Elliott, S. N., & Cravens, X. (2007, March). *Assessing learning-centered leadership: Connections to research, professional standards, and current practices.* New York: Wallace Foundation. Accessed at https://wallacefoundation.org/sites/default/files/2023-09/Assessing-Learning-Centered-Leadership.pdf on January 22, 2024.

Goldsmith, M. (1996). Ask, learn, follow up, and grow. In F. Hesselbein, M. Goldsmith, & R. Beckhard (Eds.), *The leader of the future: New visions, strategies, and practices for the next era* (pp. 227–237). San Francisco: Jossey-Bass.

Goleman, D. (1998). *Working with emotional intelligence.* New York: Bantam Books.

Goleman, D., Boyatzis, R., & McKee, A. (2002). *Primal leadership: Realizing the power of emotional intelligence.* Boston: Harvard Business School Press.

Goleman, D., Boyatzis, R., & McKee, A. (2004). *Primal leadership: Learning to lead with emotional intelligence.* Boston: Harvard Business School Press.

Good, T. L., & Brophy, J. E. (1978). *Looking in classrooms* (2nd ed.). New York: Harper & Row.

Good, T. L., & Brophy, J. E. (2002). *Looking in classrooms* (9th ed.). Boston: Allyn & Bacon.

Goodreads. (n.d.). *Maya Angelou quotes.* Accessed at www.goodreads.com/quotes/5934-i-ve-learned-that-people-will-forget-what-you-said-people on February 9, 2024.

Goodwin, B. (2012). New teachers face three common challenges. *Educational Leadership, 69*(8), 84–85.

Goodwin, B., & Taylor, M. (2019). Finding the right glue. *Educational Leadership, 77*(3). Accessed at www.ascd.org/el/articles/finding-the-right-glue on January 22, 2024.

Grenny, J., Patterson, K., Maxfield, D., McMillan, R., & Switzler, A. (2013). *Influencer: The new science of leading change* (2nd ed.). New York: McGraw-Hill.

Grenny, J., Patterson, K., McMillan, R., Switzler, A., & Gregory, E. (2022). *Crucial conversations: Tools for talking when stakes are high* (3rd ed.). New York: McGraw-Hill.

Grissom, J. A., Loeb, S., & Master, B. (2013). Effective instructional time use for school leaders: Longitudinal evidence from observations of principals. *Educational Researcher, 42*(8). Accessed at https://cepa.stanford.edu/sites/default/files/grissom%20loeb%20%26%20master%20instructional%20time%20use_0.pdf on December 21, 2015.

Gruenert, S., & Whitaker, T. (2015). *School culture rewired: How to define, assess, and transform it.* Alexandria, VA: ASCD.

Guskey, T. R. (2014). Planning professional learning. *Educational Leadership, 71*(8). Accessed at www.ascd.org/publications/educational-leadership/may14/vol71/num08/Planning-Professional-Learning.aspx on December 21, 2015.

Hall, B. (2022). *Powerful guiding coalitions: How to build and sustain the leadership team in your PLC at Work.* Bloomington, IN: Solution Tree Press.

Halvorson, G. C. (2014). Getting to "us." *Harvard Business Review, 92*(9), 38.

Hamel, G. (2002). *Leading the revolution: How to thrive in turbulent times by making innovation a way of life.* Boston: Harvard Business School Press.

Hamilton, B. (2017). *Amazing dads: Love and lessons from the animal kingdom.* Washington, DC: National Geographic.

Hannigan, J., Hannigan, J. D., Mattos, M., & Buffum, A. (2021). *Behavior solutions: Teaching academic and social skills through RTI at Work.* Bloomington, IN: Solution Tree Press.

Hansen, A. (2015). *How to develop PLCs for singletons and small schools.* Bloomington, IN: Solution Tree Press.

Hanson, H., & Torres, K. (2020). *On the road to impact: Solution Tree Arkansas PLC at Work cohort 1 year 2 milepost memo* [Executive summary]. Portland, OR: Education Northwest. Accessed at https://dese.ade.arkansas.gov/Files/20201203104240_plc-at-work-excutive-summary_rv2.pdf on April 1, 2024.

Hanson, H., Torres, K., Yoon, S. Y., Merrill, R., Fantz, T., & Velie, Z. (2021). *Growing together: Professional Learning Communities at Work generates achievement gains in Arkansas.* Portland, OR: Education Northwest. Accessed at https://educationnorthwest.org/sites/default/files/plc-at-work-impact-evaluation.pdf on April 1, 2024.

Hardy, A. (2022, February 14). *The wage gap between college and high school grads just hit a record high.* Accessed at www.nasdaq.com/articles/the-wage-gap-between-college-and-high-school-grads-just-hit-a-record-high on January 26, 2024.

Hargreaves, A., & Fullan, M. (2012). *Professional capital: Transforming teaching in every school.* New York: Teachers College Press.

Hattie, J. A. C. (2009). *Visible learning: A synthesis of over 800 meta-analyses relating to achievement.* New York: Routledge.

Hattie, J. A. C. (2012). *Visible learning for teachers: Maximizing impact on learning.* New York: Routledge.

Hattie, J. A. C. (2015a, October 27). We aren't using assessments correctly. *Education Week.* Accessed at www.edweek.org/ew/articles/2015/10/28/we-arent-using-assessments-correctly.html on November 17, 2015.

Hattie, J. A. C. (2015b, June). *What doesn't work in education: The politics of distraction.* London: Pearson. Accessed at http://visible-learning.org/wp-content/uploads/2015/06/John-Hattie-Visible-Learning-creative-commons-book-free-PDF-download-What-doesn-t-work-in-education_the-politics-of-distraction-pearson-2015.pdf on September 30, 2015.

Hattie, J. A. C. (2015c, June). *What works best in education: The politics of collaborative expertise.* London: Pearson. Accessed at www.pearson.com/content/dam/corporate/global/pearson-dot-com/files/hattie/150526_ExpertiseWEB_V1.pdf on September 30, 2015.

Haynes, M. (2014, July). *On the path to equity: Improving the effectiveness of beginning teachers.* Washington, DC: Alliance for Excellent Education. Accessed at http://all4ed.org/wp-content/uploads/2014/07/PathToEquity.pdf on September 9, 2015.

Heath, C., & Heath, D. (2010). *Switch: How to change things when change is hard.* New York: Broadway Books.

Hendry, J. (2013). *Management: A very short introduction.* Oxford, England: Oxford University Press.

Herman, J., & Linn, R. (2013, January). *On the road to assessing deeper learning: The status of Smarter Balanced and PARCC assessment consortia* (CRESST Report 823). Los Angeles: National Center for Research on Evaluation, Standards, and Student Testing.

Hersey, P., Blanchard, K., & Johnson, D. E. (2001). *Management of organizational behavior: Leading human resources* (8th ed.). Upper Saddle River, NJ: Prentice Hall.

Hersey, P., Blanchard, K., & Johnson, D. E. (2013). *Management of organizational behavior: Leading human resources* (10th ed.). Upper Saddle River, NJ: Prentice Hall.

Hirsch, E. D., Jr. (1996). *The schools we need and why we don't have them.* New York: Doubleday.

Hirsch, W. (2023, September 25). *Change implementation team: What is it and why you need one* [Blog post]. Accessed at https://wendyhirsch.com/blog/implementation-teams on January 25, 2024.

Hord, S. M. (1997). Professional learning communities: What are they and why are they important? *Issues . . . about Change, 6*(1). Accessed at https://sedl.org/change/issues/issues61.html on July 12, 2023.

Hotchner, A. E. (1989). *Hemingway and his world.* New York: Vendome Press.

Individuals with Disabilities Education Improvement Act of 2004, Pub. L. No. 108-446 § 300.115 (2004).

Ingersoll, R., Merrill, L., & Stuckey, D. (2014, April). *Seven trends: The transformation of the teaching force.* Philadelphia: Consortium for Policy Research in Education. Accessed at https://files.eric.ed.gov/fulltext/ED566879.pdf on January 22, 2024.

International Coaching Federation. (2023, May 5). *What is the coaching cycle—and how to apply it* [Blog post]. Accessed at https://practice.do/blog/what-is-the-coaching-cycle-and-how-to-apply-it on January 22, 2024.

Jacob, F., John, S., & Gwany, D. M. (2020). Teachers' pedagogical content knowledge and students' academic achievement: A theoretical overview. *Journal of Global Research in Education and Social Science, 14*(2), 14–44.

Jacobs, H. H. (2001). New trends in curriculum: An interview with Heidi Hayes Jacobs. *Independent School, 61*(1), 18–22.

Jerald, C. (2005, August). *The implementation trap: Helping schools overcome barriers to change.* Washington, DC: Center for Comprehensive School Reform and Improvement.

Jimenez, K. (2022, October 24). Reading and math test scores fell across US during the pandemic. How did your state fare? *USA Today.* Accessed at www.usatoday.com/story/news/2022/10/24/naep-report-card-test-scores-reading-math/10552407002 on January 26, 2024.

Jin, Z. (2011). *Global technological change: From hard technology to soft technology* (2nd ed.; K. W. Willoughby & Y. Bai, Trans.). Chicago: Intellect.

Johnson, J., Leibowitz, S., & Perret, K. (2017). *The coach approach to school leadership: Leading teachers to higher levels of effectiveness.* Alexandria, VA: ASCD.

Johnson, S. M. (2011, Fall). Delivering on the promise of public schooling. *Voices in Urban Education, 31*, 20–27. Accessed at https://annenberg.brown.edu/sites/default/files/VUE31.pdf on January 23, 2024.

Johnson, S. M., & Kardos, S. M. (2004). Professional culture and the promise of colleagues. In S. M. Johnson, *Finders and keepers: Helping new teachers survive and thrive in our schools* (pp. 139–166). San Francisco: Jossey-Bass.

Jones, A., & Kallingal, M. (2023). *ACT reports record low scores on its college readiness exam*. Accessed at https://ktvz.com/news/national-world/cnn-national/2023/10/13/act-reports-record-low-scores-on-its-college-readiness-exam on April 1, 2024.

Joyce, B., & Showers, B. (2002). *Student achievement through staff development* (3rd ed.). Alexandria, VA: ASCD.

Joyce, K. (2022, July 12). We don't need no education: Now Arizona says teachers don't require college degrees. *Salon*. Accessed at www.salon.com/2022/07/12/we-dont-need-no-education-now-arizona-says-teachers-dont-require-college-degrees on November 7, 2023.

Kanold, T. D. (2006). The continuous improvement wheel of a professional learning community. *Journal of Staff Development, 27*(2), 16–21.

Kanold, T. D. (2011). *The five disciplines of PLC leaders*. Bloomington, IN: Solution Tree Press.

Kanold, T. D., Toncheff, M., Larson, M. R., Barnes, B., Kanold-McIntyre, J., & Schuhl, S. (2018). *Mathematics coaching and collaboration in a PLC at Work*. Bloomington, IN: Solution Tree Press.

Kanter, R. M. (1999). The enduring skills of change leaders. *Leader to Leader, 13*, 15–22.

Kanter, R. M. (2004). *Confidence: How winning streaks and losing streaks begin and end*. New York: Crown Business.

Kanter, R. M. (2005). How leaders gain (and lose) confidence. *Leader to Leader, 35*, 21–27.

Katzenbach, J. R., & Smith, D. K. (1993). *The wisdom of teams: Creating the high-performance organization*. Boston: Harvard Business School Press.

Kaye, B., & Jordan-Evans, S. (2014). *Love 'em or lose 'em: Getting good people to stay* (5th ed.). San Francisco: Berrett-Koehler.

Kaye, B., & Jordan-Evans, S. (2021). *Love 'em or lose 'em: Getting good people to stay* (6th ed.). San Francisco: Berrett-Koehler.

Kegan, R., & Lahey, L. L. (2001). *How the way we talk can change the way we work: Seven languages for transformation*. San Francisco: Jossey-Bass.

Kerr, D., Hulen, T. A., Heller, J., & Butler, B. K. (2021). *What about us? The PLC at Work process for grades preK–2 teams*. Bloomington, IN: Solution Tree Press.

Killion, J., Bryan, C., & Clifton, H. (2020). *Coaching matters* (2nd ed.). Oxford, OH: Learning Forward.

Killion, J., & Harrison, C. (2017). *Taking the lead: New roles for teachers and school-based coaches* (2nd ed.). Oxford, OH: Learning Forward.

Killion, J., Harrison, C., Bryan, C., & Clifton, H. (2012). *Coaching matters*. Oxford, OH: Learning Forward.

Knight, D. S. (2012). Assessing the cost of instructional coaching. *Journal of Education Finance, 38*(1), 52–80.

Knight, J., van Nieuwerburgh, C., Campbell, J., & Thomas, S. (2019). Seven ways principals can improve professional conversations. *Principal Leadership, 19.* Accessed at www.nassp.org/publication/principal-leadership/volume-19-2018-2019/principal-leadership-january-2019 on February 3, 2020.

Kotter, J. P. (1996). *Leading change.* Boston: Harvard Business School Press.

Kotter, J. P. (2012). *Leading change.* Boston: Harvard Business Review Press.

Kotter, J. P., & Cohen, D. S. (2002). *The heart of change: Real-life stories of how people change their organizations.* Boston: Harvard Business School Press.

Kotter International. (2015). *Eight steps to accelerate change in 2015.* Accessed at www.kotterinternational.com/ebook/Kotter-8-steps-ebook.pdf on January 26, 2016.

Koumpilova, M. (2022, February 23). In Chicago Public Schools, more principals and teachers are leaving. *Chalkbeat Chicago.* Accessed at www.chalkbeat.org/chicago/2022/2/23/22947818/chicago-public-schools-teacher-principal-resignation-retirement-covid on January 26, 2024.

Kouzes, J. M., & Posner, B. Z. (1987). *The leadership challenge: How to get extraordinary things done in organizations.* San Francisco: Jossey-Bass.

Kouzes, J. M., & Posner, B. Z. (2003). *Encouraging the heart: A leader's guide to rewarding and recognizing others.* San Francisco: Jossey-Bass.

Kouzes, J. M., & Posner, B. Z. (2006). *A leader's legacy.* San Francisco: Jossey-Bass.

Kouzes, J. M., & Posner, B. Z. (2010). *The truth about leadership: The no-fads, heart-of-the-matter facts you need to know.* San Francisco: Jossey-Bass.

Kraft, M. A., Blazar, D., & Hogan, D. (2018). The effect of teacher coaching on instruction and achievement: A meta-analysis of the causal evidence. *Review of Educational Research, 88*(4). Accessed at https://scholar.harvard.edu/files/mkraft/files/kraft_blazar_hogan_2018_teacher_coaching.pdf on January 23, 2024.

Kramer, S. V. (2015). *How to leverage PLCs for school improvement.* Bloomington, IN: Solution Tree Press.

Kruse, S., Louis, K. S., & Bryk, A. (1994). *Building professional community in schools* (Issue Report No. 6). Madison, WI: Center on Organization and Restructuring of Schools.

Kullar, J. K., & Cunningham, S. A. (2020). *Building your building: How to hire and keep great teachers.* Bloomington, IN: Solution Tree Press.

Larner, M. (2007). *Tools for leaders: Indispensable graphic organizers, protocols, and planning guidelines for working and learning together.* New York: Scholastic.

Leana, C. R. (2011, Fall). The missing link in school reform. *Stanford Social Innovation Review.* Accessed at https://ssir.org/articles/entry/the_missing_link_in_school_reform on November 7, 2023.

Leane, B., & Yost, J. (2022). *Singletons in a PLC at Work: Navigating on-ramps to meaningful collaboration*. Bloomington, IN: Solution Tree Press.

Lee-St. John, T. J., Walsh, M. E., Raczek, A. E., Vuilleumier, C. E., Foley, C., Heberle, A., et al. (2018). The long-term impact of systemic student support in elementary school: Reducing high school dropout. *AERA Open*, *4*(4).

Leithwood, K., Louis, K. S., Anderson, S., & Wahlstrom, K. L. (2004). *How leadership influences student learning*. New York: Wallace Foundation.

Leithwood, K., Louis, K. S., Wahlstrom, K. L., Anderson, S., Mascall, B., Michlin, M., et al. (2009). *Learning from district efforts to improve student achievement*. New York: Wallace Foundation.

Lencioni, P. (2003). The trouble with teamwork. *Leader to Leader*, *29*, 35–40.

Lencioni, P. (2005). *Overcoming the five dysfunctions of a team: A field guide for leaders, managers, and facilitators*. San Francisco: Jossey-Bass.

Lencioni, P. (2012). *The advantage: Why organizational health trumps everything else in business*. San Francisco: Jossey-Bass.

Lezotte, L. W. (1991). *Correlates of effective schools: The first and second generation*. Okemos, MI: Effective Schools Products. Accessed at www.effectiveschools.com/Correlates.pdf on January 6, 2006.

Lezotte, L. W. (2002). *Revolutionary and evolutionary: The effective schools movement*. Accessed at www.effectiveschools.com/images/stories/RevEv.pdf on January 10, 2010.

Lezotte, L. W. (2005). More effective schools: Professional learning communities in action. In R. DuFour, R. Eaker, & R. DuFour (Eds.), *On common ground: The power of professional learning communities* (pp. 177–191). Bloomington, IN: Solution Tree Press.

Lezotte, L. W. (2011). Effective schools: Past, present, and future. *Journal for Effective Schools*, *10*(1), 3–21.

Lezotte, L. W., & Snyder, K. M. (2011). *What effective schools do: Re-envisioning the correlates*. Bloomington, IN: Solution Tree Press.

Lieberman, A. (1995). Restructuring schools: The dynamics of changing practice, structure, and culture. In A. Lieberman (Ed.), *The work of restructuring schools: Building from the ground up* (pp. 1–17). New York: Teachers College Press.

Little, J. W. (2006, December). *Professional community and professional development in the learning-centered school*. Washington, DC: National Education Association.

Little, J. W., & McLaughlin, M. W. (Eds.). (1993). *Teachers' work: Individuals, colleagues, and contexts*. New York: Teachers College Press.

Looney, J. (2005, November). *Formative assessment: Improving learning in secondary classrooms*. Paris: Organisation for Economic Co-operation and Development.

Louis, K. S., Kruse, S. D., & Marks, H. M. (1996). Schoolwide professional community. In F. M. Newmann & Associates (Eds.), *Authentic achievement:*

Restructuring schools for intellectual quality (pp. 179–204). San Francisco: Jossey-Bass.

Louis, K. S., Leithwood, K., Wahlstrom, K. L., & Anderson, S. E. (2010, July). *Investigating the links to improved student learning: Final report of research findings*. New York: Wallace Foundation.

Lupoli, C. (2018, June 12). *Creating a culture of collaboration and coaching to improve the effectiveness of every teacher* [Blog post]. Accessed at www.ascd.org/blogs/creating-a-culture-of-collaboration-and-coaching-to-improve-the-effectiveness-of-every-teacher on January 23, 2024.

Lynch, M. (2016, August 2). High school dropout rate: Causes and costs. *The Edvocate*. Accessed at www.theedadvocate.org/high-school-dropout-rate-causes-and-costs on January 26, 2024.

Lyon, A. R. (2017). *Brief: Implementation science and practice in the education sector*. Rockville, MD: Now Is the Time Technical Assistance Center.

Mader, J., & Butrymowicz, S. (2014, October 29). For many with disabilities, special education leads to jail. *Disability Scoop*. Accessed at www.disabilityscoop.com/2014/10/29/for-sped-leads-jail/19800 on January 26, 2016.

Maeker, P., & Heller, J. (2023). *Literacy in a PLC at Work: Guiding teams to get going and get better in grades K–6 reading*. Bloomington, IN: Solution Tree Press.

Manna, P. (2015). *Developing excellent school principals to advance teaching and learning: Considerations for state policy*. New York: Wallace Foundation. Accessed at https://wallacefoundation.org/sites/default/files/2023-09/Developing-Excellent-School-Principals.pdf on January 22, 2024.

Many, T. W., Maffoni, M. J., Sparks, S. K., & Thomas, T. F. (2018). *Amplify your impact: Coaching collaborative teams in PLCs at Work*. Bloomington, IN: Solution Tree Press.

Many, T. W., Maffoni, M. J., Sparks, S. K., & Thomas, T. F. (2020). *How schools thrive: Building a coaching culture for collaborative teams in PLCs at Work*. Bloomington, IN: Solution Tree Press.

Many, T. W., Maffoni, M. J., Sparks, S. K., & Thomas, T. F. (2022). *Energize your teams: Powerful tools for coaching collaborative teams in PLCs at Work*. Bloomington, IN: Solution Tree Press.

Many, T. W., & Sparks-Many, S. K. (2015). *Leverage: Using PLCs to promote lasting improvement in schools*. Thousand Oaks, CA: Corwin Press.

Markow, D., Macia, L., & Lee, H. (2013, February). *The MetLife survey of the American teacher: Challenges for school leadership*. New York: MetLife. Accessed at https://files.eric.ed.gov/fulltext/ED542202.pdf on January 23, 2024.

Markow, D., & Pieters, A. (2010, April). *The MetLife survey of the American teacher: Collaborating for student success*. New York: MetLife. Accessed at http://files.eric.ed.gov/fulltext/ED509650.pdf on December 15, 2015.

Marshall, K. (2015). How principals can reshape the teaching bell curve. *Journal of Staff Development, 36*(4), 34–37.

Martin, M. O., Mullis, I. V. S., Foy, P., & Stanco, G. M. (2012). *TIMSS 2011 international results in science*. Amsterdam: International Association for the Evaluation of Educational Achievement. Accessed at http://timssandpirls.bc.edu/timss2011/downloads/T11_IR_Science_FullBook.pdf on January 27, 2016.

Marzano, R. J. (2003). *What works in schools: Translating research into action*. Alexandria, VA: ASCD.

Marzano, R. J. (2006). *Classroom assessment and grading that work*. Alexandria, VA: ASCD.

Marzano, R. J. (2009). Setting the record straight on "high-yield" strategies. *Phi Delta Kappan, 91*(1), 30–37.

Marzano, R. J. (2010). When students track their progress. *Educational Leadership, 67*(4), 86–87.

Marzano, R. J., Heflebower, T., Hoegh, J. K., Warrick, P., & Grift, G. (2016). *Collaborative teams that transform schools: The next step in PLCs*. Bloomington, IN: Marzano Resources.

Marzano, R. J., Warrick, P., & Simms, J. A. (2014). *A handbook for High Reliability Schools: The next step in school reform*. Bloomington, IN: Marzano Resources.

Marzano, R. J., & Waters, T. (2009). *District leadership that works: Striking the right balance*. Bloomington, IN: Solution Tree Press.

Marzano, R. J., Waters, T., & McNulty, B. A. (2005). *School leadership that works: From research to results*. Alexandria, VA: ASCD.

Maslow, A. H. (1943). A theory of human motivation. *Psychological Review, 50*(4), 370–396.

Mattos, M., & Buffum, A. (Eds.). (2015). *It's about time: Planning interventions and extensions in secondary school*. Bloomington, IN: Solution Tree Press.

Mattos, M., DuFour, R., DuFour, R., Eaker, R., & Many, T. W. (2016). *Concise answers to frequently asked questions about Professional Learning Communities at Work*. Bloomington, IN: Solution Tree Press.

McCain, A. (2023, July 9). *30 incredible teacher statistics [2023]: Demographics, salary, and the U.S. teacher shortage*. Accessed at www.zippia.com/advice/teacher-statistics on January 26, 2024.

McDonald, J. P., Mohr, N., Dichter, A., & McDonald, E. C. (2007). *The power of protocols: An educator's guide to better practice* (2nd ed.). New York: Teachers College Press.

McGregor, D. (1960). *The human side of enterprise*. New York: McGraw-Hill.

McKee, K. (2022, June 16). *How to make coaching cycles the center of instructional coaching work* [Blog post]. Accessed at www.nwea.org/blog/2022/

how-to-make-coaching-cycles-the-center-of-instructional-coaching-work on November 7, 2023.

McLaughlin, M. W., & Talbert, J. E. (2006). *Building school-based teacher learning communities: Professional strategies to improve student achievement.* New York: Teachers College Press.

McLuhan, M. (1994). *Understanding media: The extensions of man.* Cambridge, MA: MIT Press.

Mehta, J. (2014, July 16). Five inconvenient truths for reformers [Blog post]. *Education Week.* Accessed at http://blogs.edweek.org/edweek/learning_deeply/2014/07/five_inconvenient_truths_for_reformers.html on December 20, 2014.

Metz, A., & Bartley, L. (2020). Implementation teams: A stakeholder view of leading and sustaining change. In B. Albers, A. Shlonsky, & R. Mildon (Eds.), *Implementation science 3.0* (pp. 199–225). Cham, Switzerland: Springer.

Mihalic, S., Irwin, K., Fagan, A., Ballard, D., & Elliott, D. (2004, July). Successful program implementation: Lessons from blueprints. *Juvenile Justice Bulletin.* Washington, DC: U.S. Department of Justice.

Miller, A. (2019, October 2). The value of coaching for instructional leaders. *Edutopia.* Accessed at www.edutopia.org/article/value-coaching-instructional-leaders on November 7, 2023.

MindTools. (n.d.). *Coaching for team performance: Improving productivity by improving relationships.* Accessed at www.mindtools.com/am46o36/coaching-for-team-performance on November 7, 2023.

Mintzberg, H. (1994). *The rise and fall of strategic planning: Reconceiving roles for planning, plans, planners.* New York: Free Press.

Mourshed, M., Chijioke, C., & Barber, M. (2010, November). *How the world's most improved school systems keep getting better.* New York: McKinsey & Company. Accessed at www.mckinsey.com/~/media/mckinsey/dotcom/client_service/social%20sector/pdfs/how-the-worlds-most-improved-school-systems-keep-getting-better_download-version_final.ashx on December 17, 2015.

Muhammad, A. (2009). *Transforming school culture: How to overcome staff division.* Bloomington, IN: Solution Tree Press.

Muhammad, A. (2018). *Transforming school culture: How to overcome staff division* (2nd ed.). Bloomington, IN: Solution Tree Press.

Muhammad, A., & Cruz, L. F. (2019). *Time for change: Four essential skills for transformational school and district leaders.* Bloomington, IN: Solution Tree Press.

Muhammad, A., & Hollie, S. (2012). *The will to lead, the skill to teach: Transforming schools at every level.* Bloomington, IN: Solution Tree Press.

Mullis, I. V. S., Martin, M. O., Foy, P., & Arora, A. (2012). *TIMSS 2011 international results in mathematics.* Amsterdam: International Association for the Evaluation of

Educational Achievement. Accessed at http://timssandpirls.bc.edu/timss2011/downloads/T11_IR_Mathematics_FullBook.pdf on January 26, 2016.

Nanus, B. (1992). *Visionary leadership: Creating a compelling sense of direction for your organization*. San Francisco: Jossey-Bass.

National Association of Secondary School Principals & National Association of Elementary School Principals. (2013). *Leadership matters: What the research says about the importance of principal leadership*. Alexandria, VA: National Association of Elementary School Principals.

National Center for Education Statistics. (2019). *Students with disabilities*. Washington, DC: Author. Accessed at https://bit.ly/3y4XGNW on December 8, 2021.

National Center for Educational Achievement. (2009, January). *Core practices in math and science: An investigation of consistently higher performing school systems in five states*. Austin, TX: Author. Accessed at www.act.org/content/dam/act/unsecured/documents/NCEA-core_practices_in_math_and_science-01-01-09.pdf on January 23, 2024.

National Center on Response to Intervention. (2008, May 12). *What is response to intervention?* [Webinar]. Accessed at www.rti4success.org/index.php?option=com_content&task=blogcategory&id=22&Itemid=79 on January 18, 2010.

National Commission on Teaching and America's Future. (2003, January). *No dream denied: A pledge to America's children*. Washington, DC: Author.

National Geographic Society. (2023, October 19). *Apr 23, 1635 CE: First public school in America*. Accessed at https://education.nationalgeographic.org/resource/first-public-school-america on January 29, 2024.

National Governors Association Center for Best Practices & Council of Chief State School Officers. (2010a). *Common Core State Standards for English language arts and literacy in history/social studies, science, and technical subjects*. Washington, DC: Authors. Accessed at https://learning.ccsso.org/wp-content/uploads/2022/11/ELA_Standards1.pdf on January 22, 2024.

National Governors Association Center for Best Practices & Council of Chief State School Officers. (2010b). *Common Core State Standards for mathematics*. Washington, DC: Authors. Accessed at https://corestandards.org/wp-content/uploads/2023/09/Math_Standards1.pdf on January 22, 2024.

National Governors Association Center for Best Practices, Council of Chief State School Officers, & Achieve. (2008). *Benchmarking for success: Ensuring U.S. students receive a world-class education*. Washington, DC: Authors. Accessed at https://files.eric.ed.gov/fulltext/ED504084.pdf on January 23, 2024.

National Implementation Research Network. (2020). *Implementation stages planning tool*. Chapel Hill, NC: Author.

National Policy Board for Educational Administration. (2015). *Professional standards for educational leaders*. Reston, VA: Author. Accessed at www.npbea.org/

wp-content/uploads/2017/06/Professional-Standards-for-Educational-Leaders_2015.pdf on January 23, 2024.

National Staff Development Council. (1999). Developing norms. *Tools for Schools, 3*(1), 3–5.

National Turning Points Center. (2001). *Turning points: Transforming middle schools—Guide to collaborative culture and shared leadership*. Boston: Author.

Neufeld, B., & Roper, D. (2003, June). *Coaching: A strategy for developing instructional capacity—Promises and practicalities*. Providence, RI: Annenberg Institute for School Reform. Accessed at www.aspeninstitute.org/wp-content/uploads/files/content/docs/pubs/Coaching_NeufeldRoper.pdf on November 7, 2023.

New Leaders. (2023, February 28). *3 ways to work towards better implementation in schools and districts* [Blog post]. Accessed at www.newleaders.org/blog/3-ways-to-work-towards-better-implementation-in-schools-and-districts on January 23, 2024.

The New Teacher Project. (2015). *The mirage: Confronting the hard truth about our quest for teacher development*. New York: Author. Accessed at http://tntp.org/assets/documents/TNTP-Mirage_2015.pdf on January 26, 2016.

Newmann, F. M., & Associates. (Eds.). (1996). *Authentic achievement: Restructuring schools for intellectual quality*. San Francisco: Jossey-Bass.

Newmann, F. M., & Wehlage, G. G. (1995). *Successful school restructuring: A report to the public and educators*. Madison, WI: Center on Organization and Restructuring of Schools.

Newmann, F. M., & Wehlage, G. G. (1996). Conclusion: Restructuring for authentic student achievement. In F. M. Newmann & Associates (Eds.), *Authentic achievement: Restructuring schools for intellectual quality* (pp. 286–301). San Francisco: Jossey-Bass.

No Child Left Behind (NCLB) Act of 2001, Pub. L. No. 107-110, § 115, Stat. 1425 (2002).

Odden, A. R., & Archibald, S. J. (2009). *Doubling student performance . . . and finding the resources to do it*. Thousand Oaks, CA: Corwin Press.

O'Hora, D., & Maglieri, K. A. (2006). Goal statements and goal-directed behavior: A relational frame account of goal setting in organizations. *Journal of Organizational Behavior Management, 26*(1), 131–170.

O'Neill, J., & Conzemius, A. E. (2006). *The power of SMART goals: Using goals to improve student learning*. Bloomington, IN: Solution Tree Press.

Opper, I. M. (2019). *Teachers matter: Understanding teachers' impact on student achievement*. Santa Monica, CA: RAND. Accessed at www.rand.org/pubs/research_reports/RR4312.html on January 23, 2024.

Organisation for Economic Co-operation and Development. (2009, December). *21st century skills and competences for new millennium learners in OECD countries*

(Working Paper No. 41). Paris: Author. Accessed at www.oecd.org/officialdocuments/publicdisplaydocumentpdf/?cote=EDU/WKP(2009)20&doclanguage=en on February 14, 2015.

Organisation for Economic Co-operation and Development. (2014). *Education at a glance 2014: OECD indicators*. Paris: Author. Accessed at www.oecd.org/education/Education-at-a-Glance-2014.pdf on January 23, 2024.

Organisation for Economic Co-operation and Development. (2023). *Education at a glance 2023: OECD indicators*. Paris: Author. Accessed at https://www.oecd-ilibrary.org/docserver/e13bef63-en.pdf?expires=1711563675&id=id&accname=guest&checksum=83BF501C42F3B69A9D7B8302E601C9E0 on January 23, 2024.

Palmer, K. (2022). *Parentships in a PLC at Work: Forming and sustaining school-home relationships with families*. Bloomington, IN: Solution Tree Press.

Panchal, N., Saunders, H., Rudowitz, R., & Cox, C. (2023, March 20). *The implications of COVID-19 for mental health and substance use*. Accessed at www.kff.org/mental-health/issue-brief/the-implications-of-covid-19-for-mental-health-and-substance-use on January 26, 2024.

Papay, J. P., & Kraft, M. A. (2015, May 28). *Developing workplaces where teachers stay, improve, and succeed* [Blog post]. Accessed at www.shankerinstitute.org/blog/developing-workplaces-where-teachers-stay-improve-and-succeed on January 23, 2024.

Patterson, K., Grenny, J., Maxfield, D., McMillan, R., & Switzler, A. (2008). *Influencer: The power to change anything*. New York: McGraw-Hill.

Patterson, K., Grenny, J., Maxfield, D., McMillan, R., & Switzler, A. (2013). *Crucial accountability: Tools for resolving violated expectations, broken commitments, and bad behavior* (2nd ed.). New York: McGraw-Hill.

Patterson, K., Grenny, J., McMillan, R., & Switzler, A. (2002). *Crucial conversations: Tools for talking when stakes are high*. New York: McGraw-Hill.

Pellegrino, J. W., & Hilton, M. L. (Eds.). (2012). *Education for life and work: Developing transferable knowledge and skills in the 21st century*. Washington, DC: National Academies Press.

Perkins, D. (2003). *King Arthur's round table: How collaborative conversations create smart organizations*. New York: Wiley.

Perrone, F., & Meyers, C. V. (2021, September). *Teacher hiring in the United States: A review of the empirical research (2001–2020)* (EdWorkingPaper No. 21-459). Accessed at www.edworkingpapers.com/sites/default/files/ai21-459.pdf on November 7, 2023.

Peters, T. (1987). *Thriving on chaos: Handbook for a management revolution*. New York: Knopf.

Peters, T., & Austin, N. (1985). *A passion for excellence: The leadership difference*. New York: Random House.

Pfeffer, J., & Sutton, R. I. (2000). *The knowing-doing gap: How smart companies turn knowledge into action.* Boston: Harvard Business School Press.

Pfeffer, J., & Sutton, R. I. (2006). *Hard facts, dangerous half-truths, and total nonsense: Profiting from evidence-based management.* Boston: Harvard Business School Press.

Phi Delta Kappan/Gallup Poll. (2015). Testing doesn't measure up for Americans: The 47th annual PDK/Gallup poll of the public's attitudes toward the public schools. *Phi Delta Kappan, 97*(1), NP1–NP32.

Phi Delta Kappan/Gallup Poll Archive. (2014). *Archive of responses regarding quality of education.* Accessed at www.pdkmembers.org/members_online/publications/GallupPoll/k_q_quality_1.htm#519 on January 25, 2016.

Pinchot, G., & Pinchot, E. (1993). *The end of bureaucracy and the rise of the intelligent organization.* San Francisco: Berrett-Koehler.

Pink, D. H. (2011). *Drive: The surprising truth about what motivates us.* New York: Riverhead Books.

Podolsky, A., Darling-Hammond, L., Doss, C., & Reardon, S. (2019). *California's positive outliers: Districts beating the odds.* Palo Alto, CA: Learning Policy Institute.

Popham, W. J. (2008). *Transformative assessment.* Alexandria, VA: ASCD.

Popham, W. J. (2009). Curriculum mistakes to avoid. *American School Board Journal, 196*(11), 36–38.

Popham, W. J. (2013). Formative assessment's "advocatable moment." *Education Week, 32*(15), 29.

President's Commission on Excellence in Special Education. (2002, July). *A new era: Revitalizing special education for children and their families.* Washington, DC: Author. Accessed at http://ectacenter.org/~pdfs/calls/2010/earlypartc/revitalizing_special_education.pdf on December 17, 2015.

Provencio, N. (2021). *Community connections and your PLC at Work: A guide to engaging families.* Bloomington, IN: Solution Tree Press.

Psencik, K. (2011). *The coach's craft: Powerful practices to support school leaders.* Oxford, OH: Learning Forward.

Purkey, S. C., & Smith, M. S. (1983). Effective schools: A review. *Elementary School Journal, 83*(4), 427–452.

Pustkowski, R., Scott, J., & Tesvic, J. (2014, August). *Why implementation matters.* New York: McKinsey & Company.

Quate, S. (n.d.). *Conductive conversations leading to results using protocols and structures in professional learning communities.* Denver, CO: CU Denver School of Education.

Quinn, R. E. (1996). *Deep change: Discovering the leader within.* San Francisco: Jossey-Bass.

Ragland, M. A., Clubine, B., Constable, D., & Smith, P. A. (2002, April). *Expecting success: A study of five high performing, high poverty schools.* Washington, DC: Council of Chief State School Officers.

RAND Corporation. (2012). *Teachers matter: Understanding teachers' impact on student achievement.* Santa Monica, CA: Author. Accessed at www.rand.org/pubs/corporate_pubs/CP693z1-2012-09.html on January 26, 2016.

Raue, K., & Gray, L. (2015, September). *Career paths of beginning public school teachers: Results from the first through fifth waves of the 2007–08 Beginning Teacher Longitudinal Study* (NCES 2015-196). Washington, DC: National Center for Education Statistics. Accessed at http://nces.ed.gov/pubs2015/2015196.pdf on October 10, 2015.

Ravitch, D. (2014). *Reign of error: The hoax of the privatization movement and the danger to America's public schools.* New York: Vintage Books.

Read On Arizona. (2024). *Case studies: Agua Caliente Elementary and Tanque Verde Elementary.* Accessed at https://readonarizona.org/case-studies/TVUSD on April 1, 2024.

Reeves, D. (2002). *The leader's guide to standards: A blueprint for educational equity and excellence.* San Francisco: Jossey-Bass.

Reeves, D. (2004). *Accountability for learning: How teachers and school leaders can take charge.* Alexandria, VA: ASCD.

Reeves, D. (2005). Putting it all together: Standards, assessment, and accountability in successful professional learning communities. In R. DuFour, R. Eaker, & R. DuFour (Eds.), *On common ground: The power of professional learning communities* (pp. 45–63). Bloomington, IN: Solution Tree Press.

Reeves, D. (2006). *The learning leader: How to focus school improvement for better results.* Alexandria, VA: ASCD.

Reeves, D. (2009). *Leading change in your school: How to conquer myths, build commitment, and get results.* Alexandria, VA: ASCD.

Reeves, D. (2015). *Inspiring creativity and innovation in K–12.* Bloomington, IN: Solution Tree Press.

Reeves, D. (2020). *The learning leader: How to focus school improvement for better results* (2nd ed.). Alexandria, VA: ASCD.

Reeves, D. (2021). *Deep change leadership: A model for renewing and strengthening schools and districts.* Bloomington, IN: Solution Tree Press.

Reeves, D., & Eaker, R. (2019). *100-day leaders: Turning short-term wins into long-term success in schools.* Bloomington, IN: Solution Tree Press.

Rice, J. K. (2010, August). *The impact of teacher experience: Examining the evidence and policy implications* (Brief No. 11). Washington, DC: National Center for Analysis of Longitudinal Data in Education Research. Accessed at https://files.eric.ed.gov/fulltext/ED511988.pdf on January 23, 2024.

Rich, M. (2015, August 9). Teacher shortages spur a nationwide hiring scramble (credentials optional). *The New York Times*. Accessed at www.nytimes.com/2015/08/10/us/teacher-shortages-spur-a-nationwide-hiring-scramble-credentials-optional.html?_r=0 on January 26, 2016.

Riggs, L. (2013, October 18). Why do teachers quit? And why do they stay? *The Atlantic*. Accessed at www.theatlantic.com/education/archive/2013/10/why-do-teachers-quit/280699 on January 26, 2016.

Ringwalt, C. L., Ennett, S., Johnson, R., et al. (2003). Factors associated with fidelity to substance use prevention curriculum guides in nation's middle schools. *Health Education and Behavior, 30*(3): 375–391.

Roberts, M. (2019). *Enriching the learning: Meaningful extensions for proficient students in a PLC at Work*. Bloomington, IN: Solution Tree Press.

Robinson, J. (Web Producer). (2023, June 29). Michael Lewis (Season 5, Episode 1) [TV series episode]. In J. Grossberg (Executive Producer), *Tell me more with Kelly Corrigan*. PBS. Accessed at www.kpbs.org/news/2023/06/29/tell-me-more-with-kelly-corrigan-michael-lewis on August 17, 2023.

Robinson, M. A. (2010, November). *School perspectives on collaborative inquiry: Lessons learned from New York City, 2009–2010*. Philadelphia: Consortium for Policy Research in Education.

Samit, J. (2016). *Disrupt you! Master personal transformation, seize opportunity, and thrive in the era of endless innovation*. New York: Flatiron Books.

Samuels, C. A. (2010, September 8). Learning-disabled enrollment dips after long climb. *Education Week*. Accessed at www.edweek.org/teaching-learning/learning-disabled-enrollment-dips-after-long-climb/2010/09 on January 22, 2024.

Saphier, J. (2005). *John Adams' promise: How to have good schools for all our children, not just for some*. Acton, MA: Research for Better Teaching.

Saphier, J., King, M., & D'Auria, J. (2006). Three strands form strong school leadership. *Journal of Staff Development, 27*(2), 51–57.

Sarason, S. B. (1996). *Revisiting "the culture of the school and the problem of change."* New York: Teachers College Press.

Schaffer, R. H., & Thomson, H. A. (1992). Successful change programs begin with results. *Harvard Business Review, 70*(1), 80–89.

Schein, E. H. (1996). Leadership and organizational culture. In F. Hesselbein, M. Goldsmith, & R. Beckhard (Eds.), *The leader of the future: New visions, strategies, and practices for the next era* (pp. 59–69). San Francisco: Jossey-Bass.

Scheirer, M. A., & Dearing, J. W. (2011). An agenda for research on the sustainability of public health programs. *American Journal of Public Health, 101*(11), 2059–2067.

Schlechty, P. C. (2009). *Leading for learning: How to transform schools into learning organizations*. San Francisco: Jossey-Bass.

Schmoker, M. (2004a). Learning communities at the crossroads: Toward the best schools we've ever had. *Phi Delta Kappan, 86*(1), 84–89.

Schmoker, M. (2004b). Start here for improving teaching and learning. *School Administrator, 61*(10), 48.

Schmoker, M. (2006). *Results now: How we can achieve unprecedented improvements in teaching and learning.* Alexandria, VA: ASCD.

School Leader Network. (2018). *Churn: The high cost of principal turnover* (Reissued ed.). Sacramento, CA: New Teacher Center. Accessed at https://newteachercenter.org/wp-content/uploads/2021/07/Churn-The-High-Cost-of-Principal-Turnover_RB21.pdf on January 23, 2024.

Schuhl, S., Kanold, T. D., Toncheff, M., Barnes, B., Kanold-McIntyre, J., Larson, M. R., & Rivera, G. (2024). *Mathematics assessment and intervention in a PLC at Work* (2nd ed.). Bloomington, IN: Solution Tree Press.

Schwartz, T., & Porath, C. (2014, May 30). Why you hate work. *The New York Times.* Accessed at www.nytimes.com/2014/06/01/opinion/sunday/why-you-hate-work.html on December 15, 2015.

Senge, P. M., Kleiner, A., Roberts, C., Ross, R. B., & Smith, B. J. (1994). *The fifth discipline fieldbook: Strategies and tools for building a learning organization.* New York: Doubleday.

Sergiovanni, T. J. (2005). *Strengthening the heartbeat: Leading and learning together in schools.* San Francisco: Jossey-Bass.

Shannon, G. S., & Bylsma, P. (2004, October). *Characteristics of improved school districts: Themes of research.* Olympia, WA: Office of Superintendent of Public Instruction.

Sharples, J., Albers, B., Fraser, S., & Kime, S. (2019). *Putting evidence to work: A school's guide to implementation—Guidance report* (2nd ed.). London: Education Endowment Foundation.

Shaw, G. B. (2003). *Pygmalion.* London: Penguin. (Original work published 1916)

Shelton, R. (2020a, July 9). *Adaptation and future directions for sustainability research* [Webinar]. Accessed at www.youtube.com/watch?v=4pS06hrC-TA on January 25, 2024.

Shelton, R. (2020b). *Advancing sustainability research within implementation science* [Webinar]. Prevention Science and Methodology Group Virtual Grand Rounds. Accessed at Accessed at https://cepim.northwestern.edu/calendar-events/2020-11-10-shelton on January 12, 2024.

Shelton, R., & Moise, N. (2022, September 22). *Implementation science theories, models, and frameworks* [Webinar]. Accessed at www.youtube.com/watch?v=mrJpxl--DZA on January 25, 2024.

Shidler, L. (2009). The impact of time spent coaching for teacher efficacy on student achievement. *Early Childhood Education Journal, 36*(5), 453–460.

Showers, B., & Joyce, B. (1996). The evolution of peer coaching. *Educational Leadership*, *53*(6), 12–16.

Shyamalan, M. N. (2013). *I got schooled: The unlikely story of how a moonlighting movie maker learned the five keys to closing America's education gap*. New York: Simon & Schuster.

Siang, S., & Canning, M. (2023, February 23). Coaching your team as a collective makes it stronger. *Harvard Business Review*. Accessed at https://hbr.org/2023/02/coaching-your-team-as-a-collective-makes-it-stronger on November 7, 2023.

Sinek, S. (2009). *Start with why: How great leaders inspire everyone to take action*. New York: Penguin.

Smith, J. D., Schneider, B. H., Smith, P. K., & Ananiadou, K. (2004). The effectiveness of whole-school antibullying programs: A synthesis of evaluation research. *School Psychology Review*, *33*(4), 547–560.

Smith, W. R. (2015). *How to launch PLCs in your district*. Bloomington, IN: Solution Tree Press.

Solomon, D. (2013). *American mirror: The life and art of Norman Rockwell*. New York: Farrar, Straus and Giroux.

Solution Tree. (2024a). *Evidence of excellence: Greater Hartford Academy of the Arts Middle School*. Accessed at www.solutiontree.com/plc-at-work/evidence-of-excellence/greater-hartford-academy on April 1, 2024.

Solution Tree. (2024b). *Evidence of excellence: Minnieville Elementary School*. Accessed at www.solutiontree.com/plc-at-work/evidence-of-excellence/minnieville on April 1, 2024.

Solution Tree. (2024c). *Evidence of excellence: Model PLC at Work and Blue Ribbon Schools*. Accessed at www.solutiontree.com/plc-at-work/evidence-of-excellence/model-plc-and-blue-ribbon-schools on April 1, 2024.

Solution Tree. (2024d). *Evidence of excellence: Pasadena Independent School District*. Accessed at www.solutiontree.com/plc-at-work/evidence-of-excellence/pasadena on April 1, 2004.

Solution Tree. (2024e). *Evidence of excellence: Tongue River Elementary*. Accessed at www.solutiontree.com/plc-at-work/evidence-of-excellence/tongue-river-elementary on April 1, 2024.

Solution Tree. (2024f). *PLC at Work success story: Esther Starkman School (K–9)*. Accessed at https://cloudfront-s3.solutiontree.com/pdf/EOE/SolutionTreeCAN_EstherStarkman.pdf?_ga=2.222595160.2104238624.1712243703-441923646.1689021104 on April 1, 2024.

Solution Tree. (2024g). *PLC at Work success story: Fern Creek High School*. Accessed at https://cloudfront-s3.solutiontree.com/pdf/EOE/SolutionTree_EOE_Fern_Creek.pdf?_ga=2.250626373.2104238624.1712243703-441923646.1689021104 on April 1, 2024.

Solution Tree. (2024h). *PLC at Work success story: Lake County Schools.* Accessed at www.solutiontree.com/plc-at-work/success-stories/lake-county on April 1, 2024.

Solution Tree. (2024i). *PLC at Work success story: Southeast Polk Community School District.* Accessed at www.solutiontree.com/plc-at-work/success-stories/southeast-polk on April 24, 2024.

Solution Tree. (2024j). *Solution Tree in Washington.* Accessed at www.solutiontree.com/st-states/washington on April 1, 2024.

Sonbert, M. C. (2020). *Skyrocket your teacher coaching: How every school leader can become a coaching superstar.* San Diego, CA: Dave Burgess Consulting.

Sonju, B., Powers, M., & Miller, S. (2024). *Simplifying the journey: Six steps to schoolwide collaboration, consistency, and clarity in a PLC at Work.* Bloomington, IN: Solution Tree Press.

Southern Regional Education Board. (1998). *Things that matter most in improving student learning.* Atlanta, GA: Author.

Spangler, D. (2023, October 10). *PLC coaching: 12 ways to achieve effective results.* Accessed at https://corp.smartbrief.com/original/2023/10/plc-coaching-impact-cycle on November 7, 2023.

Sparks, D. (2007). *Leading for results: Transforming teaching, learning, and relationships in schools* (2nd ed.). Thousand Oaks, CA: Corwin Press.

Spiller, J., & Power, K. (2019). *Leading with intention: Eight areas for reflection and planning in your PLC at Work.* Bloomington, IN: Solution Tree Press.

Spiller, J., & Power, K. (2022). *Leading beyond intention: Six areas to deepen reflection and planning in your PLC at Work.* Bloomington, IN: Solution Tree Press.

Statista. (2023, November 3). *U.S. poverty rate 2022, by education level.* Accessed at www.statista.com/statistics/233162/us-poverty-rate-by-education on January 26, 2024.

Steeg, S. M. (2016). A case study of teacher reflection: Examining teacher participation in a video-based professional learning community. *Journal of Language and Literacy Education, 12*(1), 122–141. Accessed at http://jolle.coe.uga.edu/wp-content/uploads/2016/04/Steeg.pdf on November 7, 2023.

Steiner, E. D., & Woo, A. (2021). *Job-related stress threatens the teacher supply: Key findings from the 2021 State of the U.S. Teacher Survey.* Santa Monica, CA: RAND Corporation. Accessed at www.rand.org/pubs/research_reports/RRA1108-1.html on November 7, 2023.

Steiner, L., & Kowal, J. (2007, September). *Instructional coaching.* Accessed at www.readingrockets.org/topics/professional-development/articles/instructional-coaching on January 23, 2024.

Stevenson, H. W., & Stigler, J. W. (1992). *The learning gap: Why our schools are failing and what we can learn from Japanese and Chinese education.* New York: Touchstone.

Stiggins, R. (1999). Assessment, student confidence, and school success. *Phi Delta Kappan, 81*(3), 191–198.

Stiggins, R. (2004). New assessment beliefs for a new school mission. *Phi Delta Kappan, 86*(1), 22–27.

Stiggins, R. (2005). Assessment FOR learning: Building a culture of confident learners. In R. DuFour, R. Eaker, & R. DuFour (Eds.), *On common ground: The power of professional learning communities* (pp. 65–83). Bloomington, IN: Solution Tree Press.

Stiggins, R., & DuFour, R. (2009). Maximizing the power of formative assessments. *Phi Delta Kappan, 90*(9), 640–644.

Stigler, J. W., & Hiebert, J. (2009). Closing the teaching gap. *Phi Delta Kappan, 91*(3), 32–37.

Stone, D., Patton, B., & Heen, S. (2000). *Difficult conversations: How to discuss what matters most.* New York: Penguin.

Stone, D., Patton, B., Heen, S., & Fisher, R. (2023). *Difficult conversations: How to discuss what matters most* (Revised ed.). New York: Penguin.

Strong American Schools. (2008). *Diploma to nowhere.* Washington, DC: Author.

Sutcher, L., Darling-Hammond, L., & Carver-Thomas, D. (2016). *A coming crisis in teaching? Teacher supply, demand, and shortages in the U.S.* Palo Alto, CA: Learning Policy Institute. Accessed at https://learningpolicyinstitute.org/product/coming-crisis-teaching on November 7, 2023.

Sweeney, D. (2013). *Student-centered coaching at the secondary level.* Thousand Oaks, CA: Corwin Press.

Sweeney, D. (2018, July 23). *The research supporting student-centered coaching.* Accessed at www.dianesweeney.com/research-supporting-student-centered-coaching/ on March 27, 2024.

Sweeney, D. (2021, September 1). *Student-centered coaching cycles.* Accessed at www.dianesweeney.com/student-centered-coaching-cycles on November 7, 2023.

Symonds, K. (2004). *Perspectives on the gaps: Fostering the academic success of minority and low-income students.* Naperville, IL: North Central Regional Educational Laboratory.

Tavernise, S. (2012, February 9). Education gap grows between rich and poor, studies say. *The New York Times.* Accessed at www.nytimes.com/2012/02/10/education/education-gap-grows-between-rich-and-poor-studies-show.html?_r=1&nl=todaysheadlines&emc=tha2 on February 10, 2012.

Taylor, F. W. (1911). *The principles of scientific management.* New York: Harper & Brothers.

Thomas, T. (2019). *The implications of instructional coaches' participation in professional learning community collaboration team meetings* [Doctoral dissertation, University of Michigan-Flint]. Deep Blue Documents. https://deepblue.lib.umich.edu/handle/2027.42/152356

Thomas, T. F., & Parker, J. (in press). Fighting the good fight: Coaching quadrants in action. *AllThingsPLC Magazine, 8*(3).

Thompson, J. W. (1995). The renaissance of learning in business. In S. Chawla & J. Renesch (Eds.), *Learning organizations: Developing cultures for tomorrow's workplace* (pp. 85–100). Portland, OR: Productivity Press.

Tichy, N. M. (1997). *The leadership engine: How winning companies build leaders at every level.* New York: HarperBusiness.

Tomlinson, C. A., & McTighe, J. (2006). *Integrating differentiated instruction and understanding by design: Connecting content and kids.* Alexandria, VA: ASCD.

Torres, K., Rooney, K., Holmgren, M., Yoon, S. Y., Taylor, S., & Hanson, H. (2020). *PLC at Work in Arkansas: Driving achievement results through school transformation and innovation* [Executive summary]. Portland, OR: Education Northwest.

Trujillo, T. (2013). The reincarnation of the effective schools research: Rethinking the literature on district effectiveness. *Journal of Educational Administration, 51*(4), 426–452.

Tucker, M. S. (2014). *Fixing our national accountability system.* Washington, DC: National Center on Education and the Economy. Accessed at www.ncee.org/wp-content/uploads/2014/08/FixingOurNationalAccountabilitySystemWebV4.pdf on December 17, 2015.

Vander Ark, T., & Schneider, C. (2014, January). *Deeper learning for every student every day.* Menlo Park, CA: Hewlett Foundation. Accessed at https://hewlett.org/wp-content/uploads/2016/08/Deeper%20Learning%20for%20Every%20Student%20EVery%20Day_GETTING%20SMART_1.2014.pdf on January 23, 2024.

Vander Els, J. G., & Stack, B. M. (2022). *Unpacking the competency-based classroom: Equitable, individualized learning in a PLC at Work.* Bloomington, IN: Solution Tree Press.

Viennet, R., & Pont, B. (2017). *Education policy implementation: A literature review and proposed framework* (OECD Education Working Papers No. 162). Paris: Organisation for Economic Co-operation and Development.

Wagner, T. (2007, August 14). Leading for change. *Education Week.* Accessed at www.edweek.org/ew/articles/2007/08/15/45wagner.h26.html on November 11, 2015.

Wallace Foundation. (2013, January). *The school principal as leader: Guiding schools to better teaching and learning.* New York: Author.

Waller, W. (1932). *The sociology of teaching.* New York: Wiley.

Waterman, R. H., Jr. (1987). *The renewal factor: How the best get and keep the competitive edge.* New York: Bantam Books.

Watlington, E., Shockley, R., Guglielmino, P., & Felsher, R. (2010). The high cost of leaving: An analysis of the cost of teacher turnover. *Journal of Education Finance, 36*(1), 22–37.

Wei, R. C., Darling-Hammond, L., Andree, A., Richardson, N., & Orphanos, S. (2009, February). *Professional learning in the learning profession: A status report on teacher development in the U.S. and abroad.* Dallas, TX: National Staff Development Council.

Weichel, M., McCann, B., & Williams, T. (2018). *When they already know it: How to extend and personalize student learning in a PLC at Work.* Bloomington, IN: Solution Tree Press.

Weisberg, D., Sexton, S., Mulhern, J., & Keeling, D. (2009). *The widget effect: Our national failure to acknowledge and act on differences in teacher effectiveness.* New York: The New Teacher Project. Accessed at https://files.eric.ed.gov/fulltext/ED515656.pdf on January 23, 2024.

Wellman, B., & Lipton, L. (2004). *Data-driven dialogue: A facilitator's guide to collaborative inquiry.* Sherman, CT: MiraVia.

Westat. (2009). *28th annual report to Congress on the implementation of the Individuals with Disabilities Education Act, 2006.* Washington, DC: U.S. Department of Education.

WestEd. (2000). *Teachers who learn, kids who achieve: A look at schools with model professional development.* San Francisco: Author.

Wheatley, M. (1999). Goodbye, command and control. In F. Hesselbein & P. M. Cohen (Eds.), *Leader to leader: Enduring insights on leadership from the Drucker Foundation's award-winning journal* (pp. 151–162). San Francisco: Jossey-Bass.

Wheelis, A. (1973). *How people change.* New York: Harper & Row.

Wiggins, G. (2012, January 4). *On pacing guides* [Blog post]. Accessed at https://grantwiggins.wordpress.com/2012/01/04/on-pacing-guides on January 24, 2016.

Wiliam, D. (2007). Content then process: Teacher learning communities in the service of formative assessment. In D. Reeves (Ed.), *Ahead of the curve: The power of assessment to transform teaching and learning* (pp. 183–204). Bloomington, IN: Solution Tree Press.

Wiliam, D. (2011). *Embedded formative assessment.* Bloomington, IN: Solution Tree Press.

Wiliam, D. (2018). *Embedded formative assessment* (2nd ed.). Bloomington, IN: Solution Tree Press.

Wiliam, D., & Thompson, M. (2008). Integrating assessment with learning: What will it take to make it work? In C. A. Dwyer (Ed.), *The future of assessment: Shaping teaching and learning* (pp. 53–82). Mahwah, NJ: Erlbaum.

Will, M. (2022, April 14). Teacher job satisfaction hits an all-time low: Exclusive new data paints a picture of a profession in crisis. *Education Week.* Accessed at www.edweek.org/teaching-learning/teacher-job-satisfaction-hits-an-all-time-low/2022/04 on January 26, 2024.

Williams, K. C., & Hierck, T. (2015). *Starting a movement: Building culture from the inside out in professional learning communities.* Bloomington, IN: Solution Tree Press.

Williams, T., Perry, M., Studier, C., Brazil, N., Kirst, M., Haertel, E., et al. (2005). *Similar students, different results: Why do some schools do better?* Mountain View, CA: EdSource.

Wren, D. J. (1999). School culture: Exploring the hidden curriculum. *Adolescence, 34*(135), 593–596.

YouthTruth. (2022, Fall). *Insights from the student experience: Emotional and mental health.* Cambridge, MA: Center for Effective Philanthropy. Accessed at https://youthtruthsurvey.org/wp-content/uploads/2023/07/EMH_2022.pdf on January 26, 2024.

Zakaria, Z., Don, Y., & Yaakob, M. F. M. (2021). Teachers' well-being from the social psychological perspective. *International Journal of Evaluation and Research in Education, 10*(2), 641–647. Accessed at https://files.eric.ed.gov/fulltext/EJ1299271.pdf on November 7, 2023.

INDEX

Concise Answers to Frequently Asked Questions About Professional Learning Communities at Work®
Mike Mattos, Richard DuFour, Rebecca DuFour, Robert Eaker, and Thomas W. Many
Get all of your PLC questions answered. Designed as a companion resource to *Learning by Doing: A Handbook for Professional Learning Communities at Work®* (4th ed.), this powerful, quick-reference guidebook is a must-have for teachers and administrators working to create and sustain the PLC process.
BKF705

The Way Forward: PLC at Work® and the Bright Future of Education
Anthony Muhammad
Educator and best-selling author Anthony Muhammad explores the educational hurdles of the past in the context of present-day concerns and envisions an education system where all schools energetically embrace the PLC at Work process.
BKG159

Beyond PLC Lite: Evidence-Based Teaching and Learning in a Professional Learning Community at Work®
Anthony R. Reibel, Troy Gobble, Mark Onuscheck, and Eric Twadell
Move your school teams beyond "PLC Lite" with ten evidence-based actions that will center student agency and efficacy in curriculum, assessment, instruction, and intervention practices. Gain access to rubrics, protocols, and templates designed to build a culture of continuous improvement.
BKF913

The 15-Day Challenge: Simplify and Energize Your PLC at Work® Process
Maria Nielsen
The 15-Day Challenge offers a step-by-step process for collaborative teams that builds on the three big ideas and four critical questions of a PLC at Work. In each chapter, you'll find practical actions for how to support all students in mastering essential learning standards.
BKF969

The Foundation for Change: Focusing on the Four Pillars of a PLC at Work®
Jonathan G. Vander Els and Joshua Ray
In this book, the authors help schools shift their mindset and transform their mission, vision, values, and goals as the foundational framework of a PLC that leads to school improvement and high levels of learning for all.
BKG113